D0026757

CRITICAL ESSAYS IN MODERN LITERATURE

MIND OF WINTER

Wallace Stevens, Meditation, and Literature

□

William W. Bevis

UNIVERSITY OF PITTSBURGH PRESS

Published by the University of Pittsburgh Press, Pittsburgh, Pa. 15260
Copyright © 1988, University of Pittsburgh Press
All rights reserved
Feffer and Simons, Inc., London
Manufactured in the United States of America

Library of Congress Cataloging in Publication Data

Bevis, William W., 1941–
   Mind of winter : Wallace Stevens, meditation, and literature
William W. Bevis.
      p.   cm. — (Critical essays in modern literature)
   Bibliography: p. 331.
   Includes index.
   ISBN 0-8229-3598-8
   1. Stevens, Wallace, 1879–1955—Criticism and interpretation.   2. Meditation
(Buddhism) in literature.   3. Philosophy, Oriental, in literature.   4. Spiritual life in
literature.   I. Title.   II. Series.
PS3537.T4753Z5956 1989
811′.52—dc19   88-19814
                                                                      CIP

Quotations from the poetry of Wallace Stevens are reprinted, by permission, from
The Collected Poems of Wallace Stevens. Copyright 1923 by Alfred A. Knopf, Inc.
Excerpts from "The Waste Land" in *Collected Poems 1909–1962* by T. S. Eliot,
copyright 1936 by Harcourt Brace Jovanovich, Inc., copyright © 1963, 1964 by T. S.
Eliot, are reprinted by permission of the publisher. Faber and Faber, Ltd., has
granted permission covering foreign rights to reprint excerpts from the work of
Wallace Stevens and T. S. Eliot. "Mohini Chatterjee" is reprinted with the
permission of the Macmillan Publishing Company from *Collected Poems* by William
Butler Yeats. Copyright 1919, 1933, 1934 by Macmillan Publishing Company,
renewed 1947, 1961, 1962 by Bertha Georgie Yeats. Copyright 1940 by Georgie
Yeats, renewed 1968 by Bertha Georgie Yeats, Michael Butler Yeats and Anne
Yeats. A. P. Watt, Ltd., has granted permission covering foreign rights to reprint
excerpts from the work of William Butler Yeats.

Figure 1 is reprinted, with permission, from Daniel Goleman, *The Varieties of
Meditative Experience* (New York: E.P. Dutton, 1972), reissued as *The Meditative
Mind* (Los Angeles: J.P. Torcher, 1988). Figure 2 is reprinted, with permission,
from Francis Leukel, *Introduction to Physiological Psychology,* 3d ed. (St. Louis: C.
V. Mosby, 1976), p. 94. Figure 4 is reprinted, with permission, from *Science
Magazine* 174, no. 4012 (November 1971).

To my parents,

Herman W. and Jennie Lyde Wade Bevis

CONTENTS

Abbreviations Used in the Text

CP   *The Collected Poems of Wallace Stevens* (New York: Knopf, 1954).

L   *Letters of Wallace Stevens*, ed. Holly Stevens (New York: Knopf, 1966).

NA   *The Necessary Angel: Essays on Reality and the Imagination* (New York: Knopf, 1951).

OP   *Opus Posthumous*, ed. Samuel French Morse (New York: Knopf, 1957).

SP   *Souvenirs and Prophecies: The Young Wallace Stevens*, ed. Holly Stevens (New York: Knopf, 1977).

Acknowledgments

I would like to thank the late Roy Harvey Pearce, whose early interest in my lines of inquiry encouraged me to continue; Frits Staal of the Center for South and Southeast Asia Studies at Berkeley also answered kindly a number of questions as I began this book. Colleagues along the way reshaped many chapters—Coburn Freer, Henry Harrington, Stuart Justman, Patricia Goedicke, and especially James Buchanan, whose Taoist and postmodern expertise provided several insights, and Julie Codell, whose wide interests in art history and modern culture proved very useful. The philosophy forum at the University of Montana, thanks to Albert Borgmann, allowed me to air crucial claims in a critical atmosphere. Helen Vendler was exceptionally lucid and kind in commenting on the completed manuscript. Susan Matule and Bettina Escudero of Typing Services at U.M. were helpful in preparing the book.

Most of all, however, I would like to thank three friends and colleagues for the closest and most critical readings of the manuscript at various stages of its evolution: Mark Livingston of Berkeley, Dick Bevis of Vancouver, and Lois Welch of Missoula. Three better readers and advisors one cannot imagine.

MIND OF WINTER

Introduction

This study began in puzzlement over "The Snow Man," a puzzlement that grew rather than diminished with the years and the criticism, and that soon spread to much of Stevens' work. Not only was the poem's "the nothing that is" quite unintelligible, if taken seriously and literally, but few of us were concerned that the listener in the poem is "nothing himself" (a *nihil,* if you will, more than a nihilist), and further, that Stevens himself had insisted one might "understand and enjoy" reality through the "mind of winter"—a stance Harold Bloom has called "the worst reading possible." The inexactness and gloom of readings of "The Snow Man" bothered me, since I had the greatest respect for Stevens as an exact poet, and since that mind of winter is so centrally located in Stevens' canon.

With many other readers, I was intrigued by the various forms of nothingness, blankness, poverty, detachment, the truly remarkable vacuities in Stevens' work.

> And the sublime comes down
> To the spirit itself,
>
> The spirit and space,
> The empty spirit
> In vacant space.   (*CP* 131)

And just when we think we have located those vacancies in fin-de-siècle ennui, they become celebratory, the nihilists become jubilant while "searching for the fecund minimum," and we are left wondering just what kind of minimum this might be:

XVI

> If thinking could be blown away
> Yet this remain the dwelling-place
> Of those with a sense for simple space.   (*CP* 153)

3

In her introduction to *On Extended Wings* in 1969, Helen Vendler noted, quoting John Malcolm Brinnin, that Stevens was "burning to come to whiteness and ascetic innocence," and she commented that his ascetic nature was "the obverse of that other Stevens shown us by critics, the doctrinal poet of ideas, advocate of hedonism."[1] Our criticism has advanced since then past many ideas and advocacies, but "the nothing that is" and its attendant absences have not been explicated, nor has Stevens' asceticism been reconciled with his theory of imagination, that "supreme fiction . . . a jovial hullabaloo among the spheres." In this book I will argue that Stevens' asceticism is meditative. His meditative interests are a perfect foil to his imaginative interests and are at the core of his modernist aspects, yet the nothings and the fictions cooperate for hullabaloos of their own. The symbiosis so easily asserted, however, is not so easily achieved in the poems, nor is the opposition of imagination and meditation to be taken lightly, nor is Stevens' asceticism easily understood.

My topic is in some ways quite odd, and in other ways quite conservative. The oddness arises because *meditation,* as I use the term, is a state of consciousness—that is, an experience—and not inherently an idea or any other linguistic, aesthetic, philosophical, or religious proposition. Because my subject is a state of mind or consciousness, my method is strictly phenomenological in its foundation. And since the meditative state of consciousness is itself aconceptual, it has a problematic relation to any of the theories with which we must interpret and value it. This project, then, in a minuscule way resembles Freud's work on dreams, for the phenomenon under examination, Freud's unconscious, or this meditative state, entails mental activity foreign to critical thought.

Yet the issues I will address, far from being odd, are almost in vogue. David Walker's book, *The Transparent Lyric,* argues the absence of a dramatic speaker in many Stevens and Williams lyrics; with expressiveness removed, Walker and others explore the reader's relation to the text.[2] I certainly agree that Stevens is profoundly impersonal, that "transparent" is an apt metaphor, and that his poetry seems importantly distanced from simple expression.

More sweepingly, Marjorie Perloff, the most recent and talented Ezra Pound propounder and postmodernist critic, has argued for a modern poetry of indeterminacy, discontinuity, and impersonality from Rimbaud through Pound to John Cage and current language poets.[3] Stevens, however, she finds romantic. In part IV, I will champion Stevens under some of Perloff's banners, although my methodology and language theory are not so postmodern as hers. Stevens' poetry is impersonal, and his long poems are also indeterminate and discontinuous. In many ways, Stevens' meditations beat the *Cantos* at their own game.

Perloff poses "expressive" poetry (romantic) against "constructionist" poetry (impersonal and modern, in the tradition of vorticist "geometry"). I find, however, that Stevens regards his own expressions as constructions; that is, he takes a modern point of view toward his own romanticism—which means that he takes a meditatively detached point of view toward his own imagination.

How often we watch Stevens watch someone else (in this case "the pensive man") watch yet someone else (in this case an eagle) become involved in a geometry of revelation:

> The pensive man . . . He sees that eagle float
> For which the intricate Alps are a single nest.   (*CP* 216)

The lover of Stevens is not surprised to find the eye drawn up only to be cast back down through another eye to find (revelation in a relative clause) that the world has been changed. Our relation to that final metaphor is indeed not that of auditor to simple report; vision is subordinate (grammatically) to ordinary perception ("He sees"), and the entire eagle metaphor is disjunct and distant (separated by the poem's ellipsis, and quite a bit of altitude) from the pensive man. In part IV I will be pursuing a reading of the long poems that bears resemblances to Walker's and Perloff's theories, and that extends, I hope, our understanding of impersonality in Stevens and of how the reader may step into the vacancies of those works.

The core of my thesis is that Stevens experimented with, or at least marvelously imitated, a meditative state of consciousness that was itself selfless. Therefore I locate the ascetic and impersonal aspects of his work not so much in a language artifact removed from a speaker, as in a speaker oddly removed from himself. Let us for a moment divide Stevens criticism (rather unfairly) into expressionists versus constructionists, with Vendler on the one hand speaking for the expressive Stevens of feeling, of passion, of a poetry that reaffirms the creative, personal self, and Perloff on the other hand representing the most reasonable version of impersonal construction and postmodern language theory. This study takes Perloff's topic of impersonality and places it within a Vendlerian biographical and expressive schema:

Stevens expresses his detachment from expression as no one else has in our language.

Certainly Stevens' asceticism has hovered over recent readings. Harold Bloom's pursuit of the "first idea" in Stevens took him to the "the mind of winter," and his questions on "The Snow Man" I could take as my own: "What, we can ask about Stevens' seeing soul, can one behold in 'the nothing that is'? How can the beholder possess 'nothing,' in a positive sense of seeing-with-amazement?"[4] Those are experiential, not just critical questions, and by the end of chapter 4, I hope to have answered them.

Two aspects of this study deserve special introduction: the use of Buddhism and the use of states-of-consciousness research. Both topics arise naturally if we seek a phenomenology of Steven's detachment, yet the association of either topic with fads and cults may excite distrust. This is not a religious book; I am no more interested in the religious aspects of Buddhism than I am in religious aspects of Stevens, who seems to me brilliantly secular yet constantly flirting with ultimate concerns, "the last purity of the knowledge of good" (*CP* 294). His is "a world without heaven to follow" (*CP* 127), in which "poetry and apotheosis are one" (*CP* 378). Indeed, Stevens is almost defined by such juggling of relative absolutes.

Similarly, I am interested in meditative experience as a physiological mindset with given characteristics, not as a means of personal or philosophical salvation. This meditative state of mind is crucially related to Stevens' poetic stance in general and to many poems in particular, and the Buddhists, more than any Western tradition, have recorded an advanced phenomenology of that state. My topic requires that the state of consciousness be studied before we can make useful critical applications. Imagine, for instance, discussing disjunction in modern poetry without any knowledge of cubist, imagist, vorticist, or dadaist claims, or of the shift away from centers of authority and toward relative points of view after Darwin. In a parallel situation, the kind of detachment that colors some of Stevens' subjects, structures, and syntax (colors them white) is simply foreign to our critical awareness and vocabulary.

Many Buddhist concepts and terms are usefully related to topics some academics are currently arguing. For instance, deconstructionists voice distaste for Western logocentric preoccupations with "presence"; readers will find I am describing Stevens' talent for "absence" and for what might be called bracketing (questioning) concepts within a modern context (within what Hans Vaihinger called a philosophy of "as if"), but my approach is experiential instead of philosophical. Buddhism and Taoism for thousands of years have questioned language and presence not from within language, which often dooms deconstructionists to endlessly self-destructing discourse (and new logos creation), but from outside of language. From the perspective of meditative consciousness, language can be appreciated for what it can and cannot do, and respected, while a theory of "absence," and of the deceit of nouns including "absence," can be developed by reference to nonlinguistic, nonconceptual experience. The anxious, incestuous, and interminably redundant war of deconstructive language with itself is thus avoided, while certain cultural revisions are, I believe, more clearly set forth. Some habits of mind, then, practiced by Stevens, are relevent to the continuing modern-existential-postmodern discourse, and are best elucidated by reference to Buddhism and physiology of the brain.

I have sketched here, in a somewhat casual and personal way, the general concerns of this book. The rest of this introduction will offer a more formal overview of the major arguments.

One of Stevens' most distinguishing and pervasive characteristics, his detachment, is meditative and therefore experiential in origin, and difficult to perceive from within our culture. If I outline the argument from a logical rather than a critical point of view, it takes this structure: meditative consciousness exists as a possible mode of operation of the central nervous system with fairly stable characteristics across cultures; reports of meditative consciousness repeat certain qualities, points of view, and psychological assumptions; the meditative model, once defined, fits very well a number of Stevens' poems, passages and attitudes—precisely those which have most puzzled or dismayed readers and which have spawned the least convincing interpretations. Many of Stevens' problem passages, his enigmatic interest in *nothing,* and indeed an entire tendency of his mind toward distance without irony, are very well explained by a meditative paradigm. His life, and especially his long walks, offer plausible evidence of meditative experience.

Immediately the subject becomes cultural as well as critical. We have hardly begun to define Stevens' detachment because our culture has had very few categories and concepts for apprehending meditative passivity. Therefore we will have to borrow and create terms, encrust them with new meanings as Stevens might say, strip away old associations—in short, offer a phenomenology and terminology for this detachment. *Meditative,* for instance, throws a net over more fish and different fish than most American, British, or European readers might assume.

With a caution to readers, then, that some key concepts and terms will have to be worked out in detail, I will sketch the outline of the critical argument. Stevens' passive, blank, detached aspect—an aspect essentially comic even though words such as *passive* or *blank* often have negative connotations in our culture—is the source of much of his power and a complementary opposite of imagination. The meditative Stevens is in constant tension with the imaginative Stevens. The tension between those poles of meditation and imagination, the circulating back and forth between them, the view of one from the other, the longing for one from the other, join his ear, wit, and comic spirit to define Stevens' work.

Beyond that core argument are unexpected critical dividends; the more subtle and complex aspects of meditative experience open up correspondingly subtle habits of Stevens, so that his famous and obvious interest in "the nothing that is" becomes only a small and introductory part of this study. His perception of *the thing itself,* which has naturally been traced by Western intellectuals (and Stevens) to sources in Kant, is much more profitably compared to the thing itself meditatively perceived. For instance, the poem "Not Ideas about the Thing but the Thing Itself" (placed by Stevens at the end of his collected poems) exhibits a meditative psychology as well as phenomenology, presented by Stevens in deliberate contrast to imaginative modes of operation. Finally, the least obvious and perhaps most useful critical result of a meditative approach is a description of the long poems: what they are, why they are, and how to read them.

One consequence of this project is to revise a traditional conception of the issues in Stevens. We used to speak of imagination and reality, or imagination versus reality in Stevens' poetry. No matter how tiresome the repetition of those terms, or how reductive the readings they sometimes spawned, we knew that those terms were central to his work. They are central, but not, say, as opposing nouns in a parallel construction. Rather, imagination in Stevens is a verb, a process, a way of approaching reality; the other way is meditation. Thus Stevens is a poet who repeatedly considers imaginative versus meditative approaches to reality; he is a poet not of imagination and reality, but of imagination and meditation in relation to reality. This *imagination* is made of romantic, neo-Kantian and modernist elements familiar to us. This *meditation,* though the word has popular currency, is really quite strange both in its origin as a state of consciousness, and in its various qualities. Nevertheless, Stevens from 1879 to 1955 somehow became a master of meditative detachment, finding it the perfect foil to his romantic inheritance.

The nature of the opposition between imagination and meditation lies at the heart of our critical inquiry, and can be quickly summarized. Stevens begins with the neo-Kantian categories of *self* (noumena or mind, including thought, feeling, psyche, imagination), and *other* (phenomena outside of mind, which in Stevens are usually objects, the materialists' bare reality). In the act of creative perception, the active, imaginative self cooperates with the other to create a third category, a higher reality, the interface of self and other. A direct descendant of Kant and Coleridge, cross-bred with impressionist art and reborn in Nietzsche, this reality is the world-as-perceived, made half of objects and half of our need and use of them, a world half objective, half subjective. In Stevens' words, such reality is "not that 'collection of solid, static objects extended in space' but the life that is lived in the scene that it composes; and so reality is not that external scene but the life that is lived in it" (*NA* 25). Perhaps more than any of his romantic ancestors, Stevens abstained from assigning value to object, subject, or their combination, except on a poem-by-poem basis.

Metaphor reflects this third reality: a world actively, imaginatively perceived. In metaphor, an *A* term (an other, for example, the sea) is combined with a *B* term (offered by the self, which for example, in perception associates the flatness of the sea with glass), to create a new construct, *C* ("The sea was glass"), a metaphoric reality made half of other and half of self: "the real made more acute by an unreal" (*CP* 451). Thus Stevens is squarely within the the radically modern tradition of relativity and skepticism, which postulates that all truths are momentary, constructed agreements between subjects and objects. This is the tradition of Nietzsche's "expedient falsification"; William James's "conception . . . is a teleological instrument" and "truth" a "human device"; Ibsen's "vital lie."

Art, to Stevens, does not differ from an act of creative perception— hence in "The Idea of Order at Key West" the artist's musical epiphany is parallel to the audience's perceptual epiphany. Art is a mirror held to our perceptual mirrors, which themselves distort and create and contain their own reflections:

> The revealing aberration should appear,
> The agate in the eye, the tufted ear,
> The rabbit fat, at last, in glassy grass.   (*CP* 153)

The problem with this imaginative schema is the emphasis it places on the creative self. Just as T. S. Eliot bemoaned the "distressing emphasis on personality" in a modern age stripped of all authority beyond psyche and cortex, Stevens often tired of the triumph of self and yearned to encounter an other that was not created in his own images. Sometimes he really believed, "It is with a strange malice / That I distort the world" (*CP* 61), and it bothered him. The source of the malice was not usually an evil psyche, but the nature of imaginative perception itself, as if noumena necessarily terrorize phenomena. In such a mood, he would attack imagination and metaphor as evasions, projections, destructions, solipsisms, tragic isolations from the thing in itself, from the world wholly other, and he would therefore seek to "trace the gold sun about the whitened sky / Without evasion by a single metaphor" (*CP* 372). "Gold" in that line may be read as a color adjective, not a metaphor. His apparent contradictions were very real indeed; in one poem he could be jubilant that, as with the color gold, "description . . . is an expectation, a desire . . . a little different from reality: / The difference that we make in what we see" (*CP* 344), and in another poem he would turn against the imaginative paradigm, longing "to be without a description of to be," and achieving it (*CP* 205). Critics have increasingly noted Stevens' paradoxical attitude toward metaphor. I hope to clarify the origin and function of that paradox. If, to put it simply, we say that romantic insight produces metaphors, and that modern skepticism deconstructs those metaphors into a collage of vital lies, then meditative detachment offers a neutral point of view toward both romantic metaphors (offered as true) and modern metaphors (offered as if true), and also promises a perception without metaphor, that is, without self. We shall see that Stevens' meditative talent tends to serve his modernism but is not coterminous with it. Unlike Eliot, Stevens evolved a benign, secular, and noninstitutional alternative to the "prison of the self."

Much of Stevens' poetry describes or employs meditative perception by a passive rather than an active self. The result is at least the illusion of an other perceived in purity, without imagination. This mode of perception usually generates poetic image, not metaphor, and is often set in a context of stasis, unity, or even peace (as opposed to "the motion of thought / And its restless iteration"). Meditative passages generally denigrate knowledge and language, which in Stevens are almost synonymous with imagination and metaphor, and choose instead "a gaiety that is being, not merely knowing" (*CP* 248). Sometimes these meditative passages lead to a reality beyond the mind's rhetoric:

> And beyond the days, beyond the slow-foot litters
> Of the nights, the actual, universal strength,
> Without a word of rhetoric—there it is.   (*CP* 309)

Meditative perception by a relatively quiet, passive self saying little more than "there it is," underlies many Stevens passages of nothingness, or of the thing in itself purely perceived—the Buddhists call this a perception of *suchness,* a word with a specifically meditative denotation. For instance, the last sentence of the "The Latest Freed Man" boils down to: "It was . . . the chairs." If that is a revelation (and it is), it is a strangely minimal fecundity. Some works read by critics as poems of reality (as opposed to imagination) are, I think, poems of meditative perception of suchness. Meditative perception, then, encounters a new world by means of less self, while imaginative perception creates a new world by means of more self. Meditative perception is typically expressed through pure image, imaginative perception through metaphor. Naturally, Stevens would at times attack the meditative mode; either approach to reality, imaginative or meditative, could be embraced, cast off, or considered from the point of view of its opposite—and even then, envied or reviled.

Attempting to follow Stevens' leap from meditative perception to poetry, we find that our culture offers almost no description of meditative consciousness, or no-mind (inaction, Chinese, *wu-wei*). When we turn to our classic Western mystics such as Plato or Plotinus, the gnostics, some Catholics, or even Emerson, we find idealist conclusions or theism, something instead of nothing, even though many individuals report experiences that seem to have been meditative. Buddhists, on the other hand, have analyzed the most passive states and written about them largely in a skeptical, even atheist spirit, offering what Herbert Guenther calls a "true phenomenology, the systematic investigation of our experiences as experiences."5 As we will soon see, we must first face the enormous difference between any idea, including that of *nothing,* and a state of consciousness that is aconceptual. That is the fence dividing most Western intellectual traditions from meditative experience. We may have had meditators, but we have had very little in the way of meditative theory that defines and values passivity, and most of what we have had was pushed toward Catholic orthodoxy. Similarly, modern theories of nihilism and of the unconscious are essentially unrelated to no-mind, as we shall see. Therefore in this study I will use states-of-consciousness research into physiology of the brain, Buddhist literature, and Stevens' poetry to develop a phenomenology of no-mind.

Stevens seems to have arrived at his knowledge without significant help from Buddhists, scientists, or orientalists, and his favorite touchstone, Plato, led him to imaginative, not meditative insight; very probably the meditative state of consciousness itself, unsought, unaffected by training (Buddhists accept this possibility), was his mentor. To follow his tracks, however, if only the tracks of his poems, most us need to develop concepts and terms hitherto unavailable.

Let us begin with a working definition of the area of inquiry. A *meditative state of consciousness* is a naturally occurring physiological phenomenon, possible for any person in any culture and probably experienced by everyone to some degree. There are several characteristics common to its various stages: (1) transience, (2) ineffability, (3) sensations of time and space changed or transcended, (4) sensations of self-loss—that is, absence of thought or feeling according to later reports, and minimal cortical activity as measured by machines during meditation. Such a state of consciousness differs in report and measurable characteristics from other states such as waking, dreaming, daydreaming, and hypnotic trance, and such calm self-loss differs also from the other mystical categories of the occult, vision, and ecstasy (excited self-loss). Contrary to common Western opinion, meditative experience can include vivid sensory perception, as well as reports of nothingness. A meditative state, in various stages, has been sought by many Hindu, Buddhist, Moslem, and Christian meditators, and is characterized by passivity: no thought or feeling. Those familiar with Christian meditation and with Martz's work on seventeenth-century meditative poetry should beware a vocabulary shift: Saint John of the Cross defined meditation as a reflective, thoughtful state, while his contemplation referred to a wordless, thoughtless, and more enlightened condition. During the nineteenth century these terms were reversed: *meditation* is now used in Asian studies and popular works for the most passive, thoughtless states sought by disciplined training. *Contemplation* and *reflection* refer to more thoughtful and more ordinary conditions.

The book is divided into four parts. Part I offers an overview of meditative issues, presents several core Stevens lyrics that seem to demand a meditative reading, and reviews meditative aspects of Stevens' early poetry. By the end of part I, we will be familiar with meditative descriptions of *nothing* (Buddhist voidness), with the thing itself meditatively perceived (Buddhist suchness), with several Stevens poems of both types and with some of the history of Western attempts to approach these issues. Part II ranges (beyond fences, as the word implies) across more subtle and various meditative problems including the structure and physiology of meditative experience, definitions of self and not-self, and through a number of apposite poems by Stevens, especially those marvelous poems of the thirties, when he came to maturity. By the end of part II, most meditative issues and all of Stevens' most extreme lyric examples will have been presented. Part III, on Stevens' milieu, shows how and why other prominent contemporaries and influences (Yeats, Santayana, Pound) were not meditative, although one might expect them to have been, reviews Stevens' early reading, and presents the evidence from Stevens' life that he was familiar with meditative consciousness. Part IV argues that his later, long poems (traditionally called meditations for entirely different reasons, in the Saint John sense of reflections) are directly related to meditative detachment. The long poems exhibit the workings of ordinary consciousness as observed from the meditative point of view, and closely parallel Buddhist experiments in returning from meditative extremes not only to watch, but also to affirm the endless processes of ordinary life—although that affirmation is accompanied, again, by a detachment specifically meditative. The Buddhists call this meditative, detached immersion in the ordinary, everydaymindedness, and that, I will argue, is exactly what is going on in Stevens' long poems. Such detached observation of ordinary consciousness is radically modern, giving an open form to skepticism, fragmentation, and impersonality, and producing a poetry more honest than Pound's *Cantos* with their closed and didactic subtext. I will offer a theory of meditative form, "the comedy of consciousness," to describe Stevens' long poems, so various, difficult and disjunct, which seem to be heard, as it were, from an odd distance. Stevens himself defined that distance in a curious way: "When the mind is like a hall in which thought is like a voice speaking, the voice is always that of someone else" (*OP* 168). Finally, I will suggest that a number of long, disjunct art forms since Wordsworth's *Prelude,* including the late Beethoven quartets and jazz improvisation, may be formally related to the comedy of consciousness.

As we proceed through Stevens' poetry, four fundamental and by no means easy topics will repeatedly come before us: voidness in meditative experience, suchness in meditative experience, the structure of meditative experience, and the history of Western acceptance or rejection of meditative experience.

As we shall see, sophisticated knowledge of no-mind to the West is very recent, since 1920 for the few and since World War II for most, even though for over a hundred years we have known Buddhism as part of the history of ideas or religions. The only informed book on meditative consciousness and English poetry, written by R. H. Blyth in 1942, is both sweeping and dogmatic in its claims.[6] Even American literature scholars who know something of Buddhism and of meditation in its popular forms may expect some surprises from recent Asian studies and brain physiology. The source materials for developing a phenomenology of meditation have been available in English for perhaps twenty years. Stevens himself falls within a period, 1800–1950, that is something of an interregnum in Western meditative history, a period when formal Christian meditation had declined and formal Buddhist meditation was hardly known. The Christian meditative poets before 1800 have already received some attention, and many post-1950 writers such as Ginsberg, Merwin, Snyder, and Kinnell make conscious and informed use of Buddhist theory and practice. Writers working explicitly within a Christian or Buddhist meditative tradition deserve their own study; this book will argue the possibility that naive, unsought, unrecognized meditative experience may profoundly influence the work of a major poet.

A major poet he is. I hope to clarify the aspect of Stevens' poetry that has remained most puzzling, and to show how his meditative detachment conspires with his imaginative exuberance to define his work.

PART I

The Snow Man

This creates a third world without knowledge,
In which no one peers, in which the will makes no
Demands. It accepts whatever is as true,
Including pain, which, otherwise, is false.
In the third world, then, there is no pain. Yes, but
What lover has one in such rocks, what woman,
However known, at the centre of the heart?

"Esthétique du Mal"

1

An Issue: Nirvana

In 1782 Thomas Henry Colebrooke, son of Sir George Cole-brooke, chairman of the court of directors of the East India Company, went to Bengal as a civil service employee; in 1814 he returned to England as a professor of Sanskrit and Hindu law. That the son of a merchant lord should become a scholar is not unusual; what was unusual, according to Buddhist historian Guy Richard Welbon, was the openmindedness of his approach to a new and ticklish subject: nirvana.

In spite of the English occupation of India, knowledge of Buddhism was rare:

> Between 1820 and 1830, the two languages [Sanscrit and Pali] essential for the historical study of Buddhism began to be known in Europe. But this was still the accomplishment of only a very few scholars. And of Buddhism itself these same scholars knew scarcely anything if they were not, in fact, ignorant of it altogether.[1]

The Hindus had long practiced meditation leading to nirvana, but in the Hindu Vedas, Brahmanas, and Upanishads, references to meditative practice were usually short, vague, or intertwined with complex religious and ritual imagery. After 500 B.C., the Buddhists tended to separate meditative practice from religious belief. The Buddhists were often skeptics—Colebroooke's Hindu sources called them "atheists or rather, disowners of another world"[2]—and they were also quite utilitarian in their insistence that salvation comes not from a creed, but from a change in one's state of mind.

Western knowledge of secular meditation (that is, outside of a Christian or theistic context) has for two centuries trailed a few decades behind Western knowledge of Buddhism. More than the Hindus, the Buddhists made meditation the center of their tradition; more than the Sufis or Christians, the Buddhists wrote and wrote,

17

commenting on hundreds of thousands of texts that touch on meditative issues. In 1830, as Emerson was preparing to write "Nature," Europeans knew almost nothing of Buddhism. During the nineteenth century, we became acquainted with the older Theravadic Buddhist texts in the Pali language—the ancient canon, written mostly before A.D. 200. In the last hundred years, we have gradually gained access to more recent Mahayana Buddhist texts in Sanskrit, Chinese, and Japanese.

By sheer coincidence we have discovered those traditions in roughly the same order that they evolved as Buddhism moved northward (to China, by A.D. 500, to Japan by 800). Not so coincidentally the texts became, as the tradition evolved, increasingly clear and explicit about meditative practice. The result is that nineteenth-century editions (such as the voluminous Oxford *Sacred Books of the East,* edited by Max Muller) contain mostly southern and early works: Hindu, Theravadic, and some early Mahayana texts in Sanskrit and Pali. In spite of a few giants such as Waley and Suzuki, writing by 1930, our knowledge of Chinese and Japanese meditation (Taoism, Ch'an, and Zen) was delayed until the close of the Second World War (Chinese study, especially, awaited the concordance of 1946). In spite of some long known texts, we knew very little of Tantric Buddhism until Tibet fell to China in 1950 and religious leaders fled.

Western knowledge of the most literate and secular meditative tradition in the world, Buddhism, is therefore remarkably recent. The necessary languages have become slowly known over the last 150 years; acquaintance with meditative issues, a necessary basis for sound translation of many texts, had hardly begun before World War I. The result is that Western knowledge of meditation as a psychological condition—not as faith or prayer or revelation—has very slowly grown with our growing knowledge of Buddhism, and it is fair to say that on the crucial subject of nirvana, Emerson's Orient is not Pound's, and Pound's is not ours.

Always the first challenge for the West has been to grasp the difference between idea and experience, between a thought and a state of mind. The Brahmin Mohini Chatterji in Dublin in 1885 explained to an impatient but fascinated young man named William Butler Yeats that Hindu and Buddhist truth was "a state of mind," not "something that could be conveyed from one man's mind to another's."[3]

The extreme of the state of mind sought in Buddhist meditative practice, Colebrooke explained on the evening of February 3, 1827, to the members of the Royal Asiatic Society of London, "is *nirvana,* profound calm. In its ordinary acceptation, as an adjective, it signifies extinct, as a fire which has gone out; set, as a luminary which has gone down; defunct, as a saint who has passed away: its etymology is from *va,* to blow as wind, with the preposition *nir* used in a negative sense: it means calm and unruffled." Such was the word; what state of mind did it signify?

> In published accounts of the religious opinions of Bauddhas and Jainas, derived principally from oral information, doubts have been expressed as to the sense attached by them to the terms which they use to signify the happy state at which the perfect saints arrive. It has been questioned whether annihilation, or what other condition short of such absolute extinction, is meant to be described.[4]

Colebrooke tried to flesh out the negative category of nirvana with more positive terms: "perfect apathy . . . a condition of unmixed tranquil happiness or ecstasy (*ananda*). . . . A happy state of imperturbable apathy is the ultimate bliss."[5] But many scholars could not accept his description of nirvana as apathy: "How, they asked—attempting to follow the logic of the Buddhist system to its conclusion—could the absence of suffering (*apatheia*) be anything less than total annihilation?"[6] From Colebrooke's speech in 1827 to the present, most Westerners, including many Asian scholars before World War II, would press the issue—nirvana is annihilation—and would press it with a moral fervor. Cowell, the editor of Colebrooke's *Miscellaneous Essays* in 1873, would reprove Colebrooke in a footnote: "All existence is absolutely an evil to the Buddhist, and consequently its absolute extinction is the only summum bonum."[7]

Cowell's remark, says Welbon, "summarizes the interpretations of nirvana given by European scholars during the half-century that followed original publication of Colebrooke's essay."[8] And although here and there someone like Max Muller demurred, pointing to "the psychological impossibility involved in postulating a type of man who could ardently wish for his own annihilation,"[9] such demurrals only point the direction of the mainstream opinion: Buddhist meditators were considered unnatural nihilists (doing what is psychologically abhorrent) or worse, pure quietists, lacking the passion even to self-annihilate.

The British had little enough patience for the Orient's limp-limbed alternative to a stiff upper lip; nineteenth-century Americans hardly believed in the worldly pain that occasioned either, and they believed even less in a passive response to anything. As Thomas Colebrooke was growing up, Ben Franklin said that in America we judge a man not by what he is but by what he does, and although Franklin may have intended only to distinguish an aristocracy from a practocracy, Thoreau by 1855 (with the largest oriental library in the United States) could depend on Concord's distrust of his habit of doing nothing. Even that fine old Christian and Puritan verb, *to meditate,* meaning to concentrate, by the time of Webster's *First Dictionary* (1806) had acquired Machiavellian overtones: "Meditate, v.t. to think, muse, scheme, contrive."

Meditation as thinking, meditation as annihilation. What "other condition short of such absolute extinction" could it be? Since that evening at the Royal Asiatic Society in 1827, "the question has remained for Western Europeans substantially as Colebrooke framed it."[10] What "other condition," besides thought or annihilation, meditation might be, and how it appears in Stevens' poetry, is the subject of this study. As we shall see, reactions to Stevens' "nothings" by his critics often repeat the reactions of Colebrooke's audience.

We begin with the proposition that Western experiences, as described in Wallace Stevens' "The Snow Man," who is "nothing himself," or in Emerson's statement in "Nature," "I am nothing," may have something to do with the claim of Yung-Chia (a seventh-century Chinese Buddhist) that in meditation "the roots of mental activity itself are cut out."[11] Recent empirical experiments suggest that meditative experience is indeed a "set" of the central nervous system which, like dreaming, may have similar contours in various cultures, and many Buddhists assert that advanced meditative experience can occur, unsought, among the uninitiated. Since romantic poets right up to the present time have often sought to put on paper their most intense experiences, one might expect that some of those experiences were meditative, and that both poets and critics have been ignorant of, or even hostile to, the meditative and especially nirvanic aspects of those works.

These are problems, then, that have helped prod this study on its way: first, meditative consciousness as a physiological state of mind (like dreaming) seems to have surfaced, undetected, in the lives and works of our artists; second, meditative consciousness, when detected, has in the West been resisted as annihilation or misapprehended as thought; third, meditative passages in our literature and especially in Stevens have been either overlooked or greeted with the same resistance that has greeted reports of Buddhist nirvana.

Since meditative consciousness is a state of mind, not an idea, it is not easily, as Mohini Chatterji warned, "conveyed from one man's mind to another's." Beginning with Stevens' "The Snow Man," we will search out the range and qualities of meditative experience and explore its place in Stevens' poetry.

2

An Example: "The Snow Man"

The Snow Man

One must have a mind of winter
To regard the frost and the boughs
Of the pine-trees crusted with snow;

And have been cold a long time
To behold the junipers shagged with ice,
The spruces rough in the distant glitter

Of the January sun; and not to think
Of any misery in the sound of the wind,
In the sound of a few leaves,

Which is the sound of the land
Full of the same wind
That is blowing in the same bare place

For the listener, who listens in the snow,
And, nothing himself, beholds
Nothing that is not there and the nothing that is.   (*CP* 9–10)

When Wallace Stevens says that someone "beholds / Nothing that
is not there and the nothing that is," English-speaking readers are
eager to believe anything else: the junipers must be something, for
they are "shagged with ice";[1] or the poem is not about nothing itself,
but "nothingness, 'uncreated' reality as against 'pure' mind";[2] or
"nothing" is an inversion of the true subject: "by telling what man is
not, this poem discloses what he is";[3] or most recently the snow man
has returned to the "first idea."[4] Right or wrong, useful or useless,
each of these remarks diverts attention as quickly as possible from
"nothing" to its context or opposite. This change of stress often leads
critics to remarkably positive, tonal paraphrases of a remarkably nega-
tive, toneless poem. "The Snow Man" exhibits "supreme activity,"[5]
or is "an affirmation of primary reality,"[6] or the "world is re-

22

vealed . . . by a living consciousness."[7] Above all, the poem must be about *something*. No one takes Stevens literally. Even the most religious of our culture (such as Emerson, feeling "the currents of the Universal Being" circulate through him),[8] those at home with an ultimate positive, have trouble with its ineffable counterpart, an ultimate negative.

The single sentence of "The Snow Man" divides into three parts: in stanzas 1 and 2, the rules of the game are laid down for a potential snow man, whoever or whatever that might be ("One must have a mind of winter / To regard . . . have been cold . . . to behold"). The monosyllables are crisp, the images clean and clear. In the second part, stanza 3 those infinitives are extended by a negation: "and not to think / Of any misery." Then, pivoting on the relative clause "which is the sound" and on several incantatory repetitions of "sound" and "same," the poem turns a corner into part three, which introduces not a potential snow man but a mysterious listener who is apparently the real thing. A logjam of negations brings the whole poem up against—paradoxically enough—the ultimate assertion: "is." The three parts, then, are mainly verbal: "One must have a mind of winter *to regard . . . not to think . . . beholds* nothing."

A curious poem. It has been widely reprinted, and in the last fifteen years not only this poem, but also the themes of nothing or bareness in Stevens' work have received a great deal of attention. Each section of the poem is enigmatic by itself, in tone as much as in content, and there are few transitions to help us read one section in the light of another. One must have "a mind of winter," but what is that? And if that is the only way to regard winter, is regarding winter such a good idea? After a semicolon, we are told that one must have a mind of winter "not to think / Of any misery in the sound of the wind." *Is* there misery in the sound, misery to which a cold mind of winter is insensitive? Or is there no misery, a hard fact that the cold mind of winter perceives? Or, to be neither romantic nor naturalist, but modern: is there no misery, but one should "think" of it, invent it, anyway? As we are munching that chestnut, Stevens, in a transition prophetic of his later work, allows the poem to slip, to slide around almost unnoticed to an entirely new scene—but no, we are told this is "the same bare place"—and an entirely new character—or is it?—who seems suddenly to have accomplished all the action that in the first part was only potential. Assuming that the final listener has accomplished what was potential for the "one," all three parts could be paraphrased: one must be cold to look at this scene and perceive not misery, but nothing.

In "The Snow Man," published in *Poetry* in 1921, we have both a classic modern lyric—concise, directed, imaged—and a classic case of modern ambiguity, created partly by syntactic fragments. Within a year of this poem, T. S. Eliot in Lausanne would be writing "The Waste Land," and from Eliot to Merwin our century would experiment with syntactic as well as symbolist or imagist fragmentation. We encounter in "The Snow Man" not only Mallarmé's ambiguity, an interlocking puzzle of potential symbols ("nothing . . . the nothing") to which the author, as Symons said, has withdrawn the key;[9] we encounter not only the sudden shock of a disjunct or isolated image, as expounded by Hulme, Flint, and Pound (1910–1913); we encounter also a poem unfolding, almost unraveling by means of syntax. Yeats had tried it in the middle of "The Wild Swans at Coole" (published in the June 1917 *Little Review* a year before three of Stevens' poems), and had liked the effect so much he later placed the stanza at the end:

> Among what rushes will they build,
> By what lake's edge or pool
> Delight men's eyes when I awake some day
> To find they have flown away?

In Yeats's stanza and in the opening of "The Snow Man," the main act of perception is buried in an infinitive. That infinitive is delayed by intermediate words, delayed by the passage of seasons, hours, or days, and by our waiting for a change of line, creating a slow uncovering of the verbal idea, a kind of periphrastic striptease at the end of which the verb finally stands revealed:

> One must have a mind of winter
> To regard . . .
>
> And have been cold a long time
> To behold . . .
>
> Delight men's eyes when I awake some day
> To find . . .

Each poem, too, as a whole, is waiting for a last verb of perception: "The Snow Man" is stripping down to the final "beholds," "The Wild

Swans at Coole" comes "to find" the swans gone. Both poets prolong the pleasure with an unexpected relative clause (Stevens, "Which is the sound" and Yeats, "when I awake") that at first seems a superfluous extension, a postscript that introduces an entirely new time if not space with a new character—Yeats without swans—who like Stevens' listener will suddenly resolve the issues of the poem by redefining them. All of this syntactic sideshow sets up in Yeats's poem a characteristically charged though negative image: "flown away." During the poem, nostalgia has evolved through loss, to hints of death. Stevens, however, had little else but syntax at his disposal if he wished to end with no visualized image, no known symbol: "nothing" repeated three times. What happened to the pine trees and the junipers? At least Yeats in his relative clause had re-*imaged* his problem—swans come and go forever, then swans are gone for good—but Stevens, when his "beholds" finally falls into place, has removed its subject and object: "nothing himself, / Beholds nothing." The fragments strip to a single verb, with subject and object, perceiver and perceived, gone. Characteristically, Yeats has become more Yeats, while Stevens has slipped away.

No one will be surprised to hear that "The Snow Man" has spawned a variety of interpretations. It may be, however, that the simplest reconciliation of those three sections is the best: one must be cold to look at this scene and perceive not misery but nothing. It may be, also, that the poem's difficulty springs not from its statement but from its tone, the emotions associated with the utterance. The tone that most readers imagine emerging from the text when they hear of being cold, of being nothing, of beholding nothing, turns them against this simple statement and drives them either to reject the poem as perverse or to pervert the poem.

Let us pause a moment and see how seriously some readers react to talk of being and beholding nothing. Harold Bloom in *Wallace Stevens: Poems of Our Climate* gives this poem showcase status. He believes that the "mind of winter" is indeed an experiential category, and he traces it to Emerson's famous religious experience in "Nature"—"I become a transparent eyeball. I am nothing. I see all"—which Bloom calls "the central passage in American literature." Though he considers this passage central, Bloom also finds it quite disturbing and takes Emerson to task for "that Sublime emptiness or great American repression."[10] Although repression is a technical Freudian term, Bloom does not explain just how it fits Emerson's psyche or the passage. We are left with an implied slur—a slander—of being nothing, which understandably enough suggests to Bloom some kind of withdrawal from vitality.

Helen Vendler, an excellent reader of Stevens, uses the same passage from Emerson as a touchstone. She deplores the love of nothing and bareness throughout Stevens' work, and unlike Bloom unleashes a direct moral attack on that bareness which she sees as a sign of an "eye turned away from the imaginative and the social alike, evading poems and feelings and even, finally, evading the human, the poet's own will. In that case he becomes, in a more sinister way, Emerson's transparent eyeball, a pure sphere, hypnotized."[11] Both Bloom and Vendler agree that Stevens' nothing refers to a state of mind, even to an Emersonian state of mind; both dislike the idea of a suspension of self or will; both use current psychological terms—"repression," "hypnotized"—to phrase anew the old charge of "annihilation."

We see here two people voicing their distaste for the condition of being and beholding nothing. Bloom, in addition, shows how to our culture the antidote to this nothing (presumed a disease, though not yet described or diagnosed) is imagination. "The Snow Man," he finds, looks like Emerson's "great American repression" but is not, for "the listener, reduced to nothing, remains human because he beholds something shagged and rough, barely figurative, yet still a figuration rather than a bareness. This nothing is the most minimal or abstracted of fictions, and yet still it is a fiction."[12] The shagged and rough qualities of the scene are not mentioned at the end of the poem; nevertheless Bloom asserts that the listener is beholding *something* instead of nothing, that he does not commit the Emersonian sin of an "eye turned away from the imaginative," in Vendler's phrase. Thus "The Snow Man" is brought in line with modernist aesthetics: " 'nothing' . . . still it is a fiction."

What is so frightening about being or beholding nothing? If some human beings prefer to do it, why is it inhuman? For that matter, what is so comforting about beholding a fiction? The interpretive arguments disguise a moral judgment on a condition—being and beholding nothing—which our critical tradition has not yet described or explained.

Curiously, if Bloom wanted to call this fictive nothing *meditative,* he might gain support for his position from our foremost critic of Christian meditative poetry, Louis Martz, who has said that meditation "brings the imagination into play."[13] Martz's statement, however, is in shocking contrast to Yung-Chia's dictum that in meditation "the roots of mental activity itself are cut out." Perhaps two different meditations—or stages of meditation—are being discussed. But how do we know that Martz is not unconsciously bringing the Christian tradition into line with romantic and modernist (or Renaissance) aesthetics? Or, when we follow the careers of Saint Teresa and Saint John from "blank" states to requisite revelations, are we sure that the Catholic church was not forcing a meditative nothing into the mold of theistic positivism, just as here Bloom wishes to push nothing into an imaginative positivism?

Are Bloom and Martz right, that this beholding nothing is really imagination in disguise (and is therefore romanticism in a new guise)? Is Vendler right, that this beholding nothing is really an annihilation of one's humanity? Thought or annihilation: these are the Western reactions to nirvana since Colebrooke's speech in 1827. What "other condition short of such absolute extinction," as Colebrooke said, could all this talk of nothing signify?

Whatever the state of mind to which "The Snow Man" refers, Stevens himself certainly did not feel he was "turned away . . . evading . . . sinister," nor did he feel he was creating a fiction. Stevens said, " 'The Snow Man' is about the necessity of identifying oneself with reality in order to understand it and enjoy it" (L 464), a reading that Bloom must logically call "the worst reading possible" in order to justify his own.[14]

The pattern is familiar, especially to scholars of Buddhism: a person reports self-loss (in Stevens' poem, the listener is "nothing himself"), union (his is a "mind of winter"; he is "identifying" with reality), and joy (Stevens says the point is to "enjoy it"). Many Westerners cry annihilation, evasion, and solipsism, without first examining just what this state of mind might be. At issue is the moral argument: one must be cold, but *should one*? *Should* one think of misery? Is perceiving nothing a triumph or a failure? Or neither?

Many critics dislike the poem's final listener, who is "cold . . . nothing himself." He is called wrong, for "shagged," "rough," and "glittering" prove that the place is not quite "bare." He is called unimaginative, for he does not "think" the world into fulfillment. He is called inhumane, for he is insensitive to the misery that others, or the leaves, or the wind might feel. The poem thus becomes an exposé of the unfeeling man, but of course it becomes an exposé only in the light of certain assumptions: that imagination and feeling are desirable, that things that glitter cannot be nothing, and that negations are depressing.

On the other hand, most of those who like the snow man listener also stand on native ground: because he sees truly, because he has achieved a cold harmony with his cold world, because in conquering subjectivity he has become the perfect observer, the snow man is seen as a hero, a hard-boiled realist who wants the facts. David Walker recently said the poem's "purpose is simply to define the kind of vision necessary in Crispin's 'starker, barer world,' to suggest that in a time of disbelief and spiritual poverty one must adopt an attitude of radical skepticism, stripped of preconceptions."[15] Again, Stevens' comic spirit ("enjoy it") is conspicuously absent in these readings, as if "The Snow Man" were the same as "The Man Whose Pharynx Was Bad" or "The Plain Sense of Things," full of ennui and the blank cold of symbolist malaise. In the realist-naturalist reading, beholding nothing is a triumph. Either way, the snow man is a nihilist: to the humanist, he has, unfortunately, withdrawn to nihilism; to the naturalist, he has courageously achieved it.

Neither position is sound. The poem itself asserts no emotional response on the part of the listener, and authorizes no emotional response to him. Where is he praised or blamed, except by the connotation the reader brings to "nothing"? We seem to be issued a moral imperative, "One must have," and then, with little or no help from our culture, we are abandoned.

Whether we like him or not, the poem says the listener is right: one would have to "think" of misery, whereas the snow man can "*behold . . . the* nothing that is.*" The verb of perception, perhaps revelation, and the definite article support the listener, although the poem did not begin with that conclusion; it purged itself, riding its own melting like ice on a hot stove, as Frost said, moving from winter images to "nothing," from someone cold to someone "nothing"; in other words, from scene to no-scene, from person to no-person, from tone to no-tone. At its end the bare poem has the same quality of nonfeeling as the bare perception.

The poem is not only about bareness, although most readers take it that way and supply their own reactions to the subject. At its end the poem is itself bare, that is, a neutral description of a certain bare state of mind in which the perceiver may be described as "nothing himself." There is no basis in the poem for judging this—what: mood? idea? nihilism? irony? state of consciousness? The poem finally moves into the mind of winter, a nonfeeling poem about a nonfeeling observer of nothing.

But what do we mean by no-scene, no-person, no-tone, nonfeeling, bare? These are only elaborations of "nothing" to which one might still cry, "Annihilation." Before we react to these words, we should make certain we know what they mean.

The idea of nothing in Stevens' work has been discussed by means of many labels: poverty, bareness, whiteness, blackness, blankness, emptiness, abstraction, denial, nakedness, innocence, purity, permanence, essence, the central, and the ultimate. All the terms are used by Stevens and could describe the objects of religious perception from Plato to Meer Baba to the pope. The best phrasing of this subject is Stevens' own: "the whiteness that is ultimate intellect."[16] Most readers, then, have acknowledged the idealist strain in Stevens—that he is "burning to come to whiteness and ascetic innocence"[17] and that in his poetry some ultimate perception often occurs in a moment of revelation.

A lawyer in 1919 or 1920 in Hartford, Connecticut, was writing a poem that may have religious or ascetic overtones hovering above the tonic chord: nothing. Had he been reading Hegel, Nietzsche? What did he mean? Stevens espoused a bewildering number of ideas about the ideal—a single, ultimate reality—and each idea could be conceived in different moods. He could dismiss the possibility of any ideal in a mood of liberation ("On the Road Home") or despair ("Loneliness in Jersey City"). Or he could believe in a bogus ideal, made when the mind molds the chaos of the world into a "supreme fiction," and then find this supreme fiction sufficient ("Sunday Morning" VII) or insufficient ("The Ultimate Poem Is Abstract"). Or he could affirm a genuine transcendental ideal—not a fiction—and feel its presence ("Curtains in the House of the Metaphysician") or its absence ("The Motive for Metaphor"). Sometimes Stevens' transcendental ideal took the positive form of Plato's sun, or Emerson's oversoul, and sometimes. it was a positive abstraction such as "dominant X" or "the middle." These positive ultimates are often platonic:

> The dazzling, bulging, brightest core,
> The furiously burning father-fire . . .

> Infant, it is enough in life
> To speak of what you see. But wait
> Until sight wakens the sleepy eye
> And pierces the physical fix of things.   (*CP* 365)

On the other hand, this ideal category was at times characterized by negation, "the nothing that is," and this "poverty," as he called it, like all his other ultimate truths, Stevens could affirm, deny, enjoy, despise or simply behold. As would be expected, critics have traced these idealisms to Plato, Kant, Coleridge, and Emerson, and have referred the bareness to Bergson, Nietzsche, and Valery. The reader can pursue these possibilities in other books, and we will return to some in later chapters, but at the moment the words "nothing himself" still stand between us and every intellectual tradition. The listener cannot be thinking anything, or feeling anything—affirming, denying, caring—or he would not *be* nothing; he would be, say, a believer in nothing, and Stevens would be exaggerating. How can we understand "nothing himself"?

Intellectual traditions provide one set of coordinates for locating this "poverty," mystical traditions another. One of the first and still one of the greatest rational scholars of mysticism, William James, said that mystical states may be identified by four "marks": ineffability (Latin *ineffabilis*, unutterable), noetic quality (enlightenment), transiency, and passivity.[18] Right away "The Snow Man" is a candidate; a "nothing that is" is at least paradoxical if not ineffable, "*the* nothing" suggests enlightenment, and the listener is so passive that he does nothing but behold; indeed he *is* nothing but a beholder.

To what sort of human experience does James's list refer? Older comparative studies of culture and religion in this century have used the word *ecstasy*. Various transports, drug-induced or natural, calm or hysterical, have been called ecstasy by philosophers as diverse as James and Laski, by anthropologists as diverse as Eliade and I. M. Lewis, by gurus and psychologists such as Alpert and Tart.[19] Ecstasy refers to a condition lasting only rarely more than two hours and almost always less than one, during which the person feels somehow beyond his ordinary world of time and space. Ecstasy—as opposed to other trances such as hypnotic states, or daydreaming, or intellectual concentration—is associated with an after-feeling of enlightenment; one feels one has seen not nothing, but *the* nothing. This description— as far as it goes—fits many of the reported experiences of Asian and

American Shamans, Yogins, Buddhists, Christian mystics, and perhaps, the snow man.

Since the 1930s, empirical studies of the brain and its functions have allowed us to investigate the mechanics of various *states of consciousness,* giving us a new perspective on James's and Eliade's compendia of worldwide reports. What do we know of states of consciousness? We know, first, that by human report there are a number of states, sets of the mind that are distinct from each other and also vary independently of thought or feeling. Some of these states are: ordinary waking consciousness, nondreaming sleep, dreaming sleep, daydreaming, hallucination, hypnotic trance, meditative consciousness. We begin with the premise that a state of consciousness, though it may contain an idea or emotion, is not the same thing as thinking or feeling. The two most obvious instances, waking and dreaming, immediately suggest the possibility that a state of consciousness is a mode of operation for the entire mind, while thinking and feeling are mental phenomena occurring within one state of consciousness or another. Awake, angry or Marxist; dreaming, angry or Marxist. Ideas and emotions are to a state of consciousness as a figure is to the ground. We know, second, that metabolic and brain-wave measurement and other empirical procedures have tended to corroborate both the distinctness of states of consciousness from each other, and the distinctness of this class of experience from ideas and emotion. We know, third, that some cultures claim detailed knowledge of states we have barely identified.

Of the states listed above, many are strongly visual: waking, dreaming, daydreaming, hallucination. The first and the only widely accepted studies in our culture of nonordinary consciousness (that is, other than ordinary waking consciousness) began with Freud and have focused on dreaming and hallucination. Because dreams are visual, narrative—and to Freudians, symbolic—in this century the study of dreams, fantasies, and hallucinations has placed new emphasis on certain images, narrative patterns, and symbols in literature. But the end of "The Snow Man" contains no visions, no dreams, no hallucinations. If a man is "nothing himself" he can hardly be said to have an idea of nothing, and if he is "beholding . . . the nothing" he is not fantasizing.

The study of dreams is very different from the study of meditative consciousness. Dreams and hallucinations are generally so full of pictures, words, people, or plots that they might themselves be called works of art. Dreams and hallucinations are already imaginings, creations of the mind. Meditative states, however, are characterized by an absence of imagination, by an absence of pictures, words, plots, and even thoughts, and so are hardly subject to direct interpretation or analysis. Such states can have only an indirect relation to the verbal medium of literature, and indeed their very existence can be hard to apprehend. A Freudian approach to the sublime in romantic literature, because it must stress fantasy and interpretation, is likely to be quite different from a meditative approach to the sublime; indeed, entirely different sublime experiences are being approached.[20]

Of the content of extreme ecstatic and meditative experiences we may say little, partly because the experiences are sometimes said to have no content and partly because by testimony of the knowers such experiences are neither known nor described by means of words. What can we say of any aconceptual experience, such as being in love? But of reported qualities (mystics can "reason of these things with later reason") and its characteristic expressions we may say a good deal.

First, in extreme ecstatic or meditative experience one feels oneself to be not in ordinary time and space but in what Eliade calls sacred time and space: the eternal and the infinite. The note of ultimacy is important: these absolutes are not present in other experiences, such as dreams, that reshape ordinary time and space. This ultimacy moves many people to associate ecstasy and meditation with religious experience.

Second, some kind of self-loss occurs; the border between oneself and the external world is blurred or destroyed. One cannot tell if he is or is not (as with Emerson's "I am nothing; I see all. . . . Whether in the body or not, God knoweth"). Or perhaps one feels one's border violated by "spirit possession" from outside or "soul loss" from inside. Such reports point to a momentary loss of the sense of self; the borders of the ego or of one's identity dissolve.

In addition to sensations of transcendence of time and space, and sensations of self-loss, ecstasy is associated with either excitement or a nonfeeling mood. This nonfeeling mood is often translated from Hindu and Buddhist sources as "detachment," but it is a state of mind quite different from the detachment of Western objectivity, or Western irony. This detachment is not a distancing of the intellect but a total disappearance of intellect, and it is variously reported as containing all emotions or none; certainly no commonly understood emotion is dominant. This detachment may be what readers of "The Snow Man" find so distasteful. We will call excited self-loss, *ecstasy,* and detached self-loss, *meditation.*

It is important to remember that our description of such states of consciousness is not limited only by ineffability. Just as our discussion of snow would seem most primitive to the Eskimo who distinguishes more than seventeen types of snow by different words, so our vocabulary for states of consciousness is also limited by our lack of experience and interest. What do we call this detached self-loss: an encounter with the sublime? Rapture? Cosmic consciousness? The *Oxford English Dictionary* reminds us that a remarkable number of qualities may be associated with *sublime,* from "lofty, haughty, proud" to "exalted" or "perfect." That is, of course, quite different from an explicit evocation of all qualities or none by a single word such as *nirvana,* used to refer specifically to a certain experience in a certain state of consciousness. We lack the vocabularly for such matters because we have not yet been accustomed to making the distinctions, but only the most provincial will assume that the Theravadic Buddhists' dissection of meditative experience, for instance, into seven stages of enlightenment, is analytical bravado in the face of the unknowable.

Many states of consciousness—or emotion—may be unutterable, but that does not mean that different states may not be distinguished one from the other by the initiate—numbered one, two, three—and distinctly known, each with its peculiar qualities, just as we each know waking, daydreaming, sleeping, dreaming. In other societies the possibility of many more such distinctions seems assumed: even the uninitiated in some tribes determine by its circumstances and aftermath whether a shamanic aspirant's ecstasy is of the right kind; Zen masters distinguish between false visions and true enlightenment during Zazen meditation; a Theravadic Buddhist might compare the experience described in "The Snow Man" to the fourth stage of meditative consciousness, when "satisfaction departs and indifference begins," or perhaps to a higher state, when one says "There exists absolutely nothing." In our own culture we now distinguish dreaming from other stages of sleep by reported content, brain-wave patterns, and other physiological contours. Thirty years ago we did not even know that most people dream three or four times each night, in ninety-minute cycles related to metabolic rate, faster than elephants, slower than mice.

This exotica is more than titillating. People tend to see what they don't think about as one homogeneous lump: snow, sleep, unusual states of consciousness, faces of another race. If one can accept that we are as naive about states of consciousness as we are about varieties of snow—though many of us live in the midst of both—it may be easier to understand how the no-tone of "The Snow Man" has been exceptionally hard for us to apprehend. And remains hard for us to discuss. A meditative detachment—that is, a meditative approach to *nothing*—seems to beg a superlative form of "ineffable"; it lacks an image (Jesus, the Virgin Mary), an idea (God), a single accepted word (sublime?), accepted ways of testing authenticity and even a roughly definable emotional quality. Which is perhaps why those traditions emphasizing meditative states attach such value to silence—or as a second best, to negation, paradox, oxymoron: "the nothing that is."

To return to "The Snow Man." The absolutely flat perception of "nothing" in the last few lines suggests that the subject of this poem might be a kind of stripping or negating of self, familiar in ecstatic and especially meditative reports. The speaker begins with the slightest possibilities of tone, the slightest distinctions, feelings, judgments: "mind of winter" and "cold" may at first seem pejorative, especially the deathlike "cold a long time," while "crusted . . . shagged . . . rough" and "glitter" associated with the "sun" seem textural, animated, warm. At that point the "mind of winter" might well seem evil, while the alternative to cold perception, thinking of "misery" in the wind, might appear attractively compassionate, suggesting a sympathetic humanism. But from the point of view of the listener in the last six lines, the feelings usually associated with such humanism disappear: "cold" and "winter" lose their sting when distilled to their ultimate state of purity ("bare"), while the listener is purified to "nothing" yet at the same time inexplicably perceptive: he "beholds." He beholds "nothing"—rationally defined—that is not there, and "the nothing"—meditatively defined—that is. He does not project or imagine, he does perceive.

The poem would be ludicrous if this perception were merely the result of blindness; the snow man listener sees the crusted, shagged, and rough trees glitter in the sun, for this is "the same bare place," but he sees them as "nothing." Our description of just what he perceives must here slow down, but what he does *not* perceive is "misery" and the poem clearly evinces a mystical and anti-intellectual epistemology: what one might "think of" is not there, while what one simply "beholds" (when one is "nothing") "is."

Such self-loss and enlightenment, as well as removing the sting from cold and, if need be, death, also makes possible a standard mystical version of compassionate love: instead of feeling sympathy for another (by hearing misery in the wind), the listener has obliterated otherness by realizing his oneness with the whole ("mind of winter . . . nothing himself . . . beholds nothing"). While this condition must be phrased in the negative, it is not necessarily depressing. As Stevens said, "The Snow Man" is about "the necessity of identifying oneself with reality in order to understand it and enjoy it." The self has disappeared; "nothing" is left. The listener is not judged by the poem; his perception has all the marks of a certain kind of meditative moment—self-loss, nonfeeling, an ineffable enlightenment— which the poem expresses in a model of mystical style: the final line is a classic paradox of ultimate negation and assertion, "nothing . . . is," said with detachment.

The snow man is in harmony with his world, but this is no cause for rejoicing. If the self has become nothing, who has triumphed? What is triumph? Because of the detached quality of this perception it is hard to agree with Vendler and Bloom that Stevens' blank is Emerson's: "The ruin or blank which we see when we look at nature is in our own eye."[21] "Beholds . . . *the* nothing that is" does not suggest ruin or depression. The tones of the two statements are utterly opposed.

For the moment, let us say only that a few issues have been raised: there are possible parallels between the poem's negations and assertions and James's "passivity," or self-loss, coupled with enlightenment. By taking this tack we have avoided an appeal to *ideas* of nothing (Heidegger, Bergson, Valery, Nietzsche), for there is no indication that the listener has any ideas at all; we have made a start (and no more) at understanding "nothing himself" as a literal description of a certain experience; we have accounted for the feeling of ineffable enlightenment; and most important, we have withheld emotional reaction, as does the poem, by treating the statements not as theories but as reports of a state of mind.

Certainly it is tempting to look for states of mind in Stevens. Throughout his career he would occasionally identify the ultimate as *being* itself, beyond imagination, metaphor, description. This being seems a kind of noumenon treated as an ultimate phenomenon, what is left of what we need when all the rest is stripped away:

> What is it that my feeling seeks?
> I know from all the things it touched
> And left beside and left behind.
> It wants the diamond pivot bright.
> It wants Belshazzar reading right
> The luminous pages on his knee,
> Of being, more than birth or death.   (*CP* 207)

This Stevens epiphany straddles, or combines, active and passive asceticisms. The repetition of "It wants" is interesting, as if Stevens first tried an ecstatic metaphor out of the platonic-romantic-Emersonian tradition, "diamond pivot bright," then erased it in favor of a more simple, ultimate abstraction, "being," which better completes the conceit of stripping away; yet that ultimate simplicity is still set within the context of desire, and the Belshazzar myth.

Always in Stevens the "Gaiety that is being, not merely knowing" (*CP* 248) is a nonintellectual category, and always it is the happiest of existentialisms:

> there is an hour
> Filled with expressible bliss, in which I have
>
> No need, am happy, forget need's golden hand,
> Am satisfied without solacing majesty,
> And if there is an hour there is a day,
>
> There is a month, a year, there is a time
> In which majesty is a mirror of the self:
> I have not but I am and as I am, I am.   (*CP* 404–05)

One may wonder how we have leapt from "nothing himself" to hours filled with the bliss of "I am." I am suggesting that both "nothing" and "being" reflect states of mind, not philosophical positions; that both have overtones of ultimacy and enlightenment; and that Stevens' equation of "nothing himself" with reality and enjoyment, implying a possible link between "nothing" and "bliss," may prove right on the mark. The "mind of winter" could be immersed in that

> white
> In which the sense lies still, as a man lies,
> Enormous, in a completing of his truth.   (*CP* 431)

At least that kind of language, laced through Stevens' work, should make us quick to the possibility of revelations oddly vacant, simple, static, and peaceful, especially when compared to Stevens' imaginative epiphanies, his more famous

> Seraphic proclamations of the pure
> Delivered with a deluging onwardness.   (CP 45)

Once "The Snow Man" is seen as a possible analogue to meditative experience—a possibility obvious enough for Lucien Stryk to print the last stanza as the epigraph to his *Zen Poems, Prayers, Sermons, Anecdotes, Interviews* and for poet Gary Snyder to use the poem at a Modern Language Association panel on Zen in literature—this study comes to a fork in the road. One direction leads to a compilation of ecstatic passages—Wordsworth's and Tennyson's spots of time, Blake's and Yeats's visions, the *ding an sich* in Keats and Stevens—on the assumption that all ecstasies and meditations are similar. The other direction leads to new distinctions and categories in the area of mystical experience, so that beyond James's four marks the various qualities of various experiences become known and named; then the special properties of a passage might be referred to a special possibility of consciousness. This is the road not yet taken, and the road recently opened up by physiology and Asian studies, and of course it is the road we will follow. There is no reason to violate our sense of taste by asserting an identity of Blake, Whitman, Tennyson, Virginia Woolf, E. M. Forster, and Wallace Stevens, even in passages explicitly related to enlightened self-loss, when every aspect of their styles, like the landscape at the end of *A Passage to India,* cries "No, not yet." If being nothing is not annihilation, just what is it? How frequent and important are echoes of this experience in our literature?

Many problems arise within the poetry of Stevens alone. The term *self-loss* is at once incredible and general, referring to many different situations or none. We need to define more exactly and even physiologically what meditative self-loss might mean, a goal that implies a definition of "self" as well as a reasonable description of how it may be "lost" short of death. Such an attempt would speak to the heart of our Western fear of meditation. And even if we can explain self-loss, not to mention "the nothing that is," we must admit that "The Snow Man" is unique in Stevens' canon, almost perfectly negative and abstract.

The general remarks by James and the anthropologists cannot do much more than suggest that there are, indeed, various types of consciousness, just as Eskimos might readily persuade us that snow comes in many forms. For a description of specific crystalline structures, however, and how they trigger avalanches—do not poems slide on their own melting?—we will have to dig deeper into the mind of winter.

3

Four Types of Mysticism

Mysticism as popularly understood can be divided into four categories: the occult, vision, ecstasy, and meditation. Although commentators such as James have drawn examples of mystical experience from all four categories, the more professional the interest in mysticism the more specifically the commentator (such as Underhill, Jones, Stace, Staal) has insisted an ecstasy and meditation as the most valid categories of mysticism, for those are the areas in which claims to ultimate or religious knowledge are most often made. Evelyn Underhill in *Mysticism* (1911), a book still used occasionally as a college text, makes it clear that she is writing not of the occult but of enlightenment, and she echoes Saint Theresa's disparagement of both vision and the more excited moments of self-loss. The list, from the point of view of most practicing mystics and scholars of mysticism, runs therefore from impure to pure: from the occult's science fiction, to vision's tricks of the mind's eye, to ecstasy's excitement, to meditation's pure tranquility. This study will concentrate only on ecstasy and meditation, which in some ways are similar and have not usually been separated by previous commentators.

For two reasons at least, ecstasy and meditation have not been separated. First, our cultural bias against passivity has apparently encouraged us to recognize the excited quality of ecstasy but to overlook the more passive quality of meditation; second, most commentators have been either practicing mystics (Jones, Underhill), philosophers (Stace), or interested in the history of religion (James, Staal), and to those commentators the *noetic* quality of mystical experience is paramount. If ecstatic and meditative practitioners both report an encounter with a unified, ultimate reality, resulting in conversion, those interested in belief (mystics, philosophers, historians of religion) will tend to see a single phenomenon. The literary critic and the psychologist, however, are apt to ask a different question: what is the

39

quality of the experience—its mood, tone, motivation, expressive result—regardless of its noetic content? Many traditional meditative disciplines distinguish excited insights from calm ones, and psychologists have begun to make the same separation, using physiological contours as well. In discussing literature—the tone of a passage, or appropriate reader responses—the separation of occult claims, visionary images, excited ecstasy, and calm meditation can be crucial.

It seems best to gain an overview right away by defining the four types of mysticism, so that the reader can see how much we are attempting and how much we are not, and can appreciate why Madame Blavatsky's seances, for instance, drop out of our picture while her Buddhist work in Ceylon does not.

The Occult

The new field of parapsychology is the occult dressed in a lab coat. Much of what we associate with magic and the supernatural falls into this category. Charles Tart, an influential spokesman for states-of-consciousness research, turned to parapsychology and defined four subtopics (the description of each topic is mine):

1. *telepathy* (extrasensory perception, ESP); the knowledge of what is in another's mind. An explanation of this phenomenon would require only the existence of subtle waves, like radio waves, emitted by one mind and received by another.
2. *clairvoyance* (also called ESP); knowledge of distant events not necessarily being experienced or transmitted by another mind. Such claims present different spatial and mechanical problems from telepathy.
3. *precognition* (foreknowledge, future or fortune telling); knowledge of events before they occur. Explanation would require new theories of time as well as space.
4. *psychokinesis* (levitation); the ability to affect objects by mental will. Explanation would require a medium of mental force much stronger than the electromagnetic brain waves we now know, or a new description of the relation of mind to matter.

Tart defines these phenomena as part of parapsychology because in each case, "no known physical energy can act as the carrier of the information or force."[1] That may be true, but it begs the question: when gravity, static electricity, magnetism, and sunlight were not "known physical energy," or their "carriers" were not (or are not) known, we didn't consider those phenomena occult; everyone *saw* something occurring that demanded explanation. Occult events are not only inexplicable; they are also rare. Parapsychology might best be defined as an interest in rare events that defy both known scientific law and consensual reality. That does not mean the field is bunk; the doctrines of a round earth and heliocentric solar system once defied science and consensus reality. But those doctrines dealt with everyday events—at least the sun had risen and a ship had sunk from sight. Imagine discussing magnetism without anyone having observed a magnet at work. The first task of parapsychology is still to prove to the community that a phenomenon exists to be studied; the second task is to define and explain the physical energy causing the phenomenon.

This book is not directly concerned with parapsychology or with the aspects of magic, witchcraft, or shamanism that might be called parapsychological, partly because the empirical literature is unimpressive (though the stories are wonderful), and partly because the occult is remarkably irrelevant to English literary study. Occultists tend to stress the event itself more than the particular knowledge gained, and perhaps it is this non-noetic quality that has made parapsychology unimportant to writers—with the notable exception of Yeats. But even to Yeats, the occult was not so much a mode of knowledge as a thrilling event: that George Pollexfen's servant Molly was "second-sighted" (telepathic and clairvoyant) fascinated him, but he was not so interested in what she saw.

Naturally, when occult events are organized into theories of knowledge and reality, as in alchemy, astrology, the caballa, or tarot, there is much to interest the intellectual and the writer. Symbolic and noetic extensions of the occult properly belong to intellectual history, however, and not to a study of meditative experience and art.

Many observers would argue that not a single instance of parapsychological power has ever been proved and that therefore the entire category should be dissolved, probably into hypnosis, hallucination, imagination, and fraud. Actually the laboratory evidence for ESP is supportive, if not irrefutable—depending often on the experimenter's definition of significant statistical variation—and ESP is not at all theoretically preposterous. No matter what one thinks of the occult, anyone perusing parapsychological literature will be struck by the unavoidable and embarrassing choice of either accepting some very tall tales or calling some apparently disinterested and sane people liars.

A belief in rare and unlikely events, from alchemy to levitation to faith healing, is often considered part of mysticism and is hotly debated within the Buddhist as well as the Christian world.[2] A separate category for occult events is useful if only to keep the skepticism that such claims generate from spreading to the other categories—vision, ecstasy, meditation—in which something definite occurs, within the mind.

Vision

We will define *vision* in life as hallucination, and in art, as the representation of hallucinatory phenomena. *Visionary* is the related adjective or personifying noun.

Vision in literary or art criticism is often a vague, honorific metaphor, implying that the artist's understanding in some area is powerful, profound, complete: Melville's vision of evil in *Moby Dick*, Hawthorne's vision of sin, Faulkner's vision of time. In this use, vision need have no visual connotation at all; it is a metaphor comparing the author's understanding to a visual revelation: his understanding is powerful, profound, complete. The mysterious epistemology suggested by vision is common in visual metaphors: "epiphany" (from *phainein*, to show forth), "revealed," "manifest," "shown."

So used, vision has a mystic flavor in that we use it for works of art. No rational discourse, no logical argument however powerful, profound, and complete would be called a vision, although a highly imaginative and moving discourse such as Martin Luther King's "I have a dream" might be welcomed to the fold. The mystery behind this use of vision is the mystery of art: it is a repetition of Socrates' observation in the *Apology* that artists do what they do not by any rational or conventional thought—σοφία—but by a sort of enthusiasm—ἐνΘουσίαςοντες—natural grace and divine possession such as that experienced by soothsayers and oracle interpreters.[3] The result in both cases is vision: for the soothsayer, sometimes a visual vision, sometimes a verbal one; for the artist, an understanding as inexplicably powerful, profound, and complete as an oracle's epigram. The Cumean sybil, hanging in her cage at the beginning of Eliot's "Waste Land," looms before all art.

Although we may admire the way in which the word *vision* preserves the flavor of an inscrutable epistemology behind works of art, the term so used has little place in a technical discussion of mystical or literary categories. We would do better to substitute "sense" (or "apprehension" or just plain "understanding"): Melville's sense of evil, Faulkner's sense of time. We should take care with the word because some authors have visions of a very different kind.

A second common use of vision refers not to the mystery of artistic knowledge but to a specific enlightenment experience: Emerson's vision in part I of "Nature." Upon examination, such visions also, though perhaps full of the metaphors of seeing, may have no visual content:

> Standing on the bare ground,—my head bathed by the blithe air and uplifted into infinite space,—all mean egotism vanishes. I become a transparent eyeball; I am nothing; I see all; the currents of the Universal Being circulate through me; I am part or parcel of God.

What did he see? The rhetorical effect of this nonvisual passage is quite different from Blake's visual vision:

> "When the Sun rises, do you not see a round disc of fire somewhat like a Guinea?" O no, no, I see an Innumerable company of the Heavenly host crying 'Holy, Holy, Holy is the Lord God Almighty.'[4]

There is imagery in both passages; we might "see" Emerson's transparent eyeball. But Blake chooses to say he saw something, whereas Emerson does not. Blake's image is complete and persuasive, especially when choiring angels evoke an entire tradition familiar to the audience, while Emerson's infinite space, divine currents, and transparent eyeball are confusing, fragmentary, and even a bit disgusting. The difference is that Blake's vision, whether a hallucination in life like his famous "angels in the trees" report, or simply a visionary image in art, has a kind of benign tyranny over us; Blake's choir is a powerful and intelligible picture, complete with characters and situation, that circumscribes for a moment our own experience. We are made passive in Blake's world as in a theater; though we may respond, we are responding to the intelligibility of *his* imaginings. His is a sufficient world, filling the senses and requiting desire. Emerson's passage, on the other hand, does not create an intelligible scene, does not create what the Renaissance called a universe. We scramble to follow Emerson but we follow at some distance, with confusion and skepticism. In Emerson's passage we are more on our own.

Emerson's passage is ecstatic; Blake's is visionary. The confusion, vagueness, and variety of Emerson's imagery point not necessarily to a lack of imaginative talent; those qualities reflect the anti-intellectual and antiverbal—the ineffable—quality of ecstatic experience. That is, the ineffable quality of Emerson's experience would be misrepresented by an effable scene. Conversely, the specific content and ready power of Blake's picture is typical of visionary literature. Visionary literature warps, creates, hallucinates time and space. Ecstatic literature explodes or transcends it.

I am suggesting that visionaries tend to be intellectual tyrants, forcing upon us their powerful and fascinating—and imaginable—worlds. Ecstaticians and meditators, on the other hand, tend to be anti-intellectual mavericks, upsetting and confusing us with open-ended and contradictory hints of ineffable—and unimaginable—worlds. Blake was unconventional and irrational, but he was intellectual, meaning that he apprehended imaginatively a coherent world. Not so with Emerson; he stressed instead a certain state of mind that spurned intellectual coherence. As we shall see in part IV, Stevens' love of variety and fragmentation in his long poems has more to do with Emerson's essays than with Blake's visionary epics. This is a sample of later arguments; the issue is that Blake and Emerson, though both were similar in doctrine and therefore are confused by historians of religion, were different not only in style but perhaps also in the experiences they valued. Indeed, the qualities of their different experiences may have led directly to pervasive differences in their work and in how they should be read. Blake's visualization is not just a literary tool; Emerson's fragmentation does not necessarily indicate an empty tool box or despair.

We should keep visual reports apart from abstract enlightenment reports such as Emerson's; not only do we react differently to passages with and without images, but in practice Saint Teresa, Tantric Buddhists, and many others have sharply distinguished between visions and deeper stages (chapter 5) of nonvisual, nonimaginative enlightenment.

We will restrict vision to its literal meaning: hallucination, seeing something that cannot be there in consensual reality. In visionary literature some *thing* is accurately described. A famous example would be Blake's "The Prophets Isaiah and Ezekiel dined with me." There is nothing ineffable about Blake's scene in *The Marriage of Heaven and Hell*. Of course, the dinner party might be only a metaphor for a mental event, but whatever Blake meant, the result is no more unutterable that any other sensory experience, just more impossible.

The difference between the occult and vision is at times a difference of attitude and emphasis on the part of the experiencer, an attitude that certainly affects the resultant literature. Occultists stress action; visionaries stress knowledge. While the occultist is fascinated by the event itself, the visionary often takes his hallucination quite lightly, no matter how vivid it is, and is more interested in what it means. At times either view could be taken of the same event. Blake, for instance, said that his dead brother Robert appeared to him and described the reverse etching method of printing. Had Blake stressed that it was really his brother returned from the dead, he would have taken an occult view of the event. But since he assumed it was his brother—whether in the flesh, vision, or dream hardly mattered—and was interested instead in the printing process, the knowledge gained, we could say he took a visionary point of view.

The difference between visionary and occult claims gives life to the rest of Blake's statement in *The Marriage of Heaven and Hell:* "The Prophets Isaiah and Ezekiel dined with me, and I asked them how they dared so roundly to assert that God spoke to them; and whether they did not think at the time that they would be misunderstood."

As Northrop Frye has suggested, Blake wasn't scared of his ghosts; he commanded them to sit while he sketched. Here Blake fears that Isaiah's and Ezekiel's claim of hearing God, like his own similar visionary claims, might be considered occult. Blake is intrigued—"I asked them how they dared"—by the presumption of his visionary characters, whom Marianne Moore would have called real toads in an imaginary garden. The presence of the biblical prophets is taken for granted; the point of view is not occult. Their knowledge is the center of interest; the point of view is visionary. "A firm persuasion that a thing is so" making it so, the dinner party proceeds in vivid detail.

We need a category for simple hallucination (which includes dreaming) and that category is vision. Unlike occult claims, visions need not be projected upon the ordinary time-space world. Unlike ecstasy and meditation, vision need not imply transcendence of time and space, enlightenment, or self-loss. Quite the opposite. Blake with Ezekiel has certainly not lost his self: he is, as usual, full of it, his prophets are substantial enough to be hungry, and instead of having a revelation Blake gets right down to professional prophetic shoptalk. Vision is a vivid sensory experience, and although in "The Second Coming" when Yeats's sphinx begins moving its slow thighs we may not be in a world as confident as Blake's, we are in a world just as visually precise, for all about us reel "shadows" of the indignant desert birds. Visionary scenes are not ineffable.

The reader might at this point protest that the examples show unutterable states of mind made utterable through imagery, and that to say an *image* is utterable is pure tautology: Yeats's fear was unutterable until it emerged in vision. But that would imply that Emerson was simply inexpressive. What makes the issue interesting is that certain states of mind seem *not* to be utterable through hallucinatory imagery; some mystics, in other cultures and in our own, deliberately and consistently deny such visions in deep meditative experience, and avoid such imagery in meditative passages. "The Snow Man" does not report angels in the trees. Such imagery is avoided, perhaps, because the content of such states is nothing so substantial as Yeats's fear, or as Blake's excitement. Therefore the Buddhists distinguish meditation from dreams and, by analogy, from ordinary consciousness ("the six paths of existence"):

> While in a world of dreams, the six paths
>   of existence are vividly traced,
> But after the wakening there is vast
>   Emptiness only.[5]

All images suggest a positive quality to the experience. What if the listener is "nothing himself," beholding "nothing"? Stevens has almost no occult or visionary poetry, and remarkably little dream imagery. His posited visions, the "angels of as if," are usually silenced in favor of the human voice; then, at times, that too is silenced.

Visionary experience is visual, though sometimes acknowledged as fantasy; occult experience makes claims about the ordinary world of time and space. Once the difference between vision and the occult is recognized, it can also be used to great effect. In Spenser's *Faerie Queene*, book IV, Prince Arthur recites a dream vision of a royal maid who came and lay down beside him in the grass. "But whether dreams delude, or true it were," he says, he loved her, and she told him she was queen of the fairies. On his awakening, the dream is of course gone; it has, however, left its mark on the grass. Before our eyes a vision becomes occult:

> But whether dreams delude, or true it were,
> Was neuer hart so rauisht with delight,
> Ne lieing man like words did euer heare,
> As she to me deliuered all that night;
> And at her parting said, She Queen of Faeries hight.
> When I awoke, and found her place deuoyd,
> And nought but pressed gras, where she had lyen,
> I sorrowed all so much, as earst I ioyd,
> And washed all her place with watery eyen.[6]

Ecstasy

Ecstasy denotes an excited self-loss, meditation a calm one. Otherwise the two conditions are similar, sharing three of James's four marks: transience, ineffability, and sometimes, noetic quality. Only in relation to passivity do ecstasy and meditation differ.

The most common and clearest example of some degree of ecstasy is sexual orgasm, often accompanied by a momentary feeling of self-loss, so that one feels he or she has died and come back. The physiological context of orgasm is excitement: metabolic rate, heart rate, blood pressure are all far above normal for the individual. Corresponding to this physical activity is a positive emotional state; the emotion may be unnameable, but ecstasy is usually reported as some kind of thrill, or joy, or *something*—not as nothing.

Emerson, like Whitman and unlike the more meditative Thoreau, seems characterized by ecstatic experience: "Crossing a bare common, in snow puddles, at twilight, under a clouded sky, without having in my thoughts any occurrence of special good fortune, I have enjoyed a perfect exhilaration. I am glad to the brink of fear" ("Nature," I). Although the emotion may be paradoxical, the words "exhilaration" and "glad" certainly suggest the presence of a positive feeling, and it is this positive quality which the traditional word "rapture" effectively evokes, as in Princess Marie's account of Rilke's experience in 1912:

> He wandered absent-minded, dreaming, through the undergrowth and maze of briars, and suddenly found himself next to a huge old olive tree which he had never noticed before. . . . The next thing he knew he was leaning back into the tree, standing on its gnarled roots, his head propped against the branches. . . . An odd sensation came over him so that he was fixed to the spot, breathless, his heart pounding. It was as though he were extended into another life, a long time before, and that everything that had ever been lived or loved or suffered here was coming to him, surrounding him, storming him, demanding to live again in him. . . . "Time" ceased to exist; there was no distinction between what once was and now had come back, and the dark, formless present. The entire atmosphere seemed animated, seemed unearthly to him, thrusting in on him incessantly. And yet this unknown life was close to him somehow; he had to take part in it.[7]

Unlike vision, ecstasy contains no identifiable thought or imagining: intellectually, it is blank. But unlike meditative enlightenment, ecstasy is accompanied by definite feelings and physiological excitement; emotionally, ecstasy is not blank. The presence of strong emotions in ecstasy leads some to say that ecstasy is less passive than deep meditation, when all feeling as well as all thought ceases; some meditative traditions make that distinction and apply that judgment: the presence of excitement is the presence of an active self.

Within our culture *ecstasy* has stood for almost all mystical experience: feelings of unity, of merging, of thrills on mountaintops, drug highs, orgasm—these might all be called ecstasies, though with widely varying degrees of self-loss and noetic content. Other mystical terms floating about in our vocabularies also seem to refer to ecstasy: "cosmic consciousness," "peak experience," "revelation," and "rapture" connote excitement.

Most Western writers on the sublime have thought that all mystical enlightenment, including Christian meditative enlightenment, is ecstatic; therefore our most excited transcendentalists or visionaries are our most widely recognized mystics: Blake, Yeats, Whitman, most clearly; Emerson, Wordsworth. Conversely, those authors most interested in meditative experience, because that category has simply not existed in our minds or language, tend to be overlooked as mystics: Stevens, Salinger, Woolf, for example.

The artists have had no better conceptual categories than the critics, and of course our artists often emphasize excitement, or (to judge from their writings) mistake their own meditative experience for ecstasy, since passive enlightenment has not existed as a category for them either. Thoreau stands almost alone in American literature before 1950 as a *conscious* spokesman for meditative experience.

For the rest of this study we will be defining ecstasy and meditation by example and by direct analysis. This chapter circumscribes the area: ecstasy is a transient feeling of self-loss and ineffable enlightenment, accompanied by physiological excitement and strong emotion. Ecstasy is what most of us think of when we hear the words "mystical revelation," though we may have been vague about its characteristics. Stevens has ecstatic poems ("Curtains in the House of the Metaphysician," "Meditation Celestial and Terrestrial"), but not many, and their positive qualities usually lead to platonic conclusions.

Meditative consciousness is what we have not imagined at all. Suggest the topic "Mysticism in English and American Literature since 1800" to a professor of English. He or she will probably think first of the visionaries—if not occultists—Blake and Yeats, then of the ecstatic transcendentalists, and possibly not at all of the meditative writers. This is a perfect inversion of the priorities of major mystical traditions, Hindu, Buddhist, Sufi, which tend to regard the most passive mystical conditions as the most characteristic and profound.

Meditation

> If life has a base that it stands upon; if it has a bowl that one fills and fills—then my bowl without a doubt stands upon this memory. It is of lying half-asleep, half-awake, in bed in the nursery at St. Ives. It is of hearing the waves breaking, one, two, one, two, and sending a splash of water over the beach; and then breaking, one, two, one, two, behind a yellow blind. It is of hearing this blind draw its little acorn across the floor as the wind blew the blind out. It is of lying and hearing this splash and seeing this light and feeling it is almost impossible that I should be here; of feeling the purest ecstasy I can conceive. . . . I am hardly aware of myself, but only of the sensation. I am only the container of this feeling of ecstasy.[8]

Woolf's "ecstasy" I would call a lower stage of meditative consciousness. Meditation is a calm state—lowered metabolism, blood pressure, heartbeat, blood sugar, brain-wave length—which can lead to a feeling of self-loss, including cessation of all thought and cessation of all emotion (while remaining awake), and to a sense of ineffable enlightenment characterized not by joy or rapture or bliss but by . . . nothing. "Not only are the means of expression destroyed, but the roots of mental activity itself are cut out."[9] By "mental activity" the Chinese meant, quite correctly, emotion as well as thought. Where, then, is Emerson's glad exhilaration? With strange zest, cut out. It is this absence of any particular quality that makes meditation hard to perceive, hard to discuss, and hard to represent in art. Deep meditation does not contain vision's imagery; it also does not encourage ecstasy's excited metaphors, especially the most venerable of ecstatic metaphors: "I am the lover of uncontained and immortal beauty." Emerson's "lover" captures the passion of ecstasy, but not the detachment of meditation, and is of a piece with Emerson's other thrilling and theistic expressions. Although Stevens says the snow man listener is "nothing himself," tremendous tonal differences exist between Stevens' detached triple negative and Emerson's passionate affirmation: "I am nothing. . . . The currents of the Universal Being circulate through me. I am part or parcel of God."

The reader can see that in the separation of ecstasy and meditation,

James's mark of passivity is the unexplored territory toward which we have set our course. Transience, ineffability, noetic quality are all clear enough, but what is this vaguely benign passivity, this purity beyond thought and feeling, beyond the mind?

> Where is that summer warm enough to walk
> Among the lascivious poisons, clean of them,
> And in what covert may we, naked, be
> Beyond the knowledge of nakedness, as part
> Of reality, beyond the knowledge of what
> Is real, part of a land beyond the mind?   (*CP* 252)

Stevens thought we could occasionally reach such a covert, a kind of humanist heresy. But where is it? We have introduced several terms that indicate direction: self-loss of some sort is involved. It is the self that is increasingly passive in meditative experience, and when one's self is lost, how can there be a sense of anything other than self? The two concepts, self and other, are mutually dependent. To lose self is to lose other; and if there is no self and no other, then all may seem one. We see here—in logical progression, not in ecstasy—that feelings of merger or unity, of self and other being indivisible, might follow from a loss of self. Time as well as space may become a unity in such moments, and feelings of transcendence of time and space— really a loss of the sense of time and space—may be a natural correlative of self-loss. This is a passive state of mind, frighteningly pure, with which Stevens clearly flirted:

> In this chamber the pure sphere escapes the impure
>
> Because the thinker himself escapes. And yet
> To have evaded clouds and men leaves him
> A naked being with a naked will
>
> And everything to make. He may evade
> Even his own will and in his nakedness
> Inhabit the hypnosis of that sphere.   (*CP* 480)

Later we will consider the evidence for just what happens to the central nervous system in these transient moments, so discomfiting to many readers.

Ecstasy is beyond thought but not beyond feeling; deep meditation is beyond both thought and feeling. That is why we say meditation is more passive, with more thorough self-loss than ecstasy, and physiological measurement indicates that meditation is indeed a calmer or more passive state. Both states can go beyond visualization as well as thought, and need not imply occult claims.

To explore meditation further, let us pick up Stevens' trail, for thirty years later he himself returned to the scene of "The Snow Man" and retold the listener's story with a new twist: "nothing" gives way to "the thing itself." If this twist also is meditative, we are facing a lingering concern on the part of this lawyer and executive, and a precise concern too.

4

Meditative Perception: "The Course of a Particular"

Stevens returned in 1951 to the windswept scene he had so carefully sketched and erased thirty years before. Often in the intervening years he had conjured up the basic slate of winter, but in 1951 he returned as if no more than a day had passed, and he added one single sensation, a sound, to the scene of meditative nothingness. This addition takes us in entirely new directions.

The Course of a Particular

Today the leaves cry, hanging on branches swept by wind,
Yet the nothingness of winter becomes a little less.
It is still full of icy shades and shapen snow.

The leaves cry . . . One holds off and merely hears the cry.
It is a busy cry, concerning someone else.
And though one says that one is part of everything,

There is a conflict, there is a resistance involved;
And being part is an exertion that declines:
One feels the life of that which gives life as it is.

The leaves cry. It is not a cry of divine attention,
Nor the smoke-drift of puffed-out heroes, nor human cry.
It is the cry of leaves that do not transcend themselves,

In the absence of fantasia, without meaning more
Than they are in the final finding of the ear, in the thing
Itself, until, at last, the cry concerns no one at all.[1]

The same scene as in "The Snow Man," and the same issue: is the mind of winter "part of everything"? Should it be? What interested him in 1951 was again "the sound of a few leaves" (a line from "The Snow Man") and whether or not one should hear misery in the sound: a "cry." In "The Snow Man" the cry had disappeared—concern with the sound of "misery" had given way to "nothing." Now a "cry" persists right to the end of the poem. This listener does not become nothing, apparently; he remains attentive to the "cry," a word that suggests misery. Is "The Course of a Particular" an answer to the cold listener of "The Snow Man"? In retaining perception, is it antimeditative? The relationship of this cry to a nothingness "still full of icy shades" is the issue that remained interesting to Stevens (after thirty years) and that we must face.

The opening pattern—"Today . . . yet . . . still"—resembles the equivocation at the opening of Stevens' "The Idea of Order at Key West," and here also the equivocal voice accompanies discomfort, discomfort in a world of self separate from object, a world in which one is not "part of everything." The rest of the poem is an attempt to go beyond equivocation. In the second stanza the listener in the snow stops his equivocal repartee and attends the sound of a few dry leaves:

> The leaves cry . . . One holds off and merely hears the cry.
> It is a busy cry, concerning someone else.
> And though one says that one is part of everything,
>
> There is a conflict, there is a resistance involved;
> And being part is an exertion that declines:
> One feels the life of that which gives life as it is.

"The leaves cry. . . ." In this second stanza the attention has been narrowed to the cry: no branches, no wind, no today. We don't know just what he means by "holds off," but we do know that he is not entirely successful; he more than "merely hears," for there is "conflict" and "resistance." He "says that one is part of everything," but apparently he doesn't feel it. Unity seems to be an uphill struggle, a theory only. His epistemology is the problem; the conflict between the method of saying and the goal of being makes "being part . . . an exertion that declines." And since he is at the moment *not* part of everything, since he is not in a state of unity, we are back in the moral dilemma some critics have found at the end of "The Snow Man": without a state of unity, passivity is ennui and apathy is inhumane.

At a turning point now, he gives up on his intellect, exhausted, and "feels"—the epistemological shift from "says" to "feels" is crucial— "feels" the possibility of pure being, the alternative to his own conflict and exertion: "One feels the life of that which gives life as it is." This is a very important line, one that has received a good deal of attention. It seems to be a cry of his own to go beyond saying and thinking, beyond the conflicts and exertions of the intellect, to a more pure yet sensate existence. Such anti-intellectual envy of nonsentient, nonhuman life is both common and radical in Stevens:

> To change nature, not merely to change ideas,
> To escape from the body, so to feel
> Those feelings that the body balks,
> The feelings of the natures round us here:
> As a boat feels when it cuts blue water.   (*CP* 234)

> The night knows nothing of the chants of night.
> It is what it is as I am what I am.   (*CP* 146)

Or, as he says in "The Latest Freed Man," he wishes "to be without description of to be," to feel on awakening as strong and dumb as an ox, "himself at the centre of reality." One is reminded of Emerson's envy of the roses beneath his window in "Self-Reliance": "They are for what they are; they exist with God today. There is no time to them. There is simply the rose; it is perfect in every moment of its existence. . . . But man postpones or remembers. . . . He cannot be happy and strong until he too lives with nature in the present, above time."

The Buddhist meditative tradition links nonsentient awareness and living in the present to meditative consciousness, a formal discipline that Emerson and Thoreau wished for but could not find in the Western or oriental texts of their time. "When Liang-chieh came to Yun-yen, he asked him, 'What kind of man is able to hear the teaching of Dharma through non-sentient things?' Yun-yen replied, 'The Dharma taught by non-sentient things will be heard by non-sentient things.' "[2] Liang-chieh correctly understood that the meditative man has become "non-sentient," and thereupon composed a poem:

> It is strange indeed!
> It is strange indeed!
> Dharma taught by non-sentient things is unthinkable.
> Listening through your ear you cannot understand;
> But you will be aware of it by listening with your eyes.

That is, Emerson and the Buddhists, like Stevens, have expressed admiration for the pure existence of nonsentient life beyond conflict and resistance, and the Buddhists have described a practice of becoming nonsentient through changes in the way we perceive. Stevens is eloquent about nonsentient but perceptive moments when

> to breathe is a fulfilling of desire,
> A clearing, a detecting, a completing,
> A largeness lived and not conceived, a space
> That is an instant nature, brilliantly.   (*CP* 301)

In his anti-intellectual search for "life as it is," Stevens brings his wandering mind back for the third time to the cry, pure and simple. Why? Apparently this poem is not about the wandering mind ("It can never be satisfied, the mind, never"), which is Stevens' favorite subject; it is about the moment when the mind does not wander, Stevens' second favorite subject.

> The leaves cry. It is not a cry of divine attention,
> Nor the smoke-drift of puffed-out heroes, nor human cry.

The best defense is a good offense, and Stevens, like Thoreau, finds his spirits lifting as he goes on the attack. It is a typically meditative attack, a string of denials: the cry is not a cry by a god, calling to us through leaves, nor (the English genitive being so vague) is it perhaps a cry to or for a god, a "too, too human god, self-pity's kin / And uncourageous genesis," as he writes in "Esthétique du Mal." The cry is not the cry of gods, of heroes, or of just plain folks. All those propositions would surround the cry with new rings of suggestion and significance, when what he wants is the thing itself. He concentrates a fourth and final time on the cry, and now makes a strong assertion of perception but a perception that is once again, as in "The Snow Man," full of negations:

> It is the cry of leaves that do not transcend themselves,
>
> In the absence of fantasia, without meaning more
> Than they are in the final finding of the ear, in the thing
> Itself, until, at last, the cry concerns no one at all.

"Things stop in that direction," as Stevens said: "final . . . thing itself, until, at last . . . no one at all." Like "The Snow Man," this poem is a model of poetic closure, and it too closes with the listener detached from any misery in the wind, in a state of "final" perception.

The speaker has worked past a theory of unity to a practice of merely hearing. He has progressed in the poem beyond thought ("says"), beyond imagination ("fantasia"), and beyond feeling ("concern"), to some ultimate perception, a "final finding of the ear," which "at last" issues in negation: "no one at all." There is enough ultimacy, noetic quality, and negation here to make the critic stop and think, as William James said of ecstatic reports.

That last stanza might be meant to represent merely hearing, but as in "The Snow Man" we have trouble with tone unless we know just what Stevens is talking about. Is this "merely hearing" a kind of withdrawal? Affirmation? Rejection? The moral issue of "The Snow Man" resurfaces: should this cry of leaves concern one or not?

A new problem has arisen. How many a sense perception be a "*final* finding," unless it is symbolic, for surely to most of us there is a vast difference between an ultimate abstraction such as "nothing" or "all" and the sound of a dry leaf in January merely heard. Or to pose it as a literary question: what is the relation of the image to ultimate claims in meditative art? Must it be a symbol? Stevens says the leaves "do not transcend themselves," yet he also says this is a "final finding." What gives the sound ultimacy? How many sense data constitute a final perception that does not imply transcendence?

The problem is addressed by the Buddhist tradition in its theory, practice, and art. The question is, how may sensation imply ultimacy without transcendence? Let us follow the course of one particular, the sound of a hand cricket heard by meditating Zen masters.

In 1966 Kasamatsu and Hirai reported results of an electroencephalographic (EEG) study of meditating Zen masters and disciples. They found, as have many such studies since, a pronounced shift of electromagnetic brain waves toward slower and more uniform rhythms during meditation, indicating relaxation (lowered nerve cell metabolism).[3] The meditative patterns do not resemble those of ordinary waking, thoughtful concentration, hypnotic trance, or dreaming; they *do* resemble patterns at the onset of sleep, but the meditator, unlike the person falling asleep, does not continue into the stage 1 EEG of beginning sleep. Some might surmise that meditative consciousness is a holding in a transitional relaxed state usually leading to sleep, but which in meditation is fixed and deepened. Brain-wave patterns alone cannot prove this; brain waves are at most one physiological correlate, origin essentially unknown, for a given state of consciousness.

One aspect of Kasamatsu's and Hirai's experiment surprised them: when a hand cricket was clicked during a Zen master's meditation, the deep alpha (and at times theta) brain-wave patterns showed a momentary interruption for 2–3 seconds, then immediately resumed.

The meditator heard the sound (and later reported so) but did not stop to think about it, or the purpose of the experiment, or the rudeness of behaviorists, et cetera. Had he, the EEG would have shown the beta waves of cognitive thought.

That pattern demonstrates sensory awareness within meditation, but the more interesting wrinkle follows:

> To the first stimulus the alpha blocking [the interruption of alpha activity] occurs for 2 seconds. With the regular intervals of 15 seconds, the click stimuli are repeated 20 times, the alpha blocking is always observed for 2–3 seconds. . . . In control subjects [nonmeditators sitting with closed eyes] the alpha blocking time decreases rapidly [with successive clicks], but in Zen masters, the alpha blocking time is fairly constant; . . . there is almost no adaptation . . . during Zen meditation.[4]

So not only do Zen masters hear the sound without thinking about it at all; they also do not habituate, that is, become accustomed to the sound and subsequently deal with it through subcortical or unconscious pathways. To explain: all along the route of a stimulus from any nerve ending through the midbrain's reticular activating system (RAS) up through the thalamus and on to appropriate areas of the cortex, decisions are made by the brain. Not every sound awakens us at night. We discriminate finely between on the one hand the safe and familiar, on the other hand the dangerous and unknown. These discriminations occur down in the midbrain, in the reticular activating system, which has learned by experience (that is, has modified neuronal pathways as a result of experience) to leave the cortex asleep during one stimulus and to awaken it during another.

Usually when the RAS and the thalamus pass a stimulus on to the cortex, the cortex goes right to work remembering, comparing, and concluding, firing off neuronal connections all over the brain in what we call cortical association activity, the "thought" that would show up on an electroencephalograph as a chaos of beta waves.

The cortex cannot possibly process every stimulus bombarding it during every second while waking, so it tries to reserve its attention for the very few stimuli that qualify as necessary considerations— "necessary" here suggesting, of course, the full range of human interests. If a given stimulus proves insignificant, the cortex quickly learns not to bother with it next time at the conscious level, or to tell the thalamus and RAS to stop forwarding such information at all. In other words, what we are not interested in we usually do not hear, and interest is based on precedent, on credentials; the mind is conservative. Not every visitor enters the door of the president.

Unless, evidently, the president is a Zenist. The Zen masters allow the click to reach the cortex and claim some kind of response (alpha interruption). Note that the response is itself negative in the purest sense; it is merely a momentary cessation of alpha activity unaccompanied by thought or emotion. Not only does the Zen master not process this stimulus in any ordinary way, thinking about it, becoming upset or concerned at the interruption, but also he refuses to program his brain (unlike the control subjects) to cut off the stimulus the next time and to handle it at lower levels of consciousness. Most remarkably, the Zenist not only remains absolutely open, repeatedly, without screening or prejudgment, to the most insignificant stimulus; he also reports that in such a state the stimulus is heard more vividly:

> The Zen masters reported to us that they had more clearly perceived each stimulus than in their ordinary waking state. In this [meditative] state of mind one cannot be affected by either external or internal stimulus, nevertheless he is able to respond to it. He perceives the object, responds to it; yet is never disturbed by it. Each stimulus is accepted as stimulus itself and treated as such. One Zen master described such a state of mind as that of noticing every person one sees on the street but of not looking back with emotional curiosity.[5]

"Respond" is probably the wrong verb; "perceived" and "notice" are better. That last analogy may be physiologically apt: the afterthought of looking back on a perception, that is, normal cortical processing of a stimulus, or in plain English, reflection, is just what is absent in the meditative mind.

We have peeled William James's category of passivity back several layers, past the ear, the RAS, and the thalamus to the cortex, though we must remember his brother's warning that the onion has no center. In aware meditation, the cortex is passive in that it does not process the stimulus in cognitive and emotional ways, and also passive in that it refuses—or "neglects," as Professor Godbole in *A Passage to India* would say—to become accustomed to the stimulus. This is one aspect of the Buddhist practice of nonattachment. One can see how different this is from the inventions of vision or the excitement of ecstasy.

The import of Kasamatsu's experiment, or of the phenomenon it investigates, is more apparent when the Zen response is compared to results of an entirely different experiment with North India Yogins (closer to Hindu tradition): "Yogis generally claim that during *samahdi* they are oblivious to their external and internal environments, and in the present experiments their alpha rythm could not be blocked by external stimuli."[6] Charles Tart, comparing the two experiments, states an interesting conclusion.

> The Zen monks are striving to exist in the here-and-now, in the immediacy of the phenomenal world; thus if one interprets the adaptation to stimulation invariably seen in ordinary subjects as the substitution of abstract cognitive patterns for the raw sensory experience, the Zen monks are apparently managing to stay in the here-and-now of immediate sensory experience. Yoga philosophy, on the other hand, has a strong world-denying quality, a belief that the phenomenal world is all illusion and ensnarement (maya), which the yogin must learn to transcend. Thus it makes sense that they show no EEG response to stimulation and also report being unaware of the stimulation when questioned after the meditative state is terminated.[7]

We have outlined three courses of a particular: in Yogic unaware meditation or sleep the particular stimulus—"the sound of a few leaves," perhaps—may be suppressed below the cortical level of awareness and memory. In ordinary waking consciousness, the sound may be allowed to reach awareness and memory and to set off chain reactions of thought and feeling. In Zen aware meditation, the sound is allowed to reach the cortical level of awareness and memory but it engenders no reaction, "concerns no one at all." It is merely heard.

Consider what aware meditation places before us: a model of heightened awareness that does not involve interpretive thought, symbolism, vision, emotion, or imagination. That reopens the door to perception of the *ding an sich* in romantic literature; to ideas of innocence and pure image; to our models for the perceiving self. So many of our romantic artists have addressed the question of fresh seeing, of apprehending in some dramatic way the thing itself, but not with precisely this conceptual model at hand. Keats may well have been grasping for such a model in his "negative capability," which in part involved the suppression of the identity of the poet, in contrast to Wordsworth's "egotistical sublime." And in this condition, Keats believed, one could take part in other existences. Certainly ecstatic identities characterized romantic literature; perhaps Keats strained to conceive of a meditative alternative.

The conceptual model of aware meditation is very important in Buddhist history, and helps us apprehend and discuss meditative perception. Mahayana Buddhism had developed by A.D. 300 a reaction against the Yogic mind-only doctrine. The reaction, led by Nagarjuna in his famous Middle Way treatises (Madhayamika Buddhism, see chapter 6) emphasized the nondifference of mind and things. Middle Way practice as well as theory explored sensory awareness; the experience of pure meditative perception of a thing became associated with such key terms as nirvana,[8] *sunyata* (emptiness or voidness),[9] *dharma* (truth),[10] and most specifically, *tathata,* which "means things as they are in absolute reality. It is often used to mean 'suchness' or 'thusness.' "[11] Again we must remind ourselves that Buddhists have a large vocabulary for experiences, and that *suchness* refers not to the *idea* of the thing itself, not to a theory of "no ideas but in things," but to the *experience* of perceiving the thing itself with meditative detachment, in a state of no-mind. We must further remind ourselves that especially in Madhayamika Buddhism, terms such as "emptiness" or "voidness" can mislead the Westerner, because we are not disposed to equate emptiness with sensory perception, any more than we are disposed to regard "the nothing that is" as benign. Yet in meditative experience, voidness and thingness can be joined. In Conze's explanation, "From another point of view emptiness is called '*Suchness,*' because one takes reality such as it is, without superimposing any ideas upon it."[12]

The experience and attendant idea of suchness, the thing itself meditatively perceived, became the center of much Chinese and Japanese art stressing ordinariness or everydaymindedness: "Every hour of the day, what one hears and sees are ordinary things and ordinary actions. Nothing is distorted. One does not need to shut one's eyes and ears to be non-attached to things."[13] With this advice, Kuei-shan (771–853) is refuting the earlier closed-senses schools, and was one of many Chinese masters who had a good deal of fun substituting suchness for abstraction, doctrine, or thought. The following reply by Master Tung-shan Shou-ch'u (d. 990), for instance, is not at all symbolic:

> *Monk:*   Now the audience is all gathered together here. Please point out the essence of Ch'an, and tell us its general principles.
>
> *Master:*   Bubbles on the surface of the water reflect all kinds of color; frogs from the depth of the pond croak under the bright moonlight.[14]

It is not surprising that the flowering of Middle Way Ch'an Buddhism in China, 600–900, coincided with the flowering of the simple, concise, clear-image Chinese poetry which was the basis of haiku, and which so impressed both Pound and Stevens. The Chinese combination of humor, lightness, and attention to the thing itself appealed to Stevens in the years of his early poetry. (Part III will take this subject up in detail.) He loved that kind of simplicity and used it:

> In my room, the world is beyond my understanding;
> But when I walk I see that it consists of three or
>   four hills and a cloud.   (*CP* 57)

Let us take one moment to notice the role of meditative perception in two 1688 haikus by Basho, the Japanese poet who began studying Zen in 1681. Henderson's translations are as follows:

> Near the Great Shrine, Tse
>
> From what tree's bloom
>   it comes, I do not know,
>   but—this perfume!
>
>   Where the Cuckoo Flies
>
> Where the cuckoo flies
>   till it is lost to sight—out there
>   a lone island lies.[15]

In both poems a specific perception arises out of ignorance and negation. In the first poem, what arises is clearly a sense perception, and the idea of living in the present of sensation, having abandoned all thinking, questioning, and analysis, is clear. The perception itself is a fragment, lacking the inherent thoughtfulness of a sentence. In Henderson's word-for-word translation, this sudden and asyntactic conciseness is even more dramatic.

> *Nan-no-ki-no* / *hana*   / *to-wa*   / *shirazu* / *nioi* / *kana*
> What tree's / blossom / as-for-that / know-not / scent / kana

Kana is an emphatic, meaning perhaps "ooh" or "ah"—an exclamation point. The word order thus jams together three stages of meditative progress: questioning, ignorance, suchness (scent). Those are the three stages also of Stevens' "The Course of a Particular."

The second poem is more subtle. The process of ignorance giving way to perception is still clear—the cuckoo must be "lost to sight" before its island can be found—but in this poem the suchness that is finally perceived, we might call "imagined." Since, however, the cuckoo is a land bird, the island is not so much imagined as hypothesized on the basis of sound evidence. I believe a Middle Way Buddhist might say this island suggests, more forcibly than does "scent," the indivisibility of voidness and suchness. Certainly, in the original word order, the thing itself, the island that is present and not present, the *one* island on which *one* cuckoo must land, is dramatically specific, revealed at last by the stripping negations:

> *Hototogisu* / *kie-yuku* / *kata*   / *ya*   / *shima* / *hitotsu*
> Cuckoo   / vanish-go / direction: / island / one

In the Middle Way Buddhist tradition, then, meditative perception has been practiced, has been linked in many ways to respect for the physical world, and has become intertwined with art. For artists, the suchness of meditative perception has most usually encouraged an emphasis on the single image (not a symbol or metaphor), or the single perception, excluding fantasy or thought. This clear image is regarded sometimes with exclamation, but always with a noninterpretive detachment.

The idea of suchness answers, I believe, the question of how sense data may result in a final perception that does not imply transcendence, although the ultimacy here derives of course from an absolute not of idea, but of experience. A number of these issues—innocence, self, the nature of perception, we will take up in later chapters, but as soon as we understand the experiential claims behind suchness we can appreciate that meditative consciousness need not deny the senses, and may equate the simplest perception with enlightenment. As Chang Chung-Yuan explains:

> It is traditionally said by Ch'annists that before one is enlightened one sees a mountain as a mountain and a river as a river; in the process of attaining enlightenment, mountains are no longer mountains, rivers no longer rivers; but when one has finally achieved enlightenment, mountains are once more mountains, rivers once more rivers.[16]

It is not surprising that the suchness of meditative perception has been overlooked in our theories, though not in our art. Christian meditative theory stressed the more positive experiences of vision and ecstasy and insisted on a theistic context for meditation, although

Christian practice was various, and the oriental traditions known to the nineteenth century were largely Yogic, Theravadic, and Hindu: world-denying. Knowledge of later Ch'an and Zen aware meditation is more recent; wide dissemination of that knowledge could perhaps be dated from D. T. Suzuki's and Arthur Waley's work in the nineteen-twenties. Only in the last fifty years have we learned of sensory awareness (besides vision) in meditation, and only once, forty years ago by R. H. Blyth, has this knowledge been applied to our literature.

Looking back, we may wonder if suchness, as well as "the nothing that is," was part of Stevens' poetry from the beginning. The answer, I think, is not really, but the tendencies are there. "The Snow Man" was written near the end of Stevens' first period, 1913–1922. Although he knew something of meditative states, as we shall see in part III, the poems of *Harmonium,* his first book, are not at all laced with meditative themes. He seems to have been intent first on exploring the styles and claims of his modernist theory of imagination, "the magnificent cause of being, / The imagination, the one reality / In this imagined world" (*CP* 25). He always had, however, a sense of humor and whimsy that prompted him to back off from theoretical claims, and he was always drawn to the simplicity and clarity he found in impressionist still life, and oriental art and poetry. In "Thirteen Ways of Looking at a Blackbird" and "Six Significant Landscapes," he imitated imagist and Chinese forms. From the beginning Stevens also espoused absolute categories, such as "the ultimate Plato, / Tranquillizing with this jewel / The torments of confusion" (*CP* 27), categories that might seem to have been on a collision course with a theory of the endless proliferation of relative knowledge.

Given the importance of his imaginative theory to his early work, however, the congeniality of its whimsical, brilliant style, and the thoroughly successful apotheosis—or depotheosis—of that theory in "Sunday Morning," it is surprising that from 1918 to 1922 Stevens turned against imagination as much as he did. He turned against it not only on the ecological, folks-in-nature grounds of "Primordia," his 1917 collection of poems in the magazine *Soil.* In "Nuances of a Theme by Williams" and "Anecdote of the Jar" he chafed against invention, finding it irrelevant or sterile (both poems will be treated in detail later) and in "The Snow Man" he turned imagination inside out. Most surprising, however, is the proportional importance he gave to "a starker, barer self" in "The Comedian as the Letter C," his long, unsuccessful, and dazzling autobiographical poem of 1922 that began, one could say, his seven-year silence.

For someone who had written only a few Platonist-Emersonian passages, a few demurrals from modernist imagination, and the thoroughly enigmatic "The Snow Man," Stevens in 1922 devoted a good deal of time to his poet-hero Crispin's reduction to some ill-defined minimum of perception, which functioned explicitly as a foil to imagination. In part I, "The World without Imagination," Stevens brought his Crispin up against an oceanic *other* that inundated *self*, even though the narrator's style was still full of its own preciosity:

> Crispin was washed away by magnitude.
> The whole of life that still remained in him,
> Dwindled to one sound strumming in his ear,
> Ubiquitous concussion, slap and sigh,
> Polyphony beyond his baton's thrust.   (*CP* 28)

In passages that would define his imagination-reality dichotomy for some time, Stevens painted Crispin-the-various against the wash of the ultimate sea. First the Triton myth "dissolved," "Triton incomplicate with that / Which made him Triton, nothing left of him," then

> Just so an ancient Crispin was dissolved . . .
>
>   . . . .
>   until nothing of himself
> Remained, except some starker, barer self
> in a starker, barer world . . .
>
>   . . . .
> Here was the veritable ding an sich, at last,
> Crispin confronting it . . .
>   a visible thing,
>
>   . . . .
>   free
> From the unavoidable shadow of himself
> That lay elsewhere around him. Severence
> Was clear. The last distortion of romance
> Forsook the insatiable egotist. . . .
>
>   . . . . . .
> Here was no help before reality.
> Crispin beheld and Crispin was made new.
> The imagination, here, could not evade,
> In poems of plums, the strict austerity
> Of one vast, subjugating, final tone.   (*CP* 29–30)

The passage sketches not just self and other, Crispin versus reality, but two selves, two Crispins: on the one hand the active Crispin of "romance," the "egotist," with an "imagination" that could "evade" the "final tone" by means of "poems of plums," and on the other hand the more passive Crispin "dissolved," "some starker, barer self" who is free of "the unavoidable shadow of himself" and confronts "the veritable ding an sich." The passage posits two approaches to reality: the one imaginative, the other, of course, the subject of this book. Stevens apparently knew, once he had written "The Snow Man," that his nihilism had a benign potential: Crispin "the nihilist, / Or searcher for the fecund minimum" (*CP* 35). Indeed, much of "Comedian" sets in opposition not imagination and reality, but a fecund maximum and a fecund minimum, each reflecting its own habits of mind and psychologies.

Stevens had no conceptual vocabulary for this alternative to imagination, and he next had Crispin

> stop short before a plum
> And be content and still be realist.
> The words of things entangle and confuse.
> The plum survives its poems. . . .
>
> . . . .
> So Crispin hasped on the surviving form,
> For him, of shall or ought to be in is.   (*CP* 40–41)

"Realist" is the term that our culture offered to Stevens to define, as alternative to romantic, a meditative perception of suchness. It is quite misleading. Crispin's perception of the plum as the thing in itself, which may seem at first like Williams Carlos Williams raiding the refrigerator, eschews language ("words of things") and value judgments ("ought to be") in favor of pure being ("is"). Nothing is eaten; desire is absent. Crispin may be a kind of "realist," but his is hardly the realism of, say, Twain, James, and Dreiser. A constant among them all may be the preference for phenomena over noumena; Crispin and James's heroines are equally abashed before reality. But clearly Crispin's realism is perceptive, not theoretical, social, or historical, and therefore closer to Manet's "naturalism of the senses" than to a Jamesian fate.

That is, no matter what one makes of "The Comedian as the Letter C," it forces on us Stevens as self-conscious phenomenologist of experience, asking of his hero the kind of nature-of-perception questions we have been asking about "The Snow Man," and setting the imaginative egotist against some "starker, barer self." He assigns to the antiimaginative, antiverbal, and passive mode the task of perceiving "the fecund minimum." We find in "Comedian" the major psychological and philosophical corollaries of meditative perception of suchness, although Stevens had not yet written its poem. When he took up poetry again in earnest almost a decade later, as we will see in part II, he seems to have been fully aware of both modes of perception, of their several claims to value and of their opposition. The imagination sometimes creates a romantic and modern reality, and sometimes evades a meditative one.

"Evade" is quite severe. When Stevens turned on his own propensities, he could be extreme. He and his critics most often criticize his asceticism by accusing it of transcendence as well as apathy:

> The greatest poverty is not to live
> In a physical world. (*CP* 325)

But in the case of many meditative poems, that is an inaccurate charge. The world is not illusion to every meditator and meditative tradition; in Stevens' meditative poetry the physical world is often purely perceived.

At times Stevens lived with the greatest poverty in a physical world. Although he never acquired a conceptual model with which to apprehend this experience, he repeatedly called such perception a "poverty," one that led to a fecund minimum, even to an ultimate "centre":

> So that if one went to the moon,
> Or anywhere beyond, to a different element,
> One would be drowned in the air of difference,
> Incapable of belief, in the difference.
> And then returning from the moon, if one breathed
> The cold evening, without any scent or the shade
> Of any woman, watched the thinnest light
> And the most distant, single color, about to change,
> And naked of any illusion, in poverty,
> In the exactest poverty, if then
> One breathed the cold evening, the deepest inhalation
> Would come from that return to the subtle centre. (*CP* 258)

Where is any hint here of imagination, of an active self beyond a beholding, of a reality created half by one's own invention? That "centre" seems beyond us, yet we are united—returned—to it simply by breathing in this moment of "naked . . . exactest" perception of the minimum: "cold . . . thinnest light . . . single color . . . one breathed [without any scent] . . . returned to the subtle centre." The mature Stevens would take seriously this asceticism that was neither realism, nor nihilism, nor a denial of the senses.

One moment of poverty in a physical world may occasion "The Course of a Particular": "One holds off and merely hears the sound." When "merely hearing" is said to go beyond thought and feeling and imagination to "a final finding," an apprehension of "the thing itself," accompanied by a sudden detachment ("concerns no one at all"), one is tempted to call this perception *suchness,* the thing itself, perceived not in Kant's intellectual tradition, but in a context of meditative concentration. Stevens himself said that "the essence of art is insight of a special kind into reality" (*OP* 238), and it may well be that at times the special insight was a "state of clairvoyant observation" (*OP* 166) when "consciousness takes the place of imagination" (*OP* 165).

Much of the argument over "The Snow Man" turns on its verbs of perception. The act of "holding off" while perceiving, of "merely hearing" without thought or emotion, is so difficult to represent that the Japanese Zen tradition has evolved a verb often translated as "to regard," and meaning "to be aware in a meditative sense," to perceive suchness:

> When just as they are,
> White dewdrops gather
> On scarlet maple leaves,
> Regard the scarlet beads![17]

The bead is a symbol of the meditative self, neutral and colorless, taking on moment by moment the color of its world in "the exactest poverty," receiving stimuli, we might say, without processing them. At that level, the reader is being instructed. But at the second level there is no symbolism; the tone at the end of the poem, the tone of the verb "regard" is itself colorless, inviting the reader to move beyond symbolic interpretation and become a neutral consciousness simply regarding not a symbol or metaphor but a dewdrop, "the thing itself." As the passive dewdrop becomes one with the leaf ("regard the scarlet beads!"), the passive mind might become one with the dewdrop.

Obviously neither writer nor reader can be in a deep meditative state while writing or reading, but the rhetoric of no-tone, with its special verb "regard" signifying peception without reaction, and the rhetoric of the pure image, stripped of all significance, mirror the passive yet regardant quality of meditative perception. Stevens' verb "beholds" in "The Snow Man" seems an attempt to collapse all knowledge to an abstract "nothing" (as in Yogic meditation), while his verbal phrase "merely hears" in "The Course of a Particular" seems an attempt to collapse all knowledge to a single definite perception (as in Zen meditation). Both verbs—"beholds" and "merely hears"— in situation, meaning, and tone, resemble the detached perception suggested at the end of many meditative poems.

Although it is a remarkable poem, "The Snow Man" is a dead end. Not every poem can or should come to "the nothing that is." But in "The Course of a Particular" a single sensory detail, the cry of the leaves, instead of being purged from the poem, is heard with detachment. Such detachment we define as allowing something to happen at the sensory level (one is receptive), while one remains nothing at the level of thought and emotion. The physical world remains; the self is lost. Obviously we are implying a definition of self as the association activity of the cortex, and since that activity is the part of us that rises above automatic response and is shaped by each person's unique cortical history, it is not a preposterous place to locate self. We will pursue this issue in chapters 8 and 9. Once we acknowledge the possibility of such a detached meditative perception, the subject of meditative poetry leaps from the ineffable abstractions of "The Snow Man" back to a physical world, to a world full of poetry, a poetry full of the earth. Mountains are mountains; rivers are rivers. And that is why Stevens' favorite divine, "the priest, / The priest of nothingness who intones," speaks of the most minute particulars:

> The iron settee is cold.
> A fly crawls on the balustrades.
>
> ("This as Including That," *OP* 88)

We have added a qualification to meditative experience: self-loss need not imply a transcendence of time and space; it may designate a sense of being, here and now, in a vivid time and space, without the thoughts and desires that define the self. Sensory meditative experience, instead of stressing nothing, stresses suchness, the thing itself perceived in a special poverty, accompanied by a special detachment that is not ennui. Stevens not only uses meditative elements in his poetry; he appears to be remarkably faithful to the intellectual and poetic correlaries of advanced meditative experience.

Obviously, *meditative experience* is itself a complex category. Although all meditators may share a transient experience of self-loss, some are passive in that they perceive nothing, while others are passive in that they perceive something with a pure detachment. Stevens seems to have written poems reflecting both kinds of experience. If we are to know what qualities to look for in his meditative poetry, we need to know more about the range of possibilities within meditative consciousness.

PART II

Meditation and Stevens' Lyrics

I do not for a moment mean to indulge in mystical rhetoric, since for my part, I have no patience with that sort of thing. That the unknown as the source of knowledge, as the object of thought, is part of the dynamics of the known does not permit of denial. It is the unknown that excites the ardor of scholars, who, in the known alone, would shrivel up with boredom. We accept the unknown even when we are most skeptical. We may resent the consideration of it by any except the most lucid minds; but when so considered, it has seductions more powerful and more profound than those of the known.

Stevens, OP 227–28

We define poetry as an unofficial view of being.

Stevens, NA 40

5

The Structure of Meditative Experience

When Stevens published his second book, *Ideas of Order,* thirteen years after *Harmonium,* he was much more aware of the several alternatives of style, subject matter, and perception he had managed to make available to himself. He opened the volume with "Farewell to Florida," announcing his return from the florid tropics to a rather nasty North, as if he wished to dissociate himself, in the reader's mind, from his previous poetry. The title poem, "The Idea of Order at Key West," his primary exposition of his theory of imagination, is set eleven poems into the volume; in between, in "Sailing after Lunch," he dismissed the old "romantic . . . in what the French commonly call a *pejorative* sense" (*L* 277), in order to reinvigorate the romantic with "something constantly new," when "the most casual things take on transcendence." The poem was important to him; he wanted it placed at the beginning of the volume. It is also an odd poem:

> But I am, in any case,
> A most inappropriate man
> In a most unpropitious place. (*CP* 120)

The aesthetic of "Sailing after Lunch" is significantly different from "The Idea of Order at Key West." In "The Idea of Order" the active minds of artist and audience produce products (the song and the transformed perception of the harbor) that lead easily to highly developed metaphors. "Sailing after Lunch," on the other hand, is much less theoretical than "The Idea of Order," and more phenomenological:

> This heavy historical sail
> Through the mustiest blue of the lake
> In a really vertiginous boat
> Is wholly the vapidest fake. . . .

73

It is least what one ever sees.
It is only the way one feels, to say
Where my spirit is I am,
To say the light wind worries the sail,
To say the water is swift today.

To expunge all people and be a pupil
Of the gorgeous wheel and so to give
That slight transcendence to the dirty sail,
By light, the way one feels, sharp white,
And then rush brightly through the summer air.   (*CP* 120–21)

The dramatic and difficult shift of rhythmn and antecedent ("It" as "historical sail"; then "It" as "the way one feels") changes the poem, and propels us toward a kind of reduction ("Where my spirit is I am") even though the human self still gives the transcendence to the sail, and what one feels is still spoken.

A few poems later, however, in "Waving Adieu, Adieu, Adieu," Stevens takes the human "spirit" (the word is central to all three poems) yet another step toward passivity. The opening is a primer on how to read intensity within this poet's reticence:

That would be waving and that would be crying,
Crying and shouting and meaning farewell,
Farewell in the eyes and farewell at the centre,
Just to stand still without moving a hand.   (*CP* 127)

The departure is not by a human lover, but by "a world without heaven to follow." The poem then turns strangely for and against one's self:

To be one's singular self, to despise
The being that yielded so little, acquired
So little, too little to care, to turn
To the ever-jubilant weather, to sip

One's cup and never to say a word,
Or to sleep or just to lie there still,
Just to be there, just to be beheld,
That would be bidding farewell, be bidding farewell. (*CP* 127–28)

Whether or not the "being" of giving and taking, yielding and acquisition is one's historical being (and I think it is; he is saying "the world is too much with us . . . getting and spending"), certainly the "singular self" grows singularly passive, and the opening conceit of a mute witness to the ever departing flux of things becomes an almost comic stasis: "never to say a word . . . to sleep or just to lie there still." No one is singing; no one is speaking. This stasis achieved, the poem comes to a jubilation not made by the active, artistic self of "The Idea of Order at Key West," or even by the neoromantic of expressed feeling in "Sailing after Lunch"; this jubilation comes from relocating spirit in the other, the "sun." Theoretically, this may resemble the Wordsworthian external romantic that Stevens burlesques and dismisses in "The Idea of Order at Key West" (the "outer voice of sky and cloud"), but I am suggesting that passivity of the self, and the phenomenological epistemology it implies, is the important variable:

> Ever-jubilant,
> What is there here but weather, what spirit
> Have I except it come from the sun?   (*CP* 128)

"Spirit" here originates beyond a passive body laid to rest; yet the result is "jubilant." This is a fecund minimum.

Over the next few years Stevens would rigorously pursue this passivity of self as an alternative to creative imagination, and by 1942 he would, I believe, have a thorough and exact understanding of his opposing modes of perception. To follow this "exactest poverty," we ourselves will have to become more exact about its possibilities, its stages and structures.

Visuddhimagga

"The vase was a hell of a lot bluer this time than it has been before . . . it was darker and more luminous at the same time."[1] "The outlines of the vase shift. At that point they seem almost literally to dissolve entirely . . . and for it to be a kind of fluid blue . . . a very fluid kind of thing . . . kind of moving."[2] We will use two sources to sketch the structure of meditative experience: Arthur Deikman's 1963 report on naive meditative consciousness in his laboratory, and first, its opposite, the *Visuddhimagga*, a Buddhist text offering a thorough breakdown of eight stages of meditation.

When a body of knowledge remains on the fringe of a society but never penetrates it, never permeates it, each generation of that society must rediscover the same arcana. Every European generation since Sir William Jones has rediscovered the East. Daniel Goleman found himself on the Harvard-Himalaya-Woodstock circuit from 1970 to 1976, in the company of "thirty or forty Western pilgrims . . . students of virtually every major spiritual tradition: of the various kinds of Indian yogas, of different sects of Tibetan Buddhism, of Sufism, of Christian contemplation, of Zen, of Gurdjieff, of Krishnakmurti, and of innumerable individual swamis, gurus, yogis, and babas. Each brought his or her own small treasure of favored books . . . I sorted out for myself."[3] He finally found the *Visuddhimagga.* In the foreword to Goleman's book, *The Varieties of the Meditative Experience,* Ram Daas (Richard Alpert) tells a similar story; after looking since 1961 for a "labelling system," in 1971 he found it in the *Visuddhimagga:* "Finally I, a Western psychologist, was truly humbled intellectually. For I saw what 'psyche logos' was really about."[4]

Both men could have saved themselves a good deal of trouble by beginning with Edward Conze's *Buddhism: Its Essence and Development* (1951), which gave an excellent summary of the *Visuddhimagga* on "trance," and his *Buddhist Meditation* (1956) which used the *Visuddhimagga* extensively. This is not to mock the spiritualist's emphasis on experience rather than research, but to observe that first-rate scholarship on the East is now available in English, and that those who want a "labelling system" should be able to find it in reputable works. For instance, Rick Fields's history of Buddhism in America, *How the Swans Came to the Lake* (1981) is an excellent step toward sensitive professionalism in popular Eastern studies.

The *Visuddhimagga* is a fifth-century summary by a monk, Buddhaghosa, of certain meditative portions of the *Abhidharma,* a huge core text in Pali of Theravadic Buddhism. Many Western scholars have found it the most useful single text on traditional Buddhist meditation, and we will use summaries of it by Goleman, Conze, and others to describe the lower stages of meditative experience.

Figure 1 reproduces Goleman's chart of concentration meditation as described by the *Visuddhimagga.* A number of key terms require discussion, and we will reduce his eight stages to four, which stand well enough for major stages of lower meditative consciousness in all traditions and which provide us with meditative categories for the rest of this study. We will use the term *detachment* for each stage because it keeps before us the salient quality of meditation: a noninvolvement of self at each level of consciousness.

Stage 1. *Relaxed detachment.* This is a state of waking revery, different in report and physiology from daydreaming or intellectual concentration, void of fantasy or thought and accompanied by long, slow brain waves and some feeling of timelessness. This state is very common, probably experienced at some time by everyone, and might be said to find its traditional American expression in the rocking

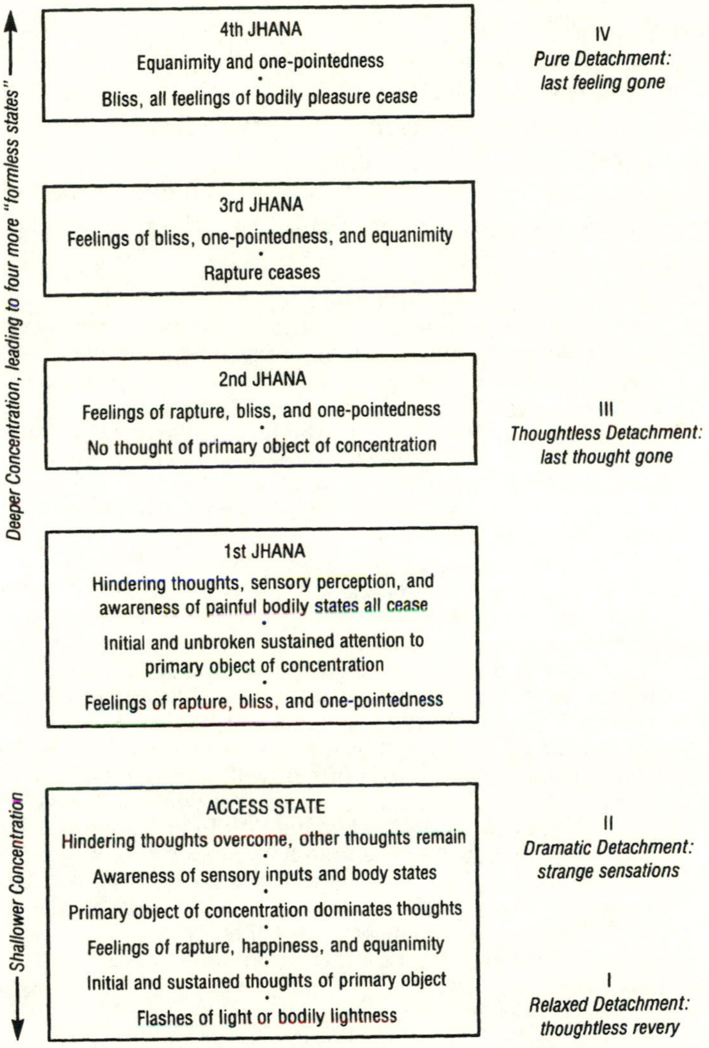

Deeper Concentration, leading to four more "formless states" ↑

4th JHANA	IV
Equanimity and one-pointedness	Pure Detachment:
Bliss, all feelings of bodily pleasure cease	last feeling gone

| 3rd JHANA |
| Feelings of bliss, one-pointedness, and equanimity |
| Rapture ceases |

2nd JHANA	III
Feelings of rapture, bliss, and one-pointedness	Thoughtless Detachment:
No thought of primary object of concentration	last thought gone

1st JHANA

Hindering thoughts, sensory perception, and
awareness of painful bodily states all cease
•
Initial and unbroken sustained attention to
primary object of concentration
•
Feelings of rapture, bliss, and one-pointedness

↓ Shallower Concentration

ACCESS STATE

Hindering thoughts overcome, other thoughts remain
•
Awareness of sensory inputs and body states
•
Primary object of concentration dominates thoughts
•
Feelings of rapture, happiness, and equanimity
•
Initial and sustained thoughts of primary object
•
Flashes of light or bodily lightness

II
Dramatic Detachment:
strange sensations

I
Relaxed Detachment:
thoughtless revery

Figure 1. Stages of Meditation
Adapted from Goleman, *The Varieties of Meditative Experience.*

chair. Decreased metabolic rate and decreased muscular tension (in contrast to intellectual concentration) and the absence of fantasy (or daydreaming) distinguish this type of revery: one is not lost in fantasy or thought, blind to one's senses; on the contrary, there may be a vivid, thoughtless sense of present reality—the sun on the coffee cup, the sound of the siren, "the freshness of the oak-leaves, not so much / That they were oak-leaves, as the way they looked," as Stevens says in "The Latest Freed Man."

Thoreau clearly cultivated this stage of meditation in "Sounds," in *Walden,* and others also have no doubt used the term *revery* in his meditative sense:

> Sometimes, in a summer morning, having taken my accustomed bath, I sat in my sunny doorway from sunrise till noon, rapt in a revery, amidst the pines and hickories and sumachs, in undisturbed solitude and stillness, while the birds sang around or flitted noiseless through the house, until by the sun falling in at my west window, or the noise of some traveller's wagon on the distant highway, I was reminded of the lapse of time. I grew in those seasons like corn in the night, and they were far better than any work of the hands would have been. They were not time subtracted from my life, but so much over and above my usual allowance. I realized what the Orientals mean by contemplation and forsaking of works. For the most part, I minded not how the hours went. The day advanced as if to light some work of mine; it was morning, and lo, now it is evening, and nothing memorable is accomplished. Instead of singing like the birds, I slightly smiled at my incessant good fortune. As the sparrow had its trill, sitting on the hickory before my door, so had I my chuckle or suppressed warble which he might hear out of my nest. My days were not days of the week, bearing the stamp of any heathen deity, nor were they minced into hours and fretted by the ticking of a clock; for I lived like the Puri Indians, of whom it is said that "for yesterday, today, and tomorrow they have only one word, and they express the variety of meaning by pointing backward for yesterday, forward for tomorrow, and overhead for the passing day." This was sheer idleness to my fellow-townsmen, no doubt; but if birds and flowers had tried me by their standard, I should not have been found wanting.

Thoreau was measuring himself by the standard of Emerson's roses, which grow outside of time and memory. His day was not spent in intellectual concentration: thinking, imagining, composing paragraphs. No Blakean visions, just "sheer idleness," timelessness, and a heightened sense perhaps of the sparrow's trill—the thing itself. That such a revery is a distinct state of consciousness is suggested by the feeling of "waking up" out of it. The sensations of suspended time, ineffable pleasure, and passivity—no-mind—are admirably captured by Thoreau, and he correctly compares those sensations to oriental "contemplation and the forsaking of works" (which he knew, in 1846, mainly through the *Bhagavat-Gita* and the *Laws of Manu*).

The *Visuddhimagga* assumes, rather than describes, this most amateur stage of meditative consciousness. Detached relaxation contains no dramatic enlightenment experience, which is one reason that philosophical and religious commentators may overlook it. Relaxation lies before Goleman's "access state" in figure 1. But some American movements, notably transcendental meditation, have clearly encouraged this eperience under the name of meditation, and physiological studies[5] as well as reports such as Thoreau's, place detached relaxation within the spectrum of meditative consciousness. When popular American movements stop at this stage, however, they are likely to miss the Buddhists' point, as Staal dryly observes: "The Buddha sought the causes of suffering, and its elimination, not a feeling of relaxation."[6]

Stage 2. *Dramatic detachment*. This stage is equivalent to Goleman's "access state" and first *jhana*. At this level a person knows something strange is happening, though whether the experience is later valued or remembered is another question. Thought and feeling are present, but one is dramatically aware either of the object of concentration or of some general expansion of being. Warpings of time and space may occur and exceptional imaginative phenomena may emerge: hallucination, sensations of levitation, flashes of light. Strong feelings of pleasure or displeasure may sweep over the meditator. Thought is still present. Conze translates the following description of the first *jhana:* "Detached from sense-desires, detached (also from the other four) unwholesome states, he dwells in the attainment of the first jhana, which is accompanied by applied and discursive thinking, born of detachment, rapturous and joyful."[7]

The term *dramatic detachment* calls attention to the paradoxical nature of this stage: on the one hand physiological relaxation continues; on the other hand, while passivity deepens with respect to body and intellect, the imagination and emotions may become exceptionally active. Some sects, notably among Tantric Buddhists of Tibet, encourage the dramatic phemonena of this stage, treating the phenomena psychoanalytically as yielding information about the meditator. They value that information for signs of what kind of self must be worked through to achieve self-loss. Reports of vision and ecstasy and popular terms such as "rapture," "Cosmic consciousness" and "peak experience" often refer to this stage of meditation, and especially in Tantric literature such reports are full of bizarre imagery and strange metaphors.

In the *Visuddhimagga,* these dramatic experiences within a meditative framework are signs that the student has taken the first step into an access state. So also in the Zen tradition, *makio* or false visions are signs of beginning meditative experience. But while in our culture these phenomena are almost synonymous with enlightenment—revelation, vision, rapture, excitement, strange occurrences—in most meditative systems this stage, though it is considered a sign of meditative progress, is also considered the opposite of enlightenment, because it is so active and imaginative: an expression of self.

Stage 3. *Thoughtless detachment.* Without thought, but with feeling, this category covers Goleman's second and third *jhanas.* Virginia Woolf's childhood ecstasy (chapter 3) would be a second or third *jhana.* We are moving toward "The Snow Man," but we are not there yet, for some kind of extraordinary emotion is still present, lending a positive though ineffable quality to such experiences. What kind of emotion is the question. Goleman's terms "rapture" and "bliss" and "one-pointedness" beg explanation:

> There is a subtle distinction between rapture and bliss. Rapture at the level of the first jhana is likened to the initial pleasure and excitement of getting a long-sought object; bliss is the enjoyment of that object. Rapture may be experienced as raising of the hairs on the body, as momentary joy that flashes and disappears like lightning, as waves showering through the body again and again, as the sensation of levitation, or as immersion in thrilling happiness. Bliss is a more subdued state of continued ecstasy. One-pointedness is the property of mind that centers it in the jhanic state. The first taste of jhana lasts but a single moment, but with continued efforts, the jhanic state can be held for longer and longer intervals.[8]

The movement from rapture to bliss to cessation of bliss indicates a movement away from excitement toward passivity and nonfeeling, a condition reportedly harder to achieve than nonthinking. Meanwhile, some mental concentration (one-pointedness) which we are told over and over is not thinking, continues. One-pointedness may well refer to the internal monitoring by which the cortex holds itself in this state, giving up more and more cortical activity without falling asleep.

This internal effort to make no effort, willed will-lessness, may in turn be one of the experiential paradoxes behind Zen dynamism and *koans* (Chinese and Zen verbal riddles designed to stop the mind). At the level of thoughtless detachment, thought has disappeared, feeling is disappearing, and the intense concentration may be the central nervous system toeing this line. Clearly, although both visions and ecstasy can occur within a meditative context as well as outside it, this Theravadic meditative tradition is interested in moving past both visions and excitement.

Stage 4. *Pure detachment.* We are studying Western literature, not Buddhism, and it would be futile for us, without training, to try to follow the *Visuddhimagga* into four more formless states beyond cessation of thought and feeling. We are as far as language can go. At this stage there is no cortical activity we can identify except the maintenance of the state itself—a pure being and, in some traditions, a pure perceiving, without the ordinary responses of self (thinking and feeling). The self is felt to be lost, and the categories of self and other no longer structure the world. Let us review the *jhanas*, and their relation to our four categories, through Conze's summary. After the initial state of relaxed detachment,

> The first stage of trance [Goleman's first *jhana,* our dramatic detachment] is achieved when one can suppress for the time being one's unwholesome tendencies—i.e., sense-desire, ill-will, sloth and torpor, excitedness and perplexity. One learns to become detached from them and is able to direct all one's thoughts unto the chosen object. At the second stage [Goleman's second *jhana,* our thoughtless detachment] one goes beyond the thoughts which went towards and round the object. One ceases to be discursive and adopts a more unified, peaceful and assured attitude of confidence, which the texts call "Faith." This attitude of groping or stretching oneself out toward something which one does not know discursively, but which one knows would be more satisfying than anything known discursively, results in elation and rapturous delight. In a manner of speaking, this elation is still a blot and a pollution, and in its turn it has to be overcome. This task is achieved in the next two stages [Goleman's third and fourth *jhanas;* entering our pure detachment] so that in the fourth Dhyana one ceases to be conscious of ease and disease, well-fare and ill-fare, elation and dejection, promotion or hindrance as applied to oneself. Personal preferences have become so uninteresting as to be imperceptible. What remains is a condition of limpid, translucent and alert receptiveness *in utter purity of mindfulness and evenmindedness.* Above this, there are four "formless" dhyanas.[9]

Several principles, I hope, are clear. First, the borders of particular *jhanas* are not so important as the broad movements away from thought and feeling. Therefore, I have made four categories for the uninitiated: (1) relaxation, (2) dramatic detachment (with thought and feeling, ecstatic), (3) detachment without thought, and finally (4) detachment without feeling. Beyond this are categories irrelevant, so far as I know, to English literary study (perhaps a master would disagree). The second principle is that beyond the first *jhana* (dramatic detachment) everything tends toward passivity of some sort, while concentration deepens. A third principle is that progressive passivity is progressive self-loss.

The passivity of this final self-loss defies paraphrase. *Any* phrasing will generate its own problems. *Penetration,* for instance, suggests a self/other dichotomy. What is there to penetrate? Who is penetrating? This is only to say that nouns themselves depend upon distinctions and that when all distinctions are dissolved, when the borders of self are gone, yet one—what one?—is vividly aware of an undifferentiated reality, the experience cannot be captured by language. No *one* can be singled out as the subject of a verb; no single action can be isolated as the predicate for a subject: Unity, then, usurps all nouns, and stasis usurps all verbs.

Within a steady detached state, or within lower meditative ones, there may occur a sudden sense of enlightenment, of penetration to an ultimate reality. The importance of a steady meditative state versus a sudden enlightenment experience within that state is hotly debated in meditative traditions. In Japan the Rinzai Zen sect seeks sudden enlightenment (*satori*), while the Soto Zen sect insists that steady meditation (*zazen*) is *satori*. Curiously enough, steady meditative practice—about which we know so little—is much more central to many mystical traditions than is dramatic enlightenment, James's "noetic quality."[10] For literary study we need only be aware of the two experiental possibilities: steady meditative self-loss and sudden enlightenment.

The *Visuddhimagga* may have the virtue of mapping a venerable meditative system which, being based on a thousand years of practice, demands respect, but it also has the disadvantage of being so complete and remote, not to mention reduced to language, translated, and popularized, that we can hardly follow its abstractions. For that reason, the reported experience of untrained Americans is perhaps as persuasive in establishing the existence not just of a meditative state of consciousness, but of roughly the same four stages—relaxation, dramatic phenomena, cessation of thought, cessation of feeling—in the same order of occurrence.

Deikman's Experiment

In the early sixties Arthur Deikman asked a number of friends, most of them professionally involved in psychiatry, to participate in an experiment. Each person was to sit in an armchair, in a plain room twelve feet square, facing a blue vase on the table. Twelve sittings of fifteen minutes were planned. Deikman wanted to study some aspects of meditation; he had read "mystic literature" and had planned to play various tapes to measure the subjects' ability to block distracting stimuli. That aspect of his experiment need not concern us, but the reported experiences of his subjects—ignorant of most meditative phenomena and unmotivated, not seeking salvation—reveal that even the most antimystical writer might experience various stages of meditative consciousness.

Deikman's directions are close to Mahayana Zen directions in his tolerance of sensory phenomena (in contrast to Yogic and most Theravadic traditions) and in his anti-intellectualism, although Deikman unwittingly strikes an extremely willful and goal-directed stance:

> The purpose of these sessions is to learn about concentration. Your aim is to concentrate on the blue vase. By concentration I do not mean analyzing the different parts of the vase, or thinking a series of thoughts about the vase, or associating ideas to the vase, but rather, trying to see the vase as it exists in itself, without any connections to other things. Exclude all other thoughts or feelings or sounds or body sensations. Do not let them distract you but keep them out so that you can concentrate all your attention, all your awareness on the vase itself. Let the perception of the vase fill your entire mind.
>
> While you concentrate I am going to play a variety of sounds on the tape machine. Try not to let the sounds occupy your attention. Keep the sounds out so that they do not disturb your concentration. Likewise, if you find you have drifted into a stream of thought, stop and bring your attention back to the vase. At the end of about five minutes (ten minutes and 15 minutes for the second and subsequent sessions respectively) I will tell you that the session is over. Take as much time as you like to stop.[11]

Because of the unusual nature of the state of mind sought, Deikman's subjects often needed further direction: "For example, one S revealed by his retrospective account of the meditation that he had been systematically scanning the vase. It was explained to him that his intent should be to suspend thinking about the vase, or analyzing it, so that he could perceive it as directly, as completely, as intensely as possible."[12]

After every session Deikman quizzed his subjects about their experiences. *All* subjects by the end of the experiments reported, among other things:

> 1. "Alteration of their perception of the vase." The color changed "to a deeper and more intense blue" . . . "more vivid" . . . "luminous." In addition, the shape or size seemed to change: "undulating up and down." Subject A, session 4: "The outlines of the vase shift. At that point they seem almost literally to dissolve entirely . . . and for it to be a kind of fluid blue . . . kind of moving."
> 2. Time-shortening in proportion to reported success in concentrating. The sessions seemed to pass very quickly.
> 3. Contradictions within reports. Deikman labeled this "conflicting perceptions," but his examples do not necessarily show evidence of tension within a single perception or between perceptions—only conflicts at the verbal level in reports. This is our first brush with the affinity between the ineffable and oxymoron: "It certainly filled my visual field. . . . It didn't fill the field by any means" . . . "a great deal of agitation . . . but it isn't agitating." "It's very hard to put into words"—"a frequent comment," said Deikman.[13]

What people considered worth reporting seems to have begun with stage 2 phenomena: dramatic sensations of warped time and space, sometimes accompanied by strong feelings. Consider subject C's report after the ninth session:

> It started radiating. I was aware of what seemed like particles . . . seemed to be coming from the highlights there and right to me. I seemed fascinated with that. I felt that it was radiating heat. I felt warm from it and then realized that it was all shut out, that everything was dark all around, a kind of brown, lavender, eerie color and it was during this incandescent kind of radiating inner glow thing I could feel my pulse beating in my head and then there was . . . a twinge in my penis, I could feel my pulse beating in my penis and in my temples. . . . I felt that there was a light coming down from above, too, that something was happening up there and I started getting an erection and this thing danced and it was very active. It moved, it pulsated and it also jumped around like this. It seemed like many colors around the edge of the table.[14]

Subject C reported a more passive experience in his next session: "I felt this whole other plane where I was nothing, I mean where my body was nothing. I wasn't aware of my body I could not have been there and I wouldn't be surprised."[15] Or as Emerson said of his highway epiphany in "The Transcendentalist," "whether in the body or out God knoweth."

Subject A was most adept. She moved quickly into dramatic warpings of time and space and then to more passive feelings of self-loss, although she "had no conscious knowledge of the mystic literature and her retrospective account emphasized the strangeness, the unexpectedness and the startling quality of her experience."[16] Let us look at some of her reports in order of occurrence: "One of the points that I remember most vividly is when I really began to feel, you know, almost as though the blue and I were perhaps merging, or that [the] vase and I were. I almost got scared to the point where I found myself bringing myself back in some way from it. . . . It was as though everything was sort of merging and I was somehow losing my sense of consciousness almost."[17] A clear description of self-loss accompanying feelings of merging. The element of fear, which persisted in her responses even though she consistently enjoyed the sessions, reminds us that her state of mind was both unsought and unexpected.

The breakdown of the borders of self, as noted in chapter 2, can allow sensations of passage in either direction: sensations of soul loss from the inside or of possession from the outside. Both seem to be associated with self-loss and merging. The self can move out into the vase; the vase can move into, occupy, take over the self. After her sixth session: "As one point it felt . . . as though the vase were in my head rather than out there: I knew it was out there but it seemed as though it were almost a part of me."[18]

We do not yet know—though it may be knowable—why passivity of the cortex accompanied by waking concentration encourages self-loss, but it is tempting to think that we define ourselves, moment by moment, by means of cortical action, that *self* is as much a verb as a noun. To lose the process, then, of manipulating data may be to lose self. After the same session, subject A also reported total Yogic blocking of stimuli accompanied by feelings of self-loss before she "came back":

> I am sure that at that point all sounds were obliterated. At that point somehow everything was out of my consciousness; . . . when I came back my awareness that suddenly I could hear the tape again and for whatever infinitesimal space of time it was . . . it seemed that I heard absolutely no sound; . . . it was as though the world was absolutely silent during that time.[19]

It seems that subject A is here approaching a noetic experience; rather than simply insisting that sounds were not heard—as the dog and the child are not heard while one is reading—she seems to strain for absolutes and to move easily into "the world": "all sounds . . . obliterated . . . everything was out . . . absolutely no sound . . . the world was absolutely silent." Perhaps this is only a dramatic tone, an excited report. But certainly we can imagine such a personality, given a context of Buddhist tradition, making a leap of faith and choosing to find this silence more fundamental than the noise surrounding it. Such a choice might be prompted by the purity (that is, passivity) of one's meditative experience.

In later and longer sessions "Subject A described a 'film of blue' that developed as the boundaries of the vase dissolved. It covered the table on which the vase sat and the wall behind it, giving them all a blue color." After the eleventh session (a longer one): "I am convinced that what I initially . . . called merging was this kind of thing that happened (now) for practically 30 solid minutes. . . . it lost its boundaries and I might lose mine too. . . . I was swimming in a sea of blue and felt for a moment I was going to drown."[20] Afterward she admitted anxiety but also felt the experience was desirable. One might compare this kind of self-loss to the less meditative crisis of Isabel Archer, facing the hard manhood of Caster Goodwood at the end of *Portrait of a Lady,* excited, and scared she was drowning—like Emerson "glad to the brink of fear," or quite over. One also thinks of the currency of the term *oceanic feeling* for ecstatic and meditative mergings. The situations of subject A and Isabel were very different, since Isabel was experiencing a unique crisis of the individual psyche, drowning perhaps in her own fear of life and sex, while subject A and Emerson were experiencing an impersonal and universal form of self-loss, yet in both cases the giving up of the ego (that familiar ghost) implies an immersion in some more fluid reality, an immersion accompanied by simultaneous feelings of pleasure and of fear.

Because she was so adept and interested, subject A came back for more sessions after the experiment had ended. In session 21 she certainly reached at least the third stage, detachment without thought, and perhaps was at the door of the fourth stage when fear pulled her back from pure detachment:

> She reported that a diffuse blue occupied the entire visual field and that she felt merged completely with that diffuseness. She had a

sense of falling, of emptiness, of loneliness and isolation as if she were in a vacuum. Her sudden realization that there were absolutely no thoughts in her mind made her anxious and she searched for thoughts to bring herself back. "It was as if I leaped out of the chair to put the boundaries back on the vase . . . because there was nothing there . . . the vase was going and I was going with it."[21]

Subject A's willingness to refer to herself as lost and to the vase as nothing may remind us of the listener who, "nothing himself, Beholds nothing." Certainly her report resembles numerous mystical reports. As Deikman observes, her description follows well enough the admonition in the thirteenth-century Christian tract, *The Cloud of Unknowing:* "At the first time when thou dost it, thou findst but a darkness and as it were a cloud of unknowing, thou knowest not what."[22]

Transcience, ineffability, passivity are there. Again, noetic quality is conspiciously absent. Deikman points out that none of the subjects had "a sense of ineffable communication with the absolute, of profound illumination into the nature of Reality, nor of being in a state of Unity,"[23] although subject A's last report of merging is close. What did occur, Deikman observes, seems similar to the ineffability, transcendence of time and space, and "absence of specific content such as images or ideas" reported in many mystic traditions.[24] In addition, he says, what occurred seemed neither expected by the subject nor encouraged by the experimenter—subject A reported surprise at the merging phenomena, for instance—and therefore relatively independent of cultural influence.

A comparison of Deikman's results with the *Visuddhimagga* reveals several similarities. First, the deeper the concentration of Deikman's subjects, measured by their own opinion and by the sequence of their reports, the greater the self-loss and passivity. Visions and flashes of radiant light came easily; the more adept the subject, the more quickly passive experiences ensued. Subject A was first to experience dramatic warpings and first also to move on to self-loss. Therefore, we can conclude that Deikman's naive meditation experiment and the venerable *Visuddhimagga* both suggest a natural (not theoretical) movement in meditative experience toward the more passive states. Relaxed concentration is followed by dramatic sensations of warped time and space, then by cessation of thought, and last, if at all, by cessation of feeling—all concurrent with progressive breakdowns of the borders of self and object (and therefore progressive loss of time and space) leading to sensations of nothingness.

We saw that both "The Snow Man" and "The Course of a Particular" move past thought, implying a sequential structure to meditative experience. Both poems introduce metaphors and vivid images early, then introduce thoughts and feelings only to deny them ("not to hear any misery"; "not the cry of gods") and move finally into negation and ultimate detachment: "nothing"; "concerns no one at all." In structure as well as in content and tone, both poems seem to imitate the stages of meditative experience.

A second conclusion is that James's category of noetic quality is relatively unimportant. James, although a psychologist, approached mysticism as a philosopher of religion with an interest in reports of ultimate knowledge or belief. But both the *Visuddhimagga* and Deikman's study show that many noteworthy experiences short of ultimate enlightenment are part of meditative consciousness, and indeed Buddhist sects disagree on the importance of sudden enlightenment compared to steady meditative practice.

Almost every commentator in our culture has approached meditation as a means to knowledge, not as simply a state of mind that might be achieved by any person regardless of theoretical persuasions. We have already seen that meditative experience and meditative art may include vivid awareness of the physical world. We now see also that meditative experience need not make claims to ultimate perception or belief.

If, in defining meditative experience, we include physical sensation and exclude—or at least hold in abeyance—ultimate belief, we enlarge considerably the common conception of what might be called meditative, and we begin to realize that meditative concentration may be practiced by many who, like Deikman's subjects, have no knowledge of meditative tradition and no mystical intent. Such concentration might be practiced by one walking. A neighbor in Hartford, Florence Berkman, described Stevens' walk: "He had a very interesting walk. It was slow and rather symmetrical. He almost walked in cadences. Every Sunday he used to walk over to the park. Rain, or sometimes it'd be sleeting, he'd walk over. He'd spend an hour; all kinds of weather."[25] The *Visuddhimagga* and Deikman describe meditative practice, but for what the meditator perceives and how it may affect his view of the world, we will turn to the subtlest of meditative traditions and return to our subtlest of poets, that ponderous walker of parks.

6

The Middle Way: "A Clear Day and No Memories"

In the last two chapters, a number of statements about meditation and assumptions about Stevens have accumulated: meditative consciousness may include sensation stressing the thing itself, need not imply enlightenment or transcendence, may include warped perception and strange feelings, has many stages, tends toward calm and passivity, and may be experienced by anyone practicing a certain kind of thoughtless concentration.

We cannot and should not try to go directly from Deikman to Stevens: direct reports prove little, and Stevens, like many masters, might by sensibility as well as comprehension make no claims to enlightenment. What Ch'an and Zen look for, instead, is the kind of understanding, in one's speech and poetry, that proceeds from— reflects, is corollary to—meditative experience. While the experience itself may be nonintellectual and transient, it can certainly enter one's daily outlook and alter one's point of view. What kind of understanding might enter a mediator's art? What we find in Stevens is not Yogic doctrine, or Christian, or Theravadic, but something very close to the most subtle and interesting of the secular, sensate Mahayana traditions: the Middle Way. We will in this chapter leap from meditative practice to the kinds of things Madhayamika meditators say afterward, placing the Buddhist allusions in this book in some historical perspective and returning, armed with meditative theory as well as practice, to Stevens' poems.

Perhaps no single doctrine can be asserted of all Buddhist schools: some popular movements seem theistic, some Chinese movements almost world-affirming. However, the vast majority of schools and the most influential have held fairly closely, if subtly, to the Buddha's sermon at Benares, in which he defined all life as ill, an illness originating in craving and cured by that renouncing of craving achieved by, among other things, the "right concentration" of meditation. Since this sermon, springing directly from Buddha's meditative enlightenment and preached right after it, introduces every major Buddhist concept in less than 200 words, it deserves to be quoted:

> 1. What then is the Holy Truth of Ill? Birth is ill, decay is ill, sickness is ill, death is ill. To be conjoined with what one dislikes means suffering. To be disjoined from what one likes means suffering. Not to get what one wants, also that means suffering. In short, all grasping at (any of) the five skandhas (involves) suffering.
>
> 2. What then is the Holy Truth of the Origination of Ill? It is that craving which leads to rebirth, accompanied by delight and greed, seeking its delight now here, now there, i.e. craving for sensuous experience, craving to perpetuate oneself, craving for extinction.
>
> 3. What then is the Holy Truth of the Stopping of Ill? It is the complete stopping of that craving, the withdrawal from it, the renouncing of it, throwing it back, liberation from it, non-attachment to it.
>
> 4. What then is the Holy Truth of the steps which lead to the stopping of Ill? It is this holy eight-fold Path, which consists of: Right views, right intentions, right speech, right conduct, right livelihood, right effort, right mindfulness, right concentration.[1]

The five *skandha*s (heaps) are categories into which all things associated with individual existence can be placed: (1) material things, including the body, (2) feelings, (3) perceptions, (4) impulses, (5) acts of consciousness. As Conze explains, "The belief in individuality or personality is said to arise from the invention of a 'Self' over and above those five heaps."[2] The very first Buddhist writings expounded the mechanism by which involvement with the *skandha*s produces suffering. The doctrine of *conditioned coproduction* describes the endless cause-and-effect chain of action and reaction, "this being, that becomes; from the arising of this, that arises, etc."[3] Buddhists trace this chain past individual existence through cycles of rebirth. In effect, one breaks out of the chain by having no reaction, by achieving the extinction of nirvana.

The world made up of the five *skandha*s and obeying the law of conditioned coproduction is close enough, in most schools, to the world or law of karma for us, to use that more familiar word. Karma, then, in this study refers to the situation of all things and events in the world of cause and effect. This is our conditioned world of *skandha*s which the Buddha described as the source of ill. Nirvana, on the other hand, is an unconditioned category that takes us out of the cycle of cause and effect.

The psychological component of these categories is so strong that *karma* is almost synonymous with the world as perceived in our ordinary state of consciousness, and *nirvana* with what is perceived in a meditative state of consciousness. Guenther says: "It is this tendency to react by emotions that is called 'the world,' Samsara, as opposed to the tranquil equanimity of Nirvana which is attained by a radical change of attitude." And he quotes the *Abhidharma:* "Karman and the emotions are the reason for the way of the world."[4] *Karman* Guenther interestingly defines as "the potential and kinetic energy of a process" heaped up in its potential stage (*apacita*) and developing (*vipacyate*) in its kinetic stage "toward a certain effect."[5] The sermon at Benares, then, provides the historical and philosophical context for the Buddhist emphasis on meditation and there can be no doubt that renunciation of action and reaction, within the psyche, is a dominant theme.

It is commonly said that "Hindus, on the whole, believe that there is a self (atmavada); Buddhists, on the whole, that there is no self (anatmavada). . . . But yoga, which makes no assumptions about the self, is practiced by either."[6] It is also commonly said that Hindus believe physical reality is illusion (*maya*), while Buddhists variously find it deluding (*samsara*), or real, or indisguishable from nirvana. However, the concepts of self and reality are so slippery within meditative traditions that such statements are only introductions to topics. In practice, writes Frits Staal, the two religions have traded a good deal: "The Buddha had adopted Upanishadic notions, and the Advaita school of the Vedanta in turn incorporated notions from the Buddhist Madhayamika school."[7] Facing this variety, Conze defines Buddhism as comprising "all those teachings which are linked to the original teaching by historical continuity, and which work out methods leading to the extinction of individuality by eliminating the belief in it."[8] "Eliminating the belief" refers to the psychological changes wrought by meditative practice.

The historical continuity of Buddhism soon divided into attentuated and cross-woven threads. After a council meeting that took place about 400 B.C., Buddhism split into camps: the Hinyana (lesser vehicle, Old Wisdom school) in the south, and the Mahayana (greater vehicle, New Wisdom school) in the north. The Hinyana schools included Theravadic Buddhism, which spread south to Ceylon where its major texts were recorded in the Pali language between 400 and 100 B.C. This Pali canon is our most important source for early Buddhist texts, and along with a few Sanskrit texts, the only source for nineteenth-century European knowledge of Buddhism. Other Hinyana schools (most notably Savastivadins in India) need not concern us in this study: Theravadins represent the oldest and most conservative strain of Buddhism.

Unlike the "peoples of the book"—Jews, Christians, Moslems— who have a Bible, the Buddhists have no authoritative word, by meditative inclination have little trust in words, and by paradoxical result have composed more scriptures than any other religious tradition. Thousands of sutras (purported conversations with the Buddha, sometimes "recorded" centuries later) and *shastras* (commentaries by monks), many now lost, were composed in a variety of languages for about a thousand years after the Buddha's death. For instance, the oldest Chinese Buddhist catalogue, A.D. 518, lists 2,113 works, of which 276 have survived. One of the two Tibetan collections includes 2,664 commentaries on Tantric texts, in 86 volumes.[9] Or again, a "single text" in name, such as the crucial *Prajnaparamita* (Perfection of Wisdom) *Sutra,* was first composed by numerous authors during two hundred years, then elaborated for two hundred years, then summarized and edited and commented on for a thousand years, so that "text" may be the oldest Prajnaparamita version in 8,000 lines, other versions in 18,000, 25,000 or 100,000 lines, or some very famous later "summaries": the *Heart Sutra* in 25 (or 14!) lines or the *Diamond Sutra* in 300 lines. The text itself seems to disappear before our eyes, as a flame that has been extinguished, a saint who has gone away.

We therefore cannot even begin a survey of central texts for each branch of Buddhism. For Theravadic Buddhism, however, one might keep in mind the *Abhidharma,* a collection of oldest Buddhist works, and its codification in A.D. 400 by Buddhagosa, in his *Visuddhimagga.*

In the north, Mahayana Buddhism formed many different schools, most notably to us the Madhayamika or Middle Way school, which influenced Tantric Buddhism in Tibet, Ch'an in China, and Zen in Japan. Again, many important sects such as Amidism, a popular devotional movement, have no place in our search for a meditative phenomenology that fits Stevens. The differences between Theravadic and Mahayana monks are easy to exaggerate, for at first they often shared the same monastery, the same monastic rules, and the same meditative practice. The Theravadics, however, tend to stress the transcendence of the absolute and denial of the senses (closer to Yogins) while the Mahayanists often stress the immanence of the absolute and acceptance of the senses. Similarly, more than Theravadins the Mahayanists emphasize the ideal of the *bodhisattva,* the enlightened man who voluntarily comes back from enlightenment, or even renounces it, returning to this miserable earth like a captain to a sinking ship, vowing to save everyone else and be the last to leave.

As Mahayana Buddhism mingled with Taoism from 100 B.C. to A.D. 500, it found ways to conform to Chinese respect for nature and to the "anti-establishment, anarchist and laissez-faire attitude" of Taoism.[10] As Chinese Ch'an Buddhism then moved to Japan to become Zen, many of those tendencies were sharpened. The crucial conformation of Buddhism to Taoism and Chinese character was given direction by Nagarjuna about A.D. 200.

An Indian philosopher of Brahmin background, Nagarjuna in his Middle Way (Madhayamika) sutra rigorously applied the idea of voidness to voidness itself; that is, the experience of voidness must eliminate the concept of voidness, and all attempts to give voidness (or nirvana, *samadhi,* oneness) a positive form or shape or quality, all attempts to make nothing into something, should be—yes—avoided. Within a meditative tradition this was not so much a heresy as a purifying return to fundamentals, an attempt, often repeated in Buddhist history, to clear the cobwebs of idea, doctrine, and verbalization from meditative insight, to wrench *nirvana,* once again, from a noun back to a verb. Within Buddhist history, then, Nagarjuna demoted the concept of voidness, which in Theravadic nirvana and in Yogic "mind-only" doctrines had approached an absolute or transcendental category.

As he demoted nirvana, however, Nagarjuna also elevated this world of ordinary perception, *samsara.* Indeed, the core of his doctrine was that "Void and being are not conceived of as two. This is called the Middle Way."[11] His ideas became the central feature of Mahayana Buddhism as it was moving north into China, and represent the best thinking in the world on the subject of meditative sensation. Nowhere else can we find more subtly examined and expressed the various interpenetrations of consciousness and reality as seen from a meditative point of view. Since Nagarjuna was essentially renouncing doctrinal and theoretical history in favor of pure, sensate experience, he was also developing a meditative phenomenology in a way that might transfer most usefully to a Western *ingenu* like Stevens, who knew nothing but the state of consciousness itself as an undefined mode of being and perceiving. We will look at Nagarjuna's approach to voidness, recall the suchness of being (presented in chapter 4) that he saw as inseparable from voidness, mention briefly some antidoctrinal Chinese Middle Way traditions rich in artistic suggestion, and examine the epistemology of meditative practice. This may seem a survey of far fields, but I believe we will find ourselves perfectly focused on another Stevens poem, and on his major psychological assumptions from 1935 on. We will also have located our most subtle meditative points within one historical tradition, perhaps the most compelling and profound for those interested in the relation of meditation to ordinary life and art. Frits Staal introduces the tradition:

> The Buddhist Madhyamika system holds that reality is ultimately *sunya* "empty, void," a doctrine that by its nature is difficult to express adequately or interpret meaningfully, but that has given rise to a voluminous literature, ancient as well as modern. Now the nature of *sunyata* is not a matter of pure speculation; it is grasped in and through meditation. . . . *Sunyata*, accordingly, is not a theory; in fact, it is regarded as the end of all theories.[12]

Conze helps us understand the qualities of this category, asserted to be unknowable by theoretical thought, in his discussion of *sunyata*'s etymology:

> The sanskrit word *sunya* is derived from the root SVI, to swell. *Sunya* means literally: "relating to the swollen." . . . Thus the root SVI, Greek KY, seems to have expressed the idea that something which looks "swollen" from the outside is "hollow" inside. . . . Thus our personality is *swollen* in so far as constituted by the five skandhas, but it is also *hollow* inside, because devoid of a central self. . . . It is a great pity that these connotations of the world *sunyata* are lost when we speak of *emptiness*. . . . Particularly to the uninitiated, this emptiness will appear as a mere nothingness, just as Nirvana did.[13]

Clinging, then, to this metaphor of voidness as swollen, or perhaps to the image of a hollow seed or gourd, let us push further towards what we can discuss: the historical sources and the theoretical results of such "voidness-being."

Emptiness or voidness in Nagarjuna's treatise "means the identity of yes and no" (reminiscent of Chuang-Tzu's identity of being and nonbeing), and:

The germ of this idea is formed in an early saying, which the scrip-
tures of all schools have transmitted. The Buddha says to Katyayana
that the world usually bases its views on two things, existence and
non-existence. "It is," is one extreme; "it is not" is another. . . .
Avoiding both extremes, the Tathagata teaches a Dharma in the
middle between them, where alone the truth can be found. This
Dharma is now called *emptiness*. The Absolute is emptiness and all
things also are empty.[14]

Nagarjuna's way of looking at things, which we must trust is only
truly understood through meditation, produced a formula which ap-
pears over and over, in one form or another, throughout subsequent
Mahayana Buddhism: "Everything is such as it is, not such as it is,
both such as it is and not such as it is, and neither such as it is nor such
as it is not."[15] This Socratic construction pretty much covers the bases
in the field of language and thought. We thought we knew that which
we did not know, and we are not surprised to hear that "the purpose
of Nagarjuna's dialectics was not to come to any definite conclusion
at all, but to destroy all opinions and reduce all positive beliefs to
absurdity."[16]

Having slid from the sublime to the ridiculous by denying any
difference, we may now return to reason with the remembrance that a
noncognitive state—indeed, a noncognitive state of perception—lies
behind such *sunyata* doctrine. In such a state, neither *I* nor *other* is
felt to exist and yet both are felt to be swollen together, and that
therefore either nothing or all or both may be appropriately reported.
In Guenther's words,

> It is the indisputable merit of the Madhayamikas and Tantriks. . . .
> to have pointed out the fallacies of these one-sided interpretations
> and to have solved the problem [of dualistic thought] by recapturing
> the living spirit of Buddhism in immediate experience where such
> predications as "existence" and "non-existence" are wholly out of
> place and where the claim of an ontological object corresponding to
> the experience is a sign of bad reasoning.[17]

We see that Nagarjuna demoted nonexistence and promoted exis-
tence, within Buddhist history, not by preferring one over the other
but by asserting their identity: "From another point of view emptiness
is called 'Suchness,' because one takes reality such as it is, without
superimposing any ideas upon it."[18]

The effect of Nagarjuna's thought, as it combined with a reaction
against Yogic mind-only doctrine and with Taoist nature worship

and a love of practicality in China, was tremendous, for here was a meditative way not of renouncing the world but of seeing it even more accurately, without the biasing preferences and blinding fears of the self. Here was an unconditioned point of view that not only respected the conditioned but identified with it: "Void and being are one."

In chapter 4 we encountered the idea of suchness and some of its physiological coordinates in meditation. We surmised that a waking mind that is neither screening nor processing data in its ordinary way might perceive an object more vividly, and we heard practitioners testify to the extraordinary vividness of their sensations. The doctrine of voidness helps explain the presence of absolute terms in a suchness report, while denying symbolism or transcendence. The thing in itself perceived in such a meditative moment *is* in some perfect, absolute way (notice the adverbial construction), but it is not *an* absolute (as is a noun). The absolute quality in such a pure perception—possibly the source of a noetic quality in the experience—is inseparable from the passivity, or negation, that makes such perception possible. It is as if the absoluteness of the thing or of being, its suchness, were merged with the negation, or voidness, of the perceiving cortex. In Stevens' own words, "I have not but I am and as I am, I am" (*CP* 405). That is as close, perhaps, as we should dare to come to an experience considered ineffable: nirvana and *samsara* are one. Here we are sashaying again around an experience that must not be allowed to become a thought. Conze observes: "When properly considered, the thought of the Buddha would really not be a thought at all, because an unconditioned thought cannot be included in the skandha of consciousness, and because it is not separated from its object, but identical with it."[19]

Kakuan's series of twelfth-century drawings and comments, one of many series on this subject, depicts a man chasing the bull of Tao, "the way" of enlightenment. He searches for the bull, perceives it (3), catches it (4), tames it (5), and rides it home (6). He then transcends the bull (7: the equivalent of transcending attachment to enlightenment) and in number eight, both "bull and self are transcended," and the picture is blank. Kakuan's poem and commentary read in part:

> Whip, rope, person, and bull—all merge in No-Thing.
> This heaven is so vast no message can stain it.
>
> *Comment:* Mediocrity is gone. Mind is clear of limitation. I seek no state of enlightenment.[20]

Here an earlier, traditional series ends, and here might be said to end the Theravadic and Yogic doctrines. Kakuan, however, following the Chinese Middle Way school, went beyond the traditional end at the eighth picture to create two more: "Reaching the Source," where again "the river flows tranquilly on and the flowers are red," and finally "In the World," where:

> Barefoot and naked of breast, I mingle with the people of the world.
> My clothes are ragged and dust-laden, and I am ever blissful.
> I use no magic to extend my life;
> Now, before me, the dead trees become alive.

In Nagarjuna's Middle Way treatise two points were central: "Never to abandon all beings and to see into the truth that all things are empty."[21] We have seen that emptiness, as Nagarjuna defined it, was an aspect of suchness. This, combined with the *bodhisattva* ideal "never to abandon all beings" and the Chinese love of nature, led to Kakuan's ninth and tenth pictures: one comes back from nirvana to "the people of the world" and to suchness, for then "the dead trees become alive." The Middle Way tradition claimed (as we shall pursue in part IV) that the transient moment of self-loss can color one's later experience of ordinary consciousness: when nirvana and *samsara* have been joined, there is no need to leave either. One is "ever blissful" while "in the world." One is "at the center of the market . . . yet he stays on top of the solitary peak."[22]

This is an experiential claim that lies behind everydaymindedness, the Ch'an and Zen encouragement of perceiving what Emerson called "the miraculous in the common." Suchness is usually associated with a meditative state of consciousness; everydaymindedness refers to preserving a sense of suchness while engaged in ordinary activity:

> Everyday-mindedness is free from intentional action, free from concepts of right and wrong, taking and giving, the finite or the infinite. . . . All our daily activities—walking, standing, sitting, lying down—all response to situations, our dealings with circumstances as they arise: all this is Tao.[23]

Clearly, simply renunciation is not the only possible consequence of meditative insight.

The Chinese invented many types of antidoctrinal exercises such as the *kung-an* or koan, questions designed to "stop the mind." The replies often suggest one's ability to avoid doctrine and to realize suchness in mundane situations. Some questions are themselves answerless ("What is the sound of one hand clapping?") while other questions are reasonable and demand subversion by means of an answerless answer. The most famous:

> A monk once asked Master Chao-chou whether a dog has the Buddha-nature. Chao-chou's answer was "Wu." The original meaning of "wu" is "to have not," or "nothing," or "non-being" . . . "wu" indicates the absolute moment. . . . So the moment one begins to meditate on "wu," one dissolves one's self in the absolute realm of "wu" or Void.[24]

More common than such a nothingness answer, however, is a remark emphasizing suchness. Perhaps the most famous of the everyday-suchness replies is also Chao-chou's (in Japanese, Joshu): "Another time Chao-chou was asked, 'Since all things return to One, where does this One return to?' His reply was, 'When I was in Tsing-chou I had a robe made which weighed seven Chin.' "[25] This was not a symbolic statement; it was a fact.

There are hundreds of such replies to the stock question "What is the meaning of Bodhidharma coming from the West?" (Bodhidharma was a monk of A.D. 500, who brought Mahayana Buddhism to China.) Answers: "The cyprus tree in the courtyard" (Chao-chou); "The blue silk fan brings the cool breeze" (Feng-Yang); silence from Ting-shu; a kick from Ma-tsu. A koan is a question that invites one to fruitless thought, doctrine, cognition on the one hand, or on the other hand to demonstrate spontaneously one's knowlege of "the identity of yes and no."

Notice that gesture, silence, or a kick, as well as speech, can serve to suggest a rejection of doctrine, and a nonintellectual insight. Tomio Hirai reports that the EEG of Renzai Zen priests answering koans resembles the EEG of meditation, and that the success of answers as judged by masters corresponded to the depth of meditation as measured by EEG.[26] This suggest that the cortical passivity of meditation can indeed be carried into more active circumstances. In the Chinese Ch'an schools from A.D. 200 to 900, a series of masters and students developed these art-in-life skills, practicing spontaneous replies to situations, replies that dramatized (1) the end of all doctrine, (2) the identity of voidness and suchness, and (3) the extinction of self. Out of thousands of stories, here is one favorite:

Another time Chao-chou went to visit Master Huang-po, who closed the door of his chamber when he saw him coming. Whereupon Chao-chou lit a torch in the Dharma Hall and cried out for help. Huang-po immediately opened the door and grabbed him, demanding "Speak! Speak!" Chao-chou answered, "After the thief is gone, you draw your bow!"[27]

Chang Chung-yuan's gloss on this story:

> Huang-po closed the door to indicate to Chao-chou that the truth of Buddhism cannot be told. . . . Chao-chou, however, understood this. He wanted to let Huang-po in turn know that one must not remain in the Void but must return from it, so he lit a fire to make Huang-po open the door. Huang-po understood this action, but wanted to make Chao-chou speak to find out if he understood correctly. However, Chao-chou's understanding went far beyond this— the demand for an explanation came much too late: "After the thief is gone, you draw your bow!"[28]

Part of the fun of such stories is that they reflect all the complex tensions of an art form: these enlightened men crave communication and competition, and they have invented grand vocabularies of speech, action, and egotism, of wanting and knowing, that become a sort of theatre of *wu*. The dominant mood of such theatre, however, is detachment, for the participants seem to take it as a game. Suchness, or one's ability to seize the moment, guides the plot.

Nagarjuna's equation of voidness and suchness, combined with Chinese irony and love of reality, produced the most thoroughly verbal, dramatic, and witty meditative arts on earth. Naturally, then, Chinese (and related Japanese) Mahayana Buddhism produces some of the best parallels to Western artists.

With some knowledge of Mahayana practice as a base, we will venture into one more area of inquiry: is there anything we can rationally learn or say about how one perceives suchness? What can we know, outside of meditation, of meditative epistemology? What do adepts say about their mode of knowing?

> The conception of Prajnaparamita is the distinctive feature of the Madhayamika system. It dominates every part of its philosophy—its metaphysics, ethics and religion. Prajna is the non-dual knowledge. . . . The dialectic reaches its fruition through three "moments," the antinomical conflict of opposed views of the real advanced by speculative systems (drstivada); their criticism, which exposes their hollowness (sunyata); and the intuition of the Real in which the duality of "is" and "is not" is totally resolved (prajna).[29]

What else can we say of this intuition called *prajna?* We can creep closer by elimination: it is not a cognitive "Eureka" experience producing an idea and therefore communicable knowledge. We can also say, however, that it is not the result of negation only: " 'sunyata' [step two] is reached by a process of manifold negation, while 'prajna' [step three] is realized by an immediate and intuitive identification."[30] Something more than pure negation is operating: the equation of voidness and suchness, the use of words like "identification," all suggest a positive quality even though we know by now not to mistake that quality for an utterable concept or any other of the five *skandha*s. I suspect that Murti, and we, and some Buddhist texts, are trying to define the *noetic* quality (*prajna*) that may or may not illumine a period of meditative negation (*sunyata*).

The most venerable Buddhist text on *prajna* is the Theravadic *Abhidharma*. Guenther, describing the *Abhidharma*'s view of *prajna*, does not shy away from some positive terms: "Far from giving a pessimistic outlook, knowledge makes man see that whatever is determinate is not all and that there is something in the nature of the determinate which is inexpressible and yet can be experienced directly and immediately and in its direct experience offers lasting happiness."[31] In direct contradiction to Western popular opinion, which assumes that Buddhism and nirvana deny the mind and knowledge, almost all Buddhist scholars emphasize the importance of some kind of knowledge in the Buddhist world: intellectual knowledge helps to expose contradiction (*sunyata*), then a suprarational knowledge produces *prajna*. Indeed, many commentators point out that the Christian God began by forbidding knowledge (of good and evil), reserving it to himself, while the Buddhists began by endorsing all intellectual functions, hoping to advance from there. While advocating meditative insight, the stopping of the mind, they do not despise simple intellect: "the intellect, in Buddhist conception, partakes of the nature of the highest and most valuable function in man, viz., discrimination (prajna), but with this difference that its way of functioning is trammeled by the veil of bewilderment-delusion, and that bewilderment-delusion associates with the other emotive bases such as cupidity and antipathy."[32]

So the *prajna* insight is to the Buddhist still a function of mind (*citta*) and consciousness, and they could well argue that it is a more intellectual category, achieved by more disciplined concentration, than is our faith.

The ineffable positivism of this category, not the positivism of "Eureka" ideas of ecstatic rapture, seems to stem from the calm, benign quality of unitive experience, a quality that persists even though the experience is beyond thought and feeling and all statements about it must be negated. Adepts do seek the experience again even if they gain it by not seeking.

The benign quality of *prajna* casts a positive tone over all this talk of no-mind and nothingness, a tone quite absent when we repeat those words in our culture. Therefore positive metaphors creep into the tradition. In the flowering of the Mahayana system A.D. 200–1000, when suchness was prized, sensation explored, and so many art forms encouraged, the metaphors of a sixth sense, or of synesthesia was sometimes used to express, as in romantic poetry, a knowledge beyond Locke's five senses: "Dharma taught by non-sentient things is unthinkable. Listening through your ear you cannot understand; But you will be aware of it by listening with your eyes."[33]

This sense beyond the five senses (the "entire body full of eyes") is not the rich surfeit of Keats's synesthesia, nor the visionary sixth sense of Blake's "imaginary forms divine." This is a sense characterized by negation of thought, negation of intellectual knowledge, and negation of self. Stevens expressed it very well:

A Clear Day and No Memories

No soldiers in the scenery,
No thoughts of people now dead,
As they were fifty years ago,
Young and living in a live air,
Young and walking in the sunshine,
Bending in blue dresses to touch something,
Today the mind is not part of the weather.

Today the air is clear of everything.
It has no knowledge except of nothingness
And it flows over us without meanings,
As if none of us had ever been here before
And are not now: in this shallow spectacle,
This invisible activity, this sense.   (*OP* 113)

Stevens' last poems are distinguished by a broad serenity; this one was published in 1954, the year before he died. The poem is built of negations: "no memories," "no thoughts," "no knowledge except of nothingness," "without meanings," "none of us . . . here before / And are not now." In this void only two positive constructions occur: "air is clear," and at the end, "in . . . this sense." "This sense" is parallel to the prior oxymorons, "shallow spectacle," "invisible activity," each of which suggests a dual nature to reality, part void (shallow, invisible) and part suchness (spectacle, activity). Those oxymorons suggest an external reality but "sense" connotes an internal reality and hence both dissolves the external scene and unites, as the final description of the scene, not only voidness and suchness, but internal and external. It is all one "sense," both this perceived world, which is the absolute "today" stripped of all "knowledge except of nothingness," and these perceivers (poet and us) who have a vivid sense of perception, as vivid as if we had never seen this before (perhaps we have not in this state of consciousness), and who have this vivid sense because of self-loss: we "are not [here] now." No memory, no knowledge, no meaning, no existence—and a vivid sense of present reality, "clear" in a single unified "sense." "If one can realize the Tao unmistakably, [his mind will be like] the great space—vast, void and clear."[34]

Within the poem, this clarity is achieved by the dramatic device of conjuring up the "people now dead," the people of whom he has "no thoughts." Those four beautiful lines place vividly before us all the possibilities of *samsara,* all the possibilities of beauty, desire, action, death: "Young and living . . . Young and walking . . . Bending in blue dresses to touch." Some critics read the entire poem negatively because that delicate beauty is now gone, because "the mind is not part of the weather."

But in stanza 2 the weather itself is gone. To read the poem negatively we must find the last word, "sense," disappointing; "the air is clear" we must find sterile; the tone must be upsetting, unquiet. I find the poem more convincing as a serene clarity achieved by calling up those memories, lovely in themselves, and then dismissing them, "just as when the birds fly away the real sky is revealed."[35]

Such a reading demands a benign quality, a kind of enjoyment in "this sense." In "The Ultimate Poem Is Abstract" (1947), Stevens had expressed a wish for this same "sense" which, like the snow man's nothingness, is a way to "enjoy":

> This day writhes with what? The lecturer
> On This Beautiful World of Ours composes himself
> And hems the planet rose and haws it ripe,
>
> And red, and right. The particular question—here
> The particular answer to the particular question
> Is not in point—the question is in point.

If the day writhes, it is not with revelations.
One goes on asking questions. That, then, is one
Of the categories. So said, this placid space

Is changed. It is not so blue as we thought. To be blue,
There must be no questions. It is an intellect
Of windings round and dodges to and fro,

Writhings in wrong obliques and distances,
Not an intellect in which we are fleet: present
Everywhere in space at once, cloud-pole

Of communication. It would be enough
If we were ever, just once, at the middle, fixed
In This Beautiful World of Ours and not as now,

Helplessly at the edge, enough to be
Complete, because at the middle, if only in sense,
And in that enormous sense, merely enjoy.   (*CP* 429–30)

It would be hard to find a better description of the Buddhist point of view towards ordinary intellect: "windings round and dodges to and fro, / Writhings in wrong obliques and distances."[36] It would be hard also to find a better description of meditative perception: "Present / Everywhere in space at once . . . at the middle, fixed . . . complete. And in that enormous sense, merely enjoy." The poem itself is a fine example of Stevens' sleight-of-hand with verbs, the prestidigitation that Vendler first revealed: "enjoy" *cannot* be parallel to either the infinitive "to be," or the adjective "complete." To be parallel, the form would have to be "to enjoy," or "enjoying." Instead, the declarative "enjoy" gives the lie to "and": there has been a hiatus, and in that hidden moment the wished-for state of mind has suddenly been accomplished. Thus it would be hard to find, also, a better example of how linear thought and language must be interrupted before meditative perception can occur.

In "A Clear Day and No Memories," Stevens seems to inhabit "that enormous sense," and to "merely enjoy." The movement of the entire poem approximates the stages of meditative knowledge: first we are offered "views of the real advanced by speculative systems" (such as memory); second, that touching reality is negated and voidness is perceived; finally, in the last word we move past a *sunyata* perception of voidness to an "intuition of the Real." The void quality of "no knowledge except of nothingness," we "are not [here] now" and the suchness quality of the scene as present "here, today" recalls Conze's definition of *sunyata,* swollen together in "this sense." Indeed, the only word that *specifically* designates "this sense" and "this sense" alone may well be *prajna*.

"A Clear Day and No Memories" appeared in the January 1955 issue of the *Sewanee Review* in a group of four poems, the last poems Stevens published, six months before his death. All four poems (*OP* 111–13) explore themes of meditation and imagination, the first, "Solitaire under the Oaks," playing with the card game as an example of concentration on "pure principles,"

> an escape
> To principiume, to meditation.
> One knows at last what to think about
>
> And thinks about it without consciousness,
> Under the oak trees, completely released.

But it is the third poem, "Artificial Populations," that goes beyond the thinking concentration of something like Christian prayer— which is the consciousness Stevens usually associated with the word *meditation*—and begins in a more empty state of "this sense":

> The center that he sought was a state of mind,
> Nothing more, like weather after it has cleared.

In the meditative reading we can account for the exact attention to "a state of mind" that permeates "A Clear Day and No Memories" even when "thoughts" and "knowledge" and "memory" are denied, we can account for the absence of words of ennui or indifference, and we can account for the insistence on "today," when "the air is clear of everything," on clarity, on self-loss, as simultaneous with ineffable perception: "this sense." In a meditative reading we can also offer a framework for the poem's structure: rejection of ordinary reality is followed by perception of the void, which is followed by intuition of a meditative reality. We saw in the last chapter that meditation has several stages, and that meditators commonly move through these stages in approaching their insights. A number of Stevens' poems seem not only to use meditative issues and points of view, but also to imitate the structure of meditative experience, an advanced, sensate, meditative experience that follows the middle way. By the late 1930s, he knew what he was doing, and right to the end he arranged his imaginative and meditative epiphanies in perfect counterpoise.

7

The Meditative Stevens: "The Latest Freed Man"

Although Stevens is widely admired as one of the great poets of this century, just why he is great is much debated. And recently, those who do not admire him have split into two camps. Some postmodern critics regret Stevens' Keatsian sensuality, his preference for committed and sonorous statement. To Perloff, Stevens becomes, like Yeats or the later Eliot or the Pound of "Mauberley," a romantic-symbolist traitor to the modern cause.

The older generation of critics, on the other hand, sometimes complaints of just the opposite. Stevens, for them, is not romantic enough. In persona, he is too impersonal and dispassionate; in diction too precious; in subject matter too aesthetic, theoretical, repetitive. In ear and wit and syntax perhaps, he is less censured—who would not admire the titles and attenuated asides?—but his older detractors paint a consistent portrait: Stevens is a "poet's poet." Always said on someone else's behalf, the phrase suggests craftsmanship without passion: "We like Jonson, but we love Shakespeare." Stevens is not "the people's poet." Both criticisms point a truth: Stevens' poetry contains simultaneous affirmation and withdrawal, passion and dispassion, strategies designed to move and yet remove the reader, and the text.

Those who love Stevens—and I am thinking now of my colleagues, friends, and students who read him in privacy, not of those who have loved him in print—seem to enjoy the fine-tuned mind and its phrase, the presence of a speaker exact and exacting, humane, considerate, witty, civilized, and yet never shallow, not a trace of Babbitt: in that way, Stevens is un-American. Like an aristocrat, like an aristocracy, he is unashamed of learning and grace. In sensibility, then, he cuts right through "Anti-Intellectualism in American Life" (Hofstadter's title); he says, to all of us, that we need not be Sandburg, or Frost, or

Whitman, aggressively democratic or agrarian or transformed. It is enough to be more subtly transformed by being humane, intelligent, observant, aware—these are qualities not to be ashamed of even in America, and whether these are the qualities of the few or the many, of this country or that, of poets or executives—all that is beside the point and can be taken up later in something less serious than poetry. For now, consider the light on the bowl, now in spring "when afternoons return." Many of us enjoy spring, decor, walking to work, and stopping to look at plants and paintings, and we consider such enjoyment important even though in America it usually seems unauthorized, a kind of "time out." I remember my delight in discovering that my high school's eighteenth-century founder, Samuel Phillips, had recommended to his charges "the greater end and real business of living," by which he meant, I think, that living is the point of living. Heresy indeed. Our American mythos may not know what to do with Stevens, but his audience is not necessarily small.

He is difficult, however, and this difficulty springs from two sources: first, a love of language over rhetoric, meaning that he doesn't think so much of persuading an audience as of word play. The second source of difficulty is his reticence: he does not wear his heart on his sleeve, and as in life or novels of manners we must be sensitive to the depth of feeling barely suggested by the phrase, the nuance, the apparently casual aside. Many poets still seek freedom by being "primitive" instead of civilized. Passion becomes a responsibility. Stevens tends to take passion for granted and seeks to be courteous and cosmopolitan in his poetry, saving his rudeness—he did not consider rudeness attractive—for private life.

Thus Stevens is also surprisingly accessible; unlike Yeats, who would write for the fisherman but demands a grand persona to do it, Stevens speaks not *as* "major man" but as someone slightly shy, even coy, a sort of poetic Jacques Tati wandering through everyday epiphanies, needing an organizing center, and then another and another. The grand debates, in Stevens, are quickly made domestic: "I also saw Marcel Duchamp in New York recently. He seemed like a cat that had been left behind" (*L* 228). While Stevens is "aesthetic" in subject, his personal aesthetic is close to common morality and common aspirations: he would be a cultured man enjoying, observing, lamenting life. This stance can anger reformers and those seeking mythic American or proletarian art, but it was his stance, and would not be so odd for, say, a Frenchman of moderate means. Stevens' poetry is full of passionate commitment to the ideal of being civilized, an ideal that many in America share and which since the eighteenth century has had few spokesmen.

Permeating these enlightenment—almost Voltairean—ideals is a rare intelligence and range of responses that save Stevens from anything like complacency. His is a model of that "examined life" which Socrates encouraged, though with the examination applied less to society and more to the nature of consciousness. The fact that he wished this or that, saw this or that, pursued this or that in such or such a way intrigued him as much as the wish, the pursuit, the way. Such self-consciousness in poetry might be called traditional since Wordsworth's "Intimations" ode, but Stevens' capacity for wit, playfulness, and detachment makes the result quite different, a bourgeois world exploded: "Home from Guatemala, back at the Waldorf" (*CP* 240). And exploded not always by understatement, but often by passionate commitment to the possibilities of ordinary life. Here the subject is the routine transformation of living figured as reading, a giant reading life as the sun reads earth, yet also (as in "The House Was Quiet and the World Was Calm"), a man reading the most ordinary things:

Large Red Man Reading

There were ghosts that returned to earth to hear his phrases,
As he sat there reading, aloud, the great blue tabulae.
They were those from the wilderness of stars that had expected
    more.

There were those that returned to hear him read from the poem
    of life,
Of the pans above the stove, the pots on the table, the tulips
    among them.
They were those that would have wept to step barefoot into
    reality,

That would have wept and been happy, have shivered in the frost
And cried out to feel it again, have run fingers over leaves
And against the most coiled thorn, have seized on what was ugly
And laughed, as he sat there reading, from out of the purple
    tabulae,
The outlines of being and its expressings, the syllables of its law:
Poesis, poesis, the literal characters, the vatic lines,

Which in those ears and in those thin, those spended hearts,
Took on color, took on shape and the size of things as they are
And spoke the feeling for them, which was what they had lacked.
                                                (*CP* 423–24)

Clearly Stevens' range of responses gave him ecstatic and lyric moments that fill the "shape and size of things as they are" with new life, and new ghosts. Since "Sunday Morning" in 1915, he had proved himself the best blank verse poet of this century, but even in the midst of sonorous rhetoric or lyric transport he often kept the subordinate, impersonal constructions that create distance:

> They were those that would have wept to step barefoot into
>   reality,
> That would have wept and been happy . . . .

The distance between the heartfelt rhymes and the considered, considerate construction—"They were those that . . . wept to step barefoot"—creates an exquisite tension, just as the lyric outpouring of the entire poem pulls against its long sentence which leads again (as in "The Snow Man") to a relative clause, a "which" that oddly subordinates the entire last stanza's emphasis on "feeling," just as an additional final clause and then another make the last realization simultaneous with yet another reflection denouement: "And spoke the feeling for them, which was what they had lacked." The rhythm forces a strong stress on the final "what." Stevens does not just get away with relative clauses; he deliberately uses abstractions and constructions as if they were images.

All this rhetoric serves ordinary life. How seldom our poets write about reading! Had Stevens instead of Keats written "On First Looking into Chapman's Homer," he would not have isolated the experience of first looking, making it dramatically unique in time and space; he would instead have presented it as one of those daily occurrences in the presence of good books: ah, the Pacific, again.

Stevens' distinctive style marries affirmative intensity to a potential or realized detachment, giving the humane, considerate, civilized flavor to his verse. Affirmation is not all, this style tells us; being is a context larger than the moment of personal feeling:

> One's grand flights, one's Sunday baths,
> One's tootings at the weddings of the soul
> Occur as they occur.   (*CP* 222)

What subjects, what *materia poetica* did this style serve? Throughout his career Stevens used a vocabulary of imagination and reality pitted against each other, now united, now divorced, now sweetly contending. And while every reader of Stevens knows to go beyond those neo-Kantian antimonies, every reader knows also that in subject matter those poles are the most constant element in his verse.

If on the one hand *reality* in its common usage refers to the external world, that "collection of solid, static objects extended in space," and if on the other hand *imagination* in Stevens' usage refers to the internal world of the perceiver selecting, using, responding to those objects, then the real reality, Stevens believed, is a third category created by the interaction of external and internal. Reality is "not that 'collection of solid, static objects extended in space' but the life that is lived in the scene that it composes; and so reality is not that external scene but the life that is lived in it" (*NA* 25). Stevens then went on to say in the next sentence, "Reality is things as they are," but in context he clearly meant things as they are to the self in a moment of imaginative perception, in "the life that is lived in the scene." Such a reality is a fresh construct of self and other: the "buxom eye" combines with the pineapple on the table to create a new reality, "the total thing, a shapeless giant forced / Upward," a reality in which the object and the reaction to the object have become one:

> The truth must be
> That you do not see, you experience, you feel,
> That the buxom eye brings merely its element
> To the total thing, a shapeless giant forced
> Upward.   (*CP* 219)

But when the eye is not "buxom" and things are not "forced," that is, when the perceiver is passive instead of active, "things as they are" is a fourth category: it is not that external "collection of solid, static objects," nor the internal self alone in its imagination, nor a fresh construct of self and other, but a fresh destruct of self and other in which the Buddhists say voidness and suchness are one. This meditative perception is less likely to emerge in the strong metaphors of "giant" and "forced," and more likely to emerge in ultimate abstractions or in a single clear image of suchness. Stevens had knowledge of two kinds of reality-as-perceived. Sometimes "things as they are" seem to be "changed upon the blue guitar," sometimes not. Sometimes "reality is an activity of the most august imagination," sometimes not.

This meditative reality of nothingness or suchness Stevens never did hold as theory: his culture did not contain the vocabulary with which to conceive of it. But he himself never thought that ideas or theories were the origin of art; he was, as the philosopher Paul Weiss observes,

> a phenomenologist—that is, somebody who is alert to what he confronts and gives it its full value, doesn't reduce it by virtue of some preconceived concept, but tries to accept things in their immediacy and their full richness. . . . I think of him as one who thinks that the world that we see every day is encrusted with all kinds of conventional meanings and that the whole function of the imagination is to penetrate beyond those and catch what the phenomenon really is as it is, there in its nakedness and full phenomenological clarity; . . . he's a man of metaphysical insight who then uses the result as an object for phenomenological examination. I always think of Stevens as involved in the immediate, confronted data, which he then sees with a philosophic or even metaphysical depth but interprets in phenomenological terms; . . . his ultimate passion was to try to get to the clean, clear ultimate reality, which required a thrust through everything that we are thinking, naming, using, saying. What I'm not clear about is what he saw when he got there.[1]

This is essentially accurate, but Weiss might have been more clear about "what he saw when he got there" had he realized that imagination, to Stevens, is not the only way to penetrate to the phenomenon "as it is." Stevens himself, though he developed no meditative theory, at times spoke for a perceptive state of mind that was anti-imaginative: "In the presence of extraordinary actuality, consciousness takes the place of imagination" (*OP* 165). And although he usually fell back on his conventional vocabulary of reality and imagination, I'm not sure that the "state of clairvoyant observation" he discusses is not meditative: "Perhaps there is a degree of perception at which what is real and what is imagined are one: a state of clairvoyant observation, accessible or possibly accessible to the poet or, say, the acutest poet" (*OP* 166). If "what is real and what is imagined" here signify other and self, as they often do in Stevens, then this acutest state of clairvoyant observation (the imagery is not imaginative, not inventive) may well refer to a meditative union.

We know for certain, as Weiss just observed, that these issues define Stevens' *materia poetica:* a phenomenologist of consciousness, Stevens sought not so much to express emotion as to examine the perceptual context in which it occurs. As he wrote: "Emotion is thought to lie at the center of aesthetic experience. That, however, is not how the matter appears to me. If I am right, the essence of art is insight of a special kind into reality" (*OP* 238). Here is the heart of Stevens: his style of considered detachment and his subject matter of perception serve to make us aware of a particular consciousness having an "insight of a special kind" at a certain time and place. "The truth is that a man's sense of the world dictates his subjects to him and that sense is derived from his personality, his temperament" (*NA* 122). We will later examine Stevens' temperament and practice (chapter 12) as they tend toward the ascetic and impersonal, but for now we can agree with Weiss that investigating experience, not espousing theory, is Stevens' subject. Therefore, Guenther's remark on Buddhism, partially quoted in the introduction, could be fairly applied to the major aspiration of Stevens' poetry: "It is true phenomenology, the systematic investigation of our experiences as experiences, and it has succeeded in giving a true and realistic picture of our emotions and the role they play even in our cognitive processes."[2]

As initial propositions, then, we can imagine four ways in which Stevens' meditative tendencies might have influenced his work, quite apart from the obvious use of meditative experience as a subject for poetry. First, his capacity for detached observation may have been encouraged by, among other propensities, meditative experience. Second, meditative experience of suchness, reality-as-it-is, offers a feeling of special insight *without* imagination, and thus serves as a foil to his major aesthetic theory. Third, his interest in experience over ideas, in consciousness over feeling, his empiricism, the phenomenological bent that stamps his subject matter, are all typical of meditators as opposed to philosophers. Fourth, his tendency to distance himself from any given moment of personal feeling or any given idea produces variety, an interest in multiple feelings and ideas all subordinate to some larger concept of being. He plays with many theories as poetic subjects, but he espouses none. Though he talks repeatedly of imagination, Stevens sometimes wallows in it, sometimes longs for it, sometimes possesses but regrets it, sometimes rejects it altogether, "As morning throws off stale moonlight and shabby sleep" (*CP* 382). Stevens always enjoyed yoked opposites, scrambling poems in *Harmonium* and publishing opposite pairs.[3] Often these pairings were imaginative versus meditative, as "Somnambulisma" placed next to "Crude Foyer" in *Transport to Summer,* or "The Course of a Particular" published with "Final Soliloquy of the Interior Paramour" in the spring 1951 *Hudson Review.* This love of variety and its possible origin in meditation we will pursue in part IV. These, then, are aspects of Stevens' work that could well be related to meditative experience: detachment, suchness as opposed to imaginative perception, phenomenology, variety.

Stevens' career may be divided into three phases: the first, 1913–1922, began when he was thirty-four and ended with his first book, *Harmonium.* His wit and wordplay earned him a reputation as "dandy, eccentric, clown," although many of the poems transcend both that reputation and his own defensive diffidence. After a long silence, Stevens began in the thirties his second phase, less clearly delineated, lasting perhaps until 1942. During this decade of steady production Stevens achieved an impressive maturity and remarkable evenness of quality, and began to write his long poems. His last phase, from about 1942 until his death in 1955, seemed to slow in pace while gaining in—yes—grace; this is an old man's art, with everything to say and nothing to prove, poems saturated with patient intensity.

In the thirties, as we have seen, he pursued more consciously this "insight of a special kind into reality" and he became more exact about its context, about the stages one moves through to attain this insight, and about the perceptive results. Perhaps the very best example of Stevens as meditative phenomenologist is his fine poem of 1938, "The Latest Freed Man";

> Tired of the old descriptions of the world,
> The latest freed man rose at six and sat
> On the edge of his bed. He said,
>   "I suppose there is
> A doctrine to this landscape. Yet, having just
> Escaped from the truth, the morning is color and mist,
> Which is enough: the moment's rain and sea,
> The moment's sun (the strong man vaguely seen),
> Overtaking the doctrine of this landscape. Of him
> And of his works, I am sure. He bathes in the mist
> Like a man without a doctrine. The light he gives—
> It is how he gives his light. It is how he shines,
> Rising upon the doctors in their beds
> And on their beds. . . ."
>   And so the freed man said.
> It was how the sun came shining into his room:
> To be without a description of to be,
> For a moment on rising, at the edge of the bed, to be,
> To have the ant of the self changed to an ox
> With its organic boomings, to be changed
> From a doctor into an ox, before standing up,
> To know that the change and that the ox-like struggle
> Come from the strength that is the strength of the sun,

Whether it comes directly or from the sun.
It was how he was free. It was how his freedom came.
It was being without description, being an ox.
It was the importance of the trees outdoors,
The freshness of the oak-leaves, not so much
That they were oak-leaves, as the way they looked.
It was everything being more real, himself
At the centre of reality, seeing it.
It was everything bulging and blazing and big in itself,
The blue of the rug, the portrait of Vidal,
Qui fait fi des joliesses banales, the chairs.

The first word is "tired." The doctor is tired of old descriptions of the world, and as the poem progresses we find him tiring of all descriptions and tiring of the intellectual activity that all descriptions imply: truth, doctrine, a point of view. The opening is negative as well as passive—"Tired of the old descriptions," "escaped from the truth," "overtaking the doctrine," "without a doctrine"—because theoretical thought is being purged. But as thought is purged a vivid sense of being, here and now, emerges within this passivity:

the morning is color and mist,
Which is enough: the moment's rain and sea,
The moment's sun . . .
Overtaking the doctrine.

The two fresh metaphors (sun as strong man, bathing in mist) are not pursued. Thinking subsides. The sensation of living in the present arises. Thinking and sensation are two buckets at opposite ends of one well rope: as one goes down, the other goes up. The psychology assumed by the poem is not *cogito ergo sum* but its opposite, the psychology of the Buddhist meditative traditions: thought and sensation, or more fundamentally, thought and being, are opposed.

Having purged thought, the doctor, like one of Deikman's subjects staring at the vase, begins to concentrate on the light, on the sun's light in the room: "The light he gives—It is how he gives his light." The dash is crucially important. In that hiatus, the doctor turns from the noun "light" to the verb "gives," from substance to process. "It is how . . . It is how . . ." Process is the work of which the doctor is sure.

"It is how he shines,
Rising upon the doctors in their beds
And on their beds. . . ."

Those ellipses and quotation marks are printed in the poem; they bring the doctor's speech to a close. Now, his mind trailing off in those dots, he falls silent. Having escaped from thought and substance, the doctor has escaped from language. Like the sun, he is now "a man without a doctrine," and he will not again speak his mind, or no-mind.

The first stanza is dominated by "escape" from doctrinal thought, by what we might call criticism of views of the real, and by some kind of pure concentration on present sensation as the doctor sits on his bed in morning light. What happens next resembles stage 2 in Deikman's experiments: dramatic sensations of an expanded self and warpings of time and space. The doctor's awareness of "how the sun came shining" suddenly creates in him a new sense of his own being, and makes us aware that this poem is about a change of state:

> To be without a description of to be,
> For a moment on rising, at the edge of the bed, to be,
> To have the ant of the self changed to an ox
> With its organic boomings, to be changed
> From a doctor into an ox . . .
>
> . . . .
> It was how he was free.

At the opening of the poem, the world was no longer described, then the light was no longer described, and now "to be" has no "description." We now realize how a landscape without description is perceived—by a being without description: "nothing himself, beholds nothing." As Yun-yen said (chapter 4), "The Dharma taught by nonsentient things will be heard by nonsentient things." And in that condition, he experiences a dramatic change. The epistemology behind the poem is throughly experiential: what the doctor seeks and finds is a change of consciousness, not a change of ideas, a change of consciousness that will purge all thought yet leave a quickened sense of being. The ox is a perfect metaphor for this newly expanded self: huge, vital, mindless, and very much there. "Where should one rest after one has attained Tao? One should become a buffalo down the hill."[4]

Having passed through purgation of thought and concentration on the sunlight, and having experienced a dramatic change of state, the doctor's ox-self now disappears from the poem, while the intensity of his sensation remains, reinforced by chords of repetition:

It was being without description, being an ox,
It was the important of the trees outdoors,
The freshness of the oak-leaves, not so much
That they were oak-leaves, as the way they looked.

The doctor notices the leaves, as the Zen master says, without looking back, without analysis and understanding, without the labeling of "oak" versus "elm."

From what tree's bloom
    it comes, I do not know,
    but—this perfume!

Theory purged, description purged, the metaphor of the ox purged, the self expanded, now suddenly the world of sun and things in process—"*how* he shines . . . the *way* they looked"—explodes into dramatic warpings of space. The doctor has a keen sense of being in the midst of bulging reality until finally that reality collapses, concentrates, into a pure image, the thing itself:

It was everything being more real, himself
At the center of reality, seeing it.
It was everything bulging and blazing and big in itself,
The blue of the rug, the portrait of Vidal,
Qui fait fi des joliesses banales, the chairs.

Here is no hint of the shaping imagination (in contrast to "The Idea of Order at Key West") that produces fresh descriptions of the world. At the end, the latest freed man uses no metaphors, no abstractions, and shows no emotion beyond an extraordinary sense of being in an extraordinary physical world. The shifting room is described not by metaphors but by hallucinatory images: "bulging and blazing and big in itself" resembles Deikman's literal reports of visual experience in the hallucinatory stage of meditative consciousness: "The vase was a hell of a lot bluer this time . . . darker and more luminous" (subject B); "The outlines of the vase shift . . . seem almost literally to dissolve entirely . . . kind of fluid blue . . . kind of moving" (subject A).

The final line has a wonderful wrinkle, suggesting the spontaneity and wit of Stevens' later, longer poems. In the midst of reporting this meditative epiphany, the poem suddenly breaks into French and into a critical consciousness to chide the bookseller Vidal ("who disdained everyday pleasures") for not apprehending what Emerson called "the miraculous in the common." Then, after this critical aside, completely disrupting the mood yet hardly more than a "click" heard in the midst of meditative concentration, the poem rushes right back to the final image of the thing itself: "the chairs." Set off by the French quotation, the hopelessly banal image of chairs is given tremendous stress by the "*joliesse*" of a remarkably strong and swift poetic closure. What has he said? "It was . . . the chairs."

> Many times the mountains have turned from green to yellow—
> So much for the capricious earth!
> Dust in your eyes, the triple world is narrow;
> Nothing on your mind, your chair is wide enough.[5]

The structure as well as the content of the poem is meditative. Tired of old descriptions, the doctor puts intellect aside. He stops thinking—no "doctrine"—and becomes mindlessly aware of the light in his room. This relaxed, mindless state "on the edge of his bed" resembles stage 1 of a meditative consciousness. As he enters stage 2, his own self expands beyond its usual borders and dramatic warpings of shapes and colors occur until he has a vivid sense of physical reality: "the chairs." The freed man has moved from a mindless revery, through expansion and contraction of self and other, to a new and pure perception of the thing itself. What was he doing? The word for Zen meditation, *zazen,* means "just sitting," which may be what Stevens did, some mornings, in his room. As Brazeau reports:

> He had a bedroom area that was furnished up like a library and spent most of his time in there, reading nights. He had a nice desk in there, lamps and a sitting chair, and, of course his bed. . . . An oil painting of Vidal by Jean Labasque hung in Stevens' bedroom, part of the furnishings mentioned in the poem "The Latest Freed Man."[6]

Many of Stevens' meditative lyrics move through stages roughly resembling those of meditative practice as described by Deikman and the *Visuddhimagga* (see table 1).

The structure of *Visuddhimagga* meditative discipline, of Deikman's subjects' experiences, and of these Stevens' lyrics suggests a single progression. Concentration on an object or scene may be followed by a quickening of imagination (the experience most sought and valued in romantic theory), then by a purgation of thought, feeling, and imagination leading to a dissolving of self and finally to a perception of nothing or the barest something—the thing itself. These lyrics repeatedly warn the reader that neither imagination nor thought can achieve the goal

Table 1. Stages of Meditation in Selected Stevens Lyrics

	1. Concentration	2. Imaginative Phenomena	3. Purgation of Thought & Feeling	4. Detachment
"The Snow Man"	"have a mind of winter to behold"	"shagged with ice, the spruces rough . . . glitter"	"and not to think"	"nothing"
"Evening Without Angels"	"The great interests of man: Light and air . . ."	"seraphim like lutanists . . . poet as eternal *chef d'orchestre*"	"Yet . . . desire for rest . . . rest and silence spreading into sleep."	"bare, bare"
"The Man on the Dump"		"The sun is a corbeil of flowers the moon Blanche . . ."	"One feels the purifying change. . . . You see the moon rise in an empty sky."	"The the"
"The Latest Freed Man"	"Escaped from the truth . . . the moment's sun"	"the ant of the self changed to an ox"	". . . not so much that they were oak-leaves . . ."	"the chairs"
"The Course of a Particular"	"the leaves cry"	"still full of icy shades and shapen snow"	"one holds off . . . not the cry of gods . . . in the absence of fantasia. . . without meaning more than they are . . ."	"the thing itself . . . concerns no one at all."
"A Clear Day . . ."	"Today the mind . . ."	"Thoughts of people now dead . . ., Young and living . . ."	"no knowledge except of nothingness"	"this sense."
"Not Ideas . . ."	"a scrawny cry"		"no longer a battered panache . . ."	"the sun was coming from outside."

of meditative perception, as Buddhists have long advised: "It has to be emphasized over and again that right view (*samyakdrsti* Pali, *sammaditthi*) is not the acceptance of a doctrine based on hypotheses, but a view gained through continuous contemplation and direct experience."[7] We find in these poems not a romantic triumph of imaginative creation by the "buxom eye," but a meditative passivity, "without a doctrine," in which we encounter the reality of the thing itself through "contemplation and direct experience."

That passivity is certainly not annihilation. Just what it is remains the most curious meditative question. In the next chapter we will examine the physiology of meditation to see if it leads us closer to an understanding of the state called in Chinese, *wu-wei,* inaction, or no-mind.

8

The Physiology of Meditation

Admiral Richard E. Byrd had planned for a small party to spend the winter of 1934 as near as possible to the South Pole. Complications arose, however, and he found himself in a hut beneath the snow and polar dark "alone," as the title of his book so simply states.

> The first days of May carried no hint of the calamities that would overtake me at the month's end. On the contrary, they were among the most wonderful days I had ever known. The blizzards departed, the cold moved down from the South Pole, and opposite the moon in a coal-black sky the cast-up light from the departed sun burnt like a bonfire. During the first six days the temperature averaged −47.03°; much of the time it was deep in the minus forties and fifties. The winds scarcely blew. And a soundlessness fell over the Barrier. I have never known such utter quiet. Sometimes it lulled and hypnotized, like a waterfall or any other steady, familiar sound. At other times it struck into the consciousness as peremptorily as a sudden noise. It made me think of the fatal emptiness that comes when an airplane engine cuts out abruptly in flight. Up on the Barrier it was taut and immense; and, in spite of myself, I would be straining to listen—for nothing, really, nothing but the sheer excitement of silence.[1]

Meditative consciousness, like any consciousness, could conceivably occur in any situation: there might be a meditative equivalent of narcolepsy, leaving the victim "a most inappropriate man, in a most unpropitious place." But usually meditative consciousness is encouraged by sensory deprivation and sensory repetition. As Byrd found in his four and a half months' isolation in a nine-by-twelve foot shack under the snow, very little input to a waking brain and the repetition of that input over and over may encourage cabin fever, diversionary thought, sleep, or meditative consciousness. Monotonous repeated activity (running, walking, singing a mantra, staring at a mandala, a vase) and monotonous barren places (desert, ocean, snow, a bare room) seem both to deprive the brain of its customary variety of

119

material, and to shake it up by repetition of a single stimulus. The brain quickly responds with its own variety: fantasy or thought. From this point of view, one can see thinking as, on occasion, a defense of ordinary consciousness, a defense against changing state. It takes about thirty seconds of restricted, repeated input to bore the brain.

The reader can watch his central nervous system trying to adapt to abnormally restricted and repetitive input: stare at a period on this page. Keep the eye from wandering, both in its large movements and in its tiny flickering actions. Now, after perhaps thirty seconds of "merely seeing" the dot, watch the mind begin to wander, making the eye momentarily "blind." You think of other things and stop seeing the dot, meaning that the cortex stops attending to it and goes off on more promising projects. Part of the fun is in watching the mind disobey the will. You are mentally uncoordinated. Advanced meditators have, of course, practiced this move. Now bring your mind back to the dot; keep your eye there. Keep your mind there. Soon peripheral vision becomes strange; keep it up and you'll feel strange. The waking cortex is just not accustomed to such restricted, repetitive input. Ordinary consciousness has been developed for survival in a fast world—we are the quick or the dead—and you can feel the mind struggling, trying to change the situation or to change state, that is, trying to find variety or to find some mode of operation appropriate to monotonous input.

The simple and direct connection between visual input and one's state of consciousness is exploited by the mantra. Try staring at the dot at the center of the mandala in figure 2, and watch the cortex cavort about the peripheral lines. A sound mantra (concentrating on a single sound) has a similar effect; repeated, restricted input changes one's mental state, as Alfred Lord Tennyson discovered:

> I have never had any revelation through anaesthetics, but a kind of waking trance (this for want of a better term) I have frequently had, quite up from boyhood, when I have been all alone. This has often come upon me through repeating my own name to myself silently till, all at once, as it were, out of the intensity of the consciousness of the individuality, the individuality itself seemed to dissolve and fade away into boundless being; and this is not a composed state, but the clearest of clearest, the surest of the surest, utterly beyond words, where death was an almost laughable impossibility, the loss of personality (if so it were), seeming no extinction, but the only true life. I am ashamed of my feeble description. Have I not said the state was utterly beyond words?[2]

Figure 2.   Mandala

The state is ineffable, noetic, based on self-loss and leads to an apparent "extinction" (nirvana) seeming "the only true life."

Such a state is apparently unstable, and for most people can be maintained for more than a few seconds only through discipline. The waking cortex, indeed the entire body, as Byrd found, resists the "evenness" and "tranquility" of restricted input:

> "The most likely explanation," I concluded that night in the diary, "is that the trouble lies with myself. . . . It may be that the evenness and the darkness and the absence of life are too much for me to absorb in one chunk. I cannot accept that as a fact, if only because I have been here but forty-three days and many months must be lived out which will be no different from the first. . . . If I am to survive—or at least keep my mental balance—I must control and direct my thoughts."
>
> Even from this distance I maintain that the attitude was a sensible one. The only fault was its glibness. . . . It was true, as I reasoned that night in May, that the concerns and practices of the outer world had not intruded into my existence. That was proved by the weeks of utter tranquility. It was also true, as I had concluded, that the way to keep them from intruding was through the censorship and control of the mind. But beyond these was a truth which that night I did not recognize; and this truth was that the whole complex nervous-muscular mechanism which is the body was waiting, as if with bated breath, for the intrusion of familiar stimuli from the outside world, and could not comprehend why they were denied.
>
> A man can isolate himself from habits and conveniences—deliberately, as I have done; or accidentally, as a shipwrecked sailor might—and force his mind to forget. But the body is not so easily sidetracked. It keeps on remembering. Habit has set up in the core of the being a system of automatic physio-chemical actions and reactions which insist upon replenishment. That is where the con-

flict arises. I don't think that a man can do without sounds and smells and voices and touch, any more than he can do without phosphorous and calcium. This is, in general, what I meant by the vague term "evenness."[3]

In Byrd's situation of enforced evenness (what could he *do*?), the passivity of meditative consciousness could be considered practical, adaptive behavior. For instance, an American economics professor and his wife, traveling for nine hours in an open truck through a locust plague in the hot plains of central India, envied the refusal of the Hindus to harm the locusts. In that situation, the professor could trace the Hindu passivity not just to a doctrine (reverence for all life based on meditative perceptions of unity) but also to a practical decision: the situation, being hopeless, is best endured in a passive and tranquil state. The Westerners in the truck could stop neither their arm-waving nor their frustration, their mind-waving, though neither did the slightest good. Such examples may raise our Western hackles—Control the locusts! Enclose the truck!—but our culture is based on not being reduced by circumstances to passivity. Ecological studies have taught us, however, that our manipulative, problem-solving behavior can produce stalemates of its own and we may yet come to admire, more than we now do, adaptation through endurance.

Byrd's account is fascinating precisely because he was so resourceful and manipulative, yet had thrown himself into solitary confinement. And there he discovered that a change of conditions can produce a change of mind—not of ideas, but of consciousness.

No matter how sophisticated the meditative tradition, it uses techniques that restrict and repeat sensory input: mantras, prayer, breath-counting, dervish-whirling. Once presented with restricted input, what will the mind do? It will probably try to think, or fantasize, or fall asleep, or meditate. That is why most meditative traditions are in part actively anti-intellectual and anti-imaginative, and why in Zen meditation halls the sleepy monks are whacked. Deikman's admonitions—do not think, do not fantasize—are traditional and crucial: the meditative state is only one of the paths the bored or "even" mind might take. If the mind takes the path of thought or fantasy, it will not take the path of meditative consciousness. No matter how rich the tradition of debate, or scholarship, or artistic imagination within, say, Buddhism, those activities are not confused with meditation. This is not to say that *only* sensory deprivation can induce meditation, or that meditation can produce only a numbing of the mind, but this *is* to say that restricted input and a restricted processing of that input, without substitution of the mind's own inventions, characterize meditative experience.

We should attempt to define that restricted processing as accurately as possible, in order to demystify our most crucial and slippery category: self-loss. How may a perceptive, waking man be "nothing himself"? In chapter 4, we raised the possibility of a perceptive cortex neglecting to respond to stimuli. Let us pursue further how that "mind of winter" might work.

In "The Physiology of Meditation," Wallace and Benson tell the results of wiring thirty-six transcendental meditation (TM) practitioners to their machines.[4] TM is basically Theravadic Buddhism sold to Americans in a way and for results that Americans respect: marketing techniques included a poster of a quarterback who had improved his reaction time x percent. However, when claims escalated to the occult (levitation), interest on campus faded.

Sitting in a comfortable position, the TM meditator concentrates on an assigned sound (a mantra, in effect). The Wallace and Benson results confirmed earlier tests by other psychologists. In meditation, metabolic rate fell sharply: the remarkable decreases in oxygen consumption, respiratory rate, blood lactate and relaxation as measured by skin resistance had no counterpart in relaxed waking, in sleep or in hypnosis; the same quieting tendencies observed in simple restfulness increased dramatically in meditation (blood lactate concentration fell at three times the rate of waking rest). In addition, brain wave patterns shifted from the chaos of ordinary waking consciousness to the alpha wave pattern of waking rest, and thence into deeper alpha intensity. On the basis of this kind of monitoring, we might call such initial meditative consciousness extraordinary rest.

Tomio Hirai (*Zen and the Mind,* 1978) reported and summarized similar experiments, many on advanced Zen monks instead of novice TM meditators. The advanced monks showed a few interesting differences such as quickened galvanic skin response and acceleration of the pulse, while the other indices of rest resembled TM novices. Hirai says, "These findings suggest that Zen meditation is not merely a state between mental stability and sleep, but a condition in which the mind operates at the optimum. In this condition, the person is relaxed but ready to accept and to respond positively to any stimulus."[5] Hirai thus finds physiological evidence for some kind of acuteness during advanced aware meditation, and also shows that this combination of traits is not present in other states such as dreams or hypnosis. As usual, *respond* and *positively* must be qualified here; the meditator is still in many ways passive.

Meditative passivity apparently occurs in the area of cortical response to neuron excitation from sensory stimuli. In the cortex, one nerve cell may receive synaptic connections from a hundred other cells, and connect to yet a hundred more, and every firing will slightly modify neuronal pathways, so that the cortex is a history of more and less probable neuronal routes, unique to that individual, as if a wiring diagram were slightly changed by each moment of use. So many cells are firing in concert that a stimulus is not one axon firing, but waves of excitation passing through myriad associated cells. Obviously, we now approach not the meditative ineffable of no-mind, but the scientific ineffable of complexity. What does the brain do with all this activity?

One is tempted to call these nerve impulses *messages,* and the metaphor aptly describes impulses to the muscles and organs which then act in accordance with commands. But in the brain, who or what is receiving the message and giving it meaning? The impulses travel around and around, branching and interconnecting, creating waves of excitation and echoes to the association areas, the memory, the motor, the sensory areas. These areas are not organs; they are simply places where the clusters of interlocking cells are mainly concerned with special roles. It is not possible to point to any part of the cortex and say this is the center, the "I."[6]

Every part of the brain connects indirectly but very quickly with every other part of the brain. The snake's rattle vibrating the eardrum's membrane and translated into neuronal excitation has in an instant looped through the thalamus up to auditory areas and to memory in the temporal lobe, while connections there (and elsewhere) have set off the adrenalin system because that type of rattle means *snake,* if that person has learned through experience or advice to associate that sound with a snake. Simultaneously other synapses have made the leg muscles contract and some neuronal pathways, going back out to eye muscles, have already changed the eyeball's shape and have prepared certain eye receptors to be supersensitive (lowered firing threshold because already partially excited) to forms low and sinuous, colors speckled and brown and diamond-shaped. If a snake isn't there, you may see one anyway. Stevens, following Kant, is right: ordinary perception is a creative act, an invention: "the buxom eye brings merely its element / To the total thing." Especially when the buxom eye is on guard.

Such loops of neuron excitation, called *cortical association* and influenced by all past neuronal activity, tied in to every capacity, memory, expectation, and desire, *are* thought and imagination and feeling, and therefore they are what we call the *self.* The self as we usually think of it is not so much the more automatic activity of the peripheral nervous system or the spine or brainstem, but the highly individualized association patterns of the cortex, created and shaped by one's personal history and one's personal needs.

Although the subtlety and complexity of thought—even how single stimuli are interpreted—is at present far beyond our descriptive capability, the routes of stimuli are not as mysterious as they once were. One important principle developed in the last twenty years is that the brain is organized vertically. In the 1950s, when the mind-body split was a prevailing myth, the brain was thought to send its impulses horizontally, back and forth across the cortex to itself, while the research in the sixties saw the brain as organized vertically so that it includes the spinal cord and the body, just as Yogins have long reported. Some of what we would call rudimentary thought can be carried on in the nerve centers of the spinal cord. Babies born with no brain above the spinal cord can still sleep, eat, suck, grasp, respond to stimuli and make facial expressions.[7] Beyond the first six months, however, development is arrested and they can be kept alive only a few years by artificial means. The spine, once thought part of an "automatic" nervous system distinct from higher centers, can think and respond in elementary ways; conversely, the automatic activities associated with spinal and nearby ganglionic nerve clusters, such as heartbeat, temperature, organ function and "smooth" muscle systems, are connected through the vertical axons of the spine to all parts of the brain, and what was once thought automatic we now know can be controlled by cortical thought, again as Yogins have reported.

This recent development in our physiological description has allowed us to comprehend, for example, how a Yogin can vary the temperature, at will, in two spots on the back of one hand, or how in half an hour a rat can learn to constrict blood vessels in one ear or the other, or to vary its pulse. A person wired to a brain wave machine that rewards, through a light or buzzer, a certain brain wavelength, can in fifteen minutes learn to produce more of that wavelength,

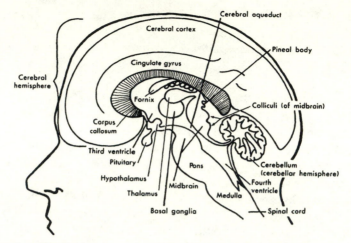

Figure 3.   The Brain
From Leukel, *Introduction to Physiological Psychology* (St. Louis: Mosby, 1976), p. 94.

although neither the subject nor the experimenter knows how it's done or what the wavelength signifies.[8] Although the mechanics of physiology usually seem to slight free will, the result of these studies is to extend our understanding of the will into areas once thought only automatic and spontaneous. Contemporary physiology not only vindicates, but also provides a primary rhetoric for the modern belief in the creativity of perception.

Let us consider some of what we know of the central nervous system's probable response in sleeping, waking, and meditative consciousness to a hypothetical stimulus: the sound of a footstep in the hall.

Asleep: In any state of consciousness, a sound or other sensory stimuli will have to approach the cortex through the brainstem, the oldest part of our brain, a bulb at the top of the spine containing many formations important in meditation, including the thalamus and hypothalamus (figure 3). The sensory stimulus, already a complex series of neuronal excitations representing the frequency, tone, volume, and duration of the sound, will come first to the brainstem reticular formation (the RAS, in the midbrain, mentioned in chapter 4). This formation is capable of learning (modifying excitation paths on the basis of past excitations and results) and discrimination, for its function is to waken the brain, to put it on alert. If the sound is familiar and safe (perhaps you live in an apartment and this particular footfall is heard every night at this time), then the RAS will do nothing, and the cortex will remain asleep, showing the brain waves of stage 2, 3, or 4 dreamless sleep, or the stage 1 EEG of dreaming sleep.

What if the footfall is not the usual one, or at the wrong hour? The RAS may awaken the entire cortex by spraying it with indiscriminate excitations. This excitation will carry no specific information; it does not vary from stimulus to stimulus. The RAS serves only to alert the brain and to prepare it to process subsequent information. The function of the RAS in this instance is to change one's state of consciousness from sleep to waking, and most people have had the experience of sitting bolt upright in bed, with no idea of what has occurred, awake and alert and straining to know what awoke them, yearning like Byrd in his silence to locate themselves in ordinary waking consciousness. The world of ordinary consciousness, of stimulus and response, is the world called *real* by Europeans, called *karma* (tragic cause-effect) by the Buddhists, called *maya* (illusion) by Hindus and Yogins. If the cortex judges that world safe, the RAS calms down; one goes back to sleep. Experiments with cats have proved the close relationship of the RAS to insomnia, and of course internal excitation as well as external can reach the RAS and set it off.

Waking: As one sits upright in bed, awake and alert, what is the course of this particular footfall in ordinary consciousness? It travels to the thalamus, where two more projection systems pass it on. The diffuse projection system, about which little is known, seems to excite many areas of the cortex most likely to be associated with that modality—in this case, sound. The specific projection system, from another part of the thalamus, sends that particular information to very precise areas of the cortex. Cats with an RAS but a severed thalamus can awaken but cannot respond to the specific stimulus. Cats with a severed RAS cannot awaken.

In an instant the excitations of all three projection systems (RAS, thalamic diffuse, and thalamic specific) are crossing and swelling or canceling each other, and each new association will release inhibiting chemicals along certain pathways, discouraging those responses, and exciting chemicals along other pathways, encouraging other responses. In the case of the footfall, for instance, waves of excitations looping through memory and sensory and association and motor areas, all modified by past experiences of all sounds ever heard, will have begun to identify the footfall as a man's or woman's, bold or sneaky—or was it the dog turning over? The outgoing motor nerves will already have tuned the ear for certain aspects of the sound— that is, will have partially excited certain receptors so that they fire readily on receiving those frequencies and tones and volumes that distinguish a dog's thump from a foot's thump, for instance, not a violin from a viola. Again we see that an active cortex is tuning sense receptors even as it interprets and responds to sensations received. Perception, then, by an active cortex is a creative act shaped by personal history, expectation and need, which is how "the buxom eye brings merely its element / To the total thing."

Meditating: Let us recall the meditating Yogins and Zen masters in such an instance (chapter 4). The brain is awake and relaxed; the brain wave pattern is a slow and steady alpha or theta rhythm. In the case of the Yogin the stimulus may be cut off at the RAS or the thalamus or, less likely, may reach the cortex without ever going on to awareness or memory. We know only that the alpha waves continue and later, no hearing of the sound is reported.

The Zen master, on the other hand, both hears and later remembers the sound, but although the stimulus has reached the cortex, the cortex does not process it in the manner of ordinary waking consciousness: assessing danger, taking action. The cortex of the Zenist remains passive, neglecting to initiate the actions not only of muscles, but also of further cortical response. One response the Zenist most probably neglects is that of tuning the sense receptors for specific information, and this perhaps is the key to the artist's interest in aware meditation, and defines "negative capability" in a way Keats might have much admired.

As we saw in chapter 4, the Zen meditator is vividly aware of stimuli but is aware without thought, reaction, or expectation. Meditative passivity probably depends not only on an absence of emotional and muscular response, which could characterize intellectual detachment as well, but also on the absence of tuning, the goal-directed selection and focusing that usually accompany sensation, making our sensation sharp in certain ways—indeed, in expected ways—and dull in others.

What makes meditative perception so vivid? Deikman attempts an explanation: "The more striking perceptions of force, movement and light . . . may possibly be the product of a de-automatization that permits the awareness of new dimensions of the total stimulus array."⁹ To put it simply, it would be very unusual for the waking brain to hear all of a sound, to see all of a scene, with sense organs untuned, messages unselected, mind unfocused. An unconventional array of sense data would then reach the cortex with unconventional force. The result, one might say, would at most times be an unconventional anarchy. Perhaps that is why Chinese and Japanese art so values simplicity: a very few stimuli apprehended fully. This tradition of simplicity, of a cherry blossom, a fan, a grass blade apprehended with meditative openness, is the opposite of the European novel tradition, which is the art of selecting and interpreting amid a wealth of detail—the art of ordinary consciousness. Wallace Stevens' "The Poems of Our Climate" tackles, in a small way, this opposition: the simplicity of "clear water in a brilliant bowl, / Pink and white carnations," is opposed to the complexity of our historical and social being, "the evilly compounded, vital I." Stevens loved both subjects, the thing itself meditatively perceived, and the complex world of "the imperfect" that is "so hot in us": karma.

The idea of an unselective, unfocused, untuned mind suggests also one kind of self-loss. In a meditative state, one's awareness would not be shaped by expectations, buried under the personal history and needs of the self. Who then is hearing? It is a cortex with a personal history of experience and biological change, to be sure, but one neglecting to follow its usual patterns of expectation and response. Such a cortex would in certain ways be neglecting its own history and personality. This is one paradigm for self-loss: unfocused sensation is partially ahistorical and impersonal.

Hindus and neurophysiologists would be quick to point out that to recognize the cherry blossom as cherry blossom, even without naming it, is a learned and therefore historical act, and it is very doubtful that an adult cortex can achieve the biological innocence of a child, for neuronal pathways have been modified by use. Objectivity in sensation is thus an illusion; all sensation is tempered by history and past desire. That is why, to many Hindus and Yogins, unaware meditation (complete withdrawal from sensation) is more pure than Mahayana Buddhist aware meditation. But the Mahayana Buddhist tradition, especially as modified by Taoist influences in China and Japan, brings us closer to the interaction of meditative consciousness and sensation, and therefore closer to Western art.

It may be that all sensation is shaped by past immersion of the self in a world of karma, or in other terms, by past immersion of the cortex in a world of cause-effect decisions, but the Mahayana Buddhists could plausibly claim that in the moment of meditative perception the historical self has been reduced to an absolute minimum; in that moment there is no present expectation or desire. The tendency then is toward as fresh and pure and passive a perception as possible:

> The freshness of the oak-leaves, not so much
> That they were oak-leaves, as the way they looked.

So the meditating mind does not simply fail to respond to an ordinary sound. It hears a different sound—all the cycles per second within the ear's range. "Merely hearing" differs from ordinary hearing in the "particular" of what is heard, as well as in one's lack of positive response. Against the background of the Antarctic silence, Admiral Byrd in his most simple of environments found his senses sharpened as if directed toward danger, when he was actually listening with new receptivity to common and unthreatening sounds:

> Underground, it became intense and concentrated. In the middle of a task or while reading a book I was sometimes brought up hard with all my senses alert and suspicious, like a householder who imagines he hears a burglar in the house. Then, the small sounds of the hut—the hiss of the stove, the chatter of the instruments, the overlapping beats of the chronometers—would suddenly leap out against the soundlessness, all seeming self-conscious and hurried.[10]

It could be that the snow man's "nothing" is the ground against which the sound of a leaf must be "merely heard." This nothing is the internal silence of the mind at rest, a still pool where the simplest intrusion is a surprise, completely heard:

> Old pond:
> Frog jump-in
> water-sound.

To Basho, sitting with his students by the pond in 1686 and speaking the last two lines as soon as the frog had jumped (the first line he added later),[11] the sound was quite possibly a "final finding of the ear . . . the thing itself." And since he had been studying Zen for five years, he might well have added with a laugh that the sound "concerns no one at all." Indeed, there had to be no concern, and no "one" in the historical and personal sense defined by cortical operations, for it to be merely heard.

Some traditional meditative exercises suggest the same areas of inquiry. The Zen master enters a strange room, sits, closes his eyes and describes every object in the room seen only fleetingly as he had entered. This could be a demonstration of his capacity for unfocused awareness, along with remarkable memory retrieval. Many of the famous Chinese and Japanese martial arts allied with meditation develop readiness, a readiness which depends upon being open to the slightest stimulus. Again, this general awareness may be heightened by one's having no expectations, and therefore, no selecting and focusing of sense receptors. Chinese and Japanese meditative exercises in verbal spontaneity similarly train the mind to think and speak without expectation, a favorite theme of Emerson's. Recall that in the brain waves of Rinzai Zen priests attempting to find answers to the koan imposed on them, Hirai found the same wavelengths as in meditating priests, and the same correspondence between stages of EEG and stages of accomplishment as judged by masters.[12]

If indeed meditative awareness opens the mind to unselected data from unfocused receptors, then the meditative emphasis on passivity, will-lessness and timelessness finds here a physiological explanation. The suspension of that focusing based on desire and expectation leads to a selfless awareness; this is the analogue of leaving the world of karma, the world of cause-effect relations based on selfish desire, and entering the world of pure awareness without self. Physiologically, such a state consists of a central nervous system awake and aware, but without habits or expectation. That is almost the same as saying a central nervous system without past or future or desire: living in the present without self. This is perhaps how "The Latest Freed Man" is free.

Such pure perception without involvement or response could be very close to talents of observation that many artists have cherished without calling the practice meditative, and certainly such pure perception could be called a kind of innocence—Blake's innocence that dwells more often with wisdom than with ignorance. Note, however, that this paradigm is opposed to fantasy, imagination, unconscious thought, or the kind of highly directed concentration that loads an object—Keats's Grecian urn, for instance—with one's strongest interests. Meditative perception is almost the perfect opposite of vision, that moment when the desiring self has recreated the world in its own image.

Meditative perception would also be different from the usual situation of the child, that romantic hero whose freshness and innocence of perception has often been compared to artistic vision. The child is certainly less "automatized," to use Deikman's term (we come trailing clouds of jargon); that is, lacking experience and habit, the child is less likely to have an automatic apprehension of phenomena, and more likely to pay attention to and interpret in some novel way what for an adult is ordinary. Psychologically, however, the child is straining to become normal, automatized, and the child is rarely as charmed as we are by his or her distance from the adult world. Not only is the child usually anxious to construct an acceptable self (as opposed to losing self), but also those charming constructions are imaginative acts. To quote Deikman again, the child's lack of habit may, like the meditator's openness, permit "the awareness of new dimensions in the total stimulus array," but the child is going the other way, trying to learn ordinary responses, and usually responds to stimuli with imaginative constructs.

It is possible, of course, that children also meditate, but that we have not distinguished between child imaginings and childhood meditations. As examples, I will offer two statements by my daughter Sarah Joy Bevis, at age four. On first tasting champagne, without a wince or a giggle, she smiled and pronounced, "angel juice." That is an excellent example of the romantic imagination at work: her innocence and experience pressed a new metaphor on an old subject, and made us look at it afresh. Another day, however, she was standing in the backyard as if in trance, stock still but alert, facing the woods a hundred yards away. "What are you doing?" I asked twice before she answered without turning her head or breaking concentration: "I am looking out of my face." No metaphor, no imagination: apparently a pure awareness of consciousness, in what I suspect was a meditative state. Both remarks certainly make us stop and reconsider our world, but only the first, I think, is accounted for by romantic theory comparing the imaginative artist to the child.

Imagination, thought, and feeling may be cortical activities—as opposed to meditation's passivity—but of course all cortical activities may involve other parts of the nervous system as well. A 1970 study of the physiology of meditation versus ecstasy—highly speculative, but continuing lines of investigation begun in Germany in the 1930s—attempted to distinguish parts of the nervous system active in thought, imagination, hallucination, and ecstasy from those parts active in meditation.[13] Whether or not Roland Fischer's conclusions hold up, it is

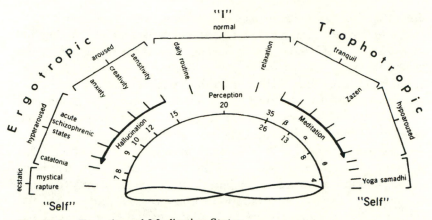

Figure 4.   Ecstatic and Meditative States
From Fischer, "A Cartography of the Ecstatic and Meditative States," p. 898.

noteworthy that he groups ecstasy with imagination, while meditation remains counterpoised to all active states. At their extremes, however, ecstatic enlightenment and meditative enlightenment are said to close the circle, becoming indistinguishable. Fischer's groupings, at least, repeat traditional meditative admonitions not only against thought, but also against drugs, hallucinations, and excitement, as being somehow different from meditative pursuits. (See figure 4.)

Fischer's approach was physiological; he used metabolic rate, eye movements, and brain wave patterns as well as behavior to suggest that experiences in the ecstatic continuum employ mainly ergotropic centers (in the sympathetic nervous system, used for body arousal in emotional states), while experiences in the meditative continuum employ mainly trophotropic centers (in the peripheral nervous system, used for body monitoring and maintenance, digestion, and so forth). Although the beginning meditator may pass through a stage of heightened excitation, Fischer's study supports the contention that some kinds of vivid perception useful to artists may not be comprehended by dramatic aesthetic theories stressing excitement or imagination.[14]

Let us update James's four marks of mystical experience, and narrow the description to meditation. The meditative experience is transient, but not necessarily as short as we once thought: although several hours of deep meditation are unusual, advanced practitioners apparently have to self-hypnotize to come out of deeper states at all, and there are cases of advanced meditation lasting for three days.[15]

James's point still stands in principle, however: the meditative state is unstable (current research on lowered metabolism in hibernation and in meditation addresses this issue), and therefore many meditative sects seek some carryover, in state of mind or in ethics, from the transient meditative experience to ordinary consciousness.

The meditative experience is essentially passive. The absence of certain activities—thought and feeling, excitation in association and other cortical areas—indicates that one can be awake and alert in the sensory world without new associations or learned responses. This passivity also defines a type of self-loss: if the self is the history of neuronal pathways in the cortex (above the brainstem), and therefore the tendency of any new excitation to take certain routes, then the refusal to focus or process or react to information in any new or old way is an abandonment of self, much more so than other states, including dreaming and sleep, with their continuous cortical and personal activities. This same passivity explains the meditator's loss, or transcendence, of time and space—conceptual categories apparently learned and stored in the cortex and not inherent in the brainstem, spine, or peripheral nervous system.

Obviously, in meditation the entire mind is not passive, or dead, or annihilated, or destroyed; reactions to meditation using such charges speak mainly to fear on the part of the observer. Certain functions of the brain are suspended; others remain. The functions that remain, according to EEG activity, seem to be centered in the midbrain and brainstem. It is possible that biologically speaking meditation is regressive, a return to a precortical mental state such as that experienced by a young fetus or by lower forms of life with less developed cortexes: life in the hypothalamic lane. Notice, however, that such regression should be carefully distinguished from regression that goes back no farther than infancy, and therefore draws on information developed by early personal experience and stored in the cortex. Most psychological interest in regression remains interested in the childhood cortex, and similarly, our concept of the unconscious is usually—not always—tied to neuronal pathways shaped by personal experience. The cortical unconscious would seem to be environmentally determined (by one's infancy and early childhood past); the subcortical unconscious would be more genetically determined and probably quite stable throughout the species (and perhaps of more interest to Jung than to Freud).

Through meditation, we might not become Emerson's roses, but we might make it back to a tree shrew, or a three-month fetus. And who is to say that the experience of precortical existence, with gills and a tail—an experience each of us has had—might not heighten one's sense of the continuity of time and space and the unity of all things?

The ineffability of such experience, noted by James, is obvious. Not only are the language areas of the cortex not involved in meditative experience, neither are any of the categories of conceptual thought that language creates or serves. Nor is there much to tell about, whether the meditative experience has taken the form of nirvana, or "the nothing that is," or "merely hearing" or seeing "the chairs." The separation of self versus other is weakened or suspended in meditative experience, and language, coming along afterward with its separate categories, might either seem ridiculous to the meditator or make the meditator seem ridiculous to the literate: "I am nothing. I see all." Even Deikman's beginning meditators found the experience hard to express. If there were some positive cerebral activity associated with meditation, as there is in vision, imagination, and thought—some positive excitement as there is in ecstasy—then language and metaphor might be if not exactly apt, at least more constructively suggestive. The passivity of meditation, however, makes even suggestiveness inappropriate.

Should we find that meditation is a biologically regressive state of the central nervous system, we must remember that this is not grounds for devaluing it. Like other fundamental acts—love, aggression—the meditative state can be sought and cherished in the context of a fully adult and educated life; it is in that context that we encounter it in art. We may find tomorrow a thousand ways in which the cortex is active during meditation; those thousand ways, however, will probably not include thought and feeling. The point is not that we know everything about the mind, but that everything science *does* know at the moment tends to corroborate the possibilities of passivity as described in meditative reports. Unlike occult claims, meditative reports of self-loss, transcendence of time and space, and no-mind can be reconciled with what we know and guess about the functioning brain; the empirical descriptions are a kind of rhetoric that may suggest the properties of no-mind for those who do not cultivate the experience, and this state of no-mind, in turn, may underlie Stevens' intermittent distaste for imagination's metaphors, which sometimes seem to be "shrinking from / The weight of primary noon, / The ABC of being" (*CP* 288).

We began this chapter on physiology with Admiral Byrd's four-month ordeal of sensory deprivation near the South Pole. He reminds us that such meditative seclusion leads quite naturally to the Thoreauvian paradox: the ascetic, having renounced all, finds himself in love with physical existence, the "*joliesses banales*":

> It was a queer business, I felt as though I had been plumped upon another planet or into another geologic horizon of which man had no knowledge or memory. And yet, I thought at the time it was very good for me; I was learning what the philosophers have long been harping on—that a man can live profoundly without masses of things. For all my realism and scepticism there came over me, too powerfully to be denied, that exalted sense of identification—of oneness—with the outer world which is partly mystical but also certainty. I came to understand what Thoreau meant when he said, "My body is all sentient." There were moments when I felt more *alive* than at any other time in my life. Freed from materialistic distractions, my senses sharpened in new directions, and the random or commonplace affairs of the sky and the earth and the spirit, which ordinarily I would have ignored if I had noticed them at all, became exciting and portentous.[16]

Sensory deprivation and sensory repetition, by encouraging meditative consciousness, may lead not to annihilation but to "oneness with the outer world," "senses sharpened," and a universe "exciting and portentous." That is, meditative consciousness, even in a nonmeditator, can lead to art.

9
Self and Will

Man, that hairless biped without feathers, nabob of bones, has come up with a new conception of himself: knight of the uncommitted cortex. For the last thirty years (at least since Aldo Leopold and Rachel Carson) biologists have carried the flag of humanism, and human beings as biologists have defined us as the most errant, original, free—in short, uncommitted organisms on earth.

Uncommitted cortex refers to that area of the brain which is not genetically programmed at birth to serve one specific function (such as motor control, visual interpretation, and so forth). The uncommitted part of the cortex is born free, free to be used as the organism wishes. Most of the *uncommitted* cortex in human beings becomes, in Wilder Penfield's words, "devoted to interpretation of present experience in the light of past experience";[1] such general interpretive activities humanists have accurately called reflection, the act of considering "present experience in the light of past experience." On the other hand, the *committed* cortical areas always develop predictable and limited functions: motor functions are carried out in the motor area, visual functions in the visual area, etc.

As mammals have evolved, some—especially primates, whales, dolphins, and human beings—have developed more and more uncommitted cortex. In a rat, about 10 percent of the cortex is uncommitted. In a monkey, about 50 percent is uncommitted. In man, about 90 percent is uncommitted.[2] To link man's identity to the percentage of his cortex uncommitted at birth is to suggest, quite correctly, why man's highest state is not fascist: we thrive on variety and originality. Ants and bees have their own biological demands; our species, by its nature, encourages each individual to consider new information in unique ways. Variety is our universe. Originality is our fate.

If the human species is distinguished by this capacity for reflection and therefore for original, unprogrammed response, which has also

137

been a capacity for adaptation (let us hope that continues), then it seems reasonable to say that the exercise of this capacity is what we usually call the *self*. Self suggests a complex of unique responses. From this definition, the proposition follows that a rat has less self than a monkey and a monkey less self than a man. This is harmonious with current usage: the concept of *personality*, those traits which distinguish one individual from another within a species, is closely linked to our concept of self.

Although some personality traits are probably inherited, the self seems mainly to be created out of personal experience; the uncommitted cortex is the tabula rasa of the brain. The first months and years of experience, however, not only cover an empty slate with information; brain cells also grow as a result of sensory experience. Early sensory deprivation may result in very little cortex. Language deprivation to the age of seven will probably leave a physical deficiency in the language area, precluding future learning of language. Sensation actually creates brain cells; learning creates mind. The tabula in any mammal is not only erased at birth; it is unformed:

> The arrangement of barrels [nerve cell clusters] across the cortex [of a mouse] matches exactly the pattern of whiskers in the mouse's moustache, so it is thought that each barrel might be the cortical representative of a single whisker. In fact, if one row of whiskers is removed in a new-born mouse, the appropriate row of barrels is missing in its cortex later in life.[3]

The self, then, as we are defining it, is closely associated with the uncommitted cortex, that part of the brain most thoroughly shaped, stamped, and even created by one's unique personal history. And the uncommitted cortex is the part of the brain most quiet in meditation.

Our definition of self is romantic: the self is the most uniquely individual aspect of man. There are many other uses of the word *self*. A naturalistic definition of *selfish* refers to the survival interests of the individual organism, and the naturalist's concept of *self-interest* applies equally, as Jack London noted, to yeast and man. Arguments about a "personal self" versus a "cosmic self" or a "racial self" are often arguments about which area of the brain should be considered primary: the interpretive cortex, or lower, more genetically determined and even universal areas shared with all mammals. One slightly different meaning of self, however, refers not so much to a complex of personal responses as to the existence of will: a command or control capacity within the individual. What, after all, is using the uncommitted cortex? Who is in charge?

The question is so tricky that one of the most prominent experimental neurosurgeons has espoused a theory of divine afflatus, an origin for the will independent of either brain (the organ) or mind (its functions). Penfield's transcendental conclusion is not shared by all of those who admire his experiments, but it certainly illustrates our frustrating ignorance in the area of "will": how the brain directs itself. Indeed, Penfield's search for a center to mental activity rehearses, unwittingly, some of the oldest Buddhist arguments, for the Madhayamikas hold that " 'mental states' are for all practical purposes real, but 'mind' is a fiction."[4] The author of the *Atthasalini* (Theravadic) and the Yogacarins, however, believe that mind or consciousness (*citta*) exists apart from states of mind.[5] Neither group believes that mental activity reveals a stable self, as suggested by these lines from the *Visuddhimagga:*

> In truth there is here only name and form,
> And there exists here neither living being nor man.
> Void is it, and constructed like a puppet,
> A mass of misery, and like wood or straw.[6]

Penfield, using local anesthetic on this "mass of misery," peels back the scalps of conscious, volunteer participants. Inserting a long, thin electric needle into specific areas of the brain, he shocks the area with a voltage comparable to the brain's synaptic voltage. By means of this shock he inhibits synapses in targeted areas and excites synapses in more distant and unpredictable areas. The patient, awake and aware (and without pain), tells Penfield what he is experiencing. Here Penfield recounts one of the incidents that most intrigued him:

> One of my associates began to show the patient a series of pictures on the other side of the sterile screen. C. H. named each picture accurately at first. Then, before the picture of a butterfly was shown to him, I applied the electrode where I supposed the speech cortex to be. He remained silent for a time. Then he snapped his fingers as though in exasperation. I withdrew the electrode and he spoke at once:
> "Now I can talk," he said. "Butterfly. I couldn't *get* that word 'butterfly,' so I tried to *get* the word 'moth!' "
> It is clear that while the speech mechanism was temporarily blocked he could perceive the meaning of the picture of a butterfly. He made a conscious effort to "get" the corresponding word. Then, not understanding why he could not do so, he turned back for a

second time to the interpretive mechanism, which was well away from the interfering effect of the electric current, and found a second concept that he considered the closest thing to a butterfly. He must then have presented that to the speech mechanism, only to draw another blank.

The patient's simple statement startled me. He was calling on two brain-mechanisms alternately and at will. He had focused his attention on the cards and set himself the purpose of recognizing and naming each picture as it came along. At first each picture was inspected in the stream of consciousness. It was identified, named, and recorded. He was using areas of cerebral cortex that, at birth, had been uncommitted as to function. Evidently, the highest brain-mechanism, impelled by mind-decision, can carry out these transactions, calling upon previously established, conditioned reflexes one by one. When I paralyzed his speech mechanism, he was puzzled. Then he decided what to do. He reconsidered the concept "butterfly" and summoned the nearest thing to butterfly that was stored away in his concept mechanism. When the concept "moth" was selected and presented in the stream of consciousness, the mind approved and the highest mechanism flashed this non-verbal concept of moth to the speech mechanism. But the word for "moth" did not present itself in the stream of consciousness as he expected. He remained silent, then expressed his exasperation by snapping the fingers and thumb of his right hand. That he could do without making use of the special speech mechanism. Finally, when I removed my interfering electrode from the cortex, he explained the whole experience with a feeling of relief, using words that were appropriate to his thought. *He* got the words from the speech mechanism when *he* presented concepts to it. For the word "he," in this introspection, one may substitute the word *mind*. Its action is not automatic.[7]

In this incident the will is almost visible, directing like a conductor the various functions of the brain. The action of this will apparently does not originate in the higher and more recently evolved cortex. The interpretive cortex, according to Penfield, is not the seat of consciousness but rather an "elaboration level" of consciousness.[8] Since rats and tree shrews also have will, it seems reasonable that will might spring from the older brain stem common to all mammals.

We return to meditation, attacked to the present day as annihilation. Shutting down the interpretive cortex, especially the uncommitted 90 percent of the human cortex, may shut down the romantic self of unique responses, but it does not necessarily shut down the more universal self of will. Penfield's patients are able to maintain an observer's detachment toward all cortical events, including language: "I couldn't get the word 'butterfly,' so I tried to get the word 'moth.' "

Penfield's electrode in the cortex can make someone move a hand or recall vividly a forgotten event, but the patient's response is "I didn't do that. You did." Quoting Penfield again: "He remains aloof. He passes judgement on it all. He says "things seem familiar," not "I have been through this before." . . . There is no place in the cerebral cortex where electrical stimulation will cause a patient to believe or to decide."[9] So the passivity of meditation may require a cortical passivity reported as self-loss, but may not require a passivity of will.

Let us consider two very different uses of the word *will*. The first use refers to a simple, goal-directed series of physical acts: commanding muscles, tuning sense receptors. Shooting an arrow at a target requires billions of willed actions such as eye and hand coordination, trajectory calculation, and timing. This could be called *animal will*, for such actions and reactions are involved in a dog chasing a rabbit, a frog catching a fly. Animal will refers to sensory and motor operations made within the committed cortex in pursuit of a goal. This is the willfulness of the dog smelling food, the mouse responding to its whiskers.

But what about the will that decides to take up archery in the first place, or decides to shoot one more quiver before dark? That we might call *free will*, what Penfield calls our ability to believe or decide, our capacity to put the cortex to work. Free will seems to be unusually active in human beings, though it is *not* part of the enlarged uncommitted cortex. Few frogs choose not to catch flies; human beings, however, might tell the cortex to do, or not to do, anything.

We have distinguished three aspects of brain and mind. First is the uncommitted cortex, the area of elaboration and reflection, formed by experience and most closely associated with the personal self. Second is the committed cortex, the area of sensory and motor functions, closely associated with animal will. Third is free will, as yet unlocated but apparently subcortical, in the midbrain or brainstem (very possibly near the hypothalamus, according to Penfield). It seems possible that when Hindus, Yogins, and Buddhists talk of meditative will-lessness and self-loss, they are usually referring to the suspension of cortical operations, committed and uncommitted: a suspension of animal will and of reflection. They do not necessarily abandon subcortical free will: decisive control of the mind. Indeed, meditative traditions stress a strong sense of purpose: the mind is being held in a state of willed will-lessness. The paradox may very well refer to the brainstem willing the cortex will-less. Free will is retained, but is used to hold passive all other goal-seeking and reflective operations. One kind of self is then lost, the most personal and conscious and learned self and perhaps the one most aware of categories of time and space, while some kind of impersonal will is retained. The Buddhists would not call this free will a self: "There is no permanent self apart from the states of a self."[10] They would also be quick to point out that in meditation the motive force (perhaps *cetana*) must not be allied with feeling (*vedana*) as it is in ordinary consciousness. Thus our categories stand well enough for Penfield and for Buddhist meditators: the self of moment-by-moment cortical activity, and the animal will of automatic (autonomic) response can be distinguished from the free will of decisiveness, a most mysterious capacity.

Now we come to another twist. There is no reason to assume that all meditative activities are identical, though all traditions share reports of passivity and self-loss. What of Sufi whirling dervishes, Chinese and Japanese Buddhist martial arts, Zen poetry, and Sumei painting? The constant factor in meditative traditions may not be one's encouraging or suppressing always the same functions, but rather one's suppressing the uncommitted reflective cortex and then playing with other possibilities. As we noted in chapter 8, for instance, Chinese and Japanese martial, verbal (koan), and pictorial (*sumei*) arts stress freedom and speed, and claim a relationship between those qualities and advanced meditative experience. Along with Emerson, they advocate marvelously appropriate spontaneous activity: "No Thinking" is on the walls of the Japanese swordplay as well as meditation halls, and should be writ large over Emerson's library.

The Ch'an or Zen swordsman is certainly using the committed (sensory and motor) cortex, although the reflective and interpretive uncommitted cortex may be held passive. There is no reason to believe that this differs fundamentally from other sports. The ice hockey goaltender could easily use Zen terms: he holds himself in absolute readiness, mind blank as a mirror, and is often unaware of what stimulus has prompted his instant response. (As Emerson said, "One could almost say the body thought.") The martial arts, then, may exercise both animal and free will, while the uncommitted cortex is passive. In speaking exercises stressing instantaneous, unconsidered, and original replies, the Ch'an and Zen traditions seem to encourage use of the language area of the cortex while reflective activities are suppressed. If these crude paradigms are even remotely accurate, we can see how such exercises parallel known meditative practices: varying one's heartbeat, varying the temperature at two different places on one's hand, walking on coals but refusing to interpret the sensations as pain. All these activities show practice in isolating and controlling mental functions and their effects. Meditators are experiential analysts of the brain; they make distinctions by doing. Stevens writes in "Esthétique du Mal":

> And out of what one sees and hears and out
> Of what one feels, who could have thought to make
> So many selves, so many sensuous worlds.

> (*CP* 326)

A modern dancer spends a good deal of time learning to isolate parts of the body—shoulder, arm, rib cage, pelvis—until one part can be used while other parts remain relaxed. The result is a demonstrated awareness, control, and articulation far beyond common expectation or experience. Meditators have long been demonstrating by practice what neurophysiologists are now discovering by research: functions originating in separate areas of the brain can be called on separately and at will. Meditators seem to practice isolating the uncommitted cortex, holding passive its complex of historically influenced expectations, associations and reactions—the self, the world of karma—while they use the will to engage or disengage other mental functions.

On the issue of will, perhaps, Western conceptions of meditation as quietist, passive, nihilist, depart farthest from meditative testimony. Meditators believe they are strong, persevering, disciplined, courageous, decisive: this could be true, while the result is passivity in isolated functions.

Certainly, meditative activity, whatever "nothing" it leads to in speech and thought, is not annihilation. If the distinctly human operations of the uncommmitted cortex can be revoked at will, they can also be convoked at will. Control in this case precedes passivity, and we must remember that the meditative state is transient. It should not be hard to explain to an existentialist the core of the Mahayana *bodhisattva* ideal: the highest virtue is a chosen, willed return to that tragedy called ordinary consciousness, the human condition: the self.

10

Language, Mind, and No-Mind: "Not Ideas about the Thing but the Thing Itself"

Words add to the senses. The words for the dazzle
Of mica, the dithering of grass,
The Arachne integument of dead trees,
Are the eye grown larger, more intense.
("Variations on a Summer Day," *CP* 234)

There might be, too, a change immenser than
A poet's metaphors in which being would

Come true, a point in the fire of music where
Dazzle yields to clarity and we observe . . . .
("Description without Place," *CP* 341)

We saw in chapter 6 that there are four categories of reality in Stevens: the external world, the internal world, the fresh recombination of those two worlds in imaginative perception, and the passive apprehension of the thing itself in meditative perception. In Stevens' poetry, both imaginative perception and meditative perception have their own language as well as dogma.

"Dazzle" is Stevens' word for imaginative perception: an active self, "grown larger, more intense," adds "to the senses." The result of this imaginative enlargement is Stevens' precious rhetoric, a vivid display of metaphorical language that calls attention to perceiver as much as to perceived, which is appropriate because that world of dazzling mica, dithering grass, and webbed trees is half created by an excited, remembering mind inventing ideas of order. Metaphor is, at least to Stevens, the perfect analogue to the way fresh cortical associations focus one's perceptions, to the way the self creates, as it receives, the world. Metaphor is "the creation of resemblance by the imagination" (*NA* 72). Just as metaphor superimposes terms *A* and *B*

144

to create *C,* so a moment of imaginative perception superimposes self and other in a new invention, that giant Stevens often called reality.

"Clarity," in "Description without Place," defines meditative perception. As imagination yields to meditative perception, rhetoric becomes more bare: "Dazzle yields to clarity." The tone, instead of being "intense," shrinks to an immediacy more static and calm:

> There might be, too, a change immenser than
> A poet's metaphors in which being would
>
> Come true, a point in the fire of music where
> Dazzle yields to clarity and we observe,
>
> And observing is completing and we are content,
> In a world that shrinks to an immediate whole,
>
> That we do not need to understand, complete
> Without secret arrangements of it in the mind.   (*CP* 341)

"Secret arrangements" are those imaginative acts of perception, those ideas of order, that give rise to a poet's metaphors. At least since 1938 Stevens had used the idea of arrangement to represent imaginative, metaphoric perception:

> You arrange, the thing is posed,
> What in nature merely grows.   (*CP* 198)

And he had said quite clearly of the posed Mrs. Pappadopoulos on the artist's couch, "The arrangement contains the idea of / The artist" (*CP* 296). In "Description without Place," the secret arrangements being rejected in favor of clarity and wholeness, are, without doubt, the imaginative constructs made by an active self. Later in the poem we are told that description is

> an expectation, a desire,
>
> A little different from reality:
> The difference that we make in what we see.   (*CP* 344)

But when "dazzle yields to clarity," such metaphoric arrangements, originating in "expectation" and "desire" and yielding "difference," are rejected; the meditative world is "immenser than / A poet's metaphors." It is the world of "being without description," as he said in the "The Latest Freed Man," the world as it appears "Without secret arrangements of it in the mind." The language for this meditative wholeness is abstract; the tone is established not by trembling metaphors of motion ("dazzle," "dithering") or even by mental motion ("Arachne integument"), but by simple words of stasis: being, point, clarity, observe, content, whole, complete. "Observing *is* completing." A passive self participates in a wholeness not of its own making. This psychology is familiar to the Hindus, as Staal explains:

> [The Indian mystic's] seemed to be a state which is unconditioned and unrelated to previous activity. . . . It is *jnana* "knowledge" because it does not through activity establish an object, but appears to reflect a situation which was already there and a condition already attained.[1]

Meditative knowledge is the opposite of imaginative knowledge. Metaphor, especially dazzling metaphor, is the quintessential language of mind. The clear image or pure ultimate abstraction ("chairs," "nothing," "all," "whole,") is the quintessential language of no-mind.

In the late 1930s Stevens wrote some of his best poems both for and against imagination. Curiously, the psychology permeating both kinds of poems, the psychology that engenders his theory of imagination in relation to self, is more Buddhist than modern. Typical categories of our culture—reason versus passion, critical intellect versus imagination, Yeats's head versus heart—are not important in Stevens' poems of the thirties, or afterward. Instead, critical mind and creative imagination and passionate desire are equated, as he makes clear in "The Poems of Our Climate." The "never-resting mind" is allied with "delight," both are immersed in the "imperfect" world of this earth, and that imperfect combination of mind and desire "so hot in us" produces art: "flawed words and stubborn sounds." Thus (as in Fischer's diagram in figure 4, above, of ecstatic arousal versus meditative calm) the intellect, the passions, and the imagination are lumped together in defining the active self. In "The Poems of Our Climate," the whole package of self is endorsed. So also in "The Glass of Water" one sitting among "dogs and dung" would "continue to contend with one's ideas," for "It can never be satisfied, the mind, never" (*CP* 247). That last statement is not quite fair to Stevens' own work, for the imaginative mind certainly has its moments of sufficient union, but his exaggeration captures the sense of driving desire, of a system in tension, present in imaginative activity: "flawed words and stubborn sounds," "blessed rage for order," "the mind in the act of finding," never satisfied.

The unsatisfied mind, restless passion, necessarily flawed art, and the physical world: our climate, according to Stevens, resembles the conditioned world of the five *skandhas:* material things, feelings, perceptions, impulses, and acts of consciousness are heaped together. The importance of the resemblance is that to Stevens all acts of self (imaginings, ideas, feelings) are similar and, through perception, linked to this imperfect world. In Theravadic psychology, the *vipaka* consciousness arises at birth and includes the entire self of "Poems of our Climate": physical body, sensation, perception and volitional activity.[2] Ordinary consciousness links the "evilly compounded, vital I," by means of mind and desire, to the phenomenal world.

In Stevens and in Buddhism this link of the imperfect that is "so hot in us" to the imperfect of the material world produces an endless activity: the "never-resting mind" will "continue to contend" forever, just as the law of karma guarantees endless action and reaction with no rest in sight. Imagination, then, is allied with desire, and takes us into the ceaseless activity of the cause-and-effect world as Stevens succinctly and beautifully observes:

> But the priest desires. The philosopher desires.
>
> And not to have is the beginning of desire.
> To have what is not is its ancient cycle.   (*CP* 382)

In conceiving of the *I*—"your thoughts, your feelings / Your beliefs and disbeliefs, your whole peculiar plot" (*CP* 501)—as one big heap of never satisfied thought and feeling, Stevens invites not the usual European questions of whether to have more or less head or more or less heart, or whether to change one idea for another, but the meditative question of whether to have more or less *I*.

In "Not Ideas about the Thing but the Thing Itself" we will see that more or less self, quite apart from the reasonableness or the beauty of one's thoughts or feelings, is indeed the central dilemma in Stevens, and that self involves us in endless cycles of action and reaction. First, however, let us look more closely at one more crucial aspect of imagination for Stevens: how it is indivisible from everyday perception, and why there is no essential difference between life and art.

When Stevens said that "you do not see, you experience, you feel," he meant that the ordinary person responding to the world, making "secret arrangements of it" through acts of imagination and understanding, is an artist. The best illustration of the essential identity of art and perception is in "The Idea of Order at Key West" (1936). In that poem the separation of self and other ("she" and "sea") is bridged twice: first by her, the singer who through her art

> was the single artificer of the world
> In which she sang. And when she sang, the sea,
> Whatever self it had, became the self
> That was her song, for she was the maker.   (*CP* 129)

The artist through an act of imagination unites self and other in a third reality, her song. However, the more surprising move, and the better poetry, occurs in the next stanza when two members of the audience, inspired by the song, are walking back toward town and suddenly see the boats in the harbor in a new way:

> Ramon Fernandez, tell me, if you know,
> Why when the singing ended and we turned
> Toward the town, tell why the glassy lights,
> The lights in the fishing boats at anchor there,
> As the night descended, tilting in the air,
> Mastered the night and portioned out the sea,
> Fixing emblazoned zones and fiery poles,
> Arranging, deepening, enchanting night.

> Oh! Blessed rage for order, pale Ramon . . . .   (*CP* 130)

The description of masts, lights, and sea resembles a painting by Paul Klee (one of Stevens' favorite artists). A work of art by either Klee or the singer by the sea arranges self and other in a new construct; likewise a moment of imaginative perception in the life of two members of the audience arranges self and other in a new construct. The active perceiver lives a life of art: things as they are have become things as they are painted. And this imaginative perception has its oxymoronic metaphors of geometry and mystery (resembling Yeats's "cold and passionate") that combine in a moment of dazzle: "arranging . . . enchanting night." The strong feeling is caught up at the coda: "Oh! Blessed rage for order." The passionate self creates a new reality through the secret arrangements, the rage for order present in imaginative perception, and therefore imaginative perception is essentially a work of art.

We have noted three aspects of Stevens' concept of self: he lumps together imagination, thought, feeling, and creative perception; he finds this compounded self ceaselessly, endlessly involved in action and reaction within the physical world; and he believes that the imaginative act of perception is a fact of life as well as of art. The language that expresses the perceptions of the active, imaginative self is meta-phoric, for metaphor's superimposition of *A* and *B* ("the sea was glass") to create a third reality (sea-glass) imitates the imagination's superimposition of self and other ("the sea . . . became the self that was her song") to create reality-as-it-is-lived. The more active and bold the self, then the more dazzling the metaphors and the more imaginative the final reality:

> By metaphor you paint
> A thing. Thus, the pineapple was a leather fruit,
> A fruit for pewter, thorned and palmed and blue,
> To be served by men of ice.
>   The senses paint
> By metaphor. The juice was fragranter
> Than wettest cinnamon. It was cribled pears
> Dripping a morning sap.
>   The truth must be
> That you do not see, you experience, you feel,
> That the buxom eye brings merely its element
> To the total thing, a shapeless giant forced
> Upward.
>   Green were the curls upon that head.   (*CP* 219)

But as much as this imaginative self, a head that has merged with the pineapple it perceives, is admired by Stevens, it is also often questioned. The "motive for metaphor," he sometimes believed, is a desire to escape from a final reality "immenser than / A poet's meta-phors" (*CP* 341), a desire to shrink from "The weight of primary noon, / The ABC of being" (*CP* 288). Sometimes he wished to "Trace the gold sun about the whitened sky / Without evasion by a single metaphor" (*CP* 373). As we have observed, Stevens' conception of the self invites a distinction not between this imagining and that, this idea or that, but between more self and less self. The imaginative and meditative models gave him two very different ways of answering what East and West both see as a problem, to say the least: ordinary consciousness, ordinarily does not suffice. In much of Stevens, and in most romantic art, one escapes the ordinary self by developing an extraordinary, more excited self: one escapes to dazzle. But in many Stevens poems, the antidote to ordinary self is not more self, but not-self, immersion of the no-mind in sure, bare perception: one escapes to clarity. Thus meditation, in Stevens, is the complementary oppo-site of imagination.

One of Stevens' greatest poems, "Not Ideas about the Thing but the Thing Itself," which he deliberately placed at the end of his *Collected Poems,* illustrates why the dazzle of imagination, no matter how beautiful, conflicts with the clarity of meditative perception.

Not Ideas about the Thing but the Thing Itself

At the earliest ending of winter,
In March, a scrawny cry from outside
Seemed like a sound in his mind.

He knew that he heard it,
A bird's cry, at daylight or before,
In the early March wind.

The sun was rising at six,
No longer a battered panache above snow . . .
It would have been outside.

It was not from the vast ventriloquism
Of sleep's faded papier-mâché . . .
The sun was coming from outside.

That scrawny cry—it was
A chorister whose c preceded the choir.
It was part of the colossal sun,

Surrounded by its choral rings,
Still far away. It was like
A new knowledge of reality.   (*CP* 534)

The plot is simple enough. At the end of winter a man awakens at dawn. In the first two stanzas this man wonders if he is really hearing the *other,* something outside of his mind, a bird's cry that at first "Seemed like a sound in his mind." To apprehend such a phenomenon as other, as the thing itself, as external rather than internal, would be to go from winter's solipsism to spring. This is the dramatic situation of the poem. After a series of negations the man is finally certain of otherness—"The sun was coming from outside"—and then has an epiphany in which sun and bird become part of a beautiful choral metaphor, "like / A new knowledge of reality."

Almost every published critic of Stevens has taken the man's final epiphany as an unquestioned good. Helen Vendler fairly represents this point of view: "In this transparently beautiful poem, Stevens claims all that can be claimed for any sublime experience—that it confers 'a new knowledge of reality.' "[3]

The epiphany is beautiful, but within the poem it exists in a broader context that makes us see it as only one kind of sublime experience, in competition with another sublime. The epiphany is a questioned good; the poem offers a middle way between the extremities of yes and no.

Some readers of this poem suspect—wrongly, I believe—an ironic tone. They point first to the "still far away" and to *"like / A new knowledge"* as evidence that the epiphany may be qualified; those are quibbles, however, compared to the problem posed by the title. The title seems to be an expressed wish for "the thing itself" instead of "ideas about the thing." It is very hard not to connect "ideas" in the title with "knowledge" in the last line. That is, we can throw out the quibbles, grant the epiphany, call it indeed a beautiful "new knowledge of reality" and then wonder how this poem has come to be diametrically opposed to the wish expressed in the title. The last line leads back to the title, the title to the first line, the first line to the last: a wonderful example of "the pleasures of merely circulating" that Stevens so often indulged. The title seems to imply a wish for clarity, while the man winds up with dazzle. If this reading is at all justified, Stevens, in placing this poem at the end of his *Collected Poems,* must have meant to draw attention to the way in which meditative perception and imaginative perception are counterpoised.

The poem has two highly metaphoric sections. In the first, stanzas 3 and 4, dazzling language is repeatedly negated. The sun is "no longer a battered panache above the snow"; it is no longer fantastic, the creation of man's dreams:

> It was not from the vast ventriloquism
> of sleep's faded papier-mâché . . .

Still in the spirit of the title, this man is rejecting winter's dazzle and trying to apprehend the sun as a simple clarity, beyond himself. Stevens in these two stanzas has linked winter, the mind, fantasy, and metaphoric language: again, the whole package of self. His proposition is clear enough: in winter (in this poem) perception is an imaginative act. A winter man of buxom eye makes secret arrangements of the world. He therefore apprehends not the thing itself but his ideas of it, which are only fantastic projections of his own self (as the ventriloquist hears only his own voice). In winter, then, the sun is merely a ventriloquist's dummy. The winter solipsist, full of himself, speaks a precious, involuted speech: dazzle. Ideas about the thing.

In the second metaphoric section, the last two stanzas of the poem, the man constructs an elaborate and beautiful choir metaphor around the bird and sun: "chorister . . . c preceded the choir . . . colossal

sun . . . choral rings." Coleridge might have called the first meta-
phoric section fantastic, the second imaginative. In this poem, surpris-
ingly, they both spell disaster.

Let us consider the plot from a Buddhist and, I would say, from
Stevens' point of view—that is, from the point of view of meditative
psychology. A man who longs for something beyond self (as winter
longs for spring), hears a bird's cry which at first seemed like a sound
in his mind. But "He knew that he heard it" and he concentrates
again on the sound much as Stevens had kept returning to the cry of
leaves in "The Course of a Particular," three years before. Deliber-
ately denying rhetoric, metaphor, imagination ("No longer a battered
panache"), he disavows mind in an attempt to apprehend the sun
itself: "It would have been outside." Almost, but still conditional. He
denies mind and fantasy again ("not from . . . sleep"), and after
these repeated negations the conditional suddenly becomes declara-
tive: "The sun was coming from outside." A very simple line; at this
moment the sun is perceived "without description." At this moment
there is a minimum of self, a minimum of thought, imagination, and
metaphor, and a maximum of clarity. For a moment on rising, this is
another freed man, apprehending the suchness of the external world
in a state of meditative detachment. As the Chinese say, after enlight-
enment, "mountains are mountains, rivers are rivers."

But then the poem takes another twist: this man starts to think and
feel again, and therefore to describe, and therefore, to project his
self. As the Buddhists would say, he becomes "attached" to his new
apprehension of bird and sun, and as his excitement mounts, desire
and metaphor sweep back into the poem. At precisely the same
point, or dash, that the latest freed man had given up on nouns and
turned to verbal process: "The light he gives— / It is *how* he *gives* his
light. It is *how* he shines" (*CP* 205), this man imports a new noun that
will become the center of a new and dazzling metaphor:

> That scrawny cry—It was
> A *chorister* whose c preceded the choir.
> It was part of the colossal sun.

The man's excitement has led him to make new secret arrangements
of his world, to remake the world in the image of his own desire. "The
tragedy, however, may have begun, / Again, in the imagination's new
beginning" (*CP* 320). In that excitement and its attendant metaphor
he has, by means of desire, fallen back into the world of self. The

choral rings of that fall widen until he has—yes—a moving and beautiful metaphor, but alas, he also has again ideas about the thing and not the thing itself. In the words of Tsung Kao,

> This is like the sun shining in the blue sky—
> clear and bright, unmovable and immutable,
> neither increasing nor decreasing. . . .
> If you want to grasp it, it runs away from you;
> but if you cast it away, it continues to exist
> there all the time.[4]

The plot of the poem, from the Buddhist and from Stevens' point of view, is based on the tragedy of desire: to love the other is to lose it by making it oneself. To the Buddhists, "The identity of the emotion with the object . . . implies that any object whatsoever can have an effect on the individual to any degree and that any sort of emotion on the part of the individual immediately violates the object. Such a mentality, which may be called autoerotic because the individual loves himself in and through the object, is a serious handicap [in Abhidharma doctrine]."[5] To the European, union is achieved by love; to the Buddhist, union is achieved by detachment. Each tradition considers the other's attempt at union solipsistic. Curiously, the psychology of Stevens' poem is Buddhist: the physical world, the other, is most closely approached by no-mind. As the man becomes excited, he gains ideas about the thing but he loses the thing itself. According to Chung-Yuan, "For Ch-an Buddhists . . . intellectual effort . . . often resulted in mere knowledge about reality, failing to reveal reality itself."[6] If "The greatest poverty is not to live / In a physical world" (*CP* 325), this poem argues for, not against, meditative perception.

In H. D. Lewis's essay "On Poetic Truth," copied by Stevens and reprinted in *OP,* he read of the difference between a poet's need for a reality that is other, and Plato's reality that is made of human "abstract systems, ideas":

> What do we learn? Just this; that poetry has to do with reality in that concrete and individual aspect of it which the mind can never tackle altogether on its own terms, with matter that is foreign and alien in a way in which abstract systems, ideas in which we detect an inherent pattern, a structure that belongs to the ideas themselves, can never be. It is never familiar to us in the way in which Plato wished the conquests of the mind to be familiar. On the contrary its function, the need which it meets and which has to be met in some way in every age that is not to become decadent or barbarous is precisely this contact with reality as it impinges on us from the outside, the

sense that we can touch and feel a solid reality which does not wholly dissolve itself into the conceptions of our own minds. It is the individual and particular that does this. And the wonder and mystery of art, as indeed of religion in the last resort, is the revelation of something "wholly other" by which the inexpressible loneliness of thinking is broken and enriched.

Lewis here correctly uses Plato, our major Western mystic, as the hero of mind and imagination. Indeed, in book 7 of the *Republic,* Plato's ultimate reality is found a long way from the "things" of appearance. Against this imagined reality Lewis proposes a found reality: "the sense that we can touch and feel a solid reality which does not wholly dissolve itself into the conceptions of our own minds." Such conceptions are the "secret arrangements," the "ideas of order," the "ideas about a thing" that we have been discussing. Just as in the poem the thinking man is solipsistic, isolated, so in this essay the thinking man needs "the revelation of something 'wholly other' by which the inexpressible loneliness of thinking is broken and enriched." The "wholly other" is precisely what appears in the middle of "Not Ideas": "The sun was coming from outside." Then the sun gives way to ideas, metaphors, "new knowledge." Stevens seems well aware that what he wants is a change in the nature of perception, as described by Lewis: "What I desire to stress is that there is a unity rooted in the individuality of objects and discovered in a different way from the apprehension of rational connections" (*OP* 236–37).

In the context of the paragraph, not only "rational connections" but platonic "ideas" and all "conquests of the mind" have been rejected in favor of the "wholly other," which is "discovered in a different way" and is found to be "a unity." "The inexpressible loneliness of thinking" is cured by this wholeness not of our own making.

"Not Ideas about the Thing but the Thing Itself" may in one way argue for meditative perception, but the beauty of the imaginative epiphany argues also for ideas instead of things, and the poem does not support a meditative *teleology* any more than it supports an imaginative one: the reader moves through the man's nirvana and through his imaginative epiphany, back to the title, and back through the cycle of the poem. This is not exactly the endless recycling of karma, for here nirvana, instead of taking us out of the process, is part of it. So neither a meditative nor imaginative teleology is held: Stevens' is a formidably impartial humanism, embracing the fecund minimum and the fecund maximum as equal parts of a never ending cycle of no-mind and mind. Perhaps it is that detachment from both kinds of knowledge, that equality of endorsement without attachment (analogous to the most radical *bodhisattva* traditions) that led Stevens to consider this poem such a fitting end (suggesting no-end) to his collected work. Two years before publishing "Not Ideas," he wrote: "Sometimes I believe most in the imagination for a long time and then, without reasoning about it, turn to reality and believe in that and that alone. But both of these things project themselves endlessly and I want them to do just that" (*L* 747). The two "things" endlessly projected are not, I suspect, imagination and reality so much as two kinds of perception: imaginative perception, making secret arrangements, and meditative perception, encountering reality-in-itself.

In exploring the alliance of metaphor and imaginative perception on the one hand, and the alliance of image and meditative perception on the other, I hope to have defined an aspect of the blankness in Stevens that has intrigued but eluded readers. I do not mean to imply, however, that a particular literary device can serve only a particular kind of perception. Any device can serve any end. In "A Clear Day and No Memories" (*OP* 113), for instance (discussed in chapter 6), the final "sense" is a metaphor suggesting perception in a state of no-mind. The metaphor, however, is not distinguished by dazzle. Rather, its virtue is to suggest quite subtly the clarity of suchness and the calm unity of no-mind. It is a metaphor with the savor of image, plus "all."

Any single device can be used to mirror any state of consciousness. On the other hand, words must be interpreted in relation to the state of consciousness to which they refer. The import of that proposition is enormous, but the premise is unavoidable: a verbal report reflecting an experience in one state of consciousness may have very little relation to the same report reflecting the experience of another state. In a tradition stressing changes of state instead of changes of ideas, such distinctions are common. When a Hindu Advaita philosopher says "Maya is understood in three ways: by the man in the street as real, by the logician as undeterminable, and by the follower of the scripture as nonexistent,"[7] he does not refer to three ideas of *maya;* he refers to not thinking much about it, thinking much about it, and encountering it in a state of no-mind. Similarly, when the Zen master says "If you don't understand—thirty blows! If you understand—also thirty blows!" we can grasp the thought if we interpret the first "understand" as *prajna*-knowledge, and the second "understand" as intellectual knowledge. Precisely the same problem dominates the last lines of "The Snow Man":

> the listener, who listens in the snow.
> And, nothing himself, beholds
> Nothing that is not there and the nothing that is.

The first "nothing himself" suggests the self-loss of meditative consciousness. The second "nothing that is not there" is the zero of ordinary consciousness, suggesting that the man sees only what is there and projects or imagines nothing extra. The final phrase, "*the nothing*," is the perceived nothing of meditative (*prajna*) consciousness, and suggests that he "beholds" the voidness of scene and self, its *sunyata* nature.

In showing how contradictory statements from the East are often rational, Frits Staal discusses the need to refer words to a states-of-consciousness epistemology.[8] This is especially necessary, I think, because ordinary consciousness is the home of language, and any other source experience creates new tension between language and knowledge. The Greek association of *word* with reason or structured thought (*logos*) continues to seem wise. Language helps structure and manipulate the world encountered in ordinary consciousness, the world of things and ideas. Language is inherently related to our "rage for order" (perhaps that is the best translation of 1 John: "In the beginning was the rage for order"). Order and perceiving order are prerequisite to the useful manipulation of causes and effects. This is not to rule out other, more Pythagorean origins of order, but simply to observe the strong alliance between language, practical survival, and ordinary consciousness. Language manipulates karma.

When language is used to discuss the experience of nonordinary consciousness, we may expect some need for translation. An extreme example of the relation of language to states of consciousness would be our reaction to someone's report, "I saw God." Most of us, even the most devout, would have trouble taking "I saw God" as a description of a visual experience in ordinary consciousness. Right away we would try to translate *saw* or *God* not only into symbolic or metaphoric meanings but also into a report of a nonordinary state. If we said, "You mean you hallucinated?" and the person replied, "Yes," we would relax, having translated the verb and noun into meanings appropriate to another state of consciousness. By understanding the statement in relation to a hallucinatory state, we would preserve order in our world of ordinary consciousness and language. If the speaker, however, refused to trace the statement to another state or to metaphor, we might have no idea what he meant. We would only know, if he insisted that the statement made sense in relation to ordinary consciousness, that he was using the religious connotations of *God;* we would know the area in which he was making a claim.

On the other hand, that is precisely what we would *not* know if the speaker was reporting a dream. "I saw God" as a report of a dream experience we could easily understand as visual (there was an old fellow with long white robes and a starry crown), while to the dreamer this experience might have been as insignificant or banal as any other dream image: "I saw God and then a green Chevrolet. A hubcap fell off." As a report of ordinary consciousness, then, "I saw God" is so wide open in denotation that it is practically meaningless, while in connotation it is almost certainly religious. As a report of a dream or a waking hallucination, however, the statement is likely to have a precise visual denotation though it need not employ any religious connotation at all.

"I saw God" proceeding from a stage 2 meditative experience could well refer to a vivid hallucination; if the claim were seriously advanced by a Taoist, Ch'an, or Zen meditator, however, known to regard stage 2 visions as false, we could assume it refers to at least a stage 3 or 4 experience: an experience devoid of visual images, devoid of theory or doctrine, but leaving an impression of ineffable and very probably atheistic enlightenment. We would translate the words into something like "I beheld (by not being I and by not beholding) the essential reality/nonreality of the universe which some circumscribe and reify with the irrelevant concept of God."

To some extent these distinctions simply review differences between sects and religions. The point is that such differences vary not only with doctrine, but also with the state of consciousness from which the claim arises. When a major artist such as Emerson says, "I am nothing; I see all. . . . I am part or parcel of God," or when Stevens says, "The sun was coming from outside," or "It was . . . the chairs," or "this sense," or "the nothing that is," a full and sympathetic reading demands some knowledge of the states of consciousness from which such claims might issue, and some knowledge of the typical metamorphoses that perceptions undergo when exported from their original context into the ordinary consciousness of language.

The borders of nations, languages, cultures, centuries, and individual history are not the only borders; a change of state is a change of context for all mental events.

The reader may perceive here a possible ground for antipathy between the intellectual and the meditator, a ground more solid than alleged doctrinal differences: the American and European humanist intellectual, no matter how much he may at times seem the gadfly of society, skeptical or critical of the practical world of getting on, nevertheless prefers the practical and adaptive ordinary state of consciousness to the ecstatic and meditative states. Socrates would be the seminal example: even while giving up the last self-interest, he was doing it in the name of the most practical functions: reason and language. Western intellectuals are often deeply offended by the meditator's refusal to manipulate not only time and space, but also ideas and language, although the meditator may be manipulating consciousness beyond the intellectual's wildest dreams.

Any supposed opposition between ordinary and meditative consciousness, however, must be placed in perspective: all states of consciousness are temporary. We cannot be awake all the time, dream all the time, or meditate all the time. Biologically, states of consciousness are complementary, not exclusive, and one suspects that only human possessiveness leads different cultures to develop, for different states, self-justifying and exclusive doctrines. That is why Stevens' nonattachment, in "Not Ideas about the Thing but the Thing Itself," to either imaginative or meditative knowledge, to either self or not-self, seems a consummate achievement.

11

The Tragedy of Desire in "Esthétique du Mal"

In "Esthétique du Mal" (1944), Stevens pondered the meditative state and its relation to the tragedy of desire. In section XII, he sketched the difference between the world of social knowledge, the world of self-knowledge, and a third world without knowledge:

> He disposes the world in categories, thus:
> The peopled and the unpeopled. In both, he is
> Alone. But in the peopled world, there is,
> Besides the people, his knowledge of them. In
> The unpeopled, there is his knowledge of himself.
> Which is more desperate in the moments when
> The will demands that what he thinks be true?
>
> Is it himself in them that he knows or they
> In him? If it is himself in them, they have
> No secret from him. If it is they in him,
> He has no secret from them. This knowledge
> Of them and of himself destroys both worlds,
> Except when he escapes from it. To be
> Alone is not to know them or himself.
>
> This creates a third world without knowledge,
> In which no one peers, in which the will makes no
> Demands. It accepts whatever is as true,
> Including pain, which, otherwise, is false.
> In the third world, then, there is no pain. Yes, but
> What lover has one in such rocks, what woman,
> However known, at the centre of the heart?   (*CP* 323)

The first stanza proposes two categories: society ("peopled") and self ("unpeopled"). At first one seems to be "alone" in both worlds, but then the speaker realizes that in both worlds one is accompanied by "knowledge." Suddenly, without explanation, knowledge of both self and other is called "desperate" and is linked to "will" and its

159

"demands" for truth. Why is knowledge desperate? As often occurs in Stevens' long poems, a sudden remark will be clarified only later in a repetition of the theme.

In the second stanza, using impersonal and conditional constructions to create a most Stevensian tone of philosophical wit, the speaker implies that since knowledge is always a symbiosis of society and self (a proposition undeniably true of language), there can be "no secret" in the world of knowledge. Society and self know each other because they are each other: "The imagination and society are inseparable" (*NA* 28). The categories of society and self, not being separate, are false:

> This knowledge
> Of them and of himself destroys both worlds.

Perhaps that is why knowledge was called desperate: knowledge "destroys" old categories and here, at least, Stevens does not claim that it creates new ones. Knowledge satisfies the mind's desire for skepticism, but not the will's demand for truth. At this point in many of Stevens' poems we might expect (and receive) a return with renewed vigor to imaginative perception, a perception that engenders some "new knowledge of reality." But instead, the strong verb "destroys" drives the poem even farther from society and self to a very interesting passage on the meditative state:

> This knowledge
> Of them and of himself destroys both worlds,
> Except when he escapes from it. To be
> Alone is not to know them or himself.

The escape is not from "both worlds," as Westerners might expect, but from knowledge itself ("it"). The following sentence proves the pronoun no mistake: "To be alone is not to know them or himself." "Not to know": not to use those cortical functions developed by experience and therefore inherently social as well as individual. This leads to a full description of the meditative condition:

> This creates a third world without knowledge,
> In which no one peers, in which the will makes no
> Demands. It accepts whatever is as true,
> Including pain, which, otherwise, is false.
> In the third world, then, there is no pain.

This meditative third world of neither self nor other, "without knowledge, / In which no one peers," answers the will's demand for truth by abandoning all goal-seeking: "in which the will makes no / Demands." In that meditative state without will or knowledge, judgment or selection, everything is accepted and thus, as in the Ch'an tradition, the "true" is suddenly perceived everywhere precisely because the will has stopped looking for it: "It [the will] accepts whatever is as true." The verb "accepts" (as opposed to "demands") mirrors the passivity of this state.

The will also accepts "pain, which, otherwise, is false." Without will or knowledge, there can hardly be metaphysical pain, and this wrinkle also parallels Buddhist doctrine on the subject of physical suffering: sensation interpreted as pain is an idea about the thing and not the thing itself; interpreted pain is only a concept and is therefore false. On the other hand, sensation simply accepted is not painful: "In the third world, then, there is no pain." This is an accurate description of the meditative practice of receiving sense impressions while suspending cortical interpretation, a practice that lies behind walking on hot coals or, closer to home, Lamaze childbirth: the delivering woman is taught, through concentration on breathing exercises, to allow sensation to pass through her mind (to accept "whatever is as true") without interpreting those sensations as pain. The sensations, then, are "true" and are accepted (not blocked out), but "without knowledge" or "will" there is no interpretation and therefore no pain.

At this point the passage takes a wonderfully spontaneous turn. The entire meditative section had risen from the ashes of "destroys" and "escapes," from a defensive need to find a world in which "no one peers." Such aloneness has now been found, and in addition "there is no pain" or desperation, for no longer does his will demand "that what he *thinks* be true"; it accepts "whatever *is* as true." But there is no reconciling the claims of the monastic life and the claims of the domestic life; suddenly the entire world of desire comes flooding back:

> In the third world, then, there is no pain. Yes, but
> What lover has one in such rocks, what woman,
> However known, at the centre of the heart?

The images are perfect: the need of the species to survive the death of the individual engenders sexuality. Both Genesis and the Buddhists agree that death, birth, and their link, sexuality, form the heart of the world of karma, the world of cause-effect demands in historical time. That is the world to which we fall from paradise. The alternative to the meditative state is indeed the ancient tragedy of desire: a "lover . . . woman . . . at the centre of the heart." This move at first seems a welcome return to society and self, to love and time. Surprisingly, the next section begins right away with the assumption that to return to desire and historical time is indeed to return to pain:[1]

XIII

It may be that one life is a punishment
For another, as the son's life for the father's.

After that opening shot, Stevens begins a series of quick turns. He suddenly dismisses the whole tragedy of being in a remarkable passage:

But that concerns the secondary characters.
It is a fragmentary tragedy
Within the universal whole. The son
And the father alike and equally are spent,
Each one, by the necessity of being
Himself, the unalterable necessity
Of being this unalterable animal.
This force of nature in action is the major
Tragedy. This is destiny unperplexed,
The happiest enemy.   (CP 324)

The "force of nature in action" (an excellent definition of karma) is a "tragedy"; the central symbol of that tragedy is biological generation, with its "unalterable necessity." Each son and father is yoked to the system of dying generations, tragedy and pain, by individual existence: "the necessity of being / Himself." Such a tragic destiny is so obvious, simple, and true that it is "the happiest enemy." That is no country for old men.

Just how radically Stevens identifies desire with evil emerges in the rest of the passage. We return suddenly to the meditative third world without knowledge, to a monk "eased of desire":

And it may be
That in his Mediterranean cloister a man,
Reclining, eased of desire, establishes
The visible, a zone of blue and orange
Versicolorings, establishes a time
To watch the fire-feinting sea and calls it good.   (CP 324)

The reader may think it caviling at first to say that the monk's medita-
tion, "eased of desire" as he "establishes the visible," is destroyed the
moment he "calls it good." But this is precisely parallel to "Not
Ideas": to love the other is to lose it by making it oneself. The monk
has just become attached to his detached perception and begins to
make value judgments. The meditative concentration is lost: thought
("good") and language ("calls") slip back in; he is now an enthusiast,
no longer "eased of desire." And he continues to fall back into desire
("good . . . ultimate good . . . maximum") until in one dramatic
move Stevens asserts that perceiving the maximum good—that is,
making value judgments engendered by desire—is the "the assassin's
scene." Desire, that brought the "lover . . . woman . . . son and the
father alike" back into the poem *is* the assassin, the force of nature in
action, and that is why "the force that destroys us is disclosed, *within*
this maximum":

> and calls it good,
> The ultimate good, sure of a reality
> Of the longest meditation, the maximum,
> The assassin's scene. Evil in evil is
> Comparative. The assassin discloses himself,
> The force that destroys us is disclosed, within
> This maximum, an adventure to be endured
> With the polite helplessness. Ay-mi!
> One feels its action moving in the blood.   (*CP* 324)

The words "action" and "force" associated now with "assassin"
take us right back to "the force of nature in action"; "in the blood"
reminds us of father, son, and before that, lover and woman. The
assassin is normal, ordinary, natural desire. This is the passionate
assassin that did *not* kill Satan, who "was denied," in section VIII; the
equation of passion, imagination, and tragedy ("desire . . . good . . .
destroys us") had been clearly put forth in that earlier section:

> The mortal no
> Has its emptiness and tragic expirations.
> The tragedy, however, may have begun,
> Again, in the imagination's new beginning,
> In the yes of the realist spoken because he must
> Say yes, spoken because under every no
> Lay a passion for yes that had never been broken.   (*CP* 320)

That passage is usually read as a humanist triumph, but in XIII we see
its dark side: beneath the monk's "no" lies a passion for "yes," and

his "good . . . ultimate good . . . maximum" is the "imagination's new beginning." "The force that destroys us is disclosed, within / This maximum," and therefore "The tragedy . . . may have begun / Again, in the imagination's new beginning."

These are hard words for our culture to swallow, but they seem to be the words Stevens was speaking: "This force of nature in action is the major / Tragedy." Ay-mi! One could only escape *this* knowledge by non-nature, or nonaction. In 1909, while reading More and Okakura on the Orient, Stevens had noted in his journal: "Sakyamuni [the Buddha]—all evil resides in the individual will to live." A strange seed blown a long way from home. Thirty years later it matured in "Esthétique du Mal."

Desire, whether manifested in a lover or a monk sure of a reality "destroys us." The strong verb that had expressed the action of knowledge has now reappeared to express the action of desire. Knowledge destroys. Desire destroys. Thought and feeling. That pretty much covers the world as we know it, the world of ordinary consciousness.

So with characteristic good humor, wit, and irony—anticipated by "the happiest enemy"—Stevens confronts the tragedy of being in a world of desire: "Ay-mi!" He also in the best meditative tradition mocks himself right away in a delightful transition:

XIV

Victor Serge said, "I followed his argument
With the blank uneasiness which one might feel
In the presence of a logical lunatic."   (*CP* 324)

That self-mockery, that dismissal of theory, of any "description of to be," is perhaps the most meditative twist of all. It also shows Stevens' awareness that his audience might be lost.

Although he had long written poems about meditative perception and about imaginative perception, Stevens in the late thirties seemed to become more aware of how the two modes of perception—active and passive—were at odds, and how each implied a mode of being and a way of looking at the world. He could then begin to write from a meditative point of view on imagination, or from an imaginative point of view on meditation. This distance, at times the distance of intellectual irony, at times the distance of meditative detachment, helped create the extraordinary variety, wit, spontaneity and repartee of his long poems. The relation of those long poems to Stevens' meditative interests will be the subject of part IV.

In the first two parts of this study we have noted many characteristics of meditative experience that appear in Stevens' poetry, and many attitudes, values, and psychological assumptions that seem common to both meditative traditions and Stevens' work. I have asserted from the beginning that the poetry must bear the weight of evidence for Stevens' meditative interests, but if Stevens in 1909 was copying the Buddha's primary renunciation, we might well ask "Whence Stevens?" To ask the question of Stevens' relation to his milieu is to confront the mystery of individual epistemology: how did he know what he knew? That we will attempt to answer in part III.

PART III

Whence Stevens?

To see is to forget the name of the thing one sees.

Paul Valery

It is Cezanne's peculiar determination to pin down his sensation, and the exactness and intensity of notation resulting from this, that made Cezanne pre-eminent.

Graham Bell

The morality of the poet's radiant and productive atmosphere is the morality of right sensation.

It is often said of a man that his work is autobiographical in spite of every subterfuge. It cannot be otherwise.

Wallace Stevens

12

Turn of the Century

If a single thread can be said to run through movements as diverse as impressionist, cubist, and dadaist painting, and symbolist, imagist, and modern poetry, movements avidly followed by Stevens from his graduation from Harvard in 1900 to his maturity in 1935, that thread would be a respect for sensation. Symbolist poetry began with sensation and attempted to return to it through linguistic means, while in the 1870s the impressionists had begun to paint not only from nature, but also from a self-conscious examination of their perception of nature. Manet's phrase for his painting, "a naturalism of the senses," suggests a literal, even scientific rendering of the irrationality of perception, and Pound's imagism was primarily sensational.

Whether sensation-perception from an individual point of view lay behind all avant-garde art is perhaps the most profound question within the study of modernism today. To what extent does perception originate in history, culture, biology, or personality? The vorticists' "geometry" is either created by the perceiver or it is found; the "objective correlative" is either invented or it is found; the "radiant gists" of the *Cantos* are either historical, or they are Pound's. The answers determine the extent to which the modern is romantic.

Whether or not we wish to link such diverse movements, they seemed similar to Stevens, part of a *modern* art. While he wavered on Picasso as realistic or abstract, Stevens saw the modern imagination as solidly grounded in sensory perception of external reality, and therefore he was interested in the mechanics of perception:

> These men [Picasso and Bonnard] attach one to real things: closely, actually, without the interventions or excitements of metaphor. One wonders sometimes whether this is not exactly what the whole effort of modern art has been about: the attachment to real things. (*L* 601)

By 1920, surrealists had turned from literal representation of subjective perception to literal representation of dream images and to

169

more obscure states such as elaborate games of concentration on objects, games designed to produce, André Breton said in the first "Surrealist Manifesto," a "poetic consciousness of objects which I have been able to acquire only after a spiritual contact with them repeated a thousand times over."[1] To experiment with perception in the modern era was to experiment with art. Sensation was the pivot point, the axis of the seesaw.

Most impressionist and symbolist artists are therefore in a special sense autobiographical, although the moment of perception, or more abstractly the biology of individual perception, has often replaced personal history as the basis of the life (*bios*) depicted. To what extent some of the sensation at the center of symbolist, impressionist, or dadaist art was meditative is a question deserving a book in itself. One might begin with Mallarmé's experience of "pure nothingness" during the "indescribable nights" of 1866, when he wrote to Villiers de l'Isle-Adam on September 24, "My thought has thought itself through . . . you will be terrified to hear that I discovered the idea of the Universe through sensation alone—and that, in order to perpetuate the indelible idea of pure nothingness, I had to fill my brain with the sensation of absolute Emptiness."[2]

Toward the other end of the modern period, Tristan Tzara lecturing in Paris in 1922 said that dada "is a state of mind. . . . Dada is not at all modern. It is more in the nature of a return to an almost Buddhist religion of indifference."[3] And although Tzara could have been simply wrong, using a faddish oriental allusion to color his lecture, a comparison between dada and Buddhism is quite inviting on the grounds of phenomenology, spontaneity, wit, claims to unity, nothingness, and love of the bizarre. Tzara again: "Dada applies itself to everything, and yet it is nothing, it is the point where the yes and the no and all the opposites meet, not solemnly in the castles of human philosophies, but very simply at the street corners like dogs and grasshoppers."[4] Dada's negations, irreverences, paradoxes, and inconsistencies have been critically described in Freudian terms as antiauthoritarian, obstructionist, nihilist, and therefore, freeing the mind and spirit—freeing them of their fathers. But quite possibly some dadaist spontaneity and anti-intellectualism reflected an attempt to eschew abstraction and seize the thing itself in a meditative moment of perception. So quite possibly Breton was right, after reading Suzuki's *The Zen Doctrine of No-Mind* in 1952, to write to Francis

Picabia: "Tell me, was not Dada perhaps, at the best, a flake of Zen wafted as far as ourselves?"⁵

Setting aside the question of how much meditative experience was involved in modern perception experiments, we can assert that Stevens was raised on those experiments, on how "to see," on "sensation alone," on "a state of mind" as a foundation for art. When Stevens began serious writing in 1913, symbolist sensation, in its dazzling and mysterious French forms, was at that moment engendering its child and successor, imagist clarity, and Stevens was hardly surprised at Pound's imagist phenomenology, his attempts to represent the "precise instant" when a thing "outward" darts "inward." Since Baudelaire's *Fleurs du Mal,* such attempts to pin down the psychology of sensation had been immanent in modern art. By coincidence, during that modern era, England, France, and America from 1880 to 1920 were also rediscovering (how often will we do it?) the Orient. Perhaps in Stevens, as in many others, modernism and orientalism were related.

The modern interest in the subjectivity of perception may well have been the zeitgeist, the genuine spirit of the age. The popular orientalism of Stevens' formative years was more of a fad. Sir Edwin Arnold's verse biography of Buddha, *The Light of Asia,* came out in 1878, the year before Stevens was born, and ran through eighty editions, making Buddhism "a household word" as Rick Fields has said.⁶ If by 1906 Stevens was quoting the Buddha ("Sakyamuni") and by 1922 was talking of "beholding nothing" one might wonder if direct knowledge of the East produced "The Snow Man."

To assess the possible relation of Stevens' "nothing" or Tzara's "Buddhist . . . indifference" to meditative practice, we must remember that three distinct Asian traditions available to Europe had talked of meditative nothingness: Hinduism, in Sanskrit texts (including, arguably, Yogins); Theravadic (southern) Buddhism in Pali texts; and Mahayana (northern) Buddhism in Sanskrit and the languages of China, Tibet, and Japan. Knowledge of the Orient was widespread when Stevens was at Harvard in 1900, but a great deal of knowledge of the Orient could accompany very little knowledge of meditative practice. Both considerations are useful in understanding, say, Paul Elmer More, whom Stevens was reading in 1905, or T. S. Eliot, who was studying Sanskrit in 1910 and paraphrasing the Buddha's Fire Sermon in 1922.

Curiously, the orientalism of Stevens' day, instead of reviving interest in Christian mysticism, seemed to replace it. Although Christian mysticism and Buddhist meditation have much in common, the Christian discovery of God through manipulation of consciousness has never offered the shock, to the West, of the Hindu and especially the Buddhist discovery of *nothing*. In the nineteenth century, notorious new reports of becoming *nothing,* in combination with the romantics' attention to consciousness, encouraged an interest in Eastern meditation even as meditative practice was dying out of the Christian church. Moreover, the Christian meditative tradition still alive in 1800 was largely Catholic. The East provided a new and non-Catholic context for old interests. Hence the irony that the Reverend Ralph Waldo Emerson knew more of Buddha than of Saint John of the Cross. Exactly what the nineteenth century understood of a Buddhist *nothing,* however, is a more complex matter.

Reports of *nothing* began soon after the departure of Sir William Jones for India in 1783. Wished well by his friend, Ben Franklin, whose American cause had helped make Jones unwelcome in some circles of his native England, Jones set out with a knowledge of Persian and in India quickly found a wealth of material to be translated from Sanskrit. By the time he died at age forty-eight, only eleven years later, he had made the first translations of Hafiz and Rumi from Persian, of Kalidasa from Sanskrit (to the delight, a century later, of Yeats—and Jones's researches at the time were filtering back to Swedenborg and presumably Blake), had founded and published four issues of *Asiatick Researches,* discovered that Sanskrit and European languages had a common base, translated the immensely popular Hindu *Laws of Manu* and founded the Royal Asiatic Society. During this period Charles Wilkins made the translation of the *Bhagavad-Gita* read by Emerson and Thoreau. Since 1788 (the first issue of *Asiatick Researches*), some Europeans have always had at least an introductory knowledge of Hindu texts.

Major Hindu Vedas (songs), Upanishads (instructions), and epics such as the *Bhagavad-Gita* quickly entered the European intellectual community; indeed, Jones foresaw a renaissance of Asiatic influence comparable to the Renaissance caused in the fifteenth century by the texts from Greece. We shall have to see if his prophecy proves correct; the effects of the Eastern traditions are accumulating more slowly, partly because those traditions are alien and partly because they are huge: all of Homer, Plato, Aristotle, and the Periclean dramatists might equal in volume one-tenth of one version of the *Prajnaparamita Sutra,* with its commentaries.

Certainly the new texts were enthusiastically circulated. By 1814, Arthur Schopenhauer at Weimar was reading fifteen principal Upanishads (translated into Latin by Du Perron from his own French, from the seventeenth-century Persian of Dara Shukoh, a mogul emperor's mystical son, who had translated from the Sanskrit: this renaissance was indeed slow in coming). Sprinkled in with those Hindu texts were a very few treatises from Ceylon and from Tibet, where those quintessential pedants, the Jesuits, had been teaching and studying since the seventeenth century (the first Sanskrit dictionary was Jesuit and unknown to William Jones, who began from scratch). But Europeans still had almost no knowledge of Buddhism. Arthur Schopenhauer wrote: "Up till 1818, when my work appeared, there were to be found in Europe only a very few accounts of Buddhism, and those extremely incomplete and inadequate."[7]

In 1826, the year before Thomas Henry Colebrooke would first describe the Buddhist nirvana to the Royal Asiatic Society in London, Eugène Burnouf compiled the first Pali dictionary, and his history of Buddhism in 1844 (*Introduction à l'histoire du Buddhisme indien*) presented to the public some of the new Buddhist materials being sent from Ceylon and Tibet by pioneering scholars (such as Colebrooke and Hodgson). For instance, excerpts from his translation of "Le Lotus de la bonne Loi" sutra (sent by Hodgson from Tibet) had by the end of 1844 reached Margaret Fuller's *Dial,* introduced by Henry David Thoreau. Thus by 1850, major Hindu texts had been known for some time, while Theravadic texts in Pali and scattered Yogic and Mahayana texts from Tibet were just coming to light. The Buddhist atheism was disturbing to Europeans; more than Hinduism it helped dramatize the difference between meditative and theistic revelation. The Buddhist nirvana, being more obviously secular than the Hindu nirvana, was harder for the West to assimilate.

Those Hindu and Buddhist texts known by 1850 contain much discourse, philosophy, ethics, and action, but little description of meditative practice. What practice is described is almost all closed-senses, nonperceptive meditation leading to *nothing.* If then, by 1850, Europeans had only the most rudimentary knowledge of meditative practice, they had been shocked right away with the most extremely withdrawn of meditative results. Schopenhauer was one of those few who, like Colebrooke and Thoreau, were unafraid of the new reports of nothingness; indeed, he instructed the Asians in its virtues:

> We have to banish the dark impression of that nothingness, which as the final goal hovers behind all virtue and holiness, and which we fear as children fear darkness. We must not evade it, as the Indians do, by myths and meaningless words, such as reabsorption in *Brahma,* or the *Nirvana* of the Buddhists. On the contrary, we freely acknowledge that what remains after the complete abolition of the will is, for all who are still full of the will, assuredly nothing. But also conversely, to those in whom the will has turned and denied itself, this very real world of ours with all its suns and galaxies, is—nothing.[8]

Schopenhauer's famous remarks in *The World as Will and Representation* are interesting for several reasons. First of all, his pure skepticism is admirable: "We, however, who consistently occupy the standpoint of philosophy, must be satisfied here with negative knowledge." Second, he respects the benevolent moral results reported by meditators more than he fears the evil connotations of certain words in European languages: emptiness, nothingness, extinction. But most curiously, he quite correctly chides the Hindu and Buddhist texts available to him for substituting *any* concepts, any "myths and meaningless words," for the ineffable experience of the state itself. In this chiding, he sounds much like the later Mahayana texts, yet to be discovered by Europeans, grumbling about the excessive philosophizing of the Hindu and early Theravadic traditions.

It is fair to say that the Asian texts of the transcendentalists, indeed the Asian texts known until the end of the century, had introduced to Europe many meditative *issues,* but very little meditative *practice.* This exacerbated a European tendency to confuse idea and experience, and to translate all transcendental claims into some form of neoplatonism; in effect, such a translation is what Schopenhauer disliked in the very word and concept of nirvana. The concept of nothing, simply by being a concept, is a positive category, and can hardly evoke accurately the experience of having no concepts. From Lord Teignmouth's opinion in the eighteenth century that Hindusim "is pure Deism and has a wonderful resemblance to the doctrines of Plato,"[9] through Emerson and Paul Elmer More's frequent confusings of Plato and the East, through contemporary Christian writers such as Thomas Merton and right up to present critics of Wallace Stevens, the temptation to translate nothing into something has been nearly irresistible.

That first century of Asian studies finished with a flurry of activity about the time of Stevens' birth in 1879. Arnold's *The Light of Asia,* the verse biography of Buddha promoted by the aging transcendentalist, Bronson Alcott, came out in 1878 with great success. Rhys David founded the Pali Text Society in London in 1881, churning out Theravadic translations, and Burnouf's pupil Max Muller edited the voluminous series, *Sacred Books of the East,* which was coming out in the 1890s as Professor Everett was offering Harvard's first course in Asian religions just a few years before Stevens enrolled.

As *The Light of Asia* was rolling off the presses, a curious pair set sail for India. Madame Helena Petrovna Blavatsky from the Caucasus had seen "many occult things and adepts," had a bullet in her shoulder from fighting with Garibaldi in Italy, and rolled her own cigarettes.[10] Colonel Henry Steel Olcott was a respected New Yorker who had served as a special commissioner investigating Lincoln's assassination; he was at the Eddy farm in Vermont to observe the famous ghosts when he stepped to the porch, said "Permettez-moi, Madame," and lit Blavatsky's cigarette. Four years later they sailed East, leaving General Doubleday, the inventor of baseball, to guide the Theosophical Society (an appropriate heritage for our national mantra: "Getcha cold beer here"). Madame Blavatsky and Colonel Olcott are not often taken seriously, for they met over ghosts and ended as Theosophists conducting seances in London; however, in between their occult activities those two sparked a nationalist Buddhist revival in Ceylon.

In Ceylon the British were suppressing Theravadic Buddhism even as Europe was discovering it. When Blavatsky and Olcott landed in Ceylon in 1880, the island had four Buddhist schools and eight hundred and five Christian ones. Many Buddhist ceremonies (including prayers and the marriage ceremony) were outlawed or unrecognized; many Christian ceremonies (including prayers and marriage) were mandatory or necessary for advancement. Blavatsky and Olcott had done their homework; they had come to the home of Theravadic Buddhism (where almost every major Pali text was housed) to say that Blavatsky's *Isis Unveiled,* Buddhism, and freedom were right, and that the British and Christianity were wrong.

> The harbor was lined with brightly painted fishing boats, a thousand flags flew in the sun, and a white cloth was spread out on the dock to lead them to their carriage. On May 25, HPB and the colonel knelt before a Buddhist priest at a temple in Galle and performed the

ceremony of "taking *pansil*"—the five lay precepts of undertaking to refrain from killing, lying, stealing, intoxicants, and sexual misconduct. They repeated the vows in Pali, as well as the refuge in Buddha, Dharma, and Sangha, before a large crowd. "When we had finished the last of the Silas," Olcott wrote in his diary, "and offered flowers in the customary way, there came a mighty shout to make one's nerves tingle." It was the first time the Sinhalese had seen one of the ruling white race treat Buddhism with anything approaching respect, and it was (as far as we have been able to discover) the first time that Americans had become Buddhists in the formal sense—that is, in a manner recognized by other Buddhists.[11]

Always catalysts for action, controversy, and reform, Olcott and Blavatsky attracted, encouraged, and launched the brilliant and handsome young Sinhalese called Dharmapala. He and Olcott by 1884 had successfully reversed many British policies in Ceylon. In Fields's words, "To the Sinhalese, it seemed that the American Theosophist had single-handedly restored their religion and culture to them."[12]

Olcott's abilities were not only political. In what becomes a familiar message, he noted the difference between Buddhism and Western religion:

> The Sinhalese Buddhists have never yet had any conception of what Europeans imply in the etymological construction of the Latin root of this term [religion]. In their creed there is no such thing as a "binding" in the Christian sense, a submission to or merging of self in a Divine Being.[13]

In bringing the Hindu Chatterji to London and the Buddhist Dharmapala to the United States, there is no doubt that Olcott and Blavatsky were part of a surging interest in Theravadic Buddhism that reached far beyond the transcendentalists' acquaintance with a few intriguing texts. Soon after Stevens left Harvard, William James, spotting Dharmapala in the audience, said, "You are better equipped to lecture on psychology than I." And after Dharmapala had lectured on Buddhism, James said to his class: "This is the psychology everyone will be studying twenty-five years from now."[14]

But if Theravadic studies were finally becoming responsible by 1900, the study of Mahayana Buddhism had hardly begun. The beginning was not auspicious: the long closed empires of China and Japan were opened by British and American gunboats in the 1850s.

> Over the Western sea hither from Niphon come,
> Courteous, the swarth-cheek'd two-sworded envoys,

Leaning back in their open barouches, bare-headed, impassive,
Ride to-day through Manhatten.[15]

Walt Whitman, watching a few of the first Japanese to have left Japan
in two hundred years parade down Broadway on June 15, 1860, was
not the only one to anticipate great things from new passages to
India; soon the market was flooded with oriental phenomena and
noumena. Twain, slipping into his bitter last years as Stevens left
Harvard in 1900, greeted the new adventures with acidic comments
on missionary and Chinaman alike. Twain's sense of scam was right
on the money. If, after the British had occupied India for two hun-
dred years, Europeans were still struggling toward their first responsi-
ble translations of Hindu and Theravadic Buddhist texts, one can
easily guess that by 1900, thirty years of acquaintance with Chinese
and Japanese landscape scrolls, scrimshaw, and screens had done
little to advance European knowledge of Mahayana Buddhism.
Puccini's *Madame Butterfly* and Gilbert and Sullivan's *Mikado* reflect
the period's conception of Japan.

In 1893 the Japanese delegation to the World Parliament of Reli-
gions in Chicago could still say, "There is no Mahayana Doctrine . . .
translated into English."[16] (The situation would improve the follow-
ing year with Cowell's *Buddhist Mahayana Texts,* volume 49 of
Muller's *Sacred Books of the East.*) Professor Ernest Fenollosa stud-
ied Chinese and Japanese art in the 1890s and mounted an excellent
exhibition at the Boston Museum in 1902, but of the great Asian
scholars of this century, only Arthur Waley had begun his work by
1913 (he deplored Pound's and Fenollosa's *Cathay*) and neither
Waley's nor Conze's research nor Suzuki's pioneering presentations
of Zen were available until the mid-twenties, after "The Snow Man"
was published.

Since Christian mysticism was at an ebb in the late nineteenth
century, and since knowledge of Asian meditative practice was still
rudimentary, Stevens formed his notions of *nothing* during something
of an interregnum in European meditative history. There was no
meditative coterie during the fin-de-siècle orgy of coteries, although
from Mallarmé to Rimbaud and Artaud there were what might be
called cults of ecstatic anguish.

In approaching Hinduism and Buddhism with little access to
Mahayana texts, Europeans in 1900 were missing a good deal. They
were missing the Chinese tradition, transferred to Japan—to put it

very simply—of immersion of the not-self in a fleeting world of karma, rather than withdrawal of the not-self from a fleeting world of karma. The Chinese and Japanese were interested in intermediate stages of meditative experience, in aware meditative experience, and in doubling back: how does this world look after enlightenment?

Consider, then, the position of Wallace Stevens in 1900–1920, before Waley, Conze, Suzuki, and others had explained Mahayana traditions in English. The new art works arriving from China and Japan, the haiku poetry forms touted by Pound, were beautiful and fascinating in their delicacy, economy, and detail. But there was no reason to connect those art works to the Buddhism Dharmapala was expounding at Harvard, to nirvana or to the issue of *nothing* as Stevens found it in Nietzsche, Heidegger, or Schopenhauer. In other words, there was no reason to connect art or moments of perception to meditative consciousness. Almost all Buddhist texts available stressed withdrawal from sensation, and the new arts from China and Japan were not yet appreciated as Buddhist. Not until 1930, or more realistically 1950 (the first Chinese concordance came in 1946), were Mahayana studies disseminated sufficiently for Europeans to connect sensation and meditation; there was no reason for a Harvard junior, sitting in a room on a rainy day in 1899, to think that his lazy state of mind and sudden, precise perception could have anything to do with meditative consciousness and therefore Chinese art; no reason for him to think that the impressionist and symbolist interest in sensation, and the Buddhist interest in meditation, might here intersect:

> The fronds of a fern were dangling over my knees and I felt lazy and content. Once as I looked up I saw a big, pure drop of rain slip from leaf to leaf of a clematis vine. The thought occurred to me that it was just such quick, unexpected, commonplace, specific things that poets and other observers jot in their note-books.
>
> (*SP* 45)

13
Yeats's Chatterji

Against the background of a symbolist interest in sensation and a general interest in the Orient, several figures emerge who might have influenced Stevens' meditative knowledge: Yeats, Santayana, Pound. All were part of modern literature; all had direct knowledge of meditative texts; all might, one would think—instead of Stevens—be at the center of this study. If "The Snow Man" came from books, and we ask what books, what better place to start than with the books of Yeats? He was certainly in the thick of things, as he records in his autobiography:

> I found Madame Blavatsky in a little house at Norwood, with but, as she said, three followers left—the Society of Psychical Research had just reported on her Indian phenomena—and as one of the three followers sat in an outer room to keep out undesirable visitors, I was kept a long time kicking my heels. Presently I was admitted and found an old woman in a plain loose dark dress: a sort of old Irish peasant woman with an air of humour and audacious power. I was still kept waiting, for she was deep in conversation with a woman visitor. I strayed through folding doors into the next room and stood, in sheer idleness of mind, looking at a cuckoo clock. It was certainly stopped, for the weights were off and lying upon the ground, and yet, as I stood there the cuckoo came out and cuckooed at me. I interrupted Madame Blavatsky to say, "Your clock has hooted me." "It often hoots at a stranger," she replied. "Is there a spirit in it?" I said. "I do not know," she said, "I should have to be alone to know what is in it." I went back to the clock and began examining it and heard her say: "Do not break my clock." I wondered if there was some hidden mechanism and I should have been put out, I suppose, had I found any, though Henley had said to me, "Of course she gets up fraudulent miracles, but a person of genius has to do something; Sarah Bernhardt sleeps in her coffin."[1]

Yeats is telling the story thirty-five years later with an air of amused indifference. In 1887 he had been not only amused, however; the meeting was enough to convert him to Theosophy, even though the

179

authoritative (Tennyson, Gladstone, William James) Society of Psychical Research had just reported on Madame Blavatsky: "For our part we regard her neither as the mouthpiece for hidden seers, nor as a mere vulgar adventuress; we think she has achieved a title to permanent remembrance as one of the most accomplished, ingenious and interesting imposters of history."[2]

What Yeats was seeking in the madame's cuckoo clock was Shelley's old Jew, "master of all human knowledge, hidden from human sight in some shell-strewn cavern on the Mediterranean shore."[3] But unlike Stevens' more passive recluse who "in his Mediterranean cloister . . . Reclining, eased of desire, establishes / The visible" (*CP* 324), Shelley's master of wisdom (Yeats said Shelley's passage "ran perpetually in [his] ears")

> May have attained to sovereignty and science
> Over those strong and secret things and thoughts
> Which others fear and know not.[4]

The rest of Shelley's passage is full of the occult—telepathy, telekinesis, willed meteors, and winds—and that is just what Yeats was after: "Already in Dublin, I had been attracted to the Theosophists because they had affirmed the real existence of the Jew."[5] Already in Dublin in 1885 he had read Kalidasa's poetry and Sinnett's *Esoteric Buddhism* (an occult Theosophy book), and Yeats with his schoolfriend had "spent a good deal of time in the Kildare Street museum passing our hands over the glass cases, feeling or believing we felt the Odic Force flowing from the big crystals. We also found pins blindfolded."[6]

In that spirit (or medium) he had met the same year Mohini Chatterji, the young Brahmin brought from India by Madame Blavatsky, admired in Dublin by Yeats's friends, cross-examined in London by the Society of Psychical Research and seduced in Paris by Miss Leonard. Writing about Chatterji thirty-five years later, Yeats remembered "a philosophy . . . at once logical and boundless."[7] What Mohini actually said about contemplation (meditation) is less dramatic and more clear and was recorded in Yeats's journal at the time: "When I was young I was very happy. I thought truth was something that could be conveyed from one man's mind to another's. I now know it is a state of mind."[8]

Yeats heard Chatterji make the distinction between ideas and experience, a distinction that a century of Asia studies had hardly begun to grasp, but Yeats either did not understand or did not believe him, for two years later he would be in front of Blavatsky's cuckoo clock, looking for the old Jew's alchemical truth that "could be conveyed from one man's mind to another's."

Yeats's first version of his poem on Chatterji began with the Brahmin's response—as recorded in Yeats's journals—to the question of whether we should pray: "I have lived many lives. I have been a slave and a prince. Many a beloved has sat upon my knees, and I have sat upon the knees of many a beloved. Everything that has been shall be again."[9] The first three stanzas of Yeats's poem rehearse the myriad reincarnations we have each had, then the fourth stanza expresses a Hindu sense of the futility of all that karma:

> Is not thy body but the garnered rust
>   Of ancient passions and of ancient fears?[10]

The conclusion, in the fifth stanza, is the familiar Asian inversion of Christian hope: death where is thy sting if life is the stinger? But then the Hindu doctrine disappears, for quite characteristically, indeed in anticipation of "Lapis Lazuli" fifty years later, Yeats even in his extreme of oriental withdrawal will not let go of art:

> Then wherefore fear the usury of Time,
>   Or Death that cometh with the next life-key?
> Nay, rise and flatter her with golden rhyme,
>   For as things were so shall things ever be.

Though it might seem slight, Yeats's relation to Hinduism, Buddhism, and meditative consciousness is crystallized in that penultimate line. Not only is art praised, but also the verbs ("rise . . . flatter") hardly scrub away our rusty passions and fears. Instead of transcending this world, Yeats sought repeatedly to master it, to concentrate all karma into a single golden rhyme or mournful melody or golden bird that would sing of "what is past or passing or to come." The world of historical time.

Between Yeats's first version of the Chatterji poem in 1885 and his final version in 1929, much orientalism passed: Theosophists, Pound, Noh plays, Tagore's poetry of 1912–1915, and a swelling flood of information in journals and books and from friends. In a letter to Sturge Moore of February 5, 1926, Yeats drew a neat distinction between Chatterji's "early Buddhism" belief that the mirror of self should be turned away from the world of karma so that it reflects nothing, and the Mahayana Zen belief that since nothing exists the mirror can reflect the world of nothing and become one with it, "all becoming through rhythm a single act of the mind." This is a distinction no one was making in 1900; Yeats's information on Zen came from Waley's influential *Introduction to the Study of Chinese Painting* (1923) and Yeats was one of the first to appreciate the difference between unaware and aware meditative traditions, although Yeats "through rhythm" still suggests, perhaps, a golden rhyme.

In his notes for the second edition of *A Vision* Yeats measured quite accurately his distance from the Buddhists:

> I have never knowingly differed from my Instructors, but one saying of theirs long tempted me to do so. "Consciousness," they said, "is conflict"; that in itself was clear; mind without images must be unconscious; but if consciousness is indeed conflict must not the phaseless sphere from which all comes and to which all returns and source of all value be unconscious, and annihilation, as some say the early Buddhists thought, end all our effort? I have come to see, however, that their conflict resolves itself into the antinomies of Kant and that we must say of the ultimate reality as the early Buddhists themselves said, "We do not know that it exists, we do not know that it does not exist," and as the early Buddhists did not, that we can express it by a series of contradictions.[11]

One difference is conventional: Yeats interprets the consciousness attacked by Buddhist meditators as the operation of the entire mind and therefore as *being* itself, which abstraction (quite encouraged by many Buddhist texts) makes abandonment of consciousness ("mind without images" conceptualized as a platonic "phaseless sphere") seem like "annihilation." Next, he quite correctly perceives that *thinking* about meditative issues brings one right back to Kantian antinomies (*doing* meditation does not) and he faces his second difference: he will not let go of art. "Ultimate reality . . . we can express it by a series of contradictions." By way of Blake's contraries and the East, another mystic has arrived at paradox, but it is the certainty in the verb "can express" that reveals Yeats's trust in language and keeps him Irish ("the greatest talkers since the Greeks," as Wilde had said to him).

No such subtle doctrinal distinctions are necessary to enjoy the final poem on Chatterji. It is unregenerate Yeats at age sixty-four (to the Buddhist, it is generate Yeats). "The whole poem," as Ellmann says, "is now argued in terms of love":[12]

Mohini Chatterjee

I asked if I should pray,
But the Brahmin said,
"Pray for nothing, say
Every night in bed,
'I have been a king,
I have been a slave,
Nor is there anything,
Fool, rascal, knave,
That I have not been,
And yet upon my breast
A myriad heads have lain.' "

That he might set at rest
A boy's turbulent days
Mohini Chatterjee
Spoke these, or words like these.
I add in commentary,
"Old lovers yet may have
All that time denied—
Grave is heaped on grave
That they be satisfied—
Over the blackened earth
The old troops parade,
Birth is heaped on birth
That such cannonade
May thunder time away,
Birth-hour and death-hour meet,
Or, as great sages say,
Men dance on deathless feet."

The sage's advice to "pray for nothing" Yeats takes as comfort to a tempestuous youth, and in his own reaction he discovers yet another occasion for romantic lament: "Old lovers yet . . . ." Though he laughs at the futility of our desire to defeat extinction—"Birth is heaped on birth / That such cannonade / May thunder time away"—it is the dance of karma that he loves. The foulness of the rag and bone shop of the heart cannot drive Yeats from desire: by its end the poem circles around not the detachment of the Brahmin, but the poignant beauty of a futile desire which in the very next poem of *The Winding Stair*, "Byzantium," begets the final image of a "dolphin-torn, gong-tormented sea." Not an ultimate reality but a most relative one expressed by a series of contradictions. That is the dance that old man Yeats kept coming back to dance: imperfections and perfections alike are made of conflict (Greek agone):

> Dying into a dance,
> An agony of trance,
> An agony of flame. . . .

Pray for everything, get nothing, and sing of both. And so the final poem entitled "Mohini Chatterjee" ends with immortality through art and action: "Men dance on deathless feet." One wonders what Mohini Chatterji was thinking, a blind old man in London in 1929—remembering perhaps the intense young fellow in spectacles forty-three years before—as his daughter read aloud to him Yeats's poem in his name.[13]

Yeats never showed the slightest affinity for meditative detachment. From his earliest countryside memories of family fiefdoms and magic, to apartments in Dublin and London where his father's painter friends shouted each other down on life and art, to his early study of Blake, and his final metaphysics, he was immersed in passion, and from his earliest poems, such as "Ephemera," he was immersed in time:

> "Passion has often worn our wandering hearts."
> . . . .
>   "Ah, do not mourn," he said,
> 'That we are tired.'

This from a man not yet twenty-four. We might well ask ourselves, as James said of Lord Warburton, what queer temporal province he was annexing. Yeats's first three words in response to Chatterji stand for half his life and work: "Old lovers yet. . . . " Yeats was content to live in time, Stevens in the moment. Compare Yeats's "A Dialogue of Self and Soul"—"I am *content to live* it all again; . . . I am *content to follow* to its source every event"—with Stevens' "Sunday Morning":

>   "I am *content when* wakened birds,
> Before they fly, test the reality
> Of misty fields, by their sweet questionings."   (*CP* 68)

Yeats's infinitives of purpose in linear time, versus Stevens' "when," measure their differing relationships to time and contentment. From the very first, Yeats was in love not only with the heart, but with the conceit that his heart had grown old, a self-pity that perhaps helped keep him young.

Yeats's heart did not grow old, though some wished it had. In 1931 at age sixty-six he met Shree Purohit Swami and began a friendship that would bring them to Majorca together in 1935 to translate and polish selected Upanishads. That was his last affair with the East, but it was undertaken with a passion not so very different from the lust for Odic forces that had first brought a schoolboy to Chatterji. An Indian commentator said that Yeats "accepted Indian life fully and with a fanaticism even Indians are not used to,"[14] and during those swami years he also took up Hitler, Mussolini, and the Blueshirt movement, for which he wrote marching songs.

In "Meru" (1936), Yeats tried to hold a mirror to what he had learned of the passivity of Eastern thought, but he reflected instead the turbulence of his own life:

> Hermits upon Mount Meru or Everest,
> Caverned in night under the drifted snow,
> Or where that snow and winter's dreadful blast
> Beat down upon their naked bodies, know
> That day brings round the night, that before dawn
> His glory and his monuments are gone.

The lines draw their energy not from the harmony of a hermit's knowledge, but from violence. The verb "know" is almost lost in a pounding of the senses: "caverned in night . . . drifted snow . . . winter's dreadful blast / Beat down." In the world of knowledge, on the other hand, things are pretty dull: day "brings round" night. The final note is not one of mental or spiritual discovery but one of worldly loss: "His glory and his monuments are gone." Desire and the passing of time. "Meru" is a poem about Eastern withdrawal, but since, as Chatterji had pointed out nearly fifty years before, Brahmin truth is a state of mind, to write a poem in the wrong state of mind *about* Brahmin truth is to get *nowhere* fast, too fast.

At the end of those Eastern interests in 1936, Yeats wrote the lines that Eliot would call "not very pleasant":[15]

> You think it horrible that lust and rage
> Should dance attendance upon my old age;
> They were not such a plague when I was young;
> What else have I to spur me into song?

A lifetime of interest in the East had failed utterly to bring to fruition Yeats's potential interest in passivity. Yeats apparently was inoculated—by whatever: genes, father, Blake, magic, Maud, Ireland—against meditative detachment. In November 1934, within a year of departing for Majorca to translate Upanishads, Yeats in his description of the injured Captain MacManus betrayed a rather stiff-upper-lip understanding of oriental meditations: "He had cured himself by oriental meditations. Every morning he stands before his mirror and commands himself to become more positive, more masculine, more independent of the feelings of others."[16]

In his 1937 preface to their completed Upanishads, Yeats still linked "the East" to "psychical research" and spoke admiringly of Eliot's and Huxley's "Buddhistic hatred of life."[17] It is wonderful, really. Yeats could imagine giving up life, but not hate. Such was his concept of detachment. As he wrote in "The Wild Swans at Coole," "Passion or conquest, wander where they will, / Attend upon them still."

And still, and still: later in 1937 the swami wrote that his master, Shri Hamsa, wished Yeats to come to India to lecture. Yeats declined: "Please tell him of the operation I went through in London and say that although it revived my creative power it revived also sexual desire, and that in all likelihood will last me until I die."[18] Not bad for a man who was tired by the age of twenty-four. Apparently he thought that his born-again sexuality made him unfit to enlighten; more likely the problem was his pride, nurtured for seventy-two years.

His revived spirit of conquest seems indeed to have lasted until death. Even the celebrated epitaph of "Under Ben Bulben," written a year before his death and soon to become his own epitaph, perhaps his closest approach to detachment and certainly his last, begins and ends in the imperative mood:

> Cast a cold eye
> On life, on death.
> Horseman, pass by!

Yeats's mind is in the nouns, but his unwearied heart is in the verbs. He is, as the Chinese would say, attached to his new detachment; others had best take notice that Yeats says there is nothing to note—except, perhaps, his words, one last mournful melody.

In letting the Chatterji poem circle back to the long march of a lover's retreat, Yeats had responded to the Brahmin in the Western way most perfectly captured by a friend—knowing something of attachment and futility, now dead by her own hand—who, seeing a poster in Boston for the "Mahara-ji, thirteen-year-old grand master of perfect wisdom," observed: "Makes a mockery of experience, doesn't it?" Indeed it does, at least of that experience which is an accretion of knowledge in time.

To both Yeats and Stevens, much knowledge accrued. Although Yeats's nonmeditative bias stands out against the background of his Eastern interests, while Stevens' meditative bias stands out against his practical American life, the two men of very different sensibilities arrived at similar positions. Yeats's fidelity to an unwearied heart, and Stevens' fidelity to an unwearied mind, produced in both their long careers resiliency and even in old age, renewal. Yeats's grand retrospective poem, "The Circus Animals' Desertion," ends by yoking "start" and "heart," a proposition exhausting to most of us by middle age, while the work Stevens placed at the end of *Collected Poems* ends with, yet again, "a new knowledge of reality." Both men were over seventy. Both had tried the heart and knowledge many, many times. Both remain examples, unsurpassed in our language, of the moral advantages of emotional and intellectual courage practiced over a long period of time.

14

Santayana's Angels

For Stevens, knowledge of meditative issues seems not to have come from an accretion of knowledge in time. This is surprising, since as Yeats was giving up—or transferring—esoteric Buddhism to Maud Gonne and Irish politics, Stevens was attending Harvard (1897–1900). Harvard's first Asian studies course had been initiated by Professor Charles C. Everett in 1891: "Comparative History of Religions, particularly the Vedic Religion, the Hindu philosophies, Buddhism, Mazdaism, and the Chinese Religions." Stevens did not take the course, but one of Everett's colleagues in religion and philosophy was to Stevens both a mentor and a critic-spokesman for religious issues.

In the person of Professor George Santayana, with whom the youthful Stevens traded sonnets and on whose death in 1952 Stevens wrote "To an Old Philosopher in Rome," the undergraduate encountered a curious combination of New England gentility and Spanish Catholicism. Even a musty whiff of Teresa or Loyola must have been heady to the Dutch lawyer's son from Reading: "But in Spain, in Salamanca, there is a pillar in a church (Santayana told me) worn by the kisses of generations of the devout" (*L* 96). (Santayana surely said Santiago.)

Stevens' poetic eulogy fifty years later emphasizes Santayana's religion and religious roots in Rome, and Santayana's own writings flesh out the Christian mysticism Stevens may have glimpsed through him. Not surprisingly, the Harvard professor of philosophy, although he saw himself as a champion of beauty over pragmatism, somehow in transition to Cambridge had lost sympathy with the visions of Castile. Three aspects of Santayana's work may bear on Stevens' meditative poetry. First, Santayana spoke of *nothing,* nirvana, and concepts of abstention in connection with mystical experience, and may have helped put those words and concepts into Stevens' vocabulary. Sec-

188

ond, like most Catholics, he identified mystical experience with a theology (a truth that could be conveyed from one man's mind to another's), and thus gave it both a positive result in belief and a monastic result in life: the mystic gives his life to the One. This Spanish Catholic absolutism begets in the humanist philosopher a predictably negative reaction. That reaction is the third aspect of Santayana's comments on mysticism:

> The way of true wisdom, therefore, if true wisdom is to deal with the Absolute, can only lie in abstention: neither the senses nor the common understanding, and much less the superstructure raised upon these by imagination, logic, or tradition, must delude us. . . . Everything, says the mystic, is nothing, in comparison with the One. . . . The ideal of mysticism is accordingly exactly contrary to the ideal of reason; instead of perfecting human nature it seeks to abolish it . . . instead of developing our mind to greater scope and precision, it would return to the condition of protoplasm—to the blessed consciousness of an Unutterable Reality. . . . The mystical spirit . . . will never be satisfied . . . with anything short of Absolute Nothing.[1]

The argument, from Santayana's essay, "Understanding, Imagination, and Mysticism," progresses from "abstention" to "abolish" to "protoplasm," which casts an ironic tone over all ensuing "blessed consciousness." The attack is typical of attacks on mysticism to the present day, especially by some of Stevens' most admiring critics. The attack is morally intelligible in the case of solipsistic fanatics everywhere, although it is inaccurate as a description of mysticism: mystics usually find everything to be nothing not by value judgment ("in comparison with") but in its essence (therefore the One is also nothing); since wholehearted devotion to "blessed consciousness" seems uniquely human it is hard to call it an abolition of "human nature" (rather than a willed and temporary abolition of self); "protoplasm" is an obscuring exaggeration; and the tenor of the whole, by assuming that the mystic's most extreme experience excludes all other aspects of his life, shows an obsessive fear on the part of the speaker, just as those fanatically opposed to sex think of sexual people as only sexy, just as those fanatically opposed to communism think of communal people as only communal. Such fears produce a sort of racism, even in the genteel humanist: for a moment, one's sense of the universality of the human condition is set aside, while one's fear of a particular difference in behavior or belief or appearance makes the entire individual seem alien.

If Yeats's forte was openness of heart, Stevens' was openness of mind, and as Santayana's explication degenerates into attack one is struck by the misplaced passion (which Stevens would *not* share), a passion born not of vitality but of fear. This mystical subject, and many another, Stevens would entertain with sensitivity and tact, but without such self-involved reaction: the perfect host.

Santayana had his own variety. Since he really preferred Ignatius Loyola to Bertrand Russell, he had to find in fanaticism some redeeming social importance. Having despised thoroughly the thorough mystic, Santayana adds a charming twist. A pinch of mysticism leavens the loaf: "A partial mysticism often serves to bring out with wonderful intensity those underlying strata of experience."[2] This theory leads him, three pages later, to an absolute nothing of complacency: "And although mysticism, left free to express itself, can have no other goal than Nirvana, yet moderately indulged in and duly inhabited by a residuum of conventional sanity, it serves to give a touch of strangeness and elevation to the character."[3] That sort of most scrutable thinking, not the inscrutable East, later created a multimillion dollar American industry in transcendental meditation, and apparently became a Panglossian Harvard convention. Later, Stevens quoted Whitehead: "The purpose of philosophy is to rationalize mysticism. . . . Philosophy is akin to poetry, and both of them seek to express that ultimate good sense which we term civilization" (*NA* 115).

Though Santayana deserves chastisement for such a cowardly way of shooting the irrational into the veins of his ideal man, the structure his argument has followed is instructive partly because it is typical and partly because it is quite original:

1. Santayana begins with a romantic respect for irrational insight, a respect derived from—among other sources—the church and Emerson, and held aggressively at Harvard in the Age of Pragmatism.
2. He accepts an old Catholic distinction between the negation of the mystic and the positivism of the imaginative man. Such a distinction was not made by Emerson, who identified mysticism with ecstasy and wanted always to link it to art.
3. Having withdrawn from imagination, the negative mystic is seen as having withdrawn from life. This was a typical assumption by antimystics from 1850 until 1950, when knowledge of Mahayana Buddhism began to complicate our equation of meditation and withdrawal.
4. The effect, however, of a moderated mystical withdrawal is benign because it resembles imagination: "The better side of mysticism is an aesthetic interest in large unities and cosmic laws."[4] So

Santayana applauds the mystic's spiritual motivation and goals, but following the humanist and Catholic traditions, he substitutes something for nothing: "Where should we look for that expansion and elevation of the mind which the mystic seeks so passionately and so unintelligently? We can find that expansion, in the first place, in the imagination itself."[5]

As mysticism is thus skewed from negative to positive, no one is likely to notice meditative consciousness. The result is now intellectual history: a positive category—imagination—has entered the twentieth century as the inheritor of spiritual insight and the successor to God. Stevens certainly agreed.

From Santayana, although he took no courses with him, Stevens in his many conversations could have acquired both a vocabulary of nothingness and a theory of imagination. In establishing a meaningful relationship between nothingness and imagination, however, Stevens went far beyond his professor. Santayana had made nothing into something ("an aesthetic interest in large unities and cosmic laws") in order to make it harmonious with imagination. Stevens repeatedly proposes a different scenario, more respectful of meditation but also in some ways Christian: the experience of nothing is a purgation of self; this purgation allows a chastened self, and a chastened imagination, to reenter the world with new humility and wonder. Thus even in poems we might not call meditative, Stevens' knowledge of "bare" states of mind helped structure his thought.

Nowhere is this schema more beautifully displayed than in "Evening without Angels" (*CP* 136–38). The title suggests an aesthete's answer to Christianity; the poem is more of an ascetic's answer to aestheticism. The poem opens with the human imagination triumphant; the entire natural universe has been taken over by art—painting, music, metaphor—and the language is sheer dazzle:

> Why seraphim like lutanists arranged
> Above the trees? And why the poet as
> Eternal *chef d'orchestre?*

And why the questions? The epigraph from Mario Rossi beneath the title had set a simpler and more serious tone: "The great interests of man: air and light, the joy of having a body, the voluptuousness of looking." The poem is about just that: air and light, physical existence and their relation to imagination (voluptuous looking). Why seraphim?

The poem now answers most aggressively and still most wittily that seraphim are rightfully there because all meaning is a human projection: where man is not, air is vacant. (Blake: "Where man is not, nature is barren.")

> Air is air,
> Its vacancy glitters round us everywhere.
> Its sounds are not angelic syllables
> But our unfashioned spirits realized
> More sharply in more furious selves.

The universe, then, is an empty place awaiting projections of the human self. Religion ("angelic syllables") is one of those projections. And we project self in order to make the unfashioned self more fashioned, the unreal self more realized, the dull self more sharp. The result is cherubim, seraphim, and angels all over the ceiling: a dazzling display of the human imagination reaching a "furious" perfection through domination of the natural world.

The next stanza continues in this vein and the fourth stanza strikes an even more aggressive stance:

> Let this be clear that we are men of sun
> And men of day and never of pointed night . . . .

But this extreme exhortation to confidence in self—the human self—begins to generate its own reaction, and the first adversative introduces an admission that air and light may have their own voices, too:

> Yet,
> If we repeat, it is because the wind
> Encircling us, speaks always with our speech.

So the wind speaks *with* us, not just by means of our seraphic projections, and it *causes* our repetitions. Is the "*chef*" still in charge of this orchestra? From there the poem sinks in one stanza down to darkness. Light, like wind, takes on its own importance as men of sun and day are put to sleep. Night comes, at first an agent of our desire for rest, but finally an independent presence:

> Light, too, encrusts us making visible
> The motions of the mind and giving form
> To moodiest nothings, as desire for day
> Accomplished in the immensely flashing East,
> Desire for rest, in that descending sea
> Of dark, which in its very darkening
> Is rest and silence spreading into sleep.

Where are the seraphim now? The human imagination, the human self has been laid to rest, and in this tranquility the air fills with a music of its own, albeit in a different key:

> . . . Evening, when the measure skips a beat
> And then another, one by one, and all
> To a seething minor swiftly modulate.
> Bare night is best. Bare earth is best. Bare, bare . . . .

In this context there can be only one meaning for "bare": bare of the human imagination, a world without "more furious selves." What began as the partial passivity of rest and sleep has now become true negation, beyond minor music, "bare" repeated four times in one line, finally beyond even the value judgment of "best": "Bare, bare," introduces the last statement of the poem, which is not a sentence but a series of careful subordinate moves away from that ultimate negation. For a moment, "Bare, bare," "there is nothing to see, not a man nor a Buddha." Evening without angels; yes, but also evening without man.

Human beings are allowed to creep back into the poem, not as *chefs d'orchestre,* but low as Santayana's devout, kissing the pillars of this universal church:

> Bare night is best. Bare earth is best. Bare, bare,
> Except for our own houses, huddled low
> Beneath the arches and their spangled air,
> Beneath the rhapsodies of fire and fire . . . .

The humility is striking. The first metaphor reintroduced is "arches," a starker architecture than the painted vaults of the opening. And who is now the architect? And whence spangling? This dazzle doesn't come from people huddled low. Like the bird's song in "Not Ideas about the Thing but the Thing Itself," it comes from outside. Most beautifully, music now for the third time returns, no longer orchestrated by man, no longer the seething minor of bareness: it is the music of the spheres, "rhapsodies of fire and fire."

The human beings readmitted beneath this spangled air are at first completely passive, purged of "more furious selves." Then line by line we are granted thought and feeling and activity again:

> Beneath the rhapsodies of fire and fire,
> Where the voice that is in us makes a true response,
> Where the voice that is great within us rises up,
> As we stand gazing at the rounded moon.

At first our voice *responds* to light and air, and our virtue is in being true to that universe, then the "great" voice within us "rises up," taking on a life of its own. But the poem holds perfectly to its chastened spirit and we remain beneath a firmament, standing still, gazing up at the air we once thought vacant, until in one word Stevens gives us back—perhaps—the shaping spirit, a universe half perceived, half created: the moon is not round, but "rounded." Is it rounded by the rolling of the heavens bringing it full phase, or by the awestruck human beings gazing at its impossible roundness, now brought full by their own response? It is impossible to say, and that is the delicacy of the proposed symbiosis. The fullest moon is light and air in a moment of voluptuous looking.

The tone, the language, and the relation of man to nature have all changed in the course of the poem. In a dazzling manner Stevens had first proposed that air is vacant until filled with human conceits. Next humanity is purged, then readmitted to a spangled universe and finally allowed to participate in bringing it round. The fulcrum on which the poem swings is ascetic: passivity, darkness, and bareness calm the furious self, purge and prepare it for voluptuous looking. In this poem the meditative pattern that we have been describing naturalistically— self, loss of self, willed return to ordinary consciousness—becomes an analogue to the Christian moral schema of pride, penitence, salvation: "The supreme virtue here is humility, for the humble are they that move about the world with the lure of the real in their hearts" (*NA* 99). "Evening without Angels" reveals a meditative schema functioning, and functioning beautifully, within a humanist universe.

Santayana had suggested, in a different schema more typical of our culture, that mysticism could be of use only if it was imaginative, and not pursued too thoroughly. His liberal misunderstanding of mysticism became a tolerant condescension, ending in faint praise. Stevens, however, was at times willing to go all the way: the experience of bareness is the opposite of imaginative experience, it should be pursued to its essential extreme ("Bare, bare") and *then* can serve the function in our lives of a thorough asceticism, cleansing, and purging, returning us to earth and to imagination with new vigor, humility, and clarity.

On Santayana's death in Rome in 1952, just three years before his own, Stevens bowed gracefully to his friend's Catholicism "on the threshold of heaven," even though he might have had some reservations about Santayana's retreat to nuns: "He seems to have gone to live at the convent, in which he died, in his sixties, probably gave them all he had and asked them to keep him, body and soul" (*L* 761–62). But Stevens' eulogy "To an Old Philosopher in Rome" (*CP* 508–11) does not continue in a Catholic vein; it would have been an extreme of tolerance to have granted Santayana a salvation Stevens did not admire, while withholding the one he did. And to Santayana, Stevens at age seventy-three granted the salvation imagined in "Evening without Angels."

By stanza 10 of the eulogy, Santayana has been purged by "misery, the afflatus of ruin, / Profound poetry of the poor and of the dead." The Catholic bells are resented, being themselves jealous of that silence and "solitude of sense" which to Stevens was the deeper truth:

> The bells keep on repeating solemn names
>
> In choruses and choirs of choruses,
> Unwilling that mercy should be a mystery
> Of silence, that any solitude of sense
> Should give you more than their peculiar chords
> And reverberations clinging to whisper still.

But like the doctor in "The Latest Freed Man" on the edge of his bed, Santayana does gain a "solitude of sense," "dozing in the depths of wakefulness, / In the warmth of your bed, at the edge of your chair," and it is this state of mind, not Catholic theology, that brings about the epiphany of yet another freed man:

> It is a kind of total grandeur at the end,
> With every visible thing enlarged and yet
> No more than a bed, a chair and moving nuns.

Finally Stevens takes this "mystery of silence . . . solitude" leading to a peculiar state of mind and places it within Santayana's belief in thought and imagination. He will not grant him Catholic salvation, but with the word "chosen" he bestows instead a humanist and imaginative grace:

> Total grandeur of a total edifice,
> Chosen by an inquisitor of structures
> For himself. He stops upon this threshold,
> As if the design of all his words takes form
> And frame from thinking and is realized.

Evening now has angels again, as Santayana builds his edifice of thought and steps across the threshold. He is the architect, the *chef d'orchestre*.

> To use a single illustration: it may be assumed that the life of Professor Santayana is a life in which the function of the imagination has had a function similar to its function in any deliberate work of art or letters. We have only to think of this present phase of it, in which, in his old age, he dwells in the head of the world, in the company of devoted women, in their convent, and in the company of familiar saints, whose presence does so much to make any convent an appropriate refuge for a generous and human philosopher. To repeat, there can be lives in which the value of the imagination is the same as its value in arts and letters." (*NA* 147–48)

But Santayana's is not a furious self; he has passed through the silence and solitude beneath the descant of the bells. Stevens' asceticism lies at the heart of his thought, and the lifeblood of that asceticism is a meditative suspension of thought, feeling, and imagination in a moment of extraordinary watchfulness. He gave back to his teacher more than he was taught. It is remarkable that Stevens was able to find such uses for a state of mind the rest of his countrymen feared.

15
Pound's Cathay

If Stevens was going to have any help from a fearless country-
man, one might have expected that help from Pound, who was help-
ing everybody with everything (Yeats, Hilda Doolittle, Eliot) and
who, as Stevens started writing for publication in 1913, was just then
flying back to the drifting ship of English poetry with a real live
twig—not Sinnett or Madame Blavatsky—from the East. Pound
wrote in a letter:

> Three years ago in Paris I got out of a "metro" train at La Con-
> corde, and saw suddenly a beautiful face, and then another and
> another, and then a beautiful child's face, and then another beauti-
> ful woman, and I tried all that day to find words that seemed to me
> worthy, or as lovely as that sudden emotion. And that evening, as I
> went home along the Rue Raynouard, I was still trying, and I found,
> suddenly, the expression. I do not mean that I found words, but
> there came an equation . . . not a speech, but in little blotches of
> color. It was just that—a "pattern," or hardly a pattern, if by "pat-
> tern" you mean something with a "repeat" in it. But it was a word,
> the beginning, for me, of a language in color. . . .
>   A chinaman said long ago that if a man can't say what he has to
> say in twelve lines he had better keep quiet. The Japanese have
> evolved the still shorter form of the *hokku.*

>   The fallen blossom flies back to its branch:
>   A butterfly.

> That is the substance of a well-known *hokku.* . . .
>   The "one-image poem" is a form of super-position, that is to say
> it is one idea set on top of another. I found it useful in getting out of
> the impasse in which I had been left by my metro emotion. I wrote a
> thirty-line poem, and destroyed it because it was what we call work
> "of second intensity." Six months later I made a poem half that
> length; a year later I made the following *hokku*-like sentence:—

>   The apparition of these faces in the crowd;
>   Petals on a wet, black bough.

> I dare say it is meaningless unless one has drifted into a certain vein of thought. In a poem of this sort one is trying to record the precise instant when a thing outward and objective transforms itself, or darts into a thing inward and subjective.[1]

Ezra Pound's "In a Station of the Metro" began with a "sudden emotion" and led to a spontaneous expression ("there came an equation . . . in little splotches of color"). Since this equation finally took a haiku form, one is tempted to see Pound's poem, and other imagist poems, as Ch'an or Zen poems, expressions of meditative enlightenment compressed into a gnomic residue.

It is more tempting to think of Pound as a pioneer in meditative verse when we know he was reading Herbert Giles's *History of Chinese Literature* and was making his own compressions of Giles:

Fan-Piece, for Her Imperial Lord

O fan of white silk,
    clear as frost on the grass-blade,
You also are laid aside.

And even more tempting when we know that the widowed Mary Fenollosa, reading Pound's metro poem in the April 1913 *Poetry* magazine, thought Ezra Pound the man to receive her husband's notebooks on Chinese poetry.[2] By 1915 Pound had published the first fourteen Chinese translations called *Cathay*.

Since Wallace Stevens in 1913 was working on "Carnet du Voyage" and "Phases" to send to *Trend* and to Harriet Monroe at *Poetry,* and was reading Pound there and elsewhere, and since in 1919, within a year of writing "The Snow Man," Stevens had read Pound and Fenollosa's essay on "The Chinese Written Character," it is tempting to find in Pound the missing link: here was the inheritor of the symbolist's interest in sensation ("the precise instant when a thing . . . darts inward") who had not only a technical interest in reforming symbolism through clarity and objectivity but also an instinct for the concise. Add to this an avid interest in the Orient and in 1913, sole possession of the most advanced commentary on Chinese and Japanese poetry available in English, and one would *expect* Pound to fall upon the "simplicity, conciseness, intuition" that according to one master is the spirit of Ch'an and Zen; one would expect Pound in his chameleon way to try out the colors of meditative Buddhist poetry.

Nothing of the sort happened. To ask why is to ask what Pound in 1913 wanted to hear, and what the Boston Buddhists had to say.

Ernest Fenollosa, Edward Morse, and William Sturgis Bigelow were Harvard professors—philosophy, zoology, and medicine—who found themselves together in the new Japan of the 1880s, teaching and collecting art. By 1890 the Boston Museum, through their efforts, had the finest collection of oriental art in the world, and their excursions into Buddhism as well as art were attracting the attention of fellow Americans. Teddy Roosevelt, meeting Bigelow in Paris in 1887, found the subject hard to take: "He was most charming; but Cabot *why* did you not tell me he was an esoteric Buddhist? I would have been spared some frantic floundering."[3] Henry Adams, in Japan in 1886 halfheartedly "in search of Nirvana" ("It's out of season," an Omaha reporter warned as Adams and John LaFarge crossed the continent), a nirvana that later helped color the rose window as Adams saw it at Chartres, found the subject of Buddhism congenial but Ernest Fenollosa himself hard to take: "I myself was a Buddhist when I left America, but he has converted me to Calvinism with leanings toward the Methodists."[4]

Perhaps Fenollosa was less agreeable than Adams, but he was certainly more enterprising: he convinced Japan that its wholesale westernization and contempt for its own art was wrong, and he lectured Japanese on their own traditions (performing a service parallel to that of Olcott and Blavatsky in Ceylon during the same years.) By 1884 he was an imperial commissioner of fine arts in Japan, along with his pupil and translator, Kakuzo Okakura. Okakura would later manage the Boston Museum collection and write the influential *Ideals of the East,* which Stevens read in 1909. Fenollosa's Eastern knowledge was further disseminated through Arthur Dow, who developed a system of art education using many of Fenollosa's ideas and Eastern materials. Georgia O'Keeffe studied with Dow at Columbia in 1914, read Fenollosa's *Epochs of Chinese and Japanese Art,* and carried those influences to Stieglitz and his circle in New York.

Fenollosa's accomplishments, however, were not confined to art history and raising hackles. According to Rick Fields, "Fenollosa and Sturgis Bigelow were probably the first Americans to have studied (and practiced to some extent) mahayana Buddhism with a qualified teacher."[5] He studied, with Dakurai Keitoku Ajari at a temple on Lake Briva, the basic tenets and practices of the Tendai school of Shingon Buddhism. The sect emphasized painting, especially Chinese T'ang portraits, and the energetic American professor was attracted not only to the Tendai use of art but also to their encouragement of the *bodhisattva:* one who takes "a vow as early as baptism to lead the strenuous path of battling for the right, to consecrate one's career throughout any number of necessary incarnations to loving service."[6] The engagement of Mahayana Buddhism to this world was finally known to the West.

Fenollosa died suddenly of a heart attack in 1908. His widowed second wife, Mary, returned to Japan to finish his *Epochs of Chinese and Japanese Art.* When she brought the manuscript to London in 1912, she met Ezra Pound. A year later she read "In a Station of the Metro" and sent Pound the manuscripts and notes of Fenollosa's unfinished studies of Chinese poetry and Japanese Noh drama. Pound responded to the direct, concise, nondidactic qualities of Chinese poetry and character writing as heralding a new Renaissance: the early Chinese poets Pound called "a treasury to which the next centuries may look for as great a stimulus as the Renaissance had from the Greeks."[7] The essay on "The Chinese Written Character as a Medium for Poetry" Pound found in Fenollosa's notes and adopted as an imagist manifesto, while Fenollosa's notes and glosses for Chinese poems Pound reworked into the highly influential *Cathay.*

Most of Fenollosa's translations were secular, like "Fan-Piece," composed within the Chinese court, although Fenollosa had worked also on a few Taoist poems. Fenollosa, as Hugh Kenner points out, had inherited Emerson's belief that metaphor embodies the creative impulse (quite in keeping with Santayana's thinking in the same years, transmitted to Stevens), and this touch of Cambridge transcendentalism, though it led Fenollosa to emphasize the verbal processes inherent in Chinese character language, also led him to an aggressive, even ecstatic sense of what verbs do. This aggression, and a distaste for negation, are qualities admirably captured by Kenner's own spirited description of Fenollosa's spirited approach to language:

> He warred on the copula: "There is in reality no such verb . . . no such original conception; our very word *exist* means 'to stand forth,' to show oneself by a definite act." In the Chinese "is" he found "a splendid flash of concrete poetry": "to snatch from the moon with the hand." He assailed negation as parvenue ("*we* can assert a negation, though nature cannot"), and derived a Chinese sign for nonexistence from "to be lost in the forest," not a non-being but a specifiable plight.[8]

In truth Fenollosa lifted his head from Chinese characters with almost the same impression that Emerson had received from the Indian

Vedas: "The ideograph meaning 'to speak' is a mouth with two words and a flame coming out of it. . . . Metaphor, the revealer of nature. . . . The known interprets the obscure, the universe is alive with myth."[9]

The English language itself worked against an appreciation of passivity. Kenner again: "In Chinese, the language accretes processes—'Lowering, lowering, the lingering clouds . . . .' In Pound's English, a man makes affirmations—'The clouds have gathered and gathered'—affirmations, moreover, about a universe structured by western preoccupations with time and causation."[10] Which reminds one of Yeats, struggling for detachment but impaled on imperative verbs: "Cast a cold eye."

Fenollosa, then, as might be expected, during his brief and busy visits to Japan was excited to discover the intersection of Mahayana Buddhism and art, but was less prepared to grasp right away the issues of passivity and negation in Buddhist poetry. It is a compliment to Pound's instincts that in spite of such predispositions he occasionally captured traditional passivity, as in "Fan-Piece": "You also are laid aside," not cast aside, not thrown away.

Certainly Fenollosa's championing of compressed metaphors wed to clarity and conciseness suited in 1913 Pound's taste for "the laconic speech of the Imagistes . . . Objective—no slither—direct—no excess of adjectives."[11] Those imagist images are really metaphors, one image dragged in by imagination ("petals") and thrown against the thing itself ("faces") with some shock or surprise, according to T. E. Hulme.

But if Pound's linguistic ability and instincts allowed him at times to improve on Fenollosa's notes, he was simultaneously losing—or failing to perceive and transmit—the Buddhist qualities in the works before him. While Fenollosa had come to see Buddhism as the foundation of Eastern character and art (Li Po was his hero, versus the rationalist Confucius), Pound was heading in the other direction. In the *Cantos*, Confucius is a hero, Buddhism something of an antagonist.

Just how close, then, was Pound's imagism to the East? In 1969, Wai-lim Yip in *Ezra Pound's Cathay* gave an authoritative reading of the poems as translations. His book demonstrates that Pound's excitement over discovering Chinese was justified; the absence of copulas and transitions in Chinese poetry, plus the pictorial nature of the characters, create a kind of verbal cubist art. The Chinese syntax is open and uncommitted, and the ingredients are hard, clear, and precise. For instance, two opening lines of five characters each read literally:

floating   cloud(s)   wanderer('s)   thought (mood)
setting   sun   old   friend('s) feeling

Yip, himself Chinese, says right away that the indeterminacy exists for Chinese readers too: the cloud is compared to (like) a wanderer's mood, or vice versa. Or are they simply simultaneous, juxtaposed? As when the linking verb is omitted from "In a Station of the Metro," the effect here is antilinguistic, if meaningful assertion is taken as the basis of language. English language translators make "syntactical commitments," as Yip says. To say the least: Compare Giles's

> Your heart was full of wandering thought;
> For me,—my sun has set indeed.

to Pound's

> Mind like a floating wide cloud,
> Sunset like the parting of old acquaintances.[12]

Whether the statements so deduced can be justified is one issue, as Yip points out, but justified or not, in the presence of statement, the atmosphere of pure montage is lost (cloud—wanderer's mood—sun—friend's feeling). Chinese poetry was correctly perceived by Pound as challenging conventional statement and inviting comparisons to cubism: the abrupt juxtaposition of disparate images.

The next question to ask of Cathay and imagism is, to what extent did Chinese cultural context supply missing generic, if not syntactic, links? Back to the most curious part of Pound's account of "In a Station of the Metro": "I daré say it is meaningless unless one has drifted into a certain vein of thought." What a strange admission, probably encouraged by what he saw but could not comprehend in haiku. Pound, and perhaps Fenollosa, never understood the depth and breadth of tradition behind many oriental gnomic poems. The imagist may have presented "an intellectual and emotional complex in an instant of time," and may have done it with remarkable brevity, but if the experience was uniquely personal, if no profound way of regarding it was argued by the poem and if no tradition gave it breadth and depth, then such an instant of perception could produce a very slight poem which might well have benefited from another twenty-eight lines. Even in oriental court poetry, the reader is not left to "drift into a certain vein of thought"; an old tradition traces the genre behind the fragments. Buddhist poetry is very traditional in genre and style. And in English lyric poems the reader is usually pushed into a certain vein of thought by the poem itself. The wonder of "In a Station of the Metro" is how far it does go with so little traditional or poetic context. Its abrupt profundity is achieved through a tension rare in imagist poetry: the subway and crowd of the first line are opposed to the leaves and branch of the second; a vague white apparition is opposed to a photographically clear "petals on a wet, black bough"; a liquid and sibilant first line yields to crisp consonants—all these oppositions, without the fulcrum of a verb to swing on, capture the novelty, surprise, and shock of Pound's epiphany—an epiphany that seems to depend ultimately on a sudden leap from city to country, from obscurity to clarity, from mundane to sublime. There is a moral, perhaps: beauty is clear. And tone: beauty is complex, sinking downward to darkness. Maybe even plot, given Pound's letter: "a woman's beautiful face."

"In a Station of the Metro" is a poem about and deliberately suggesting an epiphanic experience, transient, perhaps noetic, perhaps passive since no verb links the two lines, almost ineffable since meaning is left to chance, and the poem is certainly part of a movement between 1910 and 1913 that made Stevens' conciseness and clarity more possible. But Pound in this poem and in others remained squarely within romantic aesthetics based on creative imagination. As his letter shows, Pound had a personal insight—a subtle but positive, definite experience—and the right metaphor and tone expressed it quite well. The two lines are not true fragments; the hiatus contains an ineffable link; the equation is expressive. The experience behind the poem might possibly be called ecstatic, but not meditative. The form is an oriental form brilliantly used for the purpose of lyric self-explanation, a purpose common enough in secular Chinese court poetry.

Although he set a standard for conciseness and clarity, Pound wrote nothing that could lead to "The Snow Man." Like most of the artists of his period, Pound had hardly considered passivity, and thought meditation allied with the occult, and therefore to be regarded as an aspect of what Santayana called imagination.

Pound's emphatic style and driving, relentless sensibility is inseparable from his conduct as an artist. It is hard to imagine a sensibility more different from Stevens', or less given to detachment: "Art very possibly *ought* to be the supreme achievement, the 'accomplished'; but there is the other satisfactory effect, that of a man hurling himself at an indomitable chaos, and yanking and hauling as much of it as possible into some sort of order (or beauty), aware of it both as chaos and as potential."[13] While the content of Pound's statement is an argument for immersion in process, the imagery is so decisive, violent, and Promethean, that one might suspect the speaker's patience in Nietzsche's "chaos of sensations." Would he not be quick to haul it into order? That was, I believe, the case. Pound was always at war with the "uncertainty principle" that lay just beneath the surface of modernism, and for different reasons from Eliot, Pound leaped at hard and fast conclusions. In my final chapter, I will argue that in this way, he was less modern than Stevens, and that his collage-like structures are essentially dishonest: conclusions with transitions removed are not the same as fragments balanced against each other.

Certainly Pound was not apt to catch the Buddhist passivity in some Chinese poems, especially as filtered through Fenollosa's transcendental excitement. Detachment, irony, equanimity in the face of alternatives was simply not his style. In fact, throughout his life he seemed (especially in what he liked) to court alienation. George Antheil, the avant-garde composer whom Pound championed, recalls the effect of Pound's writings on his behalf: "Ezra's flamboyant book, couched in language calculated to antagonize everyone first by its ridiculous praise, then by its vicious criticism of everyone else, did me no good whatsoever. . . . Nobody could have been a tenth as good as Ezra made me."[14]

Ezra Pound had found the East, and many of his translations in *Cathay* are still, to my ear, the best available, but he did not advance one step toward understanding meditative issues. Perhaps more important, however, he demonstrates some of the problems of practicing modernism *without* detachment. For the moment, we can say three things of Pound's *Cathay:* first, Chinese poems helped him explore radical disjunction in syntax and structure; second, his and Fenollosa's certainties and enthusiasms helped mask the meditative aspects of those poems; third, the Chinese and Japanese cultural context of meditative theory and practice remained unknown and unexplored in *Cathay*.

So in spite of all Europe's interest in perception and sensation, and all Europe's interest in the Orient, Stevens in 1920 as he worked on "The Snow Man" was almost at square one. His culture still offered no constructive or accurate conception of meditative passivity in a perceptive being. Thought or annihilation—as Colebrooke said, "what other condition short of such absolute extinction" might the mind of winter be?

16
Stevens' Readings

After three years of attendance, Stevens left Harvard in 1900 with no degree. It was not unusual at the time (Frost and Eliot were also "special students"); he had performed well in his school work and in his editing of the *Advocate*, for which he wrote prose and poetry. After a few years of journalism in New York, however, he felt he was getting nowhere and entered law school at his father's suggestion. In June 1904 he passed the bar and in September began a practice with Lyman Ward. Stevens was an active cosmopolite in New York: few interesting exhibits or concerts escaped him. His journal and his letters to Elsie Moll, whom he had met that summer of 1904 in Reading and would marry in 1909, mentioned almost every week something new in the world of art that had passed through his hand or ear or eye. He began traveling extensively throughout the country on business trips (in 1905 alone to New Mexico and back, to Louisiana and back), a practice that would continue past his marriage. Perhaps the most outstanding features of the young bachelor's life were his aesthetic interests, his travels, and his Sunday walks.

Those aesthetic interests included aesthetes. Stevens not only visited the galleries and concert halls, he did so with a number of friends, often literary acquaintances from Harvard days, so that his art usually came with food and drink: "My idea of life is a fine evening, an orchestra + a crowd *at a distance,* a medium dinner, a glass of something cool + at the same time wholesome, + a soft, full Panetela" (*L* 74). If his moderation seems excessive, it is perhaps because he was recovering from a rum binge with Witter Bynner (his Harvard friend who by 1929 would help translate *The Jade Mountain,* an influential anthology of Chinese poems from the T'ang dynasty). He loved the idea of Paris—the art, the food, the cafes. From his early years he had a talent for voluptuous looking, the sensuality of the gourmet aesthete, and an original eye:

205

May 2 [1906]

> A half-misty, Fantin–La Tourish night. The moisture and new
> leaves together fill the streets with a sweet, earthy perfume.   —In
> town, I lunched with Walter Arensberg at the Harvard Club. Fin-
> ished with brandied peaches and cream. Felt like licking the saucer.
> Borrowed a pile of books.   —As I came indoors a moment ago, a
> cat stole over the porch, much like a mote in one's eye.   (*L* 92)

This young man about town kept up with magazines of the art
world, often in library reading rooms where he could browse to his
whim's content. We don't know what he had been reading or seeing
that summer but in August 1905 he noted the "japonaiserie of pines"
in Louisiana, and in December he wrote that his "head was full of
strange pictures . . . ivory figurines of the Japanese. . . . Reflections
on Japanese life, on specificness, on minute knowledge as disclosing
minute pleasures" (*L* 84–85). Had he been up to the Boston Mu-
seum, where he could have seen that fall's oriental exhibit?

Over the next four years he was quite taken with the Orient as
well as with the world of modern art. In April 1906, a week before
his Fantin–La Tourish night, he was reading Paul Elmer More, the
Harvard idealist, scholar, moralist, popular philosopher, and essay-
ist on Christianity, Plato, and the Orient. Stevens disparaged More
in 1906 but admired him by 1909 for his essays on Thoreau and the
East. Earlier in April, Stevens had read and liked G. Lowes Dickin-
son's *Letters from John Chinaman* (Confucian comments on various
cultures). In April he also expressed his distaste for Arthur Symons,
who "has a great weight with several fellows I know" and in the
Saturday Review had just called women "beasts of prey" (*SP* 162–
64). That month of April 1906 is a visible cross-section of Stevens'
postcollege world: Fantin–La Tour and impressionist painting, ex-
otic news from China, the *Saturday Review* and Symons, who in
1899 while Stevens was at Harvard had published *The Symbolist
Movement in Literature,* a study of French poets Stevens loved,
dedicated to W. B. Yeats. Yeats's "Lake Isle of Innisfree" Stevens
was quoting in 1909 as he read More's essay on Thoreau. When he
wrote the poem, Yeats had been reading *Walden.* Centuries do
happen.

During 1908–1909, while more absorbed with Keats's "Endymion"
than with any other book, Stevens sharpened his interest in the East,
and from February to June in the spring of 1909, just before his
marriage, he spent a good deal of time in the Astor Library "looking

through the books of Paul Elmer More" (*L* 133). March 18 he wrote a long letter to Elsie mentioning Kakuyo Okakura's *Ideals of the East* and an oriental exhibition (Okakura was Fenellosa's friend and by then curator at Boston's oriental collection). The lists of traditional painting subjects at the exhibition Stevens thought "one of the most curious things [he] ever saw." He admired a poem by Wang-an-shih and resolved: "I am going to poke around more or less in the dust of Asia for a week or two and have no idea what I shall disturb and bring to light.—Curious thing, how little we know about Asia, and all that. It makes me wild to learn it all in a night" (*L* 138).

In a May 14 journal entry he transcribed some notes from the Astor Library, including a few not worked into his March letter to Elsie, and by June 14 he "would give last winter's hat" for the catalogue and Arthur Morrison's notes for an exhibition of Japanese prints in London (*SP* 235). He acquired the notes.

During this period he sent Elsie the "June Book," twenty poems including some he would use in the 1914 collection, "Carnet de Voyage," his first published poems since Harvard. A number of the poems play with Eastern themes, as do other early works: his play *Three Travelers Watch a Sunrise*, parts of "Six Significant Landscapes" and "Le Monocle de Mon Oncle" (all 1914–1916). Curiously, the rest of his life—quite unlike Yeats; more like Thoreau—he seems not to have pursued his interest in the Orient.

That Stevens had some oriental interests and knowledge that affected his early poetry is clear. Whether those interests and influences were meditative is another matter. And what he could have learned from More and Okakura and other casual reading is perhaps separable from what he did learn, though conversely what currents may have run deep, only to surface thirty years later, no one can say. For instance, one cannot absolutely assert that behind this passage from "Esthétique du Mal" (1944),

> It may be that one life is a punishment
> For another, as the son's life for the father's.
>
>   . . . . . .
>
> This force of nature in action is the major
> Tragedy. . . .
>
>   . . . . . . Evil in evil is
> Comparative. . . .
> The force that destroys us is disclosed.　　　　　(*CP* 323–24)

lies the single line transcribed from the Astor Library notes into his journal for May 14, 1909:

> Sakamuni—all evil resides in the individual will to live.   (*SP* 221)

But the Buddha's statement, contemplated enough, especially if contemplated in the light of meditative experience, could lead (much more directly than, say, "The sins of the fathers are visited upon the children unto the third and fourth generation") to section XIII of "Esthétique du Mal."

If that note and that poem are connected across the gap of thirty-five years, what is remarkable is not the connection (Steven threw all possible kitchen sinks into the long poems) but Stevens' ability to absorb a statement so repulsive to his culture, and to absorb it with neither devotion nor fear. The Buddha perhaps did not say that individuals should stop willing to live (notice the active verb "should stop" versus 'resides," but remember that the Buddha wrote nothing himself and Buddhist glosses are no less various than Christian translations). He might have meant that to participate in the system of willing to live is to participate in evil, a word which in that statement is sometimes translated as pain—an equation Stevens made on his own throughout "Esthétique." If one wants, then, to transcend pain, one had best stop willing to live. That need not mean dying; it might mean living without will. And that, as we saw in chapter 11, was precisely the answer to pain that Stevens had proposed in section XII: the third world, without pain, is the world without knowledge or will: meditative consciousness.

If evil is translated as pain, the Buddha's statement is well-nigh irrefutable (which is not to say one cannot choose the pain of this fallen world), but few in our culture have been willing to consider dispassionately a proposition so passive and amoral, or to react with so little defense, just as few Buddhists could face the same proposition with so little enlightenment:

> The force that destroys us is disclosed, . . .
>   an adventure to be endured
> With the politest helplessness. Ay-mi!
> One feels its action moving in the blood.   (*CP* 324)

Stevens may have gleaned important ideas from his Eastern readings, but it would be unwise to draw those ideas from the reading first instead of from the poems; so many had read the same books and in the case of Yeats and Pound, so many more. Why then, of his generation was Stevens the one to come to grips with meditative detachment?

What we can be sure he learned, as evidenced in letters and journals, is interesting but conventional. First, he was struck by the "specificness" of Japanese and Chinese visual arts—paintings, carvings, screens—and he acknowledged an epistemology behind that specificness: "minute knowledge as disclosing minute pleasures." That early sense of Japanese minutiae he kept throughout his life: "The commonest idea of an imaginative object is something large. But apparently with the Japanese it is the other way round and with them the commonest idea of an imaginative object is something small" (*NA* 143). What he and others were learning from the East of China and Japan was already quite different from what the nineteenth century (Emerson, for instance) had learned from India. The Indian Hindu arts—temple carvings and writings—were grand, epic, metaphoric, mystic, and sexual (though somewhat purged in Wilkins's translations). The Chinese and Japanese arts placed much more emphasis on the thing itself, on simplicity and economy. It was several years before even Asian scholars were realizing the meditative implications of this specificness, grounded in Taoist and Ch'an suchness. Stevens' impressions of Chinese and Japanese art seem to have been largely secular and therefore more imagist than Buddhist: "minute pleasures" are neither nothing nor all. He was drawn to such art by sensibility, as he was to Valery's "clarity of details" (*OP* 279). Had he encountered such a specific poem as the following,

> When, just as they are,
> White dewdrops gather
> On scarlet maple leaves,
> Regard the scarlet beads!

he might have been charmed by its specificness, but he would have been unprepared to recognize its Buddhist suggestion of meditative self-loss. Stevens' impression of oriental art as specific and sparse is probably best captured by his friend Witter Bynner in his 1929 introduction to *The Jade Mountain:*

> The great Chinese poets accept the world exactly as they find it in all its terms, and with profound simplicity find therein sufficient solace. Even in phraseology they seldom talk about one thing in terms of another, but are able enough and sure enough as artists to make the ultimately exact terms become the beautiful terms. If a metaphor is

used, it is a metaphor directly relating to the theme, not something borrowed from the ends of the earth. The metaphor must be concurrent with the action or flow of the poem; not merely superinduced, but an integral part of both the scene and the emotion.

Bynner also, like Stevens, had only the most rudimentary understanding of the Taoist elements in his own anthology.[1]

"The sole object of interest for me in such things is their beauty," Stevens said of jades and porcelains (*L* 169), though he was also captivated by the exotic subject matter, the specific picturesque, in G. Lowes Dickinson's decriptions of China: "The friendly Chinese pictures are interesting: 'For many miles along the valley, one after the other, they (the houses) lift their blue- or red-tiled roofs out of a sea of green; while here and there glitters out over a clump of trees the gold enamel of some tall pagoda' " (*SP* 163). Dickinson's observations are not essentially different from the charm of Frost's pastoral landscape: "here a birch / And there a clump of houses with a church" ("The Onset"). Although Stevens was also reading "the *chief* document—the New Testament" in the spring of 1909 as he poked around in the dust of Asia, there is no evidence that he went far in a comparative study of Christianity and Buddhism. Just churches and pagodas.

He copied for Elsie from his Astor Library notes the traditional subjects of Chinese painting:

> Here is the list (upon my soul!)—
>
> > The Evening Bell from a Distant Temple
> > Sunset Glow over a Fishing Village
> > Fine Weather after Storm at a Lonely Mountain Town
> > Homeward-bound Boats off a Distant Shore
> > The Autumn Moon over Lake Tung-t'ing
> > Wild Geese on a Sandy Plain
> > Night Rain in Hsaio-Hsiang
>
> This is one of the most curious things I ever saw, because it is so comprehensive. Any twilight picture is included under the first title. "It is just that silent hour when travellers say to themselves, 'The day is done,' and to their ears comes from the distance the expected sound of the evening bell."   (*L* 137–38)

Specific subjects, specific times of day and sounds—all, being traditional, "expected." It is still most curious to us, the opposite of romantic.

Stevens also copied into his journal an unattributed observation:

"It is in landscape and the themes allied to landscape, that the art of the East is superior to our own—the art of the West excels in the human drama" (*SP* 221). He certainly knew the East paralleled his own taste: "Life is an affair of people not of places. But for me life is an affair of places and that is the trouble" (*OP* 158). Stevens' landscapes and floral decorations and minute pleasures were superior to his human drama: even in his play, *Three Travelers Watch a Sunrise,* he wrote to Harriet Monroe that he did not wish "to become involved in the story or characters of the men and the girl" (*L* 194).

The delicacy, specificness, and economy of Chinese and Japanese arts certainly appealed to Stevens' sensibility; by 1913, when he was writing for publication, that economy also dovetailed with the new imagist movement as advertised by Pound in *Poetry*. Seeing old and venerated artistic traditions depend on landscape, flower arrangement, plum and cherry boughs must have strengthened Stevens' trust in his own taste, in his own habits of purely beholding, merely hearing, seeing the thing itself:

> I am always especially interested at those water-color shows in the pictures of flowers—bowls of roses and the like. It would be pleasant to make a collection of them. There was one picture of a glass vase with six or seven cyclamen in it that was particularly good. There is something uncommon about cyclamen, something rare, if not exceptionally beautiful.   (*L* 140)

A second quality Stevens perceived in Eastern thought was "balance": "To think occasionally of such things gives me a comforting sense of balance and makes me feel like the Brahmin on his mountainslope who in the midst of his contemplations—surveyed distant cities—and then plunged in thought again" (*L* 133). The things of which Stevens was thinking were grand, philosophical statements worthy of "the facade of a library" ("Philosophy . . . that searches out virtues, and expellest vices") and he said that his mood resembled "the mood that fastened me, a year or more ago, so intently on Matthew Arnold—and maxims!" He was reading Paul Elmer More's *Century of Indian Epigrams* and writing his own epigrammatic "Adagia." The "comforting sense of balance" he had gained is the balance of the worldly-wise surveying all time and space and producing comforting maxims, comforting because like all maxims they convey the speaker's illusion of secure knowledge. Stevens' Brahmin is complacent, unlike Yeats's old Chinamen on the mountain slope surveying "all the tragic scene" in

"Lapis Lazuli." What Yeats's old Chinamen perceive has earned them music—"mournful melodies"—not maxims.

Stevens' complacent conception of the Brahmin's "balance" points the danger of mistaking allusions to the Orient for understanding of the Orient, especially when the subject is the Hindu and Buddhist meditative tradition. What, for instance, did the dadaist Tzara mean in 1923 when he used the words "Buddhist . . . indifference?" As when we wonder whether one *should* hear "misery in the wind" in "The Snow Man," these echoes of detachment remind us how tricky the translation not just from one language and one culture but from one state of mind to another, from Brahmin truth to American truth. Certainly Stevens could not in 1909 connect the Brahmin's detachment to the "minute particulars" of Chinese and Japanese art. For better or worse, then, Brahmin religious culture represented to Stevens a kind of balance, the omniscience not of the enlightened but of the smug.

A third quality Stevens perceived in Eastern culture, mainly through Paul Elmer More's discussion of Hinduism, is the illusory quality of this world. More had studied Sanskrit at Harvard, had translated Indian epigrams and part of the *Bhagavad-Gita,* saw the sensuality and "gladness" in Buddhism and had brought a considerable knowledge of Plato and Christianity to bear on Hindu themes, but he knew almost nothing of meditation. The Hindu belief that this world is an illusion becomes in More a kind of feminine mystique; in this case the misunderstandings are delightfully perverse. Here is a quotation from More's Shelbourne Essay on Thoreau, copied by Stevens into his journal on May 14, 1909:

> I sometimes think a little ignorance is wholesome in our communion with Nature, until we are ready to part with her altogether. She is feminine in this as in other respects, and loves to shroud herself in illusions, as the Hindus taught in their books. For they called her Mâyâ, the very person or power of deception, whose sway over the beholder must end as soon as her mystery is penetrated.   (*SP* 220)

Deceive me, deceive me! The Hindu theory of the world's tragic illusiveness has become More's theory of the world's coy elusiveness. An American Platonist is helpless before a virgin femme fatale; nature's veil prolongs indefinitely the foreplay before her "mystery is penetrated." In such darkness, who needs enlightenment?

The innuendos were hardly lost on Stevens six months before his marriage. He copied part of the quote into a letter to his fiancée and drew the only appropriate conclusion:

More, speaking of the herbalists, botanists and the like who go about examining Nature with microscopes, says,—"I sometimes think a little ignorance is wholesome in our communion with Nature; until we are ready to part with her altogether. She is feminine in this as in other respects, and loves to shroud herself in illusions, as the Hindus taught in their books." I think that this is a very fascinating observation. It makes one aware of the love of mystery among damsels—and accounts (although you will not admit it) for a certain pair of hidden slippers—that would have looked so pretty coming down the stairs. Bo-Bo is nothing if not feminine.   (*L* 133)

More was trying to sympathize with Thoreau's anguish over the split between transcendental nature worship and scientific nature observation, a split that much absorbed Thoreau in his journals from 1851 to 1858. Thoreau knew he should value "specific knowledge" and that it must somehow be related to perception of the infinite, but he never took More's impotent way out; Thoreau never preferred the vague and the veiled to penetration of the real. Indeed, as Thoreau said, it was a Hindu philosopher who first raised the veil on that statue.

More was describing Indian traditions, stressing closed senses and transcendence of the world, and was unaware of Chinese and Japanese Mahayana practice. Okakura's *Ideals of the East,* which Stevens read in 1909, discussed Japan's art and politics but hardly mentioned meditative practice, so Stevens quite understandably continued the nineteenth-century practice of equating Buddhism and Hinduism with a rejection of the phenomenal world. Not only does "evil reside in the individual will to live," but, again from his Astor Library notes: "Ukiyoyé is the Japanese equivalent of genre. 'Pictures of the fleeting world'—it means—colored with the Buddhist reproach of all that appeals to the senses and belongs to the transitoriness of miserable mortality. It came to mean a recognized style" (*SP* 221).

He is paraphrasing Morrison's catalogue notes to a London exhibition of Japanese prints. Stevens' prejudice, or rather his expectation of Buddhist prejudice against this world, is interesting. Arthur Morrison in the *Illustrated Catalogue* of 1909 did not mention Buddhism or meditation.[2] Neither the introduction nor the notes on 268 Japanese prints from the sixteenth to nineteenth centuries raises Buddhist issues. When in his 1914 *Guide to an Exhibition of Japanese and Chinese Paintings* Morrison discussed Buddhist and Zen influence, it was in Whitmanesque and pantheistic terms: "Hints of the divine were to be found everywhere; in leaves of grass."[3] The passage that Stevens had read in Morrison's 1909 catalogue actually described not reproach of the senses, but a realism transcending class boundaries:

> The name of the school was drawn from the class of subject its members commonly treated—the nearest possible literal translation of "ukioye" being "passing-world pictures," and the nearest equivalent sense being conveyed by the word "genre." Matabei and his followers painted the ordinary lives of the Japanese of all classes in their day, though it must not be supposed that they were the first Japanese painters to do so. Many men of the Tosa school had painted "genre" before them, though only as an exception to their more usual subjects of history, court life, war, and the chase, or in accessory groupings connected with those subjects.[4]

Clearly, the man who five years later would write "Death is the mother of beauty" in "Sunday Morning" did not know that to some Buddhists "fleeting" and "transitory" are not terms of reproach. Platonism is so strong in our minds that it is difficult to follow the late, northern Buddhist embracing of those shadowy figures on the wall of the cave; Buddhists agree that sensed objects are illusions, but unlike Plato, Buddhists believe that the sun is an illusion too. In theory, then, some Buddhists do not necessarily find the mortal world inferior by comparison to some immortal world, and in practice, as we have seen, meditation can include strong and accurate sensation. Plato's positive ideal is an analogue to the inherent positivism of having ideas; Buddhists derive their theory from the passivity of meditative experience. "Pictures of a fleeting world" are not always "colored with Buddhist reproach"; such pictures may be marked by total immersion and suspension of judgment. This was a mode very congenial to Stevens, though he seems not to have learned it by studying the East, nor to have recognized that it flourished there.

Stevens read—not widely or deeply—about India, China, and Japan, he saw the exhibits of Oriental objects and read explanatory notes, and from the first he was charmed by the minute particulars of Chinese and Japanese art. Near the end of his life, according to Peter Lee, "His knowledge of East Asian Literature was based on Arthur Waley's translations from Chinese and Japanese poetry; . . . he had a strong taste for Oriental paintings."[5] A Brahmin balance and a Hindu theory of illusion were part of his vocabulary, but nowhere is there evidence that through his readings he connected Buddhist or meditative practice to his own experience, to his own ability to apprehend minute particulars with detached clarity. He simply liked Chinese and Japanese style at times, and at times it became his own:

And last of all in my package of strange things from the East, a little poem written centuries ago by Wang-an-shih:

"It is midnight; all is silent in the house; the water-clock has stopped. But I am unable to sleep because of the beauty of the trembling shapes of the spring-flowers, thrown by the moon upon the blind."

I don't know of anything more beautiful than that anywhere, or more Chinese—and Master Green-cap bows to Wang-an-shih. No: Wang-an-shih is sleeping, and may not be disturbed.   (*L* 138)

Highest praise as well as charming courtesy. The poem opens with negations: darkness, silence, the clock stopped. One might think the next lines too excited to be meditative, but the verb indicates only that he is unable to sleep—is awake, watchful, attending the moment—and the moment could hardly be more simple. No metaphors: the moon, not man's mind, has made the shadow-image on the blind. The speaker's state of mind, what he thinks or feels—if he thinks or feels—is not described; we only know he cannot sleep in the presence of these "trembling shapes," unreal as shadows on the wall of the cave, transitory as moonlight: "pictures of a fleeting world." More's Maya shimmering in her veils; indeed, nothing but shimmering veils. The clothes have no emperor. Stevens: "I don't know of anything more beautiful than that anywhere, or more Chinese."

Stevens toyed with China in 1916 in the first section of "Six Significant Landscapes" (*CP* 73–75), and in a slight way he produced a pleasing impression of the unity of all things:

I

An old man sits
In the shadow of a pine tree
In China,
He sees larkspur,
Blue and white,
At the edge of the shadow,
Move in the wind.
The pine tree moves in the wind.
Thus water flows
Over weeds.

But the lines are didactic ("thus") and the final image is imported by imagination, rather than emerging from the scene itself. The stanza is imagist, more like section II that by means of deliberate comparisons strives for effect, especially a novel effect that calls attention to the act of inventive composition:

> The night is of the color
> Of a woman's arm . . .
>
> . . . .
>
> A pool shines,
> Like a bracelet
> Shaken in a dance.

The section that does more justice to the wakefulness of Wang-an-shih is V, which begins with a series of negations and ends with a pure image that takes its effect from clarity, not dazzle, and which may well owe to China a debt deeper than allusion:

> ### V
>
> Not all the knives of the lamp-posts,
> Nor the chisels of the long streets,
> Nor the mallets of the domes
> And high towers,
> Can carve
> What one star can carve,
> Shining through the grape-leaves.

The human world constructed, an entire city of sculpting metaphors, gives way to the thing itself. This is perhaps the earliest marriage of Stevens' own taste with Eastern Buddhist tastes, and makes one look again at the star in "Nuances of a Theme by Williams" (1918). William Carlos Williams had begun by drawing attention to his own reaction. (Stevens quotes the lines at the head of his own poem):

> *It's a strange courage*
> *you give me, ancient star:*
>
> *Shine alone in the sunrise*
> *toward which you lend no part!*

Stevens, however, immediately detaches the star not just from the sunrise but also from himself, and then from humanity itself:

> ### I
>
> Shine alone, shine nakedly, shine like bronze,
> That reflects, neither my face nor any inner part
> of my being, shine like fire, that mirrors nothing.
>
> ### II
>
> Lend no part to any humanity that suffuses
> you in its own light.
> Be not chimera of morning,

Half-man, half-star.
Be not an intelligence,
Like a widow's bird
Or an old horse.   (*CP* 18)

The poem does not demand, as "The Snow Man" does, a medita-
tive reading of "mirrors nothing," but all the meditative corollaries
are there: suppression of self accompanies a brighter shining of the
star; human imagination is distrusted, for it "suffuses" the universe
"in its own light," producing a world "half-man, half-star." He ex-
horts the star not to be an "intelligence," that is, not to be appropri-
ated by human beings, "Like a widow's bird / or an old horse."

The standard reading of the poem is romantic; the star is being
exhorted, like Ahab, to stand forth "his own inexorable self." But
when "my being . . . humanity . . . intelligence" are all deplored,
when the poem in section II circles about human degradation, it is
hard to take the human self as the proper model for the ideal. Per-
haps, indeed, being—a pure being—without "intelligence," a pure
"Shine . . . shine . . . shine . . . shine . . . that mirrors nothing,"
with no reflecting and no lending, is what he suggests. Perhaps Ste-
vens means what he says, and in obvious contrast (hardly a nuance)
he has revised Williams's poem from a lesson in being oneself to a
lesson in being one's not-self.

Throughout this study we have taken the position that meditative
conciousness can occur naturally; I am suggesting that in Stevens it
did, and from early in his career led him to sympathize with Chinese
and Japanese art. His sympathy for Master Wang-an-shih came, per-
haps, not so much from his reading as from his disposition and his
walks.

17
Stevens' Walks

We should have a noun for an imaginative sensibility opposite to that of the fanatic: *balanced, moderate, impartial, detached* point the direction, but those adjectives too easily imply reasonableness or indifference or unthinking stolidity. *Intellectual* may be closest; if we admired nonfanatics we would have a more charming word. Whatever we choose to call this nonfanatic but imaginative sensibility, Stevens was. From early in his journals, just out of college, he was quick to change opinion, finding himself more committed to the process of changing opinions than to the habit of holding them: "Finally (for today) my opinions generally change even while I am in the act of expressing them. So it seems to me and so, perhaps, everyone thinks of himself. The words for an idea too often dissolve it and leave a strange one" (*SP* 165).

These changes of opinion gave him at times the air of an intellectual coquette, but after his first book in 1923 and perhaps before, this intellectual coquetry was the result not of a defensive diffidence (which he frequently felt) but of a genuine skepticism on the part of a genuine thinker. Stevens was more than most poets committed to thinking, and less than most poets committed to any thought. His dedication to process, and detachment from product, is parallel to his lifelong love of a few topics—the sun, fecundity, imagination, bareness, the thing itself—and of the way those few topics could engender so many poems. Some readers complain that his poems had only two parents: imagination and reality. One could equally marvel that those parents had so many fine children. Furthermore, Stevens was right: the truths worth discussing are few and simple, while the play of the mind about those truths is infinitely various.

If we seek a real fanaticism in the young Stevens as a counterpoise to imaginative play, we find it in his walks. In those early years, 1900–1914 (between the ages of twenty-one to thirty-five), Stevens did not just stroll or take a turn around the block. He liked "all day trips, hard and fast":

> Left the house after breakfast and went by ferry and trolley to Hackensack over in Jersey. From H[ackensack] I walked 5½ miles on the Spring Valley road, then 4 miles to Ridgewood, then another mile to Hoboken and back towards town 7 miles more to Paterson: 17½ in all, a good day's jaunt at this time of year.
> (August 10, 1902; *L* 58)

> Walking is my only refuge from tobacco + food; so today I put on an old suit of clothes + covered about twenty miles or more—to Palisades and back.   (March 13, 1904; *L* 69).

> Walked from Undercliff to Fort Montgomery yesterday, just failing of West Point. A good 42 miles. Up at four.   (April 18, 1904; *L* 71)

> I am quite shattered by the walk I took yesterday—not less than thirty miles. The walks up and down town keep me in condition; but they have been rather few and far between of late. . . . Yet it was, as you say, such a glorious day: almost a September sun (I know them all).   (August 23, 1909; *L* 158)

> I walked from Van Cortlandt Park (the Broadway end of the Subway) to Greenwich, Connecticut—say, by my route, and judging from the time it took, roughly thirty miles. . . . I got to Greenwich at about half-past seven, with the rising of the moon.
> (August 26, 1912; *L* 177)

He walked hard, numbing his body and mind (that verb will not seem extreme to readers who have walked over thirty miles a day) into a kind of submission which engendered not profound thought so much as mindless, acute attention to sensory detail. He wrote on December 27, 1898:

> Yesterday afternoon I took a walk alone over Mount Penn. . . . Clusters of green ferns spread here and there. There were some brilliant spots of moss. . . . I found a large snail, some yellow dandelions and a weed. . . . At the top of the hill I sat down on a pile of rocks. . . . I forget what I was thinking of—except that I wondered why people took books into the woods to read in summertime when there was so much else to be read there that one could not find in books. I was also struck by the curious effect of the sunlight on the tops of the trees while so much darkness lay under the limbs.
> (*SP* 24)

Conventional sentiments—he was in 1898 a sophomore at Harvard, home to Reading for Christmas—but this combination of anti-intellectual sentiment and acute sensation, begun sophomorically, would become a lifelong and radical interest.

When he returned to Harvard after Christmas he contributed a story to the *Advocate* about a student, tired of his books, who longed for "mere gazing":

> The warm afternoon beat against his windows courageously, and his face was hidden in a book whose leaves were following one another to the end. He was unconsciously enjoying the sun upon his back, though he probably imputed his good humor to the philosophy he was reading. . . . The afternoon was still full and diaphanous, and he stood there longer, perhaps, than he had intended; for he knew that whatever time he gave to the mere gazing at things was lost to Science and his own Wisdom.   (*SP* 26–27)

Off went the student on a brisk walk until "the houses getting thin, he turned back again, his eyes bright, his cheeks burning."

On those walks taken since childhood—"I have always walked a great deal, mostly alone" (*L* 125)—Stevens spent a good deal of time merely gazing:

> I lay on the edge of the Palisades basking on a rock. . . . I noted that the grass has come out of curl and stands high and straight. And such a multitude of flowers—wild honey-suckle, wood-violets, purple and white, strawberry blossoms white as crystals, dandelions, buttercups—wonderful to see. The dogwood trees were sheer white and the lilac-bushes sheer lilac.   (*SP* 224)

The white things white, the lilacs lilac. Hardly an exercise in imagination; more a mood of clarity than dazzle, and typical of his reveries halfway through hikes. He continued his solitary walks—to and from the office, in Elizabeth Park—to the end of his life.[1]

At times his mere seeing took on transcendental overtones. The following passage is very close to Thoreau's desire for *the* robin, *the* twig in "Spring" of *Walden*. The context of this epiphany is again a long walk, the forty-two miler of 1904 "just failing of West Point":

> Managed to get across the river by seven and from that time until half-past six at night, I walked without stopping longer than a minute or two at a time. How clean + precise the lines of the world are early in the morning! The light is perfect—absolute—one sees the bark of trees high up on the hills, the seams of rocks, the color + compass of things. . . . The sun blazes wonderfully then, too. The mere roofs are like pools of fire. . . . In the distance the Sound shot up a flare. . . .

> I heard a dry murmur in the reeds (may I never forget it); and I
> observed a robin sitting on a stone. For all that, there were hun-
> dreds of robins. . . .
>
> God! What a thing blue is! It is one of the few things left that bring
> tears to my eyes (or almost). It pulls at the heart with an irresistible
> sadness. It seems as if it were the dusk of the lost Pleiades, as if it
> were a twilight where any moment the fairies might light their
> lamps.   (*L* 71–72)

It is quite naive of Stevens, or of us, to think that his responses
depended only on morning or evening light (or on a perceptive indi-
vidual). A forty-two mile walk, twelve hours "without stopping
longer than a minute or two at a time," like breathing exercises or any
other sensory repetition, can make the light perfect, Long Island
Sound flare. Mountain climbers know well the sky's "heartbreak
blue." The murmur in the reeds becomes a murmur for all times.
Thoreau: "I heard a robin in the distance, the first I had heard for
many a thousand years, methought, whose note I shall not forget for
many a thousand more."

By Stevens' own testimony, his walks were not only periods of
exercise and awareness when books were neglected; he intended and
achieved dramatic physiological change:

> I doubt if there is any keener delight in the world than, after being
> penned up for a week, to get into the woods on such a day—every
> pound of flesh vibrates with new strength, every nerve seems to be
> drinking at some refreshing spring. And after one has got home,
> how delicious to slip into an easy chair + to feel the blood actually
> leaping in one's pulses, a wild fire, so to speak, burning in one's
> cheeks.   (*L* 62)

In both Yogic and Zen traditions, disciplined exercise is used to turn
off the mind and to heighten body awareness. In Zen tradition, at
least, this heightened body awareness helps one achieve an open,
thoughtless receptivity. In the following passage Stevens seems to
pass through this entire cycle, from monotonous exercise to height-
ened sensation to "just sitting" and merely seeing, and he recognizes
that such merely seeing (one wonders what lines of "Endymion" he
was reading) could be the basis of poetry:

> Just as I was starting for the pike I saw two rabbits in the road and
> stopped to watch them—they cocked up their ears to listen but
> heard only the clear, bell-like, notes of some bird high up in an

apple tree—they twitched their eyes at me and watched breath-
lessly, until I went on and left them undisturbed.

Later, when I had returned I saw a barn-swallow feeding its
young. The brood were leaning on the edge of the nest which had
been built under an eave of the barn and were waiting for the
mother bird. She was circling and skimming around the barn-yard
for insects. When she found one, she would take a swift, reconnoi-
tering wheel in front of the nest and on the next round settle down
plunging the bug, or whatever it was, into the squeaking mouth of
some unfed youngster. There was a squabble and twitter of unsatis-
fied pains from the rest and off went the mother for another bug.

In the afternoon I sat in the piano room reading Keats' "Endy-
mion," and listening to the occasional showers on the foliage out-
side. The fronds of a fern were dangling over my knees and I felt
lazy and content. Once as I looked up I saw a big, pure drop of rain
slip from leaf to leaf of a clematis vine. The thought occurred to me
that it was just such quick, unexpected, commonplace, specific
things that poets and other observers jot down in their notebooks. It
was certainly a monstrous pleasure to be able to be specific about
such a thing.   (*SP* 45)

"Lazy and content" after his exercise, he notices an "unexpected"
event: "I saw a big pure drop of rain slip from leaf to leaf of a clematis
vine." The "thing" is "specific," and he is "specific" about it. This
specific perception, with no hint of symbolism or metaphor, accompa-
nied by no reported thought, gives him a "monstrous pleasure" and
seems a proper basis for art. Why? He is taking pleasure in suchness,
when one sees what Emerson ecstatically called "the miraculous in
the common," or what the Japanese poet Bankei (1622–1693) more
meditatively regarded:

> Alone in mountain fastness,
> Dozing by the window,
> No mere talk uncovers Truth:
> The fragrance of those garden plums![2]

What has occurred in this moment of clarity, when the pure drop is
seen in its specificity, is a change in the relation of observer to ob-
served. A preparatory walk, followed by lazy relaxation, has put him
in the state of self-loss described by the Japanese Zen master, Dogen:

> As he listened,
> Mindlessly,
> The eavesdrops entered him.[3]

That is why such a "quick, unexpected, commonplace, specific
thing" is jotted in a poet's notebook without symbolism, interpreta-
tion, or even association. This perception of suchness is an experien-

tial category marked by clarity, an absence of thought, and a plea-
sure all its own.

In a long letter to Elsie, January 17, 1909, just after their becoming
engaged, Stevens described an ice storm and his own taste for icy
asceticism:

> The Park was turned to glass to-day. Every limb had its coating of
> ice and on the pines even every needle. The sun made it all glit-
> ter, . . . Yesterday afternoon I went a-Parking too. The snow was
> just commencing to fall, blowing from the North, the direction in
> which I was going, so that my cheeks were, shortly, coated with
> ice—or so they felt—It would be very agreeable to me to spend a
> month in the woods getting myself trim; for while I enjoyed that
> flow of North wind and the blowing snow, I felt as if I did not enjoy
> it quite as much as possible—as if (in so short an experience of it) it
> did not go the deepest possible.   (*L* 121–22)

It is interesting how thoroughly Stevens here equates enjoyment of
winter with both physical participation and physical change; he wants
winter to "go the deepest possible" and makes it clear that total
immersion in physical "experience" is the way to accomplish that
desire. He goes on to discuss, in the strongest terms he ever used, the
sensuality of his asceticism:

> There is as much delight in the body as in anything in the world and
> it leaps for use. I should like to snow-shoe around our hills—from
> Leesport to Adamstown, from Womelsdorf to East Berkeley—long
> trips made at a jog that would pull the air down and give one life—
> all day trips, hard, fast; and I could do it very well except for the
> need of being here.

Jogging on snowshoes all day into the blowing snow to enjoy becom-
ing one with winter. No uncertainty here: Stevens is a member of that
ascetic minority—runners, climbers, hikers—who love endurance ex-
ercise. He loves it not because it hurts, but because it makes his body
real, because it gives him a vivid sense of physical existence, because
it gives him "life." Just thinking of such trips, he feels he inhabits a
body that "leaps for use." And this exercise at its extreme gives him
the feeling of inhabiting not only his body but also winter, for then
the enjoyment of wind and snow would "go the deepest possible."

It is hard to say exactly how those ascetic habits affect the poetry of
that "damned monk," as W. C. Williams called Stevens.[4] We should
expect descriptions of suchness and of meditative being as a coun-
terpoise to imaginative being:

> as if
> There was a bright *scienza* outside of ourselves,
>
> A gaiety that is being, not merely knowing.   (*CP* 248)

His vivid sense of his body, of its delight in simply existing in action, may be responsible for his desire to empathize with other purely physical existences, to escape from his own body only to inhabit another through a kind of kinesthesia: "to feel . . . / As a boat feels when it cuts blue water." And as in Eastern traditions, there is probably in Stevens a connection between this exhaustive, repetitive physical activity resulting in a change of consciousness, and the change of consciousness that can occur in more passive states. That is, a long walk helps one see the "big, pure drop of rain slip from leaf to leaf of a clematis vine." Most certainly, such moments of passive awareness do not depend on thought, feeling, or imagination: they share self-loss. Stevens' ascetic walks may be directly related to his capacity for detachment and to the detached quality of his sensuality, a quality that stamps his work.

In his letter, Stevens comes back a few paragraphs later to bareness. He distinguishes two kinds, the bareness of the real world of routine existence, and the bareness of the icy park in January:

> Poe illustrates, too, the effect of stimulus. When I complain of "bareness"—I have in mind, very often, the effect of order and regularity, the effect of moving in a groove. We all cry for life. It is not to be found in railroading to an office and then railroading back. . . . But books make up. They shatter the groove, as far as the mind is concerned. They are like so many fantastic lights filling plain darkness with strange colors.

Here "bareness" refers to the dull routine of daily existence. The solution to such bareness is the life of the imagination—thought, art, books—in short, dazzle: "fantastic lights filling plain darkness with strange colors." That bored concept of bareness or emptiness or nothing is familiar to us—as is its antidote, a romantic aesthetic based on imagination, creativity, and a positivity endemic to our culture: "While it can lie in the temperament of very few of us to write poetry in order to find God, it is probably the purpose of each of us to write poetry to find the good which, in the Platonic sense, is synonymous with God" (*OP* 222).

Stevens goes on in his letter, however, to discuss another bareness, another real world, the park in January:

One's last concern on a January night is the real world, when that happens to be a limited one—unless, of course it is as beautiful and brilliant as the Park was this afternoon. I did not tell you that we counted eight ducks flying rapidly through the air. Walter said, "I wouldn't have missed that." It was just what was needed . . . Wild ducks!

As Stevens says in "Credences of Summer":

> This is the barrenness
> Of the fertile thing that can attain no more.   (*CP* 373)

"Limited" is the link; he is thinking of the park as another kind of barren reality. But if the first barrenness was the negative one of ordinary tedium and ordinary perception, this second bareness is the beauty and brilliance of extraordinary perception in a world limited to the thing itself: wild ducks! And in this paragraph beauty and brilliance do not come as dazzle, by way of books, art, and imagination or the good, God, and Plato, but as clarity, pure sensation of the thing itself.

The two passages contrast not only the boredom of commuting and the beauty of nature; he is speaking of two types of bareness, two aesthetics. There is one problem addressed (the dullness of the ordinary self) and there are two ways of solving it: the romantic way, which is the dazzle of more self, and the meditative way, which is the clarity of less.

Stevens was quite possibly writing "The Snow Man" in 1920. It was printed in a large group of poems, "Sur Ma Guzzla Gracile,"in the October 1921 issue of *Poetry,* so the group must have been submitted by August. Perhaps it was written in the spring of 1921, but by December 1920 he wrote to Harriet Monroe, "I shall be sending you another batch of things bye and bye," and in the previous March (1920) he had groaned,

> We have been standing by, waiting for the snow to melt. The process murders me with tedium, to such an extent that I have neither thoughts, feelings, nor interests; but merely maintain my status quo among the living. But as this state is more or less universal and with most people perennial I suppose I ought not to complain.

He is complaining of the bareness of routine existence. The vocabulary springs from ordinary consciousness, and in this context having "neither thoughts, feelings, nor interests" certainly sounds like annihilation. Most critics assume this context when Stevens says one must have a mind of winter to regard the frost, and not to think, and to behold nothing. If such negations govern our expectations, the mind of winter will look bleak indeed.

But there is another context for "The Snow Man," the "barrenness / Of the fertile thing that can attain no more," when winter goes "the deepest possible." And that is the context clearly defined by Stevens' letter: "I shall explain 'The Snow Man' as an example of the necessity of identifying oneself with reality in order to understand it and enjoy it."

The confluence of "something" and "nothing," the close relationship of "The Snow Man" to "The Course of a Particular"—a relationship suggested by Stevens' repetition of scene and imagery, but explained only by a meditative paradigm—is perhaps the subtlest of meditative issues, as we have seen in chapter 6. At least since the Ch'an master Tung-shan, enlightenment through the void (*cheng*) has been identified with "enlightenment arriving from particularity" (*p'ien*). That is, meditative passivity with respect to nothing and with respect to something produces the same result. According to one master, "When the objective event is not distorted by a subjective stain, it unites with the world of the Void."[5] In Tantric tradition also, void and suchness enlightenment ("beholds . . . the nothing" and "the thing itself") are united in meditation, which Guenther calls, "the ineffable experience of that in which tranquillity and insight were singularly blended."[6]

The psychological model on which these assertions are founded is neatly summarized in the *Abhidharma:*

> Karman and the emotions are the reason for the way of the world, and among them the emotions are the principal condition. By way of the dominating influence of the emotions, Karman is able to project a new existence (*punarbhavaksepasamartha*); it cannot be otherwise. Karman which has been enabled to project a new existence will become this new existence under the conditions of the dominating influence of the emotions; it cannot be otherwise. Therefore, the emotions are, indeed, the root of the fact that the way of the world (*samsara*) continues to exist, since it is well-known that the emotions are the principal condition. But when the power of the emotions has been exhausted then the world will cease to exist; it cannot be otherwise.[7]

Therefore, in meditative psychology the perception of suchness and voidness can occur *only* when the beholder is "nothing himself," and by definition the perception of "the thing itself . . . at last . . . concerns no one at all." Those concerned will hear a different cry: misery in the wind, perhaps.

Since "what words can express comes to a stop when the domain of the mind comes to a stop," as Staal explains,[8] these issues are not easy to discuss. One of the finest suggestions of the identity of particularity and voidness, however—of how the "lilac bushes sheer lilac" in the middle of a long walk may be an aspect of "the nothing that is"— comes in Tung-shan's reply to a monk seeking the void:

> Once a monk asked Master Tung-shan, "Winter comes and summer comes. How do we avoid them?" The Master answered, "Why should you not go where there is neither summer nor winter?" The monk persisted: "How could it be that there is neither a summer nor a winter?" The Master said, "You feel hot in summer and cold in winter."[9]

We are advised to remain in sensation itself without interpretation or abstraction: one is hot or cold, but there is neither summer nor winter. "This creates a third world without knowledge," as Stevens writes in "Esthétique du Mal." Thus to the man with experience in meditative detachment, the symbolist interest in sensation, and the imagist interest in conciseness and clarity, could serve very well to express perception in a state of no-mind. Once again, Valéry: "To see is to forget the name of the thing one sees." The dogwood trees and the lilac bushes, at first identified as abstract categories, have become only color: "sheer white and . . . sheer lilac."

The listener in the snow is not Pound in the metro, having a sudden emotion, or Yeats, alternately embracing and rejecting love, but the Zenist whom Yeats encountered in Waley a few years after "The Snow Man," for whom nothing exists and for whom the self, when it is nothing, reflects and becomes one with that reality. Such a winter state of mind is not annihilation, nor does it require any particular creed or occult assertions; it is simply an extreme of that state of mind when

> Dazzle yields to a clarity and we observe,
>
> And observing is complete and we are content,
> In a world that shrinks to an immediate whole,
>
> That we do not need to understand, complete
> Without secret arrangements of it in the mind.   (*CP* 341)

18
Overlooking Nothing: The Critics

> Being is the universal power, visible nowhere in itself and yet visible
> everywhere in all things. It is what all things share through the fact
> that they are. Being is not a thing like other things, and therefore
> can appear to man only as nothing, yet it is what all things must
> participate in if they are to exist at all.[1]

J. Hillis Miller's explanation shows why mediators shun words. His
is a fair and clear attempt to express *ideas* of nothing that might be
corollary to an *experience* of nothing, but the words trip themselves.
If being "can appear to man only as nothing," how can it appear to
Hillis Miller as being? A meditative nothing phrased as something
almost invariably appears ecstatic. If we read of a "being . . . univer-
sal power . . . present . . . visible in all things," we are reading
Emerson—"the currents of the Universal Being circulate through
me"—only one step from theism or a neoplatonic oversoul: we are
not reading Stevens' "the nothing that is." And because of these
positive words, necessitated by the inherent positivity of having ideas,
Miller's tone, like Emerson's, cannot avoid elation, élan vital, the
original vitality of being. Conversely, if we seek ideas of *nothing* that
do not suggest elation and vitality, we will find those ideas positively
negative, suggesting annihilation or at least depression. It might be an
extreme of mechnistic reduction to say that binary cortical operations
defy passivity (versus a balanced neutrality); nevertheless, it seems
that only no-mind can achieve no-tone: disappearance of self.

Without really misreading, but on the other hand without knowing
the meditative possibilities of *nothing,* Miller slides inexorably toward
an expressible ecstatic positivity. Louis Martz, considering medita-
tion in a Christian and neoplatonic framework, says it "brings the
imagination into play."[2] The same scenario was followed by Santa-
yana and is acted out by even the admirers of "The Snow Man": to be
accepted in our culture, mysticism must lead to imagination.

228

Richard Macksay shows just why imagination creeps into the picture, in Stevens' poetry as well as in our criticism. He says of "The Snow Man": "After the poet's ascesis the effect is transport (ekstasis)."[3] What is this "transport"? Macksey compares it to a passage from "Notes toward a Supreme Fiction" dominated by the following:

> It is possible, possible, possible. . . .
>
> .　.　.　.　.　.　.
> 　　To find the real,
> To be stripped of every fiction except one,
>
> The fiction of an absolute.　　　　　　　　　(*CP* 404)

But this is not the snow man; the speaker of "Notes" is walking Stevens' tightrope between the "absolute" of belief and the "fiction" of imagination, and his skepticism here is betrayed both by the verb moods—action is potential instead of accomplished—and by the avoidance of true mystical paradox: "fiction of an absolute," with its subordinating preposition, could have been said by Freud. And the poetic realization of this fiction, composed half of the imaginative self, is quite naturally expressed through triumphant metaphor:

> 　　　　　　　—Angel,
> Be silent in your luminous cloud, and hear
> The luminous melody of proper sound.　　　(*CP* 404)

In "The Snow Man" where is the melody, much less a "luminous" or even "proper" one, or—conspicuously—just plain "sound"? Even that word is purged to "nothing" while "listens" is abstracted to "beholds." The absolute of "The Snow Man" is not the melody of imagination, but of silence.

Macksey has confused two of Stevens' idealisms and some moods peculiar to each, which leads him to a remarkable conclusion: "This is the supreme activity of 'The Snow Man.' The experience is one which gives rise, for all its emptiness and its fictive realization, to a sense of power and plenitude."[4] Interestingly, both of Macksey's statements have a future ring: "After ascesis . . . comes transport" and "the experience . . . gives rise . . . to a sense of power." A sense of both transport and power may arise *after* the poem in Macksey's mind and heart, but that surge of energy is neither suggested within the poem, nor advocated by it.

Macksey (and Santayana) propose a schema that most Western critics—right through Bloom—have shared: concentration—ascesis—

imaginative transport, as best suggested in "Evening without An-
gels." Stevens, too, in imaginative moods would tolerate nothingness
only as a phase in the artist's progress, a phase preparing the beholder
for supreme and fecund fictions:

> As if nothingness contained a métier,
> A vital assumption, an impermanence,
> In its permanent cold, an illusion so desired

> That the green leaves came and covered the high rock.   (*CP* 526)

Unlike the critics, however, Stevens shows a perfect knowledge of the
anti-imaginative position: the green leaves of existence, covering the
rock of nothingness, are an "illusion" created by desire, a desire that
springs from fear of nonexistence. This is not one whit removed from
the Hindu doctrine of *maya,* nor is it far (as a plot) from subject A's
fear of nothingness and her willed return, as she put the boundaries
back on the vase (see chapter 5).

What to Stevens is a closely observed, occasional pattern of reac-
tion to nothing, his own reaction, made exciting by the shift of verbs
from conditional to declarative, is to most critics a moral imperative:
nothingness must always be resisted. Harold Bloom's reading of "The
Snow Man" in *The Poems of Our Climate,* discussed in chapter 2, is
especially interesting because more than previous critics he feels that
the poem is central to Stevens' work, that the psychological condition
to which it refers is central to both Emerson and Stevens, and that it
poses a real dilemma. Instinctively, one might say, Bloom's study and
this study have gravitated toward psychological questions clustered
around the listener in the snow. Bloom's questions have been ours:
"What, we can ask about Stevens' seeing soul, can one behold in the
'nothing that is'? How can the beholder possess 'nothing,' in a posi-
tive sense of seeing-with-amazement?"[5]

Bloom's answer is to propose for all of Stevens a three-stage As-
cetic's Progress: "One must have a mind of winter, or reduce to the
First Idea; one must discover that to live with the First Idea alone is
not to be human; one must reimagine the First Idea."[6] "The Snow
Man," one might think, represents stage 1, but Bloom consistently
passes moral judgment on stage 1 as a form of annihilation (reduc-
tion) and for some reason—perhaps because he likes the poem so
much—he decides that "The Snow Man" progresses past this reduc-
tion. Thus, as we saw in chapter 2, like Macksey and Santayana, he
must make nothing into a fiction in order to admire it:

"Being" in Stevens can live with the First Idea, but at the price of
ceasing to be a "human" being. The listener, reduced to nothing,
remains human because he holds something shagged and rough,
barely figurative, yet still a figuration rather than a bareness. This
"nothing" is the most minimal or abstracted of fictions, and yet still
it is a fiction.[7]

Bloom uses "still" twice to indicate continuation, but the stamp of
"The Snow Man" is that "shagged" and "rough" are *not* still there at
the end; nothing is. Bloom goes on to insist quite improbably that the
bareness takes place in the first half of the poem, while by its end we
have a passion (as in Macksey's reading) that hints at the return of
imaginative divinity in another poem, "Tea at the Palaz of Hoon": "I
was the world in which I walked." In order to locate bareness early in
the poem, and to make the end positive, Bloom must ride right over
Stevens' own reading. This passage reveals why:

But, before this god-making takes place in the self, the last mytholo-
gies must be stripped from the human. This appears to be the pur-
pose of the reduction in "The Snow Man." The poem does not go on
to intimate the return of the divinity to man; that takes place in its
gorgeous counterpoem, "Tea at the Palaz of Hoon." The Snow Man
is not yet Hoon, but he is going to be, and that *potentia* is felt in the
pathos of his poem's closing trope. The worst possible reading of
this poem, I suggest, is the canonical one received from Stevens
himself, when he said in a letter: "I shall explain 'The Snow Man' as
an example of identifying oneself with reality in order to understand
it and enjoy it" (*L* 464). That takes care of less than half the poem,
the part in which "reality" is "regarded," and not the larger part in
which "reality" is "beheld" and so begins to become a passion.[8]

"A passion." The battle lines are drawn. The major American
intellectual tradition of our time, a humanism cradled in New York
that has spawned not only our best minds but also our best apologies
for immersion in an imperfect world (a counterweight to California so
necessary and effective that the Mississippi seems a natural crack)—
that tradition will not tolerate self-loss. Nietzsche, Ruskin (Bloom's
models), and Santayana admired the mystic's negation only when it
led to passionate imaginings; so here, Bloom, liking the poem so,
must censor its passivity to bring it within his own canon: " 'reality' is
'beheld' and so begins to become a passion." *Nihil obstet.*

Bloom performs the same operation on other meditative passages:

There might be, too, a change immenser than
A poet's metaphors in which being would

> Come true, a point in the fire of music where
> Dazzle yields to clarity and we observe
>
> .   .   .   .
>   complete
> Without secret arrangements of it in the mind.   (*CP* 341)

Bloom says that in these lines "the world has become a poem."[9] That is curious, since a "poet's metaphors" and the mind's "arrangements" are explicitly transcended. Stevens seems to be saying that there are moments when the world is *not* a poem, yet very nice indeed. Bloom will not believe that Stevens can give up on imagination.

The fun of this issue is that we really have an argument. Vendler dislikes the same passages as Bloom; she and Bloom agree that the enemy is "mysticism." Vendler is repulsed by "high, hazy references to 'a point in the fire of music.' " At least Vendler is reading the passage and attacking its weak point: "a point in the fire of music" *is* hazy, though suggestive of stasis *in the midst of* passion (if I could trace the connection between the passivity of meditative concentration and the passivity of musical concentration—a connection that may well exist— I would). At issue is a moral judgment: Vendler does not like static models of peace. Our modern moral tradition requires tension, para-dox, anxiety. Unlike Bloom, she is straightforward (though perhaps uninformed) about the "mysticism" on the page, and she can therefore only breathe a sigh of relief that Stevens' mysticism is a minor key: "Those secret arrangements in the mind are finally more interesting to Stevens than his forced faith in an instinctual beatific vision."[10] An "instinctual beatific vision"? A high and hazy reference indeed. Bloom deflects meditative passages; Vendler smites them. To Bloom, nirvana must lead to thought. To Vendler, nirvana means annihilation: " 'What other condition short of such absolute extinction, is meant to be described?' . . . The question has remained for Western Europeans substantially as Colebrooke framed it."[11]

Vendler's moral assertions are always clarifying. She dislikes many of Stevens' epiphanies, both his earthy epiphanies (the chants in orgy of "Sunday Morning" or "Credences of Summer") and his blank epiphanies, which she usually takes as a symbolist "blank cold" signify-ing ruin, waste, decay—that *is* in Stevens too: the "silence of a rat come out to see" (*CP* 503) or "an imperium of quiet, / In which a wasted figure . . . / Propounds blank final music" (*CP* 362). But she reserves her greatest scorn for the more ascetic epiphany of nothingness, a vacuum she abhors, and therefore she seizes with understandable glee upon the passage in which Stevens, always willing to change opinion, considers his own meditative tendencies and cries, "Annihilation":

It may be that they mingle, clouds and men, in the air

Or street or about the corners of a man,
Who sits thinking in the corners of a room.
In this chamber the pure sphere escapes the impure

Because the thinker himself escapes. And yet
To have evaded clouds and men leaves him
A naked being with a naked will

And everything to make. He may evade
Even his own will and in his nakedness
Inhabit the hypnosis of that sphere.   (*CP* 479–80)

This passage occasions Vendler's attack on "an eye turned away from the imaginative and the social alike, evading poems and feelings and even, finally, evading the human, the poet's own will. In that case he becomes, in a more sinister way, Emerson's transparent eyeball, a pure sphere, hypnotized."[12] Unlike his critics, however, Stevens displays a very exact—not high and hazy—knowledge of that sphere.

"Hypnotized" expresses perfectly our culture's fear of self-loss. In hypnosis the will is not just suspended but given over to another person. We could say that in hypnosis both free will and animal will are given up—indeed, given away. There is nothing like that activity in all of Stevens, although he uses the word. For almost twenty years we have been able to document the differing physiologies of meditation and hypnosis, and for much longer we have known that meditators report neither total loss of will, nor subjugation to others, nor amnesia, while hypnotized subjects report neither self-loss nor exquisite clarity, nor revelation.[13] "Hypnosis" serves to convey Vendler's (and Stevens') fear of self-loss and to repeat, in more apparently scientific terms, the old charge of annihilation.

The great difference between Stevens and most of his critics is that even in antimeditative poems Stevens feels the gravitational pull of nakedness, or not-self, and his poems are bent, like light, as they pass through that gravitational field. Readers who will not acknowledge the pull of that force, who treat meditative consciousness as a frightening or immoral or escapist mistake, or as only a prelude to imagination, are missing a major source of tension in his work. When Frost climbs birches up *toward* heaven, then swings back down ("Earth's the right place for love"), the action is only a silly detour—and the poem only precious, and the author only a dilletante—unless we acknowledge a pull both ways. So, for instance, Bloom finds no tension in section IX of "Esthétique du Mal" because to him the concept of "lustred nothingness" is absurd from the start, as is a "prince of the proverbs of pure poverty." Such dazzling language may lead us to suspect (correctly) an antimeditative mood, but to hear the richness of the passage as it unfolds we must feel the proximity and pull of bareness, the dominant minor key:

> Effendi, he
> That has lost the folly of the moon becomes
> The prince of the proverbs of pure poverty.
> To lose sensibility, to see what one sees,
> As if sight had not its own miraculous thrift,
> To hear only what one hears, one meaning alone,
> As if the paradise of meaning ceased
> To be paradise, it is this to be destitute.   (*CP* 320–21)

If read with no sympathy for meditative issues, the passage is simply negative. But a complex tone is established by the very real possibility that "pure poverty" and "destitute" suggest nirvana, a traditional Buddhist comparison:

> My poverty of last year was not real poverty.
> This year it is want indeed.
> In last year's poverty there was room for a piercing gimlet.
> In this year's poverty even the gimlet is no more.[14]

Such valuing of "poverty" and the "destitute" was not at all alien to Stevens:

> We have excluded absolute fact as an element of poetic truth. But this has been done arbitrarily and with a sense of absolute fact as fact destitute of any imaginative aspect whatever. Unhappily the more destitute it becomes the more it begins to be precious. We must limit ourselves to saying that there are so many things which, as they are, and without any intervention of the imagination, seem to be imaginative objects.   (*NA* 60)

If "sensibility" (self), imaginative sight and "the paradise of meaning" (meaningful interpretation born of desire) are at times best lost, and if in that condition only "what one sees" and "only what one hears, one meaning alone" can become a final finding of the ear, then we may well approach "destitute" wondering what key this piece is in. For several lines Stevens floats, then he resolves the key:

> Here in the west indifferent crickets chant
> Through our indifferent crises.   (*CP* 321)

The "pure poverty" that has flirted with a meditative "one meaning" has now become ennui (as in "The Snow Man" and "The Course of a Particular," ennui would signal an indifferent passivity instead of a detached passivity) and we feel the force of his return to the tonic major, imagination: "Yet, we require / Another chant, an incantation" (*CP* 321).

For most romantics, the supreme activity of the imagination produces joy; its supreme inactivity produces despair. The reactions of critics to Stevens' meditative tendencies indicate that romantic aesthetic theory has exacerbated a popular bias against passivity. Therefore even those who wish to admire Stevens' more mystical moments are likely to get the formula wrong. Consider Frank Doggett on "The Snow Man":

> Existence as opposed to blankness or warmth and affection and consciousness as opposed to black cold and nothingness—these are the oppositions of a poet who finds extinction the only alternative to "the moment of light," the present and continuous moment of being.[15]

But in "The Snow Man" blankness *is* "existence" ("nothing . . . is"), nothingness is also a condition of "consciousness" ("nothing himself, beholds"), and therefore "extinction" (nirvana: to blow out) may well be a "moment of light."

Behind this chapter looms a single issue: is meditative, or Eastern negation genuinely alien to Western culture? The debate is only beginning, for we have hardly begun to study what the Buddhists have to say, or the mind can do. We can at present give two responses: first, most commentators agree that the *experiences* of mystics—Sufi, Hindu, Buddhist, Christian, primitive—are comparable: "we know for certain that mystical experiences in very similar forms are found throughout history and all over the world."[16] Although we may debate the names to be included on a list of meditators or ecstaticians (from Dionysius Areopagitica through Eikhart to Jones Very, Alan Watts, and Wallace Stevens), reports argue for the universality of mystical experience.

But if experience is universal, doctrine is not. The second aspect of the question is more difficult: are mystical, or meditative experiences in particular, in the Christian world almost always translated into positive doctrine, while in the Hindu-Buddhist world their negative aspects are respected? Edward Conze, and many Catholic and psychiatric writers, stress the similarity of East and West in doctrine as well as experience: "When we compare the attributes of the Godhead as they are understood by the more mystical tradition of Christian thought, with those of Nirvana, we find almost no difference at all."[17] Conze's work thirty years ago was introducing Buddhism to the West, and perhaps he strained to find introductory parallels. Unless "as they are understood by the more mystical tradition" is very narrowly interpreted, however, Frits Staal and others disagree: after the experience, Christian and Buddhist doctrines go in opposite directions.

The difference between Conze and Staal becomes quite important when brought to bear on specific examples. For instance, to Zaehner or Merton or other Christian syncretists asserting the identity of East and West,[18] Stevens' nothing might be both Nietzschean and Buddhist, but to me and to many Asian scholars it is *either* Nietzschean *or* Buddhist but cannot be both. Staal again:

> The Buddhist concentration on emptiness (*sunyatasamadhi*) is not the same as nihilism (*sunyatadrsti*), the philosophical view that "nothing exists." The latter is similar to Nietzschean, Heideggerian, or existentialist nihilisms, which try to express that "nothing" "exists" and which are sometimes erroneously compared to Buddhist doctrines. The Buddhist literature is very explicit in making this distinction. Another Chinese text, translated by Lamotte . . . has the Buddha say to Ananda:
>
> > I regard a person who adheres to the doctrine of emptiness (*sunyatadrsti*) as incurable. If someone believes that there is a personality, be it as big as Mount Sumeru, I am not surprised and I don't blame him. But if some idiot believes in the doctrine of emptiness, be it as small as the sixteenth part of a single hair, I cannot allow it.
>
> The matter is summed up in the following verse of Santideva, translated in accordance with de la Vallée Poussin: . . .
>
> > When the notion of emptiness is accepted, the notion of existence disappears. Later, through the repetition of "nothing exists," that notion itself also vanishes.
> > When an existence that has been denied is no longer perceived, how then could a nonexistence that has no further support be conceived?
> > And when neither existence nor nonexistence are conceived any more, then when there is no other way, the mind achieves peace.[19]

If nihilist and meditative approaches to nothing differ so, one can easily imagine that all systems of assertion and doctrine differ from nonconceptual Buddhist traditions, and some scholars find, reasonably enough, that even Christian meditative *practice* reflects, or prefigures, the theoretical positivity common to our culture. As Guenther explains:

> Another and very important feature of Buddhist meditation is the fact that to concentrate on an object of one's choice is not the main aim or an end in itself. To become free from all ties that fetter us intellectually and emotionally is the aim, and this also implies that freedom has to be gained even from the object on which concentrated attention has been bestowed. In this respect Buddhist meditation is diametrically opposed to the meditation practices of Ignatius of Loyola in his *exercitia,* where the object of meditation is kept constant and not transcended.[20]

Beyond doubt, significant differences in doctrine between Buddhists and Judeo-Christians or (Moslems) place even allegedly similar experiences in very different contexts. Instead of finding creation divided between the human and the natural (as in Genesis), or the divine and satanic (as in Manicheanism), or the divine and chaotic (as in Milton—depending on which Western tradition one follows), the Buddhists find all creation pretty silly. That or any other single adjective is inadequate, of course, but for all Buddhist sects this is *not* God's earth; no part of creation is divine. All life, including acts of consciousness (the fifth *skandha*), is flawed, whether silly or tragic. To Buddhists, we did not fall into this world's tragedy or farce through moral error—through overreaching pride or knowledge—but through existence: God blowing life into the clay would be for them the moment of the fall. Nothing can be made in God's image. There is no perfect garden of things.

It is often said that the oriental arts do not include tragedy. There is some truth to that: since *all* the world and consciousness is tragic, there is little hope of purging or renewal *within* this world. And such extreme distrust of this world has hardly encouraged a Greek tradition of holding an ordinary mirror to nature. However, many have noted a similar paradox in Christian tragedy: the only true salvation, to some Christians, lies in leaving this world for another. Christians (being materialists) have often conceived the problem in spatial and temporal terms: the other world of heaven is in some other space, some other time. Buddhists (being psychologists) conceive the problem in terms of consciousness: this world is ordinary consciousness, and the other world, the perfect alternative, is meditative consciousness. Salvation, then, is possible in the present moment. One can renounce all conditioned awareness for unconditioned awareness. Thus they may also say that all things are made in God's image; paradise is here.

But just as there *is* Christian tragedy, no matter how richly paradoxical its doctrinal roots, there is also Buddhist tragedy, or art of the tragic, especially in Mahayana traditions stressing immersion in this world. The differences are in style of expression and style of salvation. The Greco-Judeo-Christians ramble about in this tragic creation, exploring every nook and cranny of disaster; characters—some right, some wrong—abound, and conversations (Creon-Oedipus, Kent-Lear) are therefore important. The Buddhists, believing that all conditioned consciousness (rather than error) is the root of evil, are more clear, concise, withdrawn. Clarity, suggesting a meditative epistemology, is a primary virtue. The major characters of Buddhist tragedy are not men and women of various fates making various assertions, but self and not-self, assertion and negation. So the Christian tragic sense tends toward *plots* of redemption, the Buddhist tragic sense toward *images* of immersion. Consider this poem by Buson (1715–1785):

> I feel a sudden chill—
> In our bedroom, my dead wife's comb,
> Underfoot.[21]

Or another poem of Buson's on mandarin ducks, symbols of a long, happy marriage:

> A mandarin pair!
> But the pond is old, and its weasel is watching there.[22]

Even more chilling in its original order: "mandarin ducks / weasel's / peep / pond / is old." Raised on Japanese poetry, one Zen master finds Western art "too thickly encumbered by what is dispensable. It's as if the Western artist were trying to hide something, not reveal it."[23]

It would be misleading to suggest that the tragic mode is as characteristic of Buddhist art as it is of European, but once one has learned the qualities of meditative enlightenment, one may be surprised at the number of worldly Buddhist poems and at the Buddhist encouragement of doubt, anxiety, and disillusionment as prerequisites to true (*prajna*) knowledge. The four moods of Zen art, for instance, are *sabi*, or isolated detachment at the edge of ease and unease; *wabi*, or poverty, humility, immersion in the common; *aware*, or sadness in impermanence, bittersweet mutability; and *yugen*, or the mysterious, essential calm of nature.[24] Of these four moods only the last, *yugen*, is really alien to our modern poetry, though it was perhaps familiar to Wordsworth.

Buddhists do differ from Judeo-Christians in their emphasis on knowledge as the means to salvation. Staal says that to Buddhists ignorance is the "root of all evil," while to Christians knowledge always risks heresy.[25] To Buddhists Doctor Faustus would not be an evilly ambitious overreacher, but mistaken in his science. His *quest* they would applaud, but in a kind of negative variation on the theme of Napoleon snatching the crown, they would have Faustus destroy his ego by himself, without help from any God: Faustus neglecting to snatch the crown. So to complicate matters, we must remember that the meditative salvation through consciousness, no matter how many negations are involved, is a willed human act (or nonact), and that to many meditative traditions there is nothing higher in the universe than a perfect use of the human mind. Thus much of their art celebrates the human, and a Buddhist humanism might constitute less of a paradox than a Christian or Jewish humanism.

Perhaps the crucial difference, the sticking point in the Western response to nirvana, lies in our emphasis on tension, anxiety, self-criticism as the context of enlightenment, versus the Buddhist emphasis on serenity as the context of enlightenment. This difference could reflect a genuine figure-ground disagreement: we see activity as the universal ground against which any inactivity is isolated, and they see inactivity as the universal ground against which any activity is isolated.

Such a proposition is subject to numerous caveats. Doubt *precedes* Buddhist enlightenment, Middle Way subtleties blend action and inaction, and in practice the futile engagements of the existentialist can be hard to distinguish from the peaceful involvements of the *bodhisattva*, although perhaps continued angst is encouraged in one and not the other. This angst of the "evilly compounded, vital I" is, however, as much modern as it is Western:

> The imperfect is our paradise
> Note that, in this bitterness, delight,

> Since the imperfect is so hot in us,
> Lies in flawed words and stubborn sounds.   (*CP* 194)

Neither Socrates nor Saint Francis nor Sir Thomas More was noted for angst as opposed to serenity, and for that matter our suffering heroes have often won peace. Lear's personality change through the trauma of self-doubt ("The great rage, you see, is killed in him") may not be so different from Chinese practices stressing doubt and anxiety—even madness—as preconditions to enlightenment, and some sects (especially Ling-Chi) devalue meditative enlightenment in favor of more complexly disturbing and theatrical situations.

Still, let us return to the central proposition: on the one hand, valuing the epistemology of ordinary consciousness, the West tends to value action, conflict, and anxiety during and after enlightenment; on the other hand, valuing the epistemology of meditative consciousness, the East tends to value inaction, and serenity during and after enlightenment. Learning through suffering is, from Aeschylus to the present, different from learning the nonexistence of suffering. That is precisely the difference that sometimes angers Westerners. "In short, human thought is awareness in motion, while Samadhi is awareness at rest."[26] In this perspective, Stevens' affinity with the Buddhist orientation is clear: Stevens was primarily interested in detached consciousness. That activity out there, ordinary reality, was to Stevens always a figure against the ground of an essentially calm awareness. He was as far from being a novelist as a wordsmith can be, and even his plays strain to become a drama of serene consciousness. Stevens had little interest in the tragic mode; even in relation to consciousness he was a comic poet:

> One's tootings at the weddings of the soul
> Occur as they occur.   (*CP* 222)

If one distinguishes Western and Eastern artists along the lines of interest in cause-effect events, assertion, anxiety on the one hand, and consciousness, negation, serenity on the other, then Stevens would seem at least half oriental.

It has been enormously difficult for a culture raised on seeking wisdom through reason, language, and manipulation, to apprehend that truth which is a state of mind, not "something that can be conveyed from one man's mind to another's," as Chatterji said to Yeats. But Stevens knew somehow, from his walks or reading or temperament, that "the center that he sought was a state of mind, / Nothing more" (*OP* 112). With exceptional clarity and discipline he became a master of detachment.

Helen Vendler distinguished three Stevens "manners":

> The first, in an ecstatic idiom, proclaims, sometimes defiantly, the pure good of being, the worth of vigorous life, the earthy marriages, the secular joys of ploughing on Sunday. The second, despairingly and in tones of apathy, anatomizes a stale and withered life. The third and most characteristic form is a tentative, a diffident, and reluctant search for a middle route between ecstasy and apathy, a sensible ecstasy of pauvred color, to use Stevens' own phrase.[27]

To this list we might add a fourth manner. In an idiom of clarity, Stevens represents pure being as perceived in meditative consciousness:

> The poem of pure reality, untouched
> By trope or deviation, straight to the word,
> Straight to the transfixing object . . .
>   with the sight
> Of simple seeing, without reflection.   (*CP* 471)

PART IV

The Comedy of Consciousness: Stevens' Long Poems

*In Samadhi . . . every thought is a complete process,
containing the stages of arising, subsisting, and dissipating.*
Garma C. C. Chang

*The mind of the poet describes itself as constantly in
his poems as the mind of the sculptor describes itself in his
forms, or as the mind of Cezanne described itself in his
"psychological landscapes."*
Wallace Stevens

19

Fragments and Change

"These fragments I have shored against my ruins."

The words are T. S. Eliot's from the end of "The Waste Land," penned, apparently, in the mental institution at Lausanne in 1922. From fin-de-siècle Paris, fauves, and cubists, through Yeats's rough beast to W. S. Merwin and García Márquez, much twentieth-century art has used fragments when "the center cannot hold," to shore up ruins. A ruined twentieth century, bombed repeatedly by one fragmentation device or another, is the violent, chaotic, and frightening age we were taught to find predicted in Arnold's "Dover Beach,"

> Swept by confused alarms of struggle and flight
> Where ignorant armies clash by night.

Critical attention is—and should be—circling back to major modern fragmented works and to the issue of fragmentation in those works. What is it? By now these are cultural issues: what can we make of a fragmented world? Surrealism, Sisyphus, alienation, the absurd, catch-22, protean man, postmodern discourse, metafiction; the words associated with answers to that question have entered our vocabulary. We haven't yet comprehended, however, how some of our finest artists have approached the subject. After deciphering the symbols and allusions in "The Waste Land," Pritchard argued in 1980, we still find only a formal and rhetorical mess: "There is surely no 'tone' in which a believable 'speaker' makes this and that pronouncement; no dramatic progression, as in Yeats or Frost; no punctuation to guide us in connecting one event to the next; no qualifications or degrees of emphasis."[1] The problem is not only how to interpret, line by line, a fragmented work, but how to describe and account for its form. In modern painting, music, and dance, even more than in literature, experiments in fragmentation have often dominated or divided the field, and current discussions of movies and television versus language arts claim an inherent fragmentation in image structures, as opposed to sentence structures.

The long and fragmented poems of Wallace Stevens, called his meditations (including at least "Montrachet-le-Jardin," "Notes toward a Supreme Fiction," "Esthétique du Mal," "Credences of Summer," "An Ordinary Evening in New Haven," "The Auroras of Autumn," 1942–1950), have drawn considerable attention in the last fifteen years. A period of puzzling out stanzas has yielded to increasing bewilderment about what these poems are and what they do. The individual fragments are open to notoriously different readings, while the disjunct form itself remains a mystery. Harold Bloom approached these poems with unusual caution and admirable candor:

> "Notes" is a notoriously elusive text to write commentaries upon, and I myself am no longer particularly happy with what I have written about it in the past or with nearly anyone else's commentary either. It is all too easy to underestimate how labyrinthine the poem is in its subtle evasions and in its preternatural rhetoricity, its excessively acute awareness of its own status as text. Stevens had the uncanniness and the persistence to get about a generation ahead of his own time, and he is still quite a few touches and traces ahead of ours. His major phase, from 1942 to his death in 1955, gave us a canon of poems themselves more advanced *as interpretation* than our criticism as yet has gotten to be. My theoretical emphasis in these chapters has been on finding a critical procedure for describing disjunctions or crossings in the rhetoric of poetry, because Stevens is the most advanced rhetorician in modern poetry and in his major phase the most disjunctive.[2]

Although both "The Waste Land" and Stevens' meditations are long and disjunct, a crucial difference comes immediately to mind: Stevens is comic. His fragments are not shoring up ruins. Few readers fail to find a vivacity in Stevens' wit that makes these poems affirmative long before we understand just how and why they function. Long and disjunct works do not necessarily spring from satire or despair— symbolist, surrealist, existentialist, or otherwise. Nor are such works limited to the modern age, or to poetry. Since 1800, a number of our very best or most interesting works of art—Wordsworth's *Prelude,* Beethoven's late quartets, Emerson's late essays, novels by Joyce and Faulkner, Eliot's "Waste Land," Pound's *Cantos,* Beckett's plays, jazz forms, modern dance stressing improvisation, and Stevens' meditations—are long, disjunct works, not episodic but spontaneous and varied in special ways, quite unlike any works of art before 1800 in European civilization.

Those works raise new formal issues. My thesis is simple: the structure of *some* of those long, disjunct works is the structure of ordinary consciousness as seen from the meditative point of view. Such works are radically fragmented and essentially comic: they present a detached view of the comedy of consciousness. Such a structure differs from the stream of consciousness form, which suggests meaningful psychological connections between elements apparently fragmented but unconsciously related, and it differs from other models of fragmentation (episodic or repetitive form) proposed by Kenneth Burke, Barbara H. Smith, and others. Moreover, the meditative point of view offers us not only a description of this fragmented form, but also a way of reading and reacting that makes sense of its rhetoric. That is, meditative traditions describe the benign context that makes this kind of fragmentation comic: "passions continue to rise up and disappear in the realm of quiescent wisdom."[3] Meditative detachment thus offers a unique point of view toward the fragmentation of consciousness, and may play a role in the modern search for impersonality. So the issue before us is Stevens' long poems: what are they, how do we read them and why? The scope of the works to be considered warns the reader that as Thoreau said, we will shoot and run like a Parthian, and not, like a Roman, settle colonies.

Stevens' long poems are not easy, and a printed exegesis of even three consecutive pages would be enormously complicated and deadly dull (although these poems can be "taught" orally in the classroom quite well). We will begin with a few simple propositions.

The first proposition is that Stevens always loved variety, always loved change for its own sake. He loved changing ideas—as he said, "My opinions generally change even while I am in the act of expressing them" (*SP* 165). He loved titles that allow for change: *The Grand Poem: Preliminary Minutiae* was his first title for his first book; "Notes toward a Supreme Fiction" was one of his most ambitious works; "It Must Change" is part of "Notes." He often addressed directly the theme of change; the world ("it") is a play, or rather a theater, or rather a cloud, a cloud changing so fast that only Polonius would dare call it by name:

VI

It is a theatre floating through the clouds,
Itself a cloud, although of misted rock
And mountains running like water, wave on wave,

Through waves of light. It is of cloud transformed
To cloud transformed again, idly, the way
A season changes color to no end,

Except the lavishing of itself in change,
As light changes yellow into gold and gold
To its opal elements and fire's delight,

Splashed wide-wise because it likes magnificence
And the solemn pleasures of magnificent space.
The cloud drifts idly through half-thought-of forms.   (*CP* 416)

Stanzas 3 and 4 are simple enough, as change is *described* through the images of cloud, season, and light changing in space. But in stanzas 1 and 2, change is not only described as a process; it occurs in the noun, or pronoun. What is "it"? In these stanzas change occurs in the subject itself. It is a theatre / cloud / rock / running like water / of cloud / to cloud. Here, then, change is not a matter of some essence (cloud, season, light) changing *appearances,* but of the essence itself changing—having no single essence at all, beyond the pronoun *it.* World without antecedent. The lines are a conflation of Chinese-imagist disjunction, and syntactic assertion. And why is "it" changing? "Idly . . . to no end."

In addition to changes of appearance expressed by verbs and adjectives, and changes of essence expressed by disjunct nouns in apposition, we might expect (and find) a third type of change in Stevens: change of voice, tone, or mood. Any claim can be put forward seriously, or in jest, or indifferently, and so forth. And by whom? The above passage, in fact, is happened upon after some delightful shifts of voice:

We stand in the tumult of a festival.

What festival? This loud, disordered mooch?
These hospitaliers? These brute-like guests?
These musicians dubbing at a tragedy,

A-dub, a-dub, which is made up of this:
That there are no lines to speak? There is no play.
Or, the persons act one merely by being here.

VI

It is a theatre . . . .   (*CP* 415–16)

To the problem of shifting nouns for this life (festival / mooch / tragedy / no play / act . . . by being) Stevens adds the complication of a shifting tone, and thus we come to the entire theater-cloud passage already battered by high seriousness, flip satire, and direct change of mind ("no play / Or") within seven lines.

Plays of voice can be extremely various in the long poems; the speaker can change as well as the tone. At the opening of "Esthétique du Mal," for instance, an unknown and never personalized narrator observes a complacent man at a cafe in Naples. But who speaks the stanza's last line? Who conjures up the rattle of death?

> He was at Naples writing letters home
> And, between his letters, reading paragraphs
> On the sublime. Vesuvius had groaned
> For a month. It was pleasant to be sitting there,
> While the sultriest fulgurations, flickering,
> Cast corners in the glass. He could describe
> The terror of the sound because the sound
> Was ancient. He tried to remember the phrases: pain
> Audible at noon, pain torturing itself,
> Pain killing pain on the very point of pain.
> The volcano trembled in another ether,
> As the body trembles at the end of life.   (*CP* 313–14)

Someone, in that last line, is not just remembering clichés coined at the demise of Pompeii. For someone, pain and death seem suddenly less ancient, less remembered, more present and familiar: the death rattle shakes the body at the end of life. It is hard to read that line complacently. In the last two lines, or perhaps during the "As," another consciousness—perhaps the narrator's—has rushed into the poem.

That vivid and less pleasant consciousness disappears to allow the complacent man three more lines, shockingly venal after the death-rattle, then comes back with its own shifts of mood and tone, which I will indicate by slashes:

> As the body trembles at the end of life.
>
> It was almost time for lunch. Pain is human.
> There were roses in the cool cafe. His book
> Made sure of the most correct catastrophe. /
> Except for us, Vesuvius might consume
> In solid fire the utmost earth and know

> No pain (ignoring the cocks that crow us up
> to die). / This is a part of the sublime
> From which we shrink. / And yet, except for us,
> The total past felt nothing when destroyed.   (*CP* 314)

"Except for us:" in sudden fulsome rhetoric an unexpected, omniscient consciousness slashes again across the page, intoning the truth that nature is indifferent to our crises; nature knows no pain. The proposition, "Pain is human," has shifted from a tone of complacency to one of revelation. Then this consciousness makes a drier, more intellectual, and more ironic comment on that passionate insight: "This is a part of the sublime / From which we shrink." Finally, in a sequence similar to the "no play / Or" quoted from "Auroras," the consciousness adds an adversative "And yet" and ends the stanza with a ruminative aside, repeating the phrase "except for us" in yet another key: "And yet, except for us, / The total past felt nothing when destroyed."

Such a shifting voice creates problems quite similar to those Pritchard mentioned in "The Waste Land." Who, in the withered, caustic elegance of Eliot's first four lines, finds vitality so painful?

> April is the cruellest month, breeding
> Lilacs out of the dead land, mixing
> Memory and desire, stirring
> Dull roots with spring rain.

The voice is omniscient, speaking in the most present general tense: "is" plus participles. Although the voice has irony, it speaks impersonally. We might say this voice of ironic, eloquent omniscience is the complementary opposite of Stevens' affirmative, eloquent omniscience, which T. S. Eliot had certainly read in "Sunday Morning," published in *Poetry* magazine in 1915. Indeed, Eliot in 1922 may well have been answering a passage from "Sunday Morning." No theory of afterlife, said Stevens' omniscient voice in 1915, will satisfy this lady pondering life, death, and religion. No theory of afterlife

> has endured
> As April's green endures; or will endure
> Like her remembrance of awakened birds,
> Or her desire for June and evening, tipped
> By the consummation of the swallow's wings.   (*CP* 68)

"April's green" is immortal through constant change ("In her green going, a wave interminably flowing"—Stevens' "Peter Quince at the Clavier," also published in 1915). Stevens' woman is denying heaven by affirming her participation in the flow of time from past to future (from remembrance to desire), and in the natural cycles that, through rebirth, are a constant. April is the symbol of natural cycles within historical, linear time: desire, as the Buddhists point out, propels us down the track of linear time. In a perfect inversion of the passage seven years later, Eliot's voice finds April the cruellest month because rebirth in the flow of time from past to future ("memory and desire") is a curse. April, rebirth, memory, and desire in linear time: without Christ. Those were the issues on Sunday morning in 1915 and 1922. And since both Stevens and Eliot were regular subscribers and contributors to *Poetry* in those years, it is easy to believe we have here a crossing of those two sensibilities, Eliot essentially tragic and Stevens essentially comic.

But if Eliot took up Stevens' argument on Stevens' terms, in the very next lines he began to play with voice in ways Stevens had not yet attempted:

> Winter kept us warm, covering
> Earth in forgetful snow, feeding
> A little life with dried tubers.

Who is "us"? Did we slide from present general to past specific just because of a change of seasons?

> Summer surprised us, coming over the Starnbergersee
> With a shower of rain; we stopped in the colonnade.

By now the omniscient voice in the present general has become a specific voice narrating the definite past, and by the end of the stanza someone named Marie will say, "I read, much of the night, and go south in the winter." In just a few more lines, God will speak, as he did to Ezekiel ("Son of man"), and some omniscient prophetic "I" (surely not Marie) will show us fear in a handful of dust. So the problems mentioned by Pritchard begin. Who is speaking the first sentence, who the second, who the rest of the stanza? And what is their relation to each other? What do we make of this sequence of fragments, fragments not just of ideas or of mood, but of voice?

Before we answer those questions—quite differently for Stevens and for Eliot—let us look more closely at Stevens' love of change, and see how it shades from love of process to fragmentation. "Process" art may imitate the act of working toward something: the poem, the subject, the idea or the feeling "finds itself" as the work unfolds.

Some poems are actually written that way; others are designed to suggest a process of "wanderings in search of truth," as Pound called it, retaining the "defects inherent in a record of struggle."⁴ In several major poems such as "Sunday Morning" and "The Idea of Order at Key West," not as disjunct or as long as the meditations, Stevens showed his interest in watching the mind at work, and his opening description "Of Modern Poetry" (1940), itself a sentence fragment, has become a touchstone description of process art: "The poem of the mind in the act of finding / What will suffice."

Helen Vendler took a giant step forward in Stevens criticism when she pointed out the process of potential action becoming accomplished action through irrational shifts of verb mood, or through other fragmentations, within a single Stevens sentence. Here a sky that "never clears" gives way to "if [it] cleared" and finally to a clarity, "now":

> It was an old rebellious song,
> An edge of song that never clears;
> But if it did . . . If the cloud that hangs
> Upon the heart and round the mind
> Cleared from the north and in that height
> The sun appeared and reddened great
> Belshazzar's brow, O, ruler, rude
> With rubies then, attend me now.   (*CP* 207)

My own favorite of such Presto! passages, in which the real is pulled out of the hat of the imagined, comes in one of Stevens' last poems, "The Rock" (emphasis mine):

I

Seventy Years Later

> It is an *illusion* that we were *ever alive,*
> Lived in the houses of mothers. . . .
>
>   .   .   .   .
>   The houses still stand,
>
>   .   .   .   .
> The lives these lived in the mind are at an end.
> They never were . . . The sounds of the guitar
>
> Were not and are not. Absurd. The words spoken
> Were not and are not. It is not to be believed.
> The meeting at noon at the edge of the field *seems like*
>
> An invention, an embrace between one desperate clod
> And another in a *fantastic* consciousness,
> In a *queer* assertion of humanity;

A *theorem proposed* between the two—
Two figures in a nature of the sun,
In the sun's design of its own happiness,

As if nothingness contained a métier,
A *vital assumption,* as impermanence
In its permanent cold, an *illusion* so *desired*

That the green leaves came and covered the high rock,
That the lilacs came and bloomed, like a blindness
    cleaned,
Exclaiming bright sight, as it was *satisfied,*

In a *birth* of sight. The blooming and the musk
Were being alive, an incessant being alive,
A particular of being, that gross universe.   (*CP* 525–26)

The section is a lesson in how to go from the sterile to the fecund and from the alienated to the cosmic (for here the nothingness of nonexistence is feared) in a single sentence. In the bridge, so to speak, he says drily that the personal romance is only a "theorem proposed," then, pivoting on the image of the sun, he intensifies the feeling with "vital assumption," and finally, repeating the terms of the first line he says that "being alive" is an "illusion so desired" that it has been accomplished out of nothingness by sun and will—the will of the poet and the will of the universe. Global and personal creation are one.

Now this passage, and the Belshazzar passage, and the phrase "the mind in the act of finding / What will suffice" reflect a happy teleology: process proceeds toward the sufficient. If this lyric pattern were the sum of Stevens' love of process and change, the meditations would be very different poems. Little attention has been given to Stevens' love of moving out of, as well as into, epiphanies, his habit of watching the idle transformations come, and then go. In the long poems, when all the stops of rhetoric are pulled, the experienced reader expects even the largest, brightest cloud to dissipate. Near the end of "Notes toward a Supreme Fiction" such an epiphany dissolves as we watch:

You remain the more than natural figure. You
Become the soft-footed phantom, the irrational

Distortion, however fragrant, however dear.
That's it: the more than rational distortion,
The fiction that results from feeling. Yes, that.

They will get it straight one day at the Sorbonne.
We shall return at twilight from the lecture
Pleased that the irrational is rational,

The perfectly serious and incantatory "You remain . . . You / Become" turns into the serious but casually confident "That's it." This is the "supreme fiction" defined, and yet the *tone,* that casual, complacent, academic certainty, generates the self-mockery of the Sorbonne line. Once imagined, the Sorbonne takes on a life of its own, and suddenly we are strolling the streets of Paris. "Until." If a cat runs across its path, this poem will meow.

The process of moving out of as well as into epiphanies, ideas, and moods, is not just a possibility in the long poems, it is the rule. And this rule puts tremendous emphasis on change, variety, transformation as the subject of each poem. Such change, being endless, is not teleological. The mind is always in the act of finding the sufficient insufficient and the insufficient sufficient. Indeed, the ends of most of Stevens' long poems suggest that an endless process has been arbitrarily cut short; the poem was going nowhere, and could have gone on forever, with insights won and lost, won and lost. Consider the final lines of "Montrachet-le-Jardin," "Esthétique du Mal," "The Auroras of Autumn," and "An Ordinary Evening in New Haven":

> But let this one sense be the single main.

> And yet what good were yesterday's devotions?
> I affirm, and then at midnight the great cat
> Leaps quickly from the fireside and is gone.   (*CP* 264)

> And out of what one sees and hears and out
> Of what one feels, who could have thought to make
> So many selves, so many sensuous worlds,
> As if the air, the mid-day air, was swarming
> With the metaphysical changes that occur,
> Merely in living as and where we live.   (*CP* 326)

> In these unhappy he meditates a whole,
> The full of fortune and the full of fate,
> As if he lived all lives, that he might know,

> In hall harridan, not hushful paradise,
> To a haggling of wind and weather, by these lights
> Like a blaze of summer straw, in winter's nick.   (*CP* 420–21)

"Know" has no direct object. While he "meditates a whole," the process of knowing goes on and on, blazing and fading and blazing like the lights of the fitful aurora.

> It is not in the premise that reality
> Is a solid. It may be a shade that traverses
> A dust, a force that traverses a shade.   (*CP* 489)

Such undirected openness in the long poems forces us to consider language as medium rather than as statement (after all, "what good were yesterday's devotions?") and to read for transitions ("traverses": where will he go next and how will he get there?). But another aspect of these cloud transformations is less obvious and perhaps more important: there is no irony. The voice of these poems gives itself, sincerely, to any number of contradictory propositions, or to sincerity itself, or to irony, with wholehearted and momentary commitment. Then as each cloud dissolves, the voice lets go. The effect is a remarkable detachment, innocence and openness quite unlike the overriding irony of the voice of "The Waste Land." Eliot is consistently disillusioned, Stevens inconsistently illusioned. Stevens' poems commit themselves over and over again to each moment's perception. Compare Emerson's advice in "Self-Reliance": "Speak what you think now in hard words and tomorrow speak what tomorrow thinks in hard words again, though it contradict everything you say today." If Emerson's hardness seems more fervent than Stevens' wit, it is perhaps because Emerson was ecstatic; Stevens was meditative.

Stevens was writing a poetry of the mind in the act of finding, losing, looking, finding, and losing the sufficient. The process is endless and essentially goal-less. The wandering mind is observed, even indulged: the poem neither directs nor resists vacillations. The individual pieces are complete sentences, meaningful and moving, but the structure is cubist collage. This is the heart of Stevens' style in the long poems. They are as structurally radical as the "field of action" process poems of postmoderns, full of "unbridged transitions" and "brilliant improvisation" (Perloff's terms),[5] but as in jazz, the fragments are expressive. Let us consider one example of this wandering form in a remarkably mercurial section of "Notes toward a Supreme Fiction": "It Must Be Abstract." If we can agree on what happens in the text, then we can argue in subsequent chapters what it means.

Just before this section (VII), Stevens has proposed and dismissed a "giant of the weather," and has come happily back to "mere weather, the mere air." No matter what the giant means, the mood is one of welcome deflation, of going from large to small (probably from transcendental to mundane). The section opens, then, in a sort of exuberant commonsense tone and rhetoric. I will offer the original section entire, and afterward outline its essential structure as I read it. Here, then, is one of the more delightfully slippery sections in Stevens, which can serve as our test case of how and why he changes, how the transitions work and what kind of fragmented poems these are:

VII

It feels good as it is without the giant,
A thinker of the first idea. Perhaps
The truth depends on a walk around a lake,

A composing as the body tires, a stop
To see hepatica, a stop to watch
A definition growing certain and

A wait within that certainty, a rest
In the swags of pine-trees bordering the lake.
Perhaps there are times of inherent excellence,

As when the cock crows on the left and all
Is well, incalculable balances,
At which a kind of Swiss perfection comes

And a familiar music of the machine
Sets up its Schwärmerei, not balances
That we achieve but balances that happen,

As a man and woman meet and love forthwith.
Perhaps there are moments of awakening,
Extreme, fortuitous, personal, in which

We more than awaken, sit on the edge of sleep,
As on an elevation, and behold
The academies like structures in a mist.   (*CP* 386)

Whoever the giant is, he is gone and we first notice the simple diction and an aura of mundane ease: "It feels good. . . . The truth depends on a walk around a lake." The repetitions and the strings of appositives build a typically Stevens tone of civilized lyricism: "a walk . . . a composing . . . a stop . . . a stop . . . certain . . . certainty . . . a rest." The subject of the stanza is some nearly perfect moment when what will suffice has been found in the easiest way, in the most pleasant place. The three occurrences of "Perhaps" divide the entire section into (1) the scene by the lake, (2) a comment on that scene, and (3) an awakening into some unspecified revelation.

I choose this stanza for a test case because it is not obviously or outrageously disjunct or difficult. It could be read as a fairly consistent exposition of the way intellectual integrations ("composing . . . definition growing certain") are satisfying and may lead to more extraordinary insights ("behold"). But reading it that way, I find this mediocre poetry: long, slack, repetitive, with clumsy and unconvincing images of perfection. Instead, I find that within this apparent structure, nuances of tone and modulations of key take over and create the real subject: how the mind changes. Read this way, the section has three themes (A, B, C): A, the theme of rest by the lake; A–B, the bridge in stanza 4, in which the theme of perfect rest is found insufficient through its inherent complacency and theme B is anticipated; B, stanza 5, the complementary opposite of A: perfect rest has become mechanical sterility. Finally, theme C, in stanzas 6 and 7, introduces a totally new experience of awakening (versus rest), without the modulation of a bridge.

My description is clumsy partly because of the double vocabulary of *key* and *theme*. *Key* suffers the limitations of any musical analogy, while *theme* too easily misses the irrational nuances of tone, color, and modulation that move the passage from point to point. We have no good vocabulary for such a slippery, musical language form. A dramatic reading is best, and I will attempt to outline one here. If the reader will imagine possible reactions and alternatives to each phrase of the poem quoted, if one reads each of Stevens' statements as a basis for potential change, one comes, I think, closest to what Stevens was doing:

Stanza		Theme	
1	good as it is Perhaps truth a walk around a lake		A casual, spontaneous, easy tone and message: the ordinary will suffice. Sets up the
		A	complementary opposite: complacency.
2	body tires stop stop certain		So much stopping approaches entropy. As hepatica and defi-
3	wait certainty a rest Perhaps inherent excellence		nition grow equally certain, is complacency in bud? The key is not yet changed, but this "inherent excellence" resembles the static simplicity of "Poems of Our Climate." We are nearing an extreme of rest.
4	all Is well balances Swiss perfection		Bridge. With "all / Is well" the extreme is reached. Things
		A–B	stop in that direction.

The modulation introduces "Swiss," suggesting a new key: this lake scene is becoming too perfect, cute, sterile.

5   music of the machine
Schwärmerei   balances
balances

B

"Swiss" is taken to its extreme, and the new key is established: "good as it is" has become a mechanical sterility. The schmaltz of this music box is mocked.

6   meet and love forth-
with

We are now so balanced that human passion is also automatic. B is the dominant minor potential of the tonic A.

Perhaps   awakening
Extreme   personal

C

A dramatic change of key without modulation, although "love" may have suggested personal awakening. In spite of the parallelism of "Perhaps," the situation has totally reversed: "Awakening" replaces "rest," "extreme" and "personal" replace "balance" and "machine." The expected atmosphere of "familiar" and "forthwith" has changed to the unpredictably fortuitous. This revelation is radically disjunct.

7   more than awaken
behold academies
like structures

The theme of revelation has developed rapidly to full expression. A new metaphor is introduced, interrupting the scene by the lake.

"Academies like structures in a mist" is enigmatic: do we behold the academies' truth, or our misty distance from their academics? The vision ends on a strange note, and the curious flavor of that image will provide the transition to the next section, which Stevens begins by playing with Viollet-le-Duc's restoration of Carcassonne:

VIII

Shall we compose a castle-fortress-home,
Even with the help of Viollet-le-Duc?

I would think that at this point Stevens could have taken any number of directions. He chose, however, to react to the forced quality of his image "academies like structures" and to mock its grandiosity. Viollet-le-Duc's own obsessive restoration of the medieval town was much publicized during Stevens' youth, and now "we" set out to "compose" some analogous folly. The awakening revelation has itself quickly dissipated, and the transition to irony seems to depend solely on the characteristics of the image chosen for that revelation: "academies" (as in "Sorbonne") generated ironic humor: "A castle-fortress-home."

The primary argument for such a slippery reading is simple: "Swiss perfection," a music box with quaintly swarming notes, and loving "forthwith" strain our credulity as representations of perfection. Rather, they call into question the idea of perfection itself. And this is exactly the kind of tidy little perfection that comes of a desire for "good as it is," "All is well," and "balances . . . balances . . . balances." What is fascinating about the section and Stevens' technique is that one's distaste for such inert well-being is *not* anticipated in the text: the idea *self*-destructs. There is no irony in the first three stanzas. We all, I hope, have such moods of lake and flower perfection, and any such mood could be extrapolated to its extreme, then mocked. Stevens allows the thought full play: "The truth depends on a walk around a lake"—see "The Doctor of Geneva" for a thoroughly ironic treatment of "lacustrine man"—and the thought runs its natural course. For instance, I am not claiming that a tone or theme of entropy is developed in stanza 2: "body tires . . . stop . . . stop . . . certain." I am claiming that while the tone is still positive, a totally detached observer could see in the terms of this ideal the seeds of its demise. Entropy is simply one of several alternatives raised by the mood, probably in its essence, certainly as it finds expression. Every thought, every mood, every phrase raises possibilities of which a detached observer may be aware, possibilities that the mind may be about to follow. Such reading is not easy to perform; indeed, it is like a performance in which the pianist, say, is not "getting through" the notes, but "getting into" the piece, recreating each phrase as if it had just been found.

The consciousness behind Stevens' meditations, the ultimate voice of these poems, is that of the most detached observer watching the mind in the act of finding the sufficient insufficient, and vice versa. The speaker is really that part of the mind capable of reporting with-

out involvement or interference the rest of the mind's idle transforma-
tions of thought and feeling.

On the way to stopping the mind, most Buddhist traditions practice
concentration by watching the mind at work. According to Staal, "In
the process of meditation, such deliberation ('vitaka') initially assists
in directing the attention of the mind to its own movements."[6] The
reason the meditator watches the "windings round and dodges to and
fro" of his mind is to perceive the transitory, illusory, and insubstan-
tial quality of this *skandha* of conditioned consciousness. That is, just
as Stevens moved from love of change in the external "theatre float-
ing through the clouds / Itself a cloud, although of misted rock / and
mountains running like water" (*CP* 416), to love of change in the
internal theatre of thoughts, so also the Ch'an meditator, said master
Han Shan,

> should see all manifestations as clouds floating in the sky—changing
> and unreal. Not only the outer world, but all habitual thoughts,
> passions, distractions, and desires within one's own mind are, like-
> wise, insubstantial, non-concrete, rootless, and floating. Whenever
> any thought arises, you should try to find its source ; never let it go
> easily or be cheated by it. If you can practice like this, you will be
> doing some solid work.[7]

That last note of analytical discipline is interesting: thoughts and
passions are perceived as floating when one pays strict attention to
transitions. Han Shan continues, "Search out the point where your
thoughts arise and disappear. See where a thought arises and where
it vanishes; . . . look right at the arising point of the distracting
thought."[8] Rimbaud said he was "present at the birth of [his]
thought," and Perloff sees his discontinuity as parent to the modern
style, to "creation of a verbal field where the identity of the 'I' is
dissolved."[9]

In the lower stages of meditation, it is natural to become aware of
the flow of thought and feeling. This awareness does not interfere
with the flow; such awareness observes cortical events without becom-
ing involved. Indeed, in order to establish the calm of meditative
consciousness it is crucial *not* to oppose "distracting" thoughts, but
rather to let them pass through until a change of consciousness is
achieved and thoughts stop naturally. In this lower stage of medita-
tion, since one is not attached to the sufficiency or insufficiency of
each thought and feeling, the points of arising and disappearing—the

transitions—are unusually obvious. In ordinary consciousness, when we take seriously the *substance* of our thought and feeling, the center of each thought is noted: thought is a noun. In meditative consciousness, when we take seriously the *process* of our thought, the beginning and end of each thought is noted: thought is a verb.

Stevens, in his long poems, took the lyric process, the mind in the act of finding what will suffice, one step farther. He detached himself from the need to direct his consciousness toward the sufficient. He watched the mind going into and out of moments of lyric sufficiency; he then strung those lyrics and antilyrics along the threads of long poems; he took no ironic stance toward this process, but rather allowed each idea its day; his interest was in "the point where your thoughts arise and disappear," and thus transitions, how and why consciousness changes, come to our attention.

That part of the mind capable of detachment from the rest of the mind's "idle transformations" may well be what Wilder Penfield calls the "seat of consciousness" and Buddhists call the selfless center of pure awareness. That relatively impersonal center of awareness and will is the *ur*voice of Stevens' meditations, the single voice of not-self that allows the myriad voices of self to have their say, arising and disappearing in endless procession. This model explains the extraordinary detachment and undirected quality of the meditations, and also explains why these open, fragmented works are neither desperate nor ironic. Stevens is not rejecting or mocking the noumena of self, "so many selves, so many sensuous worlds"; rather, he is giving audience, in some remote space, to the comings and goings of his own thought: "When the mind is like a hall in which thought is like a voice speaking, the voice is always that of someone else" (*OP* 168).

Opus 130 and the Politics of Emotion

Everything [in Bach's Prelude no. 1, book two] will depend from that note and harmony. No foreign element enters into the harmonic framework of the piece. Up to the end of bar 13 [of Beethoven's Sonata in F-Sharp Major, op. 78, allegro] this is true of the Beethoven piece, also. But at the beginning of bar 14 something happens: a chord consisting of G sharp, A sharp and C double sharp, with an E sharp implied. This chord is a foreign agent to F sharp major, and it has cut across the simple F sharp major landscape without any preparation. If one listens to this music without stopping for anything, the effect of that unprepared chord will be to blot from one's mind all memory of F sharp as a tonic; in that very real character it has disappeared, so long as one continues to listen; and the effect of the music depends upon continuity of listening, since sound unfolds through time. This is a very real effect; it was the discovery of this possibility which brought the whole classical era in music of the eighteenth century in its train. Nothing like it will be found in any music prior to the eighteenth century. Once this foreign element has done its work the music can proceed to substitute a new tonality, and the elements of the dramatic conflict are all there.

This is the basis of classical sonata style; appreciation of this music depends on an ability to hear this effect and its consequences in the unfolding music, following the progress of the harmony (as distinct from the tune) as one follows the reasoning of an argument, and it is on this ability that full appreciation of Beethoven's five late quartets depends.[1]

Harold Truscott compares the progress of the harmony to the reasoning of an argument; perhaps a reasoned argument is better compared to the progress of a melodic line, with its linear development and the beauty of apparent inevitability. The harmonic shifts which Truscott says "cut across the . . . landscape without any preparation" are best compared to changes of voice, shifts of emotional and intellectual context that place even a repeated melody in a new perspective, shifts that often surprise and delight with the beauty of the unexpected. That, at least, will be my claim: that we have learned, as Truscott suggests, to listen to classical sonatas for shifts of key as much as for melodic line, but we have not yet learned to read analogous (and contemporaneous) language forms for shifts of tone rather than for argument. Our slow learning is probably due to the inevitable connection between language and statement; or as Stevens said after several bewildering shifts of voice in "Esthétique du Mal" (and after calling his narrator a "logical lunatic"): "The politics of emotion must appear / To be an intellectual structure." John Ashbery speaks of sudden clarity in a Gertrude Stein text "as though a change in wind had suddenly enabled us to hear a conversation that was taking place some distance away."[2] Let us see if transitions in the late Beethoven quartets help illuminate the open, spontaneous, and fragmented quality of "the politics of emotion" in some romantic and modern works of art.

Beethoven wrote his five last quartets from 1824 to 1826, the year before he died. In density, boldness, variety, and ambition, those quartets overpower most symphonic music as well as all other works for two violins, viola, and cello. In the last quartet, opus 135, Beethoven in the second movement painted himself into a curious corner. There are few passages like it in all European music: the three lower instruments settle into a forty-eight-bar repetition of a simple fortissimo phrase (try repeating *da-da-da-da dum* forty-eight times; that is a tremendous amount of repetition). After some vacillation, the first violin also joins with an insistent repetition of its own phrase. The effect is almost abusive, violent, as if the quartet were trying to self-destruct. Once the repetition is established, it goes on too long, then much too long, until it seems that the music is stuck. If, as Truscott says, the mere appearance of one key can blot out all memory of another, how much more true that in this passage all previous melodies, harmonies, and keys are lost. The aggressive repetition has become our universe, and as the four strings scrape away, the only question is, how will we get out? We listen and listen, as if Beethoven were listening, as if the four instruments were listening for some nuance, a single note, that could break this obsession and lead us to some other place. In bar 41 the violin is able to back away from the binding force, but the other instruments remain locked in the phrase until bar 48 when a single note is flattened a half-step by all the instruments at once. It is the end of an era, and we listen relieved and fascinated to learn where that new half-step will lead.

The effect of such unmelodic and insistent repetition is to make us anticipate change: the potential transition becomes the true subject of the passage. How and when will the transition occur, and will it lead to something more sufficient? This is "the mind in the act of finding" reduced to an absolute minimum; here for a moment is the mind prior to even the act of finding, catatonic, unable to take the first half-step. Most remarkable is the length of the passage. Had Beethoven led the instruments out earlier, he would have imposed a solution. Instead, he allows the moment full development until the music itself, in sheer exasperation or exhaustion or whatever, seems to discover a way out. Indeed, an excellent gloss on the passage is in section VII, "It Must Give Pleasure," of Stevens' "Notes toward a Supreme Fiction":

> But to impose is not
> To discover. To discover an order as of
> A season, to discover summer and know it,
>
> To discover winter and know it well, to find,
> Not to impose, not to have reasoned at all,
> Out of nothing to have come on major weather,
>
> It is possible, possible, possible. It must
> Be possible. It must be that in time
> The real will from its crude compoundings come,
>
> Seeming, at first, a beast disgorged, unlike,
> Warmed by a desperate milk. To find the real,
> To be stripped of every fiction except one,
>
> The fiction of an absolute—Angel,
> Be silent in your luminous cloud and hear
> The luminous melody of proper sound.   (CP 403–04)

The "crude" and "desperate" repetitions and the subject of potential order, only potential, always potential, create tension: "To discover . . . To discover . . . To discover . . . To discover . . . possible, possible, possible . . . possible . . . must be . . . must be . . . To find . . . To be." Finally all the potential infinitives give way to the dash, "—Angel," and the imperative mood. Melody, luminous melody, returns. And if this is a mirror and gloss to Beethoven's passage, in which "The real will from its crude compoundings come," how apt Beethoven's curious notation for opus 135, last movement, would be at the head of Stevens' poem: "The difficult resolution: must it be? It must be, it must be."[3]

Both artists, we might say, took as their subject the process of struggling into and out of difficult resolutions. They both took, also, a remarkably detached point of view toward that struggle, a remarkably detached point of view toward the mind in the act of finding. Their detachment had two consequences: first, each moment of thought and feeling is allowed its day. Stymied passages are not suppressed; on the other hand, lyric possibilities are not necessarily developed. The effect is that a flow of consciousness is discovered, not imposed, not pushed or edited always toward the sufficient. The second effect of their detachment was to emphasize transitions and to make us read or listen with a forward-looking mind: what will happen next? We are not looking backward as in a fugue or argument or linear progression, but forward to the nuance that will change one moment into another.

Beethoven's passage is unique in his work, but the way it makes us alert to transition is not. The late quartets change quickly, dramatically, unpredictably. Ideas are hinted, half-developed, or develped in three measures and thrown away. To limit the discussion, let us use opus 130, first movement, as an example. A beautiful, sonorous adagio opens for three measures, and is repeated (see figure 5). This structure is conventionally classical. Then, after a double rest, the quartet fails to continue the theme and is headed off somewhere else in a crescendo, when the four voices stop suddenly and the cello begins solo. Its phrase is picked up by the second violin and leads to a new foursome which changes color unexpectedly with the first violin's G. Suddenly the four voices stop again without warning and the violin runs off—now in 4/4 instead of 3/4 rhythm, and allegro instead of adagio—in a six-measure lilting descent against an ominous base that brings the entire quartet to a very formal and balanced crescendo. This alas, has again led nowhere and more searching begins with the reintroduction of the first theme. What were the agents of transition? A disjunction when the theme fails to repeat, a cello's phrase, a violin's G, a sudden melody, a joining in, an abrupt stop . . . any aspect of the music could become a fulcrum for change.

I do not wish to give the impression that the movement is chaotic. In Truscott's words, "Beethoven worked, in these quartets, on a basis of musical logic as strict and exact as that of any of his earlier music."[4] That is true, but in his particulars Beethoven courted an extraordinary variety that seems to represent spontaneous thought processes (though the manuscript shows much revision). We watch the music searching, trying to make up its mind. Consider part of Truscott's description of the quartet's first movement:

Figure 5. Beethoven, Opus 130

> The development is one of the wonders of music in its sheer simplicity and the complexity. . . . Beethoven here takes us step by step through his thought processes. First, at the end of the exposition there is a cadence in which a unison G flat drops to F. [I omit here a technical description of the next fifteen measures.] So that cadence, detached from its original Adagio phrase, becomes a gently rocking accompaniment to the development, still on D major. Beethoven has shown us every step of the way in detaching that cadence.[5]

The effect of this kind of composition is not to present us with a theme or a key as a fait accompli, but to show us the theme or key emerging from the music, to show us musical thought. New keys are possibilities, then hints, then probabilities, exactly as the entropic and sterile possibilities of "stop" and "perfection" come to dominate Stevens' passage from "Notes" on a walk around the lake. For instance:

> Five times this new theme (after bar 108) comes on gradually changing harmony, and not twice in succession exactly the same. The harmony moves gradually from D major to G major, the F sharp becomes F natural, hinting at C, major and minor, a normal supertonic anticipation of a perfect cadence, and this opens, without a pause, wonderfully into B flat major (bars 129–132) and the recapitulation, with a hint at the turn become an accomplished fact.[6]

Truscott (like Charles Rosen in *The Classical Style*) is intent on proving order and design in the late quartets, yet one can see that Beethoven's interest in process creates even in Truscott's view an extraordinary variety, unpredictability, and emphasis on transition, which as Truscott says is at one point "used for the reverse of a transition" having become the subject.[7] The other major book on the late quartets, by Philip Radcliffe, describes much more emphatically the varied, arbitrary, and unpredictable nature of the first movement of the quartet:

> This opens with a short phrase of great beauty which is only allowed to make a tantalizingly brief appearance . . . punctuated by the semiquaver figure . . . which becomes increasingly prominent towards the end. . . . A vigorous contrapuntal passage leads to a very broad and emphatic cadence; this is followed by a mysterious passage. . . .
> In view of the size of the whole movement this development is shorter than might be expected, but still more unusual is the fact that it contains the most relaxed music in the movement and has almost the air of being a kind of lyrical interlude. First there is a brief dialogue; . . . then the last two notes . . . quietly detach themselves. . . . Assisted by both elements they form a background for a

new theme which has no obvious connection with anything else in the movement. . . . Starting in D major, the music wanders delightfully through various keys; after hesitating for a moment between C minor and C major it eventually chooses the latter . . . semiquavers more exuberant . . . the tonality is more restless, leading through Eb minor to Db major. . . . The opening phrase . . . appears first in Db and then modulates to Bb with a wonderful lightening of colour.[8]

We might ask how we listen to this music that "wanders delightfully through various keys" and "eventually chooses" one briefly—music in which themes and keys "come on gradually" until "the hint" has become an accomplished fact, as Stevens' verbs of potential become declarative. It is the extreme of the sonata form, as Truscott notes, with the device of a key change expanded to a subject matter, an area of investigation: the mind in the act of finding.

Long before Stevens had taken his interest in transition to an extreme (as Beethoven had in his last quartets) he had toyed (as had Beethoven in the earlier Piano Sonata op. 78) with the idea of unanticipated key change. One of Stevens' best, most accessible, and most misread early poems is "Anecdote of the Jar" (1919):

> I placed a jar in Tennessee,
> And round it was, upon a hill.
> It made the slovenly wilderness
> Surround that hill.
>
> The wilderness rose up to it,
> And sprawled around, no longer wild.
> The jar was round upon the ground
> And tall and of a port in air.
>
> It took dominion everywhere.
> The jar was gray and bare.
> It did not give of bird or bush,
> Like nothing else in Tennessee. (*CP* 76)

A number of readers find here a benign call "to be definite in one's own being, like Wallace Stevens' jar in Tennessee."[9] The poem begins that way: the jar is a figure for the human imagination shaping the chaos of a slovenly, sprawling wilderness. Without doubt, in the first two stanzas, nature is a mess. And probably, ceramic order is to be admired. But in the third stanza the scene of "bird or bush" erases all memory of "slovenly" and "sprawled," suggesting a specific delicacy if not beauty, while the jar has become "gray and bare" and "did not give." The attractive jar has become unattractive; the unattractive wilderness has become attractive; the positive and egocentric verb "I placed" has given way to verbs impersonal and negative: "It did not give . . . like nothing else."

What has happened, in content, is easy enough: the poem exposes the inherent sterility of ideal solutions to the problem of chaos. Confronted with the wilderness of Tennessee, some narrator longs for the human idea of order (a jar) and he puts it there. Once that pure, ideal order is firmly established, however, the narrator longs again for the variety of nature. Both natural chaos and human order are shown to have drawbacks. So we go from chaotic nature and a beautiful jar to a sterile jar and a beautiful nature.

But how do we get there? How does the transition work? The jar was "round," and it "made" the wilderness "surround" that hill. Order and will. In the second stanza—and here is the element of capriciousness in such a work—the narrator might have found a number of things to say about this jar. Was it Keats's Grecian urn, did it have a Chinese celadon glaze? The jar is apparently very plain, and a simple "round" is repeated, followed by "ground," the fifth such rhyme in seven lines: "round . . . surround . . . around . . . round . . . ground." Forget the jar, and the pros and cons of order and will; the point of view is becoming sterile (gray and bare) and it is understandable that as a cure the next line becomes whimsical: "And tall and of a port in air." The narrator, turning from repetition to humor, comes up with another quaint construction (anticipated by "round it was") and the word "port." This is the note that has "cut across the simple F sharp major landscape without any preparation." "Port" suggests portly, fat, authoritative, wealthy, British. Just this hint of Lord Warburton generates the next line: "It took dominion everywhere." The key has changed. And if we can follow sonatas, as Truscott says, "the effect of that unprepared chord will be to blot from one's mind all memory of F sharp as a tonic." Now that the order brought to chaos has become imperial, revolution is again desired—this poem could go on forever, as Stevens realized by 1942. The development follows naturally: "port . . . dominion . . . gray and bare . . . did not give." By the end only nature's variety will suffice.

This poem moves from position A to a contradictory position B. It could have gone to C or D or F; I am suggesting that another word besides "port" could have led to entirely different conclusions. For instance, "round" in line 2 does not determine direction, nor does "made" in line 3. The poem does not begin ironically. "Made" could suggest the creative making of art ("poesis, poesis, the vatic lines"), for Stevens was well aware that "poetry" comes from the Greek *poiein,* to make. Perhaps the combination of "made" with "slovenly" helps emphasize will instead of imagination: art tidies up. Another Swiss perfection. For whatever reason, the jar's negative role in making wilderness not wild dominates lines 3–6. Even here, "the one" versus "the many" could easily be given new life, new positive connotations. In the same year Stevens wrote of the variety of clouds giving way to final perception, when the firmament "bares the last largeness, bold to see" (*CP* 62). The jar could suggest such a "one," a final perception. Instead, the poem seems stuck on the rhyme of "round." I think the best guess for the motive of change in this poem is that the narrator is seduced by an easy rhyme, and the poem is becoming dull, cheap, cute. What we do know is that Stevens allows this voice of increasing cuteness to come to a head, to reach its definitive extreme: "of a port in air" is a crisis of voice, for either the voice is ridiculously fastidious or it is sarcastically humorous. We must turn against something, the voice or the jar. The voice turns against the jar, and we can side with the voice. The crucial point is that the poem allowed a moment of thought and feeling to reach its definitive extreme and generate its own reaction, or rather, in the politics of emotion of this poem, an initial reaction was allowed to lead to revolution.

Perhaps I have exaggerated the potential of this short lyric, in which direction may be imposed as much as discovered, but certainly in the long, late poems, the older Stevens, like the older Beethoven, seems to have found the courage of pure detachment, allowing passions and ideas to flow in a natural sequence of action and reaction, encouraging the audience to anticipate the note—"port"—that signals "this real key change . . . analogous to a complete change of direction in perspective."

Beethoven's late quartets and Stevens' long poems demonstrate a logical extreme of the romantic interest in consciousness and organic form, an extreme that has possibly appeared in a number of longer, major works of our culture. At least since Wordsworth's 1805–1806 version of *The Prelude,* the development of an idea, as distinct from the final product, has been a subject of poetry:

> Some called it madness—such indeed it was,
> *If child-like* fruitfulness in passing joy,
> *If* steady moods of thoughtfulness, *matured*
> To inspiration, sort with such a name;

If prophecy be madness. . . .
                        But leaving this,

It was no madness.   (III, 149–58)

Wordsworth's string of conditional comparisons (emphasis added) creates a clear progression—"childlike . . . matured . . . prophecy"—which realizes the potential of the "if" clause, although the verb moods remain conventional and Wordsworth, finally, "leaving this" playful syntax, states the point more rationally, if less poetically.

What we might progressive appositives, or progressive comparisons, are common in Wordsworth and Stevens. At the time of Stevens' first book, Hans Vaihinger's *The Philosophy of As If* was popular among poets, and Harvard's Alfred North Whitehead (whose work Stevens admired) was saying "All thought is by analogy." Although Wordsworth went about it quite conservatively, his poetic attention to consciousness in a long form, free to wander, permitted the kinds of multiple analogies that become a record of thoughtful change:

Oft in those moments such a holy calm
Did overspread my soul, that I forgot
That I had bodily eyes, and what I saw
Appeared like something in myself, a dream,
A prospect in my mind.   (II, 367–71)

"Something," "dream," and "prospect" are quite different, and the progressive changes of analogy give a direction to the thought (inner to outer, past to future, illusion to reality) that makes the passage less of a statement, and more the record of Man Thinking.

These, however, are only hints of the "ecstatic freedom of the mind" (*NA* 35) that Beethoven and Stevens exhibit. Emerson, defining organic form, said that one's work should grow from one's soul as the shell from the shellfish. Such a single-purposed organic teleology, although it may fit Wordsworth, does not suit Beethoven or Stevens, nor does it necessarily describe all of Emerson's own work (begun as Beethoven wrote his last quartets, and inspired by the same German idealism).

The opening of Emerson's late essay, "Experience," is a case in point. Like Stevens' long poems, the essay is about a string of moods, exhibits a string of moods, and manifests the variety of transitions that can join one mood to another. The essay is not, then, like Emerson's early work, punctuated by ecstatic fragments; it is rather a continuous history of idle transformations. For instance, the essay opens with three pages of rather severe depression, stated repeatedly in structural metaphors suggesting endless linear time:

> Where do we find ourselves? In a series of which we do not know the extremes, and believe that it has none. We wake and find ourselves on a stair; there are stairs below us, which we seem to have ascended; there are stairs above us, many a one, which go upward and out of sight. . . . Sleep lingers all our lifetime, about our eyes; . . . we lack the affirmative principle; . . . souls never touch their objects. An innavigable sea washes with silent waves between us and the things we aim at and converse with. . . . In the death of my son, now more than two years ago, I seem to have lost a beautiful estate,—no more. . . . Dream delivers us to dream and there is no end to illusion. Life is a train of moods like a string of beads.

In absolutism ("souls *never* touch"), personal daring, and melancholy, those three pages are very strong. But in one more page, Emerson will again be back in an optative, ecstatic mood: "When virtue is in presence, all subordinate powers sleep; . . . at one whisper of these higher powers we awake." How and why did he awake?

It is hard to say. What we know for sure is that he finds a word, "temperament," for these beads of moods on a string. The word itself, the act of conceiving, naming, seems to arouse him, and then negative repetitions ("Of what use . . . Of what use . . . Of what use") change the tone from sleep to something more like anger. Then the doctrine of temperament-as-fate reminds him of physicians of phrenology, and his spirits definitely lift as he goes on the attack. Never mind that what he is attacking, the idea of temperament as fate is the very idea he had advocated. Like Stevens, he allows the idea to reach its absurd extreme (phrenology) and generate a reaction. There is no attempt at possessing or controlling the idea. By now his dander is up—"the grossest ignorance does not disgust like this impudent knowingness" of physicians—and a new mood dominates the text: "I carry the keys . . . I distrust the facts." "Spirit" now enters, to confine temperament's tyranny to the level of nature:

> On its own level, or in view of nature, temperament is final. . . . But it is impossible that the creative power should exclude itself; . . . at one whisper of these high powers we awake from ineffectual struggles with this nightmare. We hurl it into its own hell, and cannot again contract ourselves to so base a state.

From sleep to waking in four pages, from lethargy to violence, from lost on an endless stairway to the top of the stairs: godlike mastery hurled down on satanic foes. How did he get there? There was no irony, and no qualification, to set up the reversal or make it rational: "Souls *never* touch their objects; . . . there is *no end* to illusion." And in the last passage, although he is exhibiting yet another change of mood, there is no irony still: he shows no awareness that this newfound spirit may simply prove temperament's reign. There was no progression of argument leading to the point. There was a change of key: the modulation occurred during the attack on physicians, and it may well have begun with the idea of order inherent in the act of naming: temperament. Finding the right word, perhaps, encouraged him. "The politics of emotion must appear / To be an intellectual structure" (*CP* 324).

These examples from Beethoven, Stevens, and Emerson provide a basis for a few assertions. First of all, these works are not fragmented in the simplest sense: the order of events is fascinating. But they are fragmented in another way: the order of events is infinitely arbitrary. Second, the principles of transition are extremely various: sonata form, reasonable argument, tonal color, melodic line, a dynamic shift, reaction rational or irrational, anger, exhaustion—any aspect of the work can become the center of attention and the basis for change. Third, there is no irony: each artist shows a willingness to commit the voice thoroughly to any number of positions, to live in the moment. Fourth, in at least Stevens and Emerson, this detached point of view toward free-flowing consciousness is expressed in long, ambitious works by men with demonstrable meditative or ecstatic sensitivity. And fifth, all three artists are comic in that they affirm the unpredictable and various vitality of consciousness. Even Emerson's essay ends: "Never mind the ridicule, never mind the defeat; up again, old heart!". . . As Stevens says in "Esthétique du Mal," "who could have thought to make / So many selves, so many sensuous worlds." In this type of process art, the flow of consciousness is the subject, detached acceptance is the point of view, and transition is the focal point of the rhetoric.

The way Wordsworth revises his text and the way Emerson happens on phrenology, the way Beethoven and Stevens allow any possibility of the piece to become a momentary center of attention, resembles improvisation. That is, even Wordsworth's revisions are less a search for a more central perfect synonym than an opening out of the text in new directions, as if those directions had not been anticipated. The improvisational aspects of Stevens' late work has been noted by Frank Doggett:

> The special quality of the late style is so permeated with the effects of apposition that some criticism has felt that it resembled improvisation. That effect is given because in apposition the poet seems to deliberate about his original concept. He appears to reconsider it by seeking an equivalent in another and another version, continuously altered yet presented as though it were the same.[10]

I think it a fine irony that some of the best modern art has gone virtually unnoticed by literary champions of modernism and postmodernism. Amid the talk of fragments versus truths, the irrational versus logos, the avant-garde against the status quo, the greatest marginal, disjunct, and counterculture art of our time is often overlooked: jazz.

After the Civil War, southern blacks began gathering in their own lodges, able for the first time to purchase instruments and play what they pleased. They had for two centuries been developing their music. By 1700, traditional African dances and drumming were forbidden among southern slaves of Anglo owners (the French and Spanish were more tolerant—hence the importance of New Orleans and Caribbean connections). By 1800, most plantations had a black musician who could play either the minuets, schottisches, and cotillions for the master, *or* whatever jigs and reels were allowed for dances in the slave quarters.[11] The Great Awakening, by 1800, apparently allowed blacks to slip more ring dances and rhythm back into their culture under the aegis of tent revivals. By 1830 (the time of the Beethoven quartets), there were crude minstrel shows. Dickens in 1842 took note of black music in New York, which also had black theaters and dance halls.[12]

African music is not notated and cannot be. It is polyrhythmic, not just syncopated: a 2/4, a 3/4 and a 6/8 rhythm might be played simultaneously by one drummer and cannot be signed in measures. One could write out three different scores and try to read them simultaneously—a task for a cubist band. The music is also improvised; even in the 1920s, almost none of the black musicians could read. Terry Waldo points out that a system of notation by measure is divisive, whereas African music is additive, and notation must give dominance to one key and metric pattern. African drumming is both polyrhythmic and extremely subtle and varied in its accents (not unlike what Pound was attempting by

1909 against the iambic *da-dum*), and traditional tribal dancing had always included improvisation.

So between 1700 and 1865, blacks, forbidden their traditional music, had of necessity made accommodations to the regular beat and single melodic line of European music, while keeping as much as possible of their old arts. Then suddenly, after emancipation, the new lodges were buying and playing their own instruments. By the 1890s there were probably 150 black bands in New Orleans alone.[13] What did they play? Military bands and music were all the rage. John Philip Sousa, by 1900, was known worldwide. The cheap, available instruments from 1870 to 1900 were, of course, the drums, trombones, trumpets of the marching bands. "To rag" meant to tear apart. "Stars and Stripes Forever" was a favorite tune. They would play a tune straight, then "rag the hell out of it."[14]

We will never know just how they sounded. Old black musicians remember it as pretty crude. But the first jazz piece recorded, performed by the all-white Original Dixieland Jazz Band in 1917, was written by them in 1912. It is fairly sophisticated ("Livery Stable Blues"), and we know that both white groups and recording sessions tended to suppress improvisation and rhythmic complexity. We can assume, then, that music we would instantly recognize as jazz, improvised and complex, was heard by 1912. In that music, a standard notated beat and melody (Europe, the empire, logos, the center) was deconstructed by rhythmic and melodic attacks from the margin: Africa. The result is a tension of center and off-center, solidity and fragments, the familiar and unfamiliar. It must have been like looking at a Matisse nude.

After looking at the Fauvist and cubist nudes in the infamous Post-impressionist show at the Grafton Galleries in London in 1912, Pound and his friends could (and did) go to the Cave of the Golden Calf for a drink. There, William Wees tells us, "continental cuisine, gypsy music, ragtime, avant-garde art, and all the latest 'rages' mixed under the ministrations of August Strindberg's second wife, Madame Frida Uhl Strindberg."[15] The Cave was open from 1912 to 1914. The Bunny Hug and the Turkey Trot one patron called "vorticist dances," and Sir Osbert Sitwell recalls "a super-heated vorticist garden of gesticulating figures, dancing and talking, while the rhythm of the primitive forms of ragtime throbbed through the wide room."[16] The spirit of revelry, one participant recalls, "had its artistic counterparts in Cubism, Vorticism, Futurism, the recitals of Marinetti, the publication of *Blast*."[17] And in jazz. Every move away from convention and toward open form by Caucasian painters in Paris is remembered. The existence of jazz in concert with fragmentation, indeterminacy, de-centering, and "making it new" is hardly recognized.

As Wallace Stevens was working on "An Ordinary Evening in New Haven" in 1949, and contemplating "The Auroras of Autumn," Art Tatum was recording "Willow Weep for Me." Both Stevens' medita-tions and Tatum's maturity came when jazz improvisation had reached its height, a rebirth of improvisation unmatched since the commedia dell'arte. In two songs in the *Smithsonian Collection of Classic Jazz,* Tatum drifts through keys, melodies and tones in dazzling spontaneity. In the program notes, Dick Katz observes of "Willow Weep for Me":

> Typically, such non-thematic Tatum fragments are not lyric; they are abstract, intense, almost anti-melodic, and sometimes difficult to follow . . . a compendium of arpeggios, runs and harmonic substi-tutions that may tend to overwhelm laymen and fascinate (but traumatize) musicians.[18]

Although Katz on Tatum (like Rosen and Truscott on Beethoven) takes pains to emphasize the *aaba* structure and control of the songs, the tendency of the "non-thematic Tatum fragments" is to create a surprising, bewildering series of transitions. In "Too Marvelous for Words," says Katz,

> Tatum embarks on a harmonic flight that breaks at the very limits of the key center (G major). To these ears, it sounds as though he states the first part of a sequential phrase, and then completes it a half step higher or lower, as the case may be. However, these transi-tions (they aren't long enough to be termed modulations) are done with substitute, altered chord changes that create an effect of sus-pended animation or musical weightlessness.

André Hodeir in the Smithsonian notes on Charlie Parker is more emphatic:

> Even more astonishing is [Parker's] solo in *Klactoveedsedstene,* which is made up of snatches of phrases that sound completely disconnected, even though they follow an implacable logic. . . .
> The melodic discontinuity that we have observed in some of Char-lie Parker's choruses is occasionally matched by an equally remark-able rhythmic discontinuity. It sometimes happens, generally in moderate tempos, that the melody and the rhythm are disjointed in a way that verges on the absurd. Snatches of melody then become part of a piecemeal method of phrasing that is surprisingly intense

and expressive. The chorus of *Klactoveedsedstene* is an excellent example of this approach, in which a rest, becoming part of the phrase's contour, takes on new meaning.[19]

By July 1949, when Tatum recorded "Willow Weep for Me," chord after chord could "cut across the simple F sharp major landscape without any preparation."[20]. Stevens, writing that month the last section of "An Ordinary Evening in New Haven," offered one of his many defenses of the form explored by Beethoven, Emerson, and himself, and made part of our culture by the shifts of thought at the end of the last century:

XXXI

The less legible meanings of sounds, the little reds
Not often realized, the lighter words
In the heavy drum of speech, the inner men

Behind the outer shields, the sheets of music
In the strokes of thunder, dead candles at the window
When day comes, fire-foams in the motions of the sea,

Flickings from finikin to fine finikin
And the general fidget from busts of Constantine
To photographs of the late president, Mr. Blank,

These are the edgings and inchings of final form,
The swarming activities of the formulae
Of statement, directly and indirectly getting at,

Like an evening evoking the spectrum of violet,
A philosopher practicing scales on his piano,
A woman writing a note and tearing it up.

It is not in the premise that reality
Is a solid. It may be a shade that traverses
A dust, a force that traverses a shade.   (*CP* 488–89)

What is that implied reality, that force, that shade of final form? On May 3, 1949, Stevens wrote to Bernard Heringman of being at work on "An Ordinary Evening in New Haven": "What underlies this sort of thing is the drift of one's ideas." To Stevens, that was not a slighting of the form (*L* 636).

Perhaps the most exact contemporary counterparts to Stevens' long poems came within ten years of his death in the form of dance improvisation, improvisation that instead of offering variations on a theme, served to reflect the endless and surprising quality of an absolutely open consciousness.

In the early 1960s, the Judson Dance theatre in New York City gathered many pioneers of modern dance, including Robert Dunn, Yvonne Ranier, Trisha Brown, Steven Paxton, Lucinda Childs, Deborah Hay, Phoebe Neville. The Grand Union dance company was formed at that time and practiced dance-theatre improvisations until its final performance in 1976. The company included widely different personalities and talents (different "voices," to make the analogy clear). Douglas Dunn was an exceptionally relaxed and fluid dancer, a virtuoso in his style. Steve Paxton was the creator of contact improvisation, Barbara Dilley and Nancy Lewis were talented in deadpan, mime, and theatre as well as in dance. David Gordon's aggressive presence, verbal talent, and caustic wit provided a foil to Dunn and Paxton's fluid serenity. But the individuals did not stay within those stereotypes or roles. They didn't stay within much of anything.

An impromptu skit could develop into a complex plot. Dunn could shuffle through it and his pure dance might be taken up by the others or totally ignored. Each might pursue individual activities, unrelated. Every mood, every theatrical form might be tried. Props found backstage helped suggest possibilities. Dead time occurred: everyone sitting on stage, totally passive, waiting—not unlike forty-eight bars of a single phrase.

Modern dancers and artists in the sixties liked to talk of active and passive audiences, and sometimes sought minimalism in art in order to elicit maximum participation from the audience. I found the Grand Union dullest when watched passively, but fascinating when I watched for transitions, trying to anticipate change. In this example I am coming close to Charles Altieri's idea of *performative discourse* as a form, which David Walker uses to argue the peculiar selflessness of the modern *transparent lyric,* and the demands it places on the audience. What made the Grand Union fascinating was the performers' detachment: if change was forced, the transition was too easy and conventional. Steve Paxton, for example, although he seemed passive, was often too willful. One could almost see him casting about for what to do next; he imposed an order rather than discovered it. Lacking passivity, his transitions were often obvious and predictable, and for that matter consistent with a persona: if you connected the dots, you had a picture of Paxton. Gordon, however, though an aggressive personality, was absolutely open to suggestion. When he led the transition, the next section often seemed to emerge from the situation, not to be imposed on it, and his transitions seemed also not to reflect a consistent persona. The passivity, openness, and spontaneity necessary for such activity parallels the Zen traditions of sword and word play. The challenge for Gordon was to maintain disinterest yet be acutely aware of every nuance of tone, movement, sound, sense, argument, color, to allow those nuances to develop. Like the Zen monk, he tried to enter "the sphere where nothing exists, while retaining consciousness of mental processes."[21]

With Wordsworth as a starting point, and with late Beethoven, late Emerson, late Stevens, jazz, and the Grand Union as mature examples, let us turn to a theory of this special form, the comedy of consciousness. The rhetoric of these works encourages anticipation; they have a uniquely open structure, based on transitional fragments even if those fragments occur within a traditional framework. These works are comic, not ironic, and their structure is explained and justified by the meditative point of view towards ordinary consciousness. In the next chapter we will discuss some principles of structure. Then, perhaps, we can make the claim that a comic approach to fragmentation has indeed been, for some time, a part of our cultural heritage.

21
Four Types of Form

Truscott and Rosen take pains to show the conventional patterns and careful development underlying Beethoven's late quartets. They take such pains because the only alternatives to continuity available to them are chaos and musical fantasy. The quartets are certainly not chaotic, and they do not resemble the fantasies of, say, Debussy. Like Radcliffe, however, Truscott and Rosen also find great spontaneity, surprise, and variety in the quartets. To say that Beethoven was writing sonatas, that Art Tatum plays an *aaba* song, or that "Esthétique du Mal" is about pain, may be true, but may also miss the point. We have no positive model for an arbitrary form. Cubism is thoroughly pictorial and not necessarily arbitrary; improvisation or a fantasy in music or a stream of consciousness in literature suggest a continuous unconscious with its own consistent persona or dreamlike narrative. In our culture, the concept of fragmentation has been mainly negative (the opposite of *perfect* meaning whole), implying either chaos or despair. We need to develop a theory of comic fragmentation to account for the examples before us. In fact, our cultural prejudice against fragmentation in art may very well be related to our prejudice against meditative consciousness, for passivity is the constant. Order and will—we need that jar in Tennessee. In this chapter we will ask how these connected yet fragmented, transitional forms are put together, and what part such forms may have played in modern literature.

We find in many works of Northrop Frye, Kenneth Burke, Barbara Smith, Wolfgang Iser, and others three fundamental types of form: narrative, associative, and episodic. *Meditative fragmentation,* the structure underlying what we have been calling the comedy of consciousness, is a fourth form. These four forms may be divided as follows.

1. *Narrative form* (also called sequential, logical, or syllogistic).

"The lines or verses usually 'follow' from one another, either logically, temporally, or in accord with some principle of serial generation."[1] Examples: 1, 2, 3, and so on, which is an open sequence; sexual intercourse, a logical argument, a conventional story—a closed sequence, which comes naturally to an end. In the closed sequence, as Burke says, the "premises [force] the conclusion."[2]

2. *Associative form* (also called qualitative progression). "We are put into a state of mind which another state can appropriately follow."[3] Although the next state of mind—in associative form—cannot be predicted as clearly as in narrative form, we "[recognize] its rightness" afterward.[4] Example: "The grotesque seriousness of the murder scene [in *Macbeth*] prepares us for the grotesque buffoonery of the porter scene."[5]

3. *Episodic form* (also called repetitive, paratactic). "Repetition is the fundamental principle; . . . coherence . . . will not be dependent on the sequential arrangement; . . . the principle of generation does not cause any one element to 'follow' from another."[6] Episodic or repetitive form "is the consistent maintaining of a principle under new guises."[7]

4. *Meditative form*. A true fragmentation, made of an endless series of associations that follow one from another but which fail to progress, to maintain a single principle, or to form a coherent picture of the speaker. This form reflects the flow of consciousness as seen from the meditative point of view. Examples: Beethoven's Quartet op. 130, no. 13; Emerson's "Experience"; and Stevens' "Esthétique du Mal."

First, a crucial caveat: few works since 1800 employ only one principle of organization to the exclusion of all others. Each form is a tendency of the work. Beethoven, for instance, is radically disjunct in many particulars, but much more structured in overall organization than Stevens. Joyce, Proust, Picasso, Braque, Beckett, Eliot, Faulkner, Stevens, Tatum, Parker, Merwin, García Márquez—it is hard to name an influential modern artist who was not in some way a master of fragments. And those "modern artists" who like Frost spoke in a continuous narrative or lyric form (although Frost knew the oven bird should learn "in singing not to sing"), sometimes do not seem modern at all.

The fragmentation found in modern literature may be divided into two types: associative fragmentation and true fragmentation. In associative fragments there is an underlying order. The dots can be connected to form a picture. The fragments are apparent only; by follow-

ing the associations correctly (connect dot 1 to 2 to 3, etc.) one finds
the real narrative (logical) form hidden beneath. For example, Quentin in Faulkner's *The Sound and the Fury* seems to talk in fragments:

> You can be oblivious to the sound for a long while, then in a second
> of ticking it can create in the mind unbroken the long diminishing
> parade of time you didn't hear. Like Father said down the long and
> lonely lightrays you might see Jesus walking, like. And the good
> Saint Francis that said Little Sister Death, that never had a sister.[8]

The experienced reader of Faulkner can connect the dots: Quentin's
obsession with time, fueled by Father, with its inexorable and tragic
march from innocence to experience, an obsession originating in his
sexual love-hate of himself and his sister, has made his sister's fall into
sexuality unbearable, his own virginity unbearable, divine salvation
unnattainable, and death devoutly to be wished. He will be martyred—
that had a sister.

Such associative fragments are the heart of the stream of consciousness tradition. As in Freudian free association, the apparent fragments of the stream of consciousness are symbolic of an underlying
order. Much of Joyce and Faulkner contains apparent fragments
which, as in Joyce's *Dubliners,* are linked by a single voice, or as in
Picasso's *Guernica,* maintain a single principle (in that case, violence)
through fragmented instances. Most cubist art has a consistency of
style (think of Wyndham Lewis's *Alcibiades,* or Picasso's *Nude with
Drapery*) which makes its fragments associate—although I am uncomfortable in moving too easily from painting to words.

The second type of modern fragmentation is true fragmentation:
the dots are not connected. True fragmentation in art is denied by
Freudians, who would argue that all acts of a single artist's mind must
be connected by a persona, if we can only interpret the symbols. But
Freudians assume that all mental acts are dominated by self; even the
psychotically "split" are composed of related segments. Exactly what
we will argue is that selfless detachment allows a play of mind that
does not necessarily reveal a single coherent persona. Before we
review that claim, however, let us consider three candidates for genuine fragmentation: desperate, ecstatic, and meditative.

Desperate fragmentation remains within the Christian and Freudian
world: chaos is denied or feared. Desperate fragments really are
associated, then, in the despair of the voice. Eliot's "Waste Land" is
the prime example of a modern work of desperate fragments united

by a voice. The voice's persona is not quite revealed (as clearly as is Quentin Compson's) but its desperation is (even more clearly in the original manuscript). At least that is the argument readers may find vividly between them at the end:

> Shall I at least set my lands in order?
> London bridge is falling down falling down falling down
> *Poi s'ascose nel foco che gli affina*
> *Quando fiam uti chelidon*—O swallow swallow
> *Le Prince d'Aquitaine à la tour abolie*
> These fragments I have shored against my ruins
> Why then Ile fit you. Hieronymo's mad againe.
> Datta. Dayadhvam. Damyata.
>   Shantih shantih shantih

There is no better passage to serve as a foil to Stevens, for this is not comic. It is strange to me that many do not find the end of "The Waste Land" ironic, that they believe this voice is any closer to peace ("Shantih") by virtue of saying (shouting? crying?) the word. He protests too much. A voice stamped by ironic bitterness and fear from line one ("April is the cruellest month") has finally reached its bitter end, crying for what it has not. That is, I agree with Marjorie Perloff and most contemporaries that "The Waste Land" does not practice a poetics of indeterminacy. But we need not argue the poem here; what is interesting is that in "The Waste Land" fragments are desperate, and that those who read the end positively do not find fragments: they find meaningful associations in the allusions, a significant underlying order, even a progression, in the last nine lines. That is, they say the shoring up works; there is structure.[9] I think that the order of the last nine lines could be scrambled, and the speaker is mad. The only progression is over the course of the entire poem, from bitterness, satire, and hatred of others, to satire and hatred of self, and this mad self-awareness gives hope of therapy. The speaker has finally realized that his problems are within.

However, we all agree that in the universe of "The Waste Land," true fragmentation would signal despair. Thus we remain within the Christian universe, with two choices: chaos or order. God resides only in order.

Ecstatic fragmentation is the complementary opposite of desperate fragmentation; it is a repetitive form in which someone shouts over and over his good news. A clear example would be Thoreau's famous paragraph at the end of the second chapter of *Walden:*

> Time is but the stream I go a-fishing in. I drink it; but while I drink I
> see the sandy bottom and detect how shallow it is. Its thin current
> slides away, but eternity remains. I would drink deeper; fish in the
> sky, whose bottom is pebbly with stars. I cannot count one. I know
> not the first letter of the alphabet. I have always been regretting that
> I was not as wise as the day I was born.

In the original manuscript, most of the sentences were in a different
order. Although some readers profess to find a brilliant progression
in the final version, we could find a brilliant progression in any se-
quence and the last four sentences actually are atomistic, as Georges
Poulet said of Emerson's early work: a cluster of repetitive assertions
around a single theme. Ecstatic fragments are joined by a consistent
voice, as are desperate fragments. The above two categories, then,
even if they contain fragments, cna be comprehended by associative
or episodic models of form; desperate and ecstatic fragments are
variations on a theme or maintainings of a single principle in new
guises.

In *meditative fragments,* however, the order of sentences cannot be
rearranged. One moment generates the next in an endless series of
associative (not episodic) transitions. The voice itself is extremely
various: it may indeed be ecstatic at times, or desperate, or bored, or
logical, and the types of structures and transitions used are also infi-
nitely various. And although there may be a traditional structure as a
skeleton for the piece (sonata, lyric, an investigation of pain, the
supreme fiction, Christian reflection) the changes overwhelm the nar-
rative. The real voice, the *ur*-consciousness that chooses to report the
drift of one's ideas, is detached to the point of impersonality. I be-
lieve this form offers a sound linguistic approach to the true cubist
project of collage, an approach more successful than those that vio-
late syntax and meaning yet seek powerful juxtaposition.

These claims raise two related and interesting questions. First, are
the long poems not recognizable as the poetry of Wallace Stevens?
And do his long poems not differ from each other, as do Beethoven's
last five quartets? Yes, this is Stevens' vocabulary, style, range of
interests, and yes, "Auroras" is more austere, "Notes" more whimsi-
cal. As the Buddhists would observe, all thought and feeling and
language acts will be stamped by self (Chao-chou's enlightened re-
plies have a certain style) and each of Stevens' long poems has some
organizing center and tonal consistency.

These concessions lead to the crucial second question: in what significant way, then, are these poems selfless? The answer has two parts, because I have claimed two voices in these poems: the voice of self, various and inconsistent, speaking the fragments, and the meditative voice, a silent detachment that allows self free play and dominates the structure by *not* joining the fragments into a teleological or even coherent form.

Let us consider first the possible selflessness of the inconsistent self. While Stevens is certainly limited in his choice of subject matter and style (we know we are not reading Frost or Eliot), within that spectrum of style and interests the mind of these poems has bewildering variety. I have not seen a thorough Freudian reading of one of the long poems, and would be interested in the attempt, but I am suggesting that such an attempt to "connect the dots" would not convincingly reveal a single persona. It is possible that the subconscious, as well as the conscious, has in any one person so many possibilities, "so many selves, so many sensuous worlds" (*CP* 326), that divorced from circumstance and observed with detachment it would resolve into not one picture, but so many pictures, so many faces of Eve, that the Freudian search for *the* person, the defining persona, would break of its own weight. That, I suggest, is the case in these poems: so many Stevens emerge, all speaking his dialect, all sharing some qualities of reticent brilliance, that we find ourselves reading a poem stylistically familiar but profoundly impersonal. The text contains ideas and feelings (the fragments are individually expressive) but the endless and arbitrary series of fragments reveals no overriding persona. Instead we find a detached record of consciousness that comes closer to being unlimited than we have believed a consciousness should. One rhetorical effect of these poems, then, is identical to Buddhist theory: these poems undermine the idea of a single, stable self. The self seems to dissolve in a myriad of contradicting instances. Hence, the open and indeterminate form.

Now to the second part of the answer, the selflessness of the *ur*-voice, of the meditative detachment that characterizes these poems. One might be tempted to call these poems associative or episodic, united by meditative detachment as a constant, and that would be apt *if* we were accustomed to passivity as a principle. That is, the single uniting *ur*-voice behind these poems is an absence, not a presence. Stevens' refusing—or rather neglecting—to judge, choose, guide, become involved, allows the myriad presences to come forth, be recognized, have their day and disappear, all in a context of detachment that suggests a comic fragmentation: the comedy of consciousness. Such detachment permits a play of voices, and shifts the attention from statement to transition, from assertion to the dynamics of existence. According to Garma C. C. Chang: "In Samadhi . . . every thought is a complete *process,* containing the stages of arising, subsisting, and dissipating."[10] Compare Stevens'

> In the instant of speech,
> The breadth of an accelerando moves,
> Captives the being, widens—and was there.   (*CP* 440)

The emphasis on momentary time ("instant"), on changes of verb tense, on change itself, on commitment versus irony ("captives the being") should now seem familiar. Being free of concepts is to Buddhist meditators a kind of voidness that allows one to apprehend and report the suchness of each concept:

> What is meant by "becoming free from a concept"? One is free from a particular thought or concept if that thought always arises without the slightest unconscious tension, repression, or break in awareness of the thought as thought. Then one experiences the thought so fully that there is no time for the mind to tense and solidify the thought, so the thought ceases to be in one's way. In other words, a thought, concept, mental image, or memory has no hold over us if we always experience it totally (vipasyana) and yet remain relaxed (samatha). This is no easy matter in any case. Initial enlightenment comes when we discover that it is possible to allow our deepest moment-to-moment image of "me and mine" to arise in this full, empty way.[11]

That is why Stevens can allow such freedom to such myriad voices; they have ceased to be in any significant way his: "When the mind is like a hall in which thought is like a voice speaking, the voice is always that of someone else" (*OP* 168).

In Stevens' papers S. F. Morse found the opening lines for ten sections of a long poem that Stevens did not write. The lines provide an interesting example of radical disjunctions, changes of voice, and of the arbitrary but precise nature of his transitions:

I

I am bound by the will of other men.

II

Only one purpose exists but it is not mine

III

I must impale myself on reality

IV

Invisible fate becomes visible

V

Cry out against the commander so that I obey

VI

In the uproar of cymbals I stand still

VII

They are equally hapless in the contagion innate in their numbers

VIII

The narrative stops . . . Good-bye to the narration.

IX

As great as a javelin, as futile, as old

X

But did he have any value as a person   (*OP* xxiv)

There are many continuous elements in the proposed poem: an isolated "I" versus others in I, II, III, VII, X; implicit violence in "bound . . . impale . . . commander . . . javelin"; and something approaching despair: "I am bound . . . I must impale . . . I stand still . . . equally hapless . . . as futile, as old . . . any value?" If finished, the poem might have been one of Stevens' more tightly constructed meditations, and it could well have been the least comic. The structure he planned, however, seems neither a progressive argument, nor a Christian reflective meditation leading to deepened concentration, but a presentation of the variety of the mind as it moves about a single object—in this case, perhaps, fate versus free will, conceived as a violent opposition and entitled "Abecedarium of Finesoldier." The list ends not with a conclusion but with an entirely new direction, and Stevens in the manuscript had a heading for section XI with nothing under it. If this poem was going somewhere besides enumerating an ABCD of fate and war, the notes give no clue to its direction. Simply the method itself, of beginning with extremely strong, contrasting propositions as first lines to different sections, suggests that the tightest structure ever considered by Stevens was variations on a theme. We know that Stevens' long poems, representing "the drift of one's ideas," were arbitrary in length and very casual in subject matter and form. As Louis Martz recalls:

> So that was the genesis of "An Ordinary Evening in New Haven." We talked about that, and he described how he composed it. "I wanted to have something that would relate to the occasion but not directly. So I just fixed on this idea of a poem about a walk in New Haven, but then branching out." He said it really got so far away from the base that New Haven hardly appears in it. "It's only the title, really, but," he said, "that's the way things happen with me. I start with a concrete thing, and it tends to become so generalized that it isn't any longer a local place. I think that puzzles some people." He had written many more parts of that poem than the ones he read here. He told me that he had selected sections and put them together specially for the Connecticut Academy to suit the length of time he had to read it.[12]

As I suggested in reading the "walk around a lake" passage of "Notes," the movement in such a poem is generated by reactions to itself, or as the postmodernists might say, the commentary has entered the text. This commentary, however, is not really cultural reflection, but fresh re-action. That is why we find in these poems neither consistent commitment nor layers of irony.

Although the long poems are extremely subtle and difficult, and therefore spawn contradictory readings, they do not thrive on layers of irony—that is, they do not come alive through contradictory readings held simultaneously in tension, as, say, New Critics liked to read Shakespeare's sonnets. In Stevens, reading is usually unilateral, although a second reading may go another way. The exciting complexity of these poems lies not in layers of simultaneous assertions ironically contrasted, but in the multiple possibilities of transition each clear assertion generates. The linear development is the question, and forces the linear variety of the form. These are poems of the mind *in* the act, not layered ironic reflections on a fait accompli. The rhetorical effect, then, even in a poem on pain or war, is not reflective irony but comic variety.

Meditative fragmentation differs a bit from the classic fragmentation of point of view in modern art as we are accustomed to considering it. Modernist fragmentation, when it was not desperate, was almost always outer-directed. That is, many people can look at one object from one angle, or one object can be seen from many angles. In the words of Paul Cézanne: "The same structure seen from a different angle gives a motif of the highest interest, and so varied that I think that I could be occupied for months without changing my place—simply bending a little more to the left or right."[13]

In modern art, the variety of an object is revealed by a moving observer. The cubists represented various perspectives simultaneously on a single canvas, thus (at the same moment as Einstein) asserting that time is inseparable from space. One effect of such interests is to celebrate the variety inherent in the perception of objects, just as the inherent variety of the world is celebrated (or its uncertainty regretted) through Henry James's (or Dos Passos's) use of relative points of view. Relative points of view, or various views of one object—in neither case is the fragmentation within an individual.

Meditative fragmentation, instead of revealing the variety of an object by means of a moving observer, reveals the variety of an observer as he moves about an object. Cézanne speaks of the changes in the object as he moves; Stevens would write the poem of Cézanne moving. The variety and vitality of one mind is celebrated. The mind's transitions are endless and arbitrary, the fragments are within, yet the result is comic. If the consciousness behind the work is not detached, the result will be not meditative fragmentation but a stream of consciousness in which the self is speaking; in which desire shapes, directs and limits the voice; in which transitions are not endless and arbitrary; in which the apparent fragments are not really fragments unless the speaker is desperate. If the consciousness behind the work is detached, however, the remarkable variety of any mind and the arbitrariness of desire is exposed, a single purpose does not guide the work, transitions are endless, fragments are fragments yet the speaker is sane, watching the self (that logical lunatic) from a selfless point of view.

Stevens was well aware that his own tendency toward fragmentation, change, and improvisation was part of the modern movement.

> Now, just as the choice of subject is unpredictable at the outset, so its development, after it has been chosen, is unpredictable; . . . the true subject is not constant nor its development orderly. This is true in the case of Proust and Joyce, for example, in modern prose.
> (*OP* 221)

He was also well aware that such shiftiness was related to modernist interest in perception:

> Bergson describes the visual perception of a motionless object as the most stable of internal states. He says: "The object may remain the same, I may look at it from the same side, at the same angle, in the same light; nevertheless, the vision I now have of it differs from that which I have just had, even if only because the one is an instant later than the other."   (*NA* 25)

If, as Stevens thought, his love of unpredictable shifts of consciousness was part of a modern movement, then the concept of a selfless detachment narrating comic fragments might be useful to apply, say, to Faulkner's *As I Lay Dying* (versus *The Sound and the Fury*), to Beckett, Proust, to Joyce's *Ulysses* and *Finnegans Wake*. A number of modern works such as these seem stamped by detachment, by a kind of vacuity that is strangely comic, and they seem to suggest, as Stevens said, that the subject matter of art is not emotion but "insight of a special kind into reality"—that reality, often enough, being consciousness. Stevens quoted Henri Focillon: "The chief characteristic of the mind is to be constantly describing itself" (*NA* 46). This aspect of modernism is very close to Buddhist interests: "To be self-aware means to be aware of the results of the play of consciousness."[14]

22

The Comedy of Consciousness

The pathos of the human condition is man's inescapable exclusion
from absolute experience.

T. S. Eliot

Is it I then that keep saying there is an hour
Filled with expressible bliss, in which I have

No need, am happy, forget need's golden hand,
Am satisfied without solacing majesty,
And if there is an hour there is a day,

There is a month, a year, there is a time
In which majesty is a mirror of the self:
I have not but I am and as I am, I am.   (*CP* 404)

Stevens was not a religious poet in the usual sense of the term, for
no orthodoxy, or for that matter no particular heresy, dominated his
work. But he certainly was interested in ultimate experience and less
consistently, in ultimate issues. Thus Stevens was interested in the
phenomenology of religion, in reasoning about experiences that
might generate one belief after another.

But the difficultest rigor is forthwith,
On the image of what we see, to catch from that

Irrational moment its unreasoning,
As when the sun comes rising, when the sea
Clears deeply, when the moon hangs on the wall

Of heaven-haven. These are not things tranformed.
Yet we are shaken by them as if they were.
We reason about them with a later reason.   (*CP* 398–99)

Stevens himself often linked poetry to sensibility, to the life of the
poet at one end and, surprisingly for such an asocial poet, to the life
of the audience at the other: "His role, in short, is to help people to
live their lives" (*NA* 29). The sensibility of the man who wrote this is

one of the nicer enigmas of our time, and Peter Brazeau's book of reminiscences deepens, rather than dispels, the enigma. Certainly the "very powerful personality inside that silence" as Mary Aiken put it, kept his own counsel and in life often seemed made of the same impersonal constructions, sudden images, and civil yet radical disjunctions that characterize his work.

> He didn't argue. He meditated. He struck me all the way through as a very reflective and reticent man. He would hear something, and you could see him think about it; you could practically hear him think about it. He spoke in sentences, not in paragraphs. There was no such thing as a connected argument. What you had instead was a series of intuitive and highly perceptive remarks. When he got on a subject, he would talk with flashes of intuition. That was not a man who thought consecutively.[1]

This book has asserted that Stevens knew, practised, indulged a state of consciousness that allowed a certain kind of detachment. Such detachment could lead to perceptions of nothing, to perceptions of suchness, or to a free observation of the mind of the ephebe who in a special way "must become an ignorant man again." Because such detachment is a universal possibility of the cerebral cortex, we should expect to find it not only in Stevens' ephebe.

> We must aim at bringing about two changes in [the subject]: an increase in the attention he pays to his own physical perceptions and the elimination of the criticism by which he normally sifts the thoughts that occur to him. In order that he may be able to concentrate his attention on his self-observation it is an advantage for him to lie in a restful attitude and shut his eyes. It is necessary to insist explicitly on his renouncing all criticism of the thoughts that he perceives; . . . the whole frame of mind of a man who is *reflecting* is totally different from that of a man who is *observing* his own psychical processes. In reflection there is one more psychical activity at work than in the most attentive self-observation, and this is shown amongst other things by the tense looks and wrinkled forehead of a person pursuing his reflections as compared with the restful expression of a self-observer. In both cases attention must be concentrated, but the man who is reflecting is also exercising his *critical* faculty; this leads him to reject some of the ideas that occur to him after perceiving them, to cut short others without following the trains of thought which they would open up to him, and to behave in such a way towards still others that they never become conscious at all and are accordingly suppressed before being perceived. The self-observer on the other hand need only take the trouble to suppress his critical faculty. *If he succeeds in doing that, innumerable ideas come into his consciousness of which he could otherwise never have*

got hold. The material which is in this way freshly obtained for his self-perception *makes it possible to interpret* both his pathological ideas and his dream structures.[2]

As the last sentence indicates, the quotation is from Freud. In the introduction, I suggested that meditative studies are quite different from psychoanalytic studies, although both attempt to examine nonordinary states of consciousness and then return to literature with fresh readings. Here, in a passage from *The Interpretation of Dreams* noted by Staal, we see the close crossing of psychoanalytic and meditative techniques. Freud, however, assumes meaningful structure to the patient's association; the psychoanalytic observer listens not with detachment, but in a very goal-directed, analytical state of consciousness. The *patient* in free association, then, could well be in a meditative state, but the doctor is paid to discover self rather than not-self. Those modern artists who experimented with nonordinary consciousness, dream states, and free association, or whose technical devices are compared to those states for elucidation, may well have been practicing or imitating the style of meditative states. Neither voidness, nor suchness, nor true fragmentation, however, is likely to be found in their work by critics operating only in Western intellectual and psychoanalytic traditions.

From the meditative point of view, the mind is reported as comic: a buffoon, a child rushing this way and that, too ineffective to be feared, silly in its self-important vagaries:

> the genius of
> The mind, which is our being, wrong and wrong,
> The genius of the body, which is our world,
> Spent in the false engagements of the mind.   (*CP* 316–17)

There are many such deprecations of the mind in Stevens, but rarely are they the last note sounded in a poem. In Stevens the flow of consciousness is not just comic in its buffoonery but truly comic in its endless, changing vitality. The mind, though full of "false engagements," though leading nowhere, silly in its particulars, is usually affirmed as the form life takes in the world of longing:

> This endlessly elaborating poem
> Displays the theory of poetry,
> As the life of poetry. A more severe,
>
> More harassing master would extemporize
> Subtler, more urgent proof that the theory
> Of poetry is the theory of life,

> As it is, in the intricate evasions of as,
> In things seen and unseen, created from nothingness,
> The heavens, the hells, the worlds, the longed-for lands. (*CP* 486)

From the Buddhist point of view, the "endlessly elaborating" consciousness is truly chaotic, although full of transitions, because for all its practicality it goes nowhere and has no meaning. Consciousness has no valid progressions; the meditative point of view toward consciousness is profoundly antiprogressive. We may survive (briefly), but we will neither improve the world nor make ourselves happy, nor discover truth by means of thought and feeling. The mind separates us from the reality of unity. To the Buddhists and Stevens, ordinary consciousness is a record of "endlessly elaborating . . . intricate evasions," a record of unsatisfied desires: "The heavens, the hells, the worlds, the longed-for lands."

Within the general detachment that permeates Stevens' endlessly elaborating meditations and makes them possible, there are two different kinds of affirmation. One we have just mentioned: celebration of the vitality of endless change. That is an affirmation of the many, of Nietzsche's "chaos of sensations," and resembles Mahayana immersion in the fleeting world. There is also, however, in some poems, an affirmation of this process as the one, an affirmation not of the variety of parts but of the unity of the whole through change. Process is the one, or even suggests some *ur*-force behind the particulars of change. Stevens treads very lightly around this theme, and Buddhist traditions hotly debate whether such unity is apprehended through meditative experience or is an intellectual construct, a theory implied by, say, making a noun out of the action of process, or out of nirvana (to blow out): the term's history is one of repeated reification. If something exists only as predicate, can we say "it is"? In Stevens, such an ultimate unity behind the ultimate verb is not usually epiphanic; it appears as a theory, sometimes a very moving one, of the unity behind change:

> That's it. The lover writes, the believer hears,
> The poet mumbles and the painter sees,
> Each one, his fated eccentricity,
> As a part, but part, but tenacious particle,
> Of the skeleton of the ether, the total
> Of letters, prophecies, perceptions, clods
> Of color, the giant of nothingness, each one
> And the giant ever changing, living in change.   (*CP* 443)

It is a fine passage (and what a wonderful line: "As a par*t*, bu*t* par*t*, bu*t* *t*enacious par*t*icle"), but appropriately enough this impassioned ideological affirmation of nothingness and something united ends the relatively short (four pages) and rather consistently theoretical, continuously voiced "A Primitive Like an Orb."

In the long poems, detachment and a bewildering array of moods, tones, devices, voices, statements are the dominant constant. If one wishes to elevate variety or change itself to a principle and to regard that as an ultimate unity, that is possible, but as we have noted such absence of constancy is not a presence, and differs from those more platonic unities occasionally glimpsed in Stevens: this is the unity not of the sun, but of the dancing illusions on the wall of the cave, and detachment, not transport, reveals the nature of that unity.

Perhaps Stevens' finest evocation, then, of variety as a cosmic unity is at the end of "Landscape with Boat." This poem has often been held up as antimystical, for it rejects a *nihilistic theory* of nothing. In fact, it is antitranscendental, but a perfect expression of a Mahayana and Stevensian point of view: "if nothing/Was divine then all things were." It is also absolutely delightful in its sly movement from negative to positive, from conditional to accomplished, and in its witty detachment. If the comedy of consciousness were to suggest "the One," this is the way it might be done:

> He never supposed
> That he might be truth, himself, or part of it,
> That the things that he rejected might be part
> And the irregular turquoise, part, the perceptible blue
> Grown denser, part, the eye so touched, so played
> Upon by clouds, the ear so magnified
> By thunder, parts, and all these things together,
> Parts, and more things, parts. He never supposed divine
> Things might not look divine, nor that if nothing
> Was divine then all things were, the world itself,
> And that if nothing was the truth, then all
> Things were the truth, the world itself was the truth.
>
> Had he been better able to suppose:
> He might sit on a sofa on a balcony
> Above the Mediterranean, emerald
> Becoming emeralds. He might watch the palms
> Flap green ears in the heat. He might observe
> A yellow wine and follow a steamer's track
> And say, "The thing I hum appears to be
> The rhythm of this celestial pantomime."   (*CP* 242–43)

Stevens was a most acute observer of consciousness, and a lover of words. He became a connoisseur of his thoughts and senses, examining with precision and objectivity the perceptive actions and reactions that comprise our being. That precision and objectivity, that habit of detached observation simultaneous with mental acts, give the curiously impersonal flavor to his work. He usually expressed not himself, but his ability to observe his expression. That ability owed much to his meditative experience, and had a great deal to do with his "signature" quirks of style. No other poet in our language uses so much "it," "is," "that," so many impersonal and abstract constructions, so many "as ifs." No other poet in our language has written with such detachment while so loving words.

His detachment affected all of his work. Even in his lyrics he liked to write a nonpoem that would set up a two-line poem. He would write of the need for an image, then for a metaphor, until like Babe Ruth pointing at the stands, he delivered:

> There is one dove, one bass, one fisherman.
> Yet coo becomes rou-coo, rou-coo. How close
>
> To the unstated theme each variation comes . . .
> In that one ear it might strike perfectly:
>
> State the disclosure. In that one eye the dove
> Might spring to sight and yet remain a dove.
>
> The fisherman might be the single man
> In whose breast, the dove, alighting, would grow still.
>
> (*CP* 356–57)

The effect is to make us aware of the poem not as artifact, but as something so needed it is born. The effect is also to put us at one remove from the poem, and our need of it, just as in his poetry being at one remove from metaphor often precedes the metaphor. Stevens wished not just to perceive, but to establish a relation to perception. Those detached aspects of style are the heart and soul of his work. In the long poems those stylistics habits are joined to a structure that encourages ebb and flow, variety, and in the sheer weight of total commitment and change makes possible an affirmation of process itself.

> A bench was his catalepsy, Theatre
> Of Trope. He sat in the park. The water of
> The lake was full of artificial things,

Like a page of music, like an upper air,
Like a momentary color, in which swans
Were seraphs, were saints, were changing essences.

The west wind was the music, the motion, the force
To which the swans curveted, a will to change,
A will to make iris frettings on the blank.

There was a will to change, a necessitous
And present way, a presentation, a kind
Of volatile world, too constant to be denied,

The eye of a vagabond in metaphor
That catches our own. The casual is not
Enough. The freshness of transformation is

The freshness of a world. It is our own,
It is ourselves, the freshness of ourselves,
And that necessity and the presentation

Are rubbings of a glass in which we peer.   (*CP* 397–98)

As a meditative poet, Stevens wrote three types of poems: lyrics of nothingness, lyrics of meditative perception (suchness), and long poems of endlessly elaborating cloud transformations of change, within and without. In addition, his detachment colored all his work and provided a context for his celebrations of imagination and metaphor. It is remarkable how seldom he was ironic (rather than witty, dry, detached, sardonic), how seldom he was bitter or sarcastic. The long poems reveal most clearly his sensibility; the meditations seem to be the finest examples of a form that through fragmentation expresses neither despair, nor nihilism, nor black humor, but a genuinely comic approach to consciousness. This comic spirit is generated by one's ability to commit oneself wholeheartedly to a phrase, a moment of perception, an idea—to live in that moment—without becoming "attached" to it in a Buddhist sense. This is accomplished by immersing oneself in experience while maintaining detachment.

This comic spirit demands an emphasis on transition, on the act of arriving rather than on what one arrives at, and these formal properties demand, in turn, a different kind of listening on the part of the audience: future listening, a moment by moment expectation of change. By such listening, which highlights the unpredictability of the piece, we realize the author's intended effect: we take delight in the variety and transience of thought and feeling, we participate in being as a verb, not a noun. "The feeling of Liadoff was changed. It is / The instant of the change that was the poem" (*CP* 347).

The meditative experiences and points of view of which Stevens wrote did not harm anyone; certainly they did not annihilate him, and they provide us with a model of artistic perception quite different from imaginative models. A moral reaction to the meditative Stevens would best be based on one's view of solipsism; that is, meditative experience occurs outside of historical time and social space. The object and the perceiving consciousness are united as it were, to the exclusion of all else. That in itself is not an immoral condition, but it is fair to ask the relation of that experience to social consciousness and historical time. One answer has already been suggested: the long poems, by taking the Buddhist view that our ordinary life has always been composed of meaningless fragments, and by taking a comic view of that fragmentation, offer an alternative to angst or despair in a modern world. Such poems do not, of course, offer the slightest political or social solutions to our problems—only the advice that solutions are illusory, and that one can know this without going mad; indeed, one can know this and be quite civilized. The beauty with which that position is held in Stevens' poetry consitutes an argument by itself. It is quite possible that the interest in Buddhism during the last thirty years is due partly to the Buddhists' advice on how to live with fragments, which makes Euro-American Buddhist study a possible subtopic of modernism.

The Snow Man's *nothing* may help define Stevens' relation to society and his distance from the other greatest poet of our century: Yeats. We have seen that Yeats had no real taste for meditative detachment, that even his ideal images were social and historical, singing like a golden bird

>   To lords and ladies of Byzantium
>   Of what is past, or passing, or to come.

Stevens, on the other hand, redefined our categories. He posed not a Platonist question of whether or not to embrace the physical world, but a meditative question of whether to embrace the physical world as clarity in a state of detachment, or as dazzle in a state of desire. The mere existence of those two alternatives colored his embracing of either one in the extreme, or in the middle ground of "pauvred ecstasy" of which Vendler speaks.

When, for instance, "gazing at the rounded moon" at the end of "Evening without Angels," Stevens embraced once again the world of self, he did so with a full recognition of "bare, bare" as an alternative, as if he could—and did—stand outside of time and desire. Unlike Yeats, he knew pure "light and air" as well as "the voluptuousness of looking." So, although Stevens' evocations of the social and historical world are not so vivid as Yeats's, although "the imperfect is our paradise" is more than a little fastidious, abstract, and Latinate compared to Yeats's "raving slut who keeps the till," in Stevens that world of desire is embraced as an option. He can and does go away, and his returns derive their wry eloquence and detached rhetoric from a possibility of withdrawal that for Yeats was never really a choice. Thus Stevens' affirmations of this world have a courage, an awareness, an air of election all their own.

> Of these beginnings, gay and green, propose
> The suitable amours. Time will write them down.   (*CP* 398)

Postscript: Stevens, Meditation, and Modernism

I would like to conclude with an overview of Stevens' detachment in relation to the contemporary debate on modernism. The debate has two foci: Are the moderns still romantics, and, are you for or against the *Cantos?* Neither modernism nor respect for the *Cantos* should be wired to a binary switch, but the toggle on-off terms have helped generate a useful controversy on what our arts are and where they are going. "Pound/Stevens: whose era?" asks Marjorie Perloff in the first chapter of *The Dance of the Intellect* (1985), one of the more recent and enjoyable shots fired in the skirmish:

> If Poundians take MAKE IT NEW! as their watchword, one might say, without being at all facetious, that those who regard Stevens as the great poet of our time admire his ability to MAKE IT OLD. What matters, to Harold Bloom and Hillis Miller as to Frank Kermode and Helen Vendler, is Stevens' restatement, in chastened, qualified and ironic form, of the Romantic position, his Emersonian (for Bloom) or Coleridgean (for Kermode) or Keatsian (for Vendler) ethos. Stevens carries on the Symbolist tradition, whereas Pound's Imagism and Vorticism constitute, in Donald Davie's words, "a radical alternative to it." For Stevens, poetry is "an unofficial view of Being"; for Pound, it is, so to speak, an offical view of becoming: the "VORTEX [is] a radiant node or cluster . . . from which, and through which, and into which, ideas are constantly rushing."[1]

Perloff defines the variable between Pound and Stevens as "indeterminacy," which she says Pound practices and Stevens doesn't. "Indeterminacy," she says of late Beckett prose in *The Poetics of Indeterminacy* (1981), "is not thematic motif; it exists in the very fabric of the discourse."[2]

I share Perloff's respect for indeterminacy and its place in a distinctly modern discourse, but I would almost reverse her conclusions. In spite of Stevens' symbolist approach to meter and sound and his

300

conservative habits, he lived within indeterminacy and his poems reflect that milieu. Pound, however, for all his technical innovation, bohemian style, and theories of exploration, was not given to either openness or change in his art. Therefore I find Perloff's groupings misleading:

> And whereas Baudelaire and Mallarmé point the way to the "High Modernism" of Yeats and Eliot and Auden, Stevens and Frost and Crane, and their Symbolist heirs like Lowell and Berryman, it is Rimbaud who strikes the first note of that "undecidability" we find in Gertrude Stein, in Pound and Williams, as well as in the short prose works of Beckett's later years, an undecidability that has become marked in the poetry of the last decades.[3]

By 1985, Perloff had added John Cage, some of Ashbery, and the language poets to her list. I would take Stevens out of the high moderns, and put Pound in. Perhaps it would be useful to show why I believe Pound, not Stevens, betrayed the revolution of 1910–1914.

The foundation of modernism in art is relativity of point of view. Darwin's dictum that "the nature of species is not fixed" had a Copernican effect, encouraging challenges to every established authority; the decentering of man from God's plan was only one case in which the certainty of nouns—*man*—gave way to the uncertainty of process: something evolving from ape through man to X. In that case, what *is* it? The copula was suddenly missing, in English as in Chinese poetry. Into the new vacuum of authority, by 1900, philosophy and the arts had rushed. Impressionists were taking delight in the subjectivity of perception; no one in a James novel could agree on why Isabel had married Osmond and James said he didn't know; and Nietzsche, like Santayana, had turned to imagination and metaphor to create momentary, personal meaning in the space from which the gods had fled, and the empire was retreating. As I have mentioned earlier, key phrases from the period show the extent and depth of this new skepticism about the truth value of mental operations. Consider Nietzsche, who argued that thought is "expedient falsification," that we "misunderstand reality in a shrewd manner." Poincaré: thought is "convention." William James: "Conception . . . is a teleological instrument"; the "truest formula may be a human device." Ibsen: we live by "vital lie . . . illusion is *the* stimulating principle." Frost: "A poem is a momentary stay against confusion." Stevens: "Poetry is the supreme fiction."

By 1910, the most consistent result in the arts was a continuing turn toward surface and away from meanings external to each form: paint more conscious of itself as paint on flat canvas, instead of offering an illusory window on the world; poetry chaffing at personal expression and becoming more interested in its own rhythms and images as images; music, also, eschewing rhetoric and seeking something more spare and clear. "He took hard bits of rhythm," Pound said in praise of Stravinsky, "noting them with great care."[4] By 1910, Pound was hearing Webern, Satie, Schoenberg, Berg in London, where he had free tickets to Philarmonic rehearsals, just as Stevens was avidly following postimpressionist painting. Certainly the new skepticism with its attention to process had replaced the old vocabulary of static being, with a new Darwinian vocabulary of incessant becoming: Bergson's *durée*, Nietzsche's chaos of sensations, Bradley's immediate experience, William James's stream of consciousness. The stage was set for an art of indeterminacy and open form.

"On or about December 1910, human character changed," said Virginia Woolf.[5] By 1914 the mood in London, Paris, and New York was one of increasing attack on tradition, increasing delight in disjunction, and increasing awareness of one's process and medium as a kind of truth. In New York, Stieglitz's *291* was already publishing radical avant-garde material and William Carlos Williams was active in that circle; Picabia and Duchamp were about to arrive; and the conservative Stevens, who had hardly begun to write seriously, by 1914 was composing the imagist collage "Thirteen Ways of Looking at a Blackbird" and the aggressively anti-Christian "Sunday Morning." *Poetry* magazine in Chicago had Pound as its foreign correspondent and Yeats and Eliot as contributors. America was surprisingly up on modernism, although in retrospect our political security and love affair with nature seem to have modified the trends coming from abroad. In Paris and London, the new uncertainty principles joined a revolutionary, bohemian scene, and a rapidity of industrial progress hard for us to recall (electricity, high-rise architecture, autos, moving pictures, airplanes), to produce an atmosphere of heady change—as William Wees has ably shown.[6]

In such an atmosphere it is easy to imagine that many reactionaries, too, were bred. Eliot was one, appalled by the brave new world in Paris in 1910 and admiring the anti-Semitic Action Française, whose leader and theorist, Charles Maurras, Eliot praised throughout his life. Maurras's 1910 platform included repealing the French Revolution and democracy, and bringing back king, church, and aristocracy. C. K. Stead in *Pound, Yeats, Eliot, and the Modernist Movement* gives a chilling view of Eliot and the radical right.[7] The new age of skepticism, uncertainty, and indeterminacy could easily prompt a reactionary response.

Cubism, especially cubist collage, represents the quintessential modern art: radical disjuctions, modern subject matter, a medium aware of itself—all in a form shocking to the art establishment and the bourgeoisie. Reviews of the two postimpressionist shows in London (1910 and 1912) and of the Armory show in New York (1913) provide extraordinary glimpses of just how threatening the modern was in art.

The above is a textbook overview, but it seems best to make my assumptions visible. Now I would like to be more speculative. The self-consciously modern or avant-garde writers since 1914, right through contemporary postmodern language poets, have by and large been seeking a verbal cubism. It was a fine quest. It has failed. Direct attempts to invent an impersonal geometry or to imitate a fragmented world have failed to produce a powerful verbal art (I accept the rhetorical standard that calls for *some* form of power). Moreover, such idealistic projects have often created, ironically, a new romanticism or neoclassicism under the guise of an avant-garde. Stevens' detachment offers a better approach to a modern/cubist language art.

Early cubism in art and language (imagism) had some stylistic features we can depend on: hard, precise, delineated fragments. But philosophically—or perhaps better to say emotionally—cubism could go either of two ways: the fragments could be seen as supporting relativity of point of view because in their contrary clues they thwart understanding and suggest process, the absence of transition, the space between themselves as subject. On the other hand, the fragments could suggest a new idealism, made of hard facts, stasis, and theory—lines connecting the dots. From the very beginning, Pound was a conservative imagist, as Donald Davie observes.[8] Collage was a way to be certain. Pound was one of those who, while leading the revolution, was also reacting against it.

A prototype of what happened to Pound, Eliot, and Lewis appears at the very beginning of the period, in Ernest Fenollosa's notebooks. Studying Chinese characters, Fenollosa suddenly saw stasis as symbiotic with process:

> A true noun, an isolated thing, does not exist in nature. Things are only the terminal points, or rather the meeting points of actions, cross sections cut through actions, snapshots. Neither can a pure verb, an abstract motion, be possible in nature. The eye sees noun and verb as one, things in motion, motion in things.[9]

The Chinese ideogram, he decides, is a patterned energy like the acorn: "The forces which produce the branch-angles of an oak lay potent in the acorn; . . . the development of the normal transitive sentence rests upon the fact that one action promotes another."[10] He defines nouns as glimpses of verbs. Note that this is also a Bergsonian time-language, for each snapshot suggests another, and another, in an infinite unfolding. But Fenollosa in his Emersonian transcendentalism quickly reifies the concept, as spiritual absolutists must. You can reach that *ur*-process behind the snapshots. Metaphors *are* that patterned energy, participating in natural law. In Fenollosa's words, "All truth has to be expressed in sentences because all truth is the transference of power. The type of sentence in nature is the flash of lightning."[11] Amid this talk of process, we slid to a truth *behind* both noun and verb and to dead certain knowledge of it (Emerson's "flash of lightning faith"). Without hesitation Pound picked up this transcendental certainty and after him came Kenner, who could have taught Emerson enthusiasm.

In his fascinating and brilliant chapter in *The Pound Era* on these passages, Kenner moves from Fenollosa's ideogram to Buckminster Fuller's knot as a pattern of energy, to the vortex: "Luminous details, then, are 'patterned integrities' which transferred out of their context of origin retain their power to enlighten us."[12] The pattern is beyond culture and history, yet can be known and spoken. Kenner says that Pound's reiterated advice to translators is: "Convey the energized pattern and let go the words."[13] Words in the translation can successfully convey the spirit (energized pattern) of the original. This is more optimistic than Emerson, who had advised that "words cannot cover the confines of what is in truth."[14] The dissected surface of Chinese ideograms has become a reconstructed depth, along transcendental lines.

This energized pattern is a transcendental geometry: a universal pattern beyond time and culture, which, the vorticists believed, can be perceived and expressed. Pound comes very close in ways to Yeats's mysticism, except that Pound prefers a scientific vocabulary: iron filings shaped by a magnet. Pound's hard, precise occult of verbal fragments is to Yeats's soft, vague occult as imagist poetry is to symbolist poetry. Pound speaks:

> Thus three or four words in exact juxtaposition are capable of radiating this energy at a very high potentiality; mind you, the juxtaposition of their vortices must be exact and the angles or "signs" of discharge must augment and not neutralize each other. This particular energy which fills the cones is the power of tradition, of centuries of race consciousness, of agreement, of association; and the control of it is the "Technique of Content" which nothing short of genius understands.[15]

Such belief in the *inherent* power of words is not in the modern tradition of regarding metaphors as constructs, offered *as if* true; nor is it really in the romantic tradition of believing the truth of the metaphor while admitting that consciousness is the epistemological agent; rather, vorticist geometry yearns to be neoclassical (though without using reason, in my opinion), advocating a perceived truth while minimizing the role of personality, consciousness, and the subjectivity of perception.

Buckminster Fuller's knot and the acorn both exist in nature; the question is whether what we think will hold as well as the overhand knot. And will it have the same shape five centuries hence? In their excitement at perceiving a new systems-theory, which at its inception could have served the new interest in process, Fenollosa, Pound, and Kenner glossed right over epistemological problems, held to a Newtonian world (the knot is a constant, rather than relative to certain materials under certain conditions, etc.), and leapt to direct knowledge of unchanging truths, expressed or triggered by words. Kenner:

> Rare single words can imply, like seeds, whole energy systems. "Anaxiforminges," in the fourth Canto, belongs to Pindar, "Aurunculeia" to Catullus. Three cantos later "Smaragdos, chrysolithos" say "Propertius," and "e quel remir" says "Arnaut." "Quel remir" also says "sexual radiance," and says too that a poet once transubstantiated a common word. Such a word becomes "Gestalt seed," implicit with *maestria*. So writing in the 52nd Canto of the Emperor's duties toward the first month of summer, Pound with his eye on French phrases in Père Couvreur's *Li Ki*, page 354, "la voiture rouge" and "des pierres de prix de couleur incarnate," wrote "In red car with jewels incarnadine / to welcome the summer," bidding us remember how Shakespeare found an unforgettable word to be spoken by a king with bloody hands.[16]

The *Cantos* are not cubist. They are not made of fragments, but of bits and pieces of the pattern, from which glimpses we are supposed to perceive the knot, the integrated structure of energy flowing through the nouns and verbs. Both Pound and Kenner assume that language "says," that meaning inheres in words rather than in associations made by speaker and audience. The *Cantos* are not indeterminate. They are vision masquerading as collage. *The Four Zoas* cut up and pasted. "Quite simply," Pound said, "I want a new civilization."[17]

The *Cantos* do demand an active audience. I sincerely believe that I and every reader of this book could spend the time, learn the connections, and feel the power of selected *Cantos*. But what, then, has occurred? We have supplied the rhetoric of duration (the missing time language) and the fixed conclusions that the *Cantos* imply. And that reading might take so much energy, and indeed the connections might be so strong, that we are converted and proclaim the *Cantos* brilliant. Or we might find the ideas suspect, but the activity of deciphering worthwhile; in that case we might declare the *Cantos* a useful workout. Pumping Pound—not unlike the rationale for studying Latin earlier in this century: it strengthens the mind. The *Cantos* as religion; the *Cantos* as Nautilus equipment. If they are not collage, then the only justification for their form is the activity they require of the reader.

Davie makes a valiant attempt to read the *Cantos* as process; Yvor Winters's complaint that in the *Cantos* "we have no way of knowing if we have any ideas or not," Davie takes as a correct description of Pound's intent and accomplishment.[18] Davie tosses out the debate on structure: "Does a sea have a structure?" I wish I could believe him. The *Cantos* may be a mess and Pound may be right that they contain many wanderings and mistakes, but the goal that guides the form remains final, certain knowledge of history and culture. His phrases for his project favor fixed nouns modified toward the universal and epiphanic: luminous details, radiant gists. They exist beyond the perceiver, forever.

The scholars who have spent the time to connect the dots have come up with remarkably similar readings of most passages (as is not true of comments on Stevens' long poems). The *Cantos* are an episodic form, maintaining single principles under new guises, working by addition. Even though Hugh Kenner makes an excellent case for "the romance of things" in the early Sapphic translations, in which genuine fragments create truly open and emphatically isolated details, the later Pound is romancing not things, but theory.

The *Cantos* can be moving partly because they *are* vision, a reactionary vision of living in a culture in which all of Pound's associations would be shared, in which this apparent collage could be seen for the classic landscape it wishes to be, in which Pound, the reader, erudition, and the best of Mediterranean and Chinese culture would be one. The ways in which the *Cantos* are unreadable, then, create a rhetoric of pathos; the gaps measure the distance between our modern world of fragments and an integrated civilization. In reading the *Cantos* we see what we have, measured against Pound's wish and—alas—conviction that we have more. There is the difference between Pound and Stevens.

"Any object," said Eliot, "which is wholly real is independent of time."[19] There is no need to rehearse here the neoclassicism of Eliot, but I would like to comment on the typicality of his and Pound's objectivist stances. If we take seriously the "poetry" of the lives of T. E. Hulme, Pound, Wyndham Lewis, Eliot—meaning their metaphors and tonalities in art and out—we have a rather consistent portrait of men quite at odds with indeterminacy (unlike the shy, diffident, and withdrawing Stevens, wanting to call his first book "preliminary minutiae"). That is, Pound's autocracy (perhaps we should call it autologacy) was part of the modernist movement. American modernism was especially transcendental; articles in *291* assumed that Emerson and Whitman were the fathers of modernism, as if Nietzsche's inversion of Plato (appearances *are* reality) had never occurred. The top of the hourglass was superimposed on the bottom; even as avant-garde artists rushed, 1910–1914, to develop the techniques of modernism, they were rushing away from its rationale.

Hulme, for instance, admired the stasis of language; poetic imagery "endeavors to arrest you, and to make you continuously see a physical thing, to prevent you gliding through an abstract process."[20] As Schwartz and Materer have pointed out, when faced with a theory of flux, Hulme resisted: "It is as if the surface of our mind was a sea in a continual state of motion. . . . The artist by making a fixed model of one of these transient waves enables you to isolate it out."[21] These are the seeds of the imagist revolt against the time–merging–indistinct–ecstatic poetry of the romantics and the symbolists, and on behalf of the space–distinct–geometric–static poetry of the moderns. Especially after he had turned from Bergson to Worringer in 1913, Hulme's language became more aggressively modern: "geometric" art is "angular, lifeless," with "stiff lines and cubical shapes" versus the "vital," soft and "empathetic" romantic art. The modern should be "austere, mechanical, clear-cut and bare," a "complicated machinery."[22] In one way this seems extremely progressive, like Marinetti's "automobilism," but at the same time it is naturalistically reductive and certain. The machine—now there's a fact you can trust. One can understand that moderns saw symbolist musicality and vagueness as the enemy, and yet wonder if the avant-garde were not betraying the truer modernism of relativity of point of view.

Why was Hulme giving up on the "vital"? By the time of his famous and influential 1914 lecture on modern art, Hulme was unabashedly defining modernism as a defense against process. What had failed was not just romanticism, but nature. The modern artist wants "to create a certain abstract geometrical shape, which, being durable and permanent shall be a refuge from the flux and impermanence of outside nature."[23] This is cubist neoclassicism, and when the hard, bright bits in geometrical relation belong to a single universal system as in Pound, it is cubist vision. By 1914, the stylistic avant-garde had drifted away from the philosophic-scientific avant-garde. One can admire the new style, and yet remember that it was Darwin, not Bergson or Baudelaire, who said we live in time. The vorticists were as much a reaction against modernism as they were a part of it.

I have indicated that Pound and the vorticists were transcendental idealists at times, and also naturalists. I would like to pursue the second possibility for a moment. At the turn of the century, literary naturalists seemed to be the alter egos of the relativists, and therefore of the moderns. The literary relativists took Darwin's "the nature of species is not fixed" and followed it through to "all categories are relative" and all is uncertain. The naturalists, on the other hand, took the new Darwinian evidence of how the past causes the present and followed it through to natural law and to certainty about that law, which described the "facts" of life. Some of Darwin's descriptions of process, then, fed uncertainty, while his cause-effect deductions fed certainty. By 1900, one could trace the two strains to the relativist Henry James, say, and to the naturalist Jack London; in style, subject, and philosophy those two would seem to be opposites.

We have known that Pound loved Flaubert and the sophisticated (relativist) realism of James; we have not recognized, however, how close Pound and some moderns may have been to extreme naturalism and its reductive truths. "True art speaks plainly," said Theodore Dreiser—or was it Jack London, or Frank Norris, back from art school in Paris to the young Gertrude Stein's Oakland—or was it Pound?

Pound frequently said he was against ideas, meaning ideas as abstractions: "The artist seeks out the luminous detail and presents it. He does not comment. . . . Each historian will 'have ideas'—presumably different from other historians—imperfect inductions, varying as the fashions, but the luminous details remain unaltered."[24] So the luminous details are not part of "ideas" or "imperfect deductions." They are free of thought. Pound is trying to substitute the "facts" of perception for the "ideas" of knowledge, as if perception were not subjective, were not informed by theory, ideas, the "fashion" of culture. He is not only antirelativist, he is absolutist in the naturalist tradition of perceived fact rather than the transcendental tradition of intuited spirit. Pound says, "An abstract or general statement is GOOD if it be ultimately found to correspond with the facts."[25] Just what the facts are, of course, and when "ultimately" occurs, are left open.

Pound admired the work of naturalist Louis Agassiz, and apparently felt that his own theories of economics and history were a science, or rather the raw data for a science that each reader would perceive when presented with the facts: the luminous details lying next to each other in the layers of the *Cantos*. A character in Wyndham Lewis's *The Apes of God* (1930) commented on this vorticist pretense to scientific truth: "The 'impersonality' of science and 'objective' observation is a wonderful patent behind which the individual can indulge in a riot of personal egotism."[26]

Many readers are familiar with the following passage from Pound. Pretend for a moment that it was spoken by Jack London:

> The arts, literature, poesy, are a science, just as chemistry is a science. . . . Bad art is inaccurate art. It is art that makes false reports. . . . If an artist falsifies his report as to the nature of man, as to his own nature . . . or on any other matter in order that he may conform to the taste of his time, to the proprieties of a sovereign, to the conveniences of a preconceived code of ethics, then that artist lies.[27]

This is pretty simple-minded. An artist has a "report" to make, a report that is "accurate" concerning "the nature of man" without reference to cultural or personal point of view, and shucks, he can either tell the truth or lie. Those familiar with Jack London, the most

reductive, extreme and courageous of the American literary natural-
ists, will recognize not only London's sentiments but also his style.
Short, no-nonsense, punchy, and aggressive sentences—about the
nature of man—from a straight-talking guy:

> Life? Bah! It has no value. Of cheap things it is the cheapest.
> Everywhere it goes begging. Nature spills it out with a lavish hand.
> Where there is room for one life, she sows a thousand lives, and it's
> life eat life till the strongest and most piggish life is left.[28]

Pound, London, and Hulme (a big man who occasionally slugged
people) and many others were interested in separating themselves
from turn-of-the-century aesthetes such as Oscar Wilde. Simplistic
statements about art, especially from one as bright as Pound, proceed
partly from an emerging cultural bias (luminous irony) toward a ma-
cho art. The following is from the journal of American musician
Charles Ives, about 1907:

> It used to come over me—especially after coming from some of
> those nice Kneisel Quartet concerts—that music had been, and still
> was, too much of an emasculated art. Too much of what was easy
> and usual to play and to hear was called beautiful, etc.—the same
> old even-vibration, Sybaritic apron strings, keeping music too much
> tied to the old ladies. The string quartet music got more and more
> weak, trite, and effeminate. After one of the Kneisel Quartet con-
> certs in old Mendelssohn Hall, I started a string quartet score, half
> mad, half in fun, and half to try out, practice, and have some fun
> with making those men fiddlers get up and do something like
> men. . . . It is one of the best things I have, but the old ladies (male
> and female) don't like it at all.[29]

This macho strain of modern art was partly following the conventions
of nineteenth-century naturalist sexism. An ugly male truth ("the
strongest and most piggish") is ranged against beauty, women, and
irrelevance. The dissonant, twelve-tone compositions and the cubist
nudes were perceived as aggressively ugly; sometimes, perhaps, they
were offered in that spirit too. J. B. Yeats said to his son W. B., "The
poets loved by Ezra Pound are tired of beauty."[30] Naturalist doctrine
offered little choice to an artist who wished to tell the truth of a nasty
"science," all else being "inaccurate art . . . false reports . . . lies."
Beauty was no longer truth, truth beauty; they were opposites. In this
respect Stevens differed from Pound and "his explosive-mouthed
gang" as Ford Madox Ford called them.[31] Stevens never believed in

the truth of naturalist "fact"; he located ugliness and beauty in the eye of the beholder.

Jack London, like the Lewis and Pound of *Blast,* was a leftist ranging from socialism to revolution. In his novel *The Iron Heel,* London joyously details the coming of the communist revolution to America. His hero and the leader of the left, Ernest Everhard (I can say no more), is fond of repeating to all opposition, "the facts, the irrefragable facts," meaning Marxist theories of economic history. He is a man of certainty, hardness, clear image, not a man of fluidity and change. A space man, as Lewis would say, not a time man. Everhard speaks the dialect of the imperious Pound. I fear that Everhard's naturalist conviction that certain luminous details can simply be known, and that a great man then acts violently to correct the anarchic mess into which we have obviously fallen, prefigures Lewis's *Hitler* and Pound's "The Duce will stand . . . with the lovers of OR- DER." Right and left are joined in reaction against modern relativity, and against the tolerance of antipathies which relativity implies. It is enough to drive one back to liberalism.

If we conceive of the modernist project as the pursuit of impersonality in art, we do it the most justice, and pull the men of 1914 into the same frame of reference as Stevens' meditative consciousness. The neoscientists and transcendental geometrists were not simply tired of romanticism or symbolism, they were inheriting Marx's and Engels's refutation of romanticism: consciousness does not determine the conditions of existence; the conditions of existence determine consciousness. By 1900, the heady progress of industry and the escalation of social and environmental problems caused by it had produced a world in which private consciousness seemed increasingly irrelevant or luxurious. In that world, very powerful things coopted the imagination. Gertrude Stein said the airplane would change our view of ourselves and nature, and she was right. Wallace Stevens by 1917 was publishing his work in *Soil,* next to odes on steam shovels. Things, whether or not they were falling apart, seemed to be leading consciousness. Why pursue an art of individual expression and feeling in the midst of this new world? From that point of view, the Nietzschean emphasis on metaphor, even provisional metaphor, could seem too personal. Art would have to leave the private, and take on the new public world.

That is why Kermode was correct, I believe, to seize on Mallarmé's description of modern dancer Loie Fuller in February 1893, as a touch-stone to the coming age. Her dance, said Mallarmé, is "an artistic intoxication and an industrial achievement. In that terrible bath of materials swoons the radiant, cold dancer. . . . The pure work re-quires that the poet vanish from the utterance." Mallarmé admired Fuller's swooning out of expression and into evanescent process within a setless theatre: "Here is atmosphere . . . that is nothingness . . . visions no sooner known than scattered, limpid evocation."[31]

The crucial element is the impersonality that Fuller conveyed while enacting her highly original and fluid "industrial achievement." Ken-ner would later say of Eliot's maturity, when Eliot sought to "escape personality" through poetry, that he had "withdrawn in favor of lan-guage,"[32] and we have seen Pound bend over backward to assert a perception free of self.

The modern age is different from the romantic in that it *seeks* to dethrone private consciousness. Whether, however, in a culture so heterogeneous and secular, we can lift the burden from personality and the subjectivity of perception, is highly arguable. The modern age might be called reluctantly romantic, which is not the same as romantic; and perhaps some of our angst derives from a desire to move on from the world of consciousness in which we are still locked and which seems at increasing odds with the tyranny of our products. We are rattling bars in the prison of the self. The contemporary ecological movement may represent the first real step out of that world, for as a branch of science ecology posits an external and beauti-ful system that exists beyond self and is perceived by reason (a true neoclassicism). Ecology also mounts the first *empirical* critique in European history of the idea of progress. Ecology offers, then, a description of a transpersonal and valuable reality, and this descrip-tion is approved by science while also serving as a rallying point for reform. Logically, I can see that we may have moved on from romanti-cism and modernism although I am not aware of the effect of ecology on our art.

Certainly by 1910, a romantic, expressive "I" seemed archaic to Mallarmé, James, Pound, Eliot, Joyce, Stevens—possibly even to Yeats. The need for impersonality is the constant of the age. The argument from there on is simple. Pound and Eliot strained to find an order outside of personality, but thereby of necessity turned their backs on the radical subjectivity of the age: its relativity of point of view and skepticism. Stevens found an impersonal way of regarding that subjectivity, leaving behind romantic commitment without asserting new truth. He not only made "as if" assertions in the Nietzschean tradition, but he took a detached point of view toward those provisional assertions, making a construction of his expression, a geometry of need. Thus his meditative consciousness is quintessentially modern. This book has been an attempt to show how an impersonal relation to consciousness might be possible, a relation which holds to the suchness of things as they are in a fragmented world, yet assiduously avoids the many modern temptations to reestablish the authority of the ordering mind. Detachment may offer the *only* true collage—collage with no subtext of desire or thought.

We do live in a world of fragments. Headlines on facing pages of the *Missoulian* newspaper for June 22, 1987: "Boeing nets contract . . . Collection of canines displayed at annual Missoula dog show . . . Tornado hits suburban Detroit . . . Reagan applauded for vetoing fairness bill . . . 'What summer? Two weeks of poor sledding—that's all it is.'—Hazel Clapperton, an Arctic cleaning lady." From Marinetti's futurism of 1914 ("Light, noise, speed—you can never get enough of these") to the present, even those not personally drawn to the avant-garde must respect the attempt to represent the anarchy loosed upon our world. The various wars against beauty, melody, closed symbols, statement, syntax, logos, and narrative are not simply rebellions by *enfants terribles,* though there has been enough of that; the wars are partly an honest attempt to make art of, to represent the dead geometry of, or to coopt with vitality or even find a way to love a culture that seeks meaning in data, not story, which does not tell tales, but gathers bits of information. The fragmentation of our milieu justifies the attempts to develop new and appropriate and disjunct forms. The collected works of Hazel Clapperton are a formidable poetry indeed.

It is easy to sympathize with those impatient with Stevens—his private and thoughtful language, his universe of consciousness, his apparent divorce from events of his age. The failure to achieve verbal collage by direct means is an important failure, which leaves authors such as Woolf, Stevens, Beckett, and Ashbery looking more modernly effective than the extreme avant-garde. As the list shows— Beckett being the most extreme—writing and reading may not be the medium for this project; movies, theatre, performance, music, may be better. MTV rock videos are certainly the triumph of surrealist technique, which means only that the revolutionary awareness of one generation may become the pablum of the next.

Thought and feeling unfold in time. No matter how profound the mimetic aspirations of various moderns, our central nervous systems evolved before Marinetti's "light, noise, speed," and we still think *to* a conclusion, whether we are operating inductively or deductively. And our feelings build, sometimes to a climax, and take time to dissipate. If we wish to push our needs up against the modern world, then it is perhaps best to speak with *enough* continuity and meaning to express the thought and feeling of the author and to engage the thought and feeling of the reader. That is why, I believe, the most successful moderns have not been the radical fringe, but the more linguistically conservative yet profoundly open or disjunct authors. The effect, then, of Stevens' expressive discourse within a disjunct framework is similar to jazz, playing the left hand of authoritative statement against the indeterminate right.

Stevens took up the modern challenge. He could be sure of nothing beyond consciousness, but he did not simply commit himself to thought and feeling in the romantic tradition, nor did he simply delight in creating fresh untruths in a Nietzschean world. Instead he watched himself do both, without denying the need to think and feel, and without retreating to new certainties. He did his best to observe his own construction of being, moment by moment, as if the observer were not himself. In a meditative schema, I hope to have shown, that may be quite possible. He was a poet of imagination and meditation—that is, of personality and impersonality—in relation to reality.

NOTES
BIBLIOGRAPHY
INDEX

Notes

Introduction

1. Helen Vendler, *On Extended Wings* (Cambridge, Mass.: Harvard University Press, 1969), pp. 10–11; hereafter cited as Vendler, *Wings.*

2. David Walker, *The Transparent Lyric* (Princeton, N.J.: Princeton University Press, 1984); hereafter cited as Walker, *Lyric.*

3. Marjorie Perloff, *The Dance of the Intellect* (Cambridge and New York: Cambridge University Press, 1985); hereafter cited as Perloff, *Dance;* and *The Poetics of Indeterminacy* (Princeton, N.J.: Princeton University Press, 1981); hereafter cited as Perloff, *Poetics.*

4. Harold Bloom, *Wallace Stevens: The Poems of Our Climate* (Ithaca, N.Y.: Cornell University Press, 1977), p. 62; hereafter cited as Bloom, *Stevens.*

5. Herbert V. Guenther, *Philosophy and Psychology in the Abhidharma* (Berkeley, Calif.: Shambhala Press, 1976), p. 95; hereafter cited as Guenther, *Abhidharma.*

6. R. H. Blyth, *Zen in English Literature and Oriental Classics* (1942; rpt. New York: E.P. Dutton, 1960). For example, see p. vii.

Chapter 1.   An Issue: Nirvana

1. Henri De Lubac, *La Rencontre du Bouddhisme,* as quoted by Guy Richard Welbon, *The Buddhist Nirvana and Its Western Interpreters* (Chicago: University of Chicago Press, 1968), p. 24; hereafter cited as Welbon, *Nirvana.*

2. Welbon, *Nirvana,* p. 29.

3. Yeats's journal, quoted by Frank Tuohy, *Yeats* (New York: Macmillan, 1976), p. 35.

4. Quoted in Welbon, *Nirvana,* p. 27.

5. Quoted in ibid., p. 28.

6. Ibid., p. 29.

7. Quoted in ibid., p. 29.

8. Ibid., p. 29.

9. Ibid., p. 153.

10. Ibid., p. 27.

11. Quoted in Chang Chung-Yuan, *Original Teachings of Ch'an Buddhism* (1969; rpt. New York: Random House, 1971), p. 11; hereafter cited as Chung-Yuan, *Teachings*.

Chapter 2.   An Example: "The Snow Man"

1. Vendler, *Wings*, p. 8.

2. Roy Harvey Pearce, "Wallace Stevens: The Last Lesson of the Master" in *The Act of the Mind*, ed. Pearce and Miller (Baltimore: John Hopkins Press, 1965), p. 133; hereafter cited as Pearce and Miller, *Act*.

3. Frank Doggett, *Stevens' Poetry of Thought* (Baltimore: Johns Hopkins Press, 1966), p. 130; hereafter cited as Doggett, *Thought*.

4. Bloom, *Stevens*, p. 62.

5. Richard A. Macksey, "The Climates of Wallace Stevens" in Pearce and Miller, *Act*, p. 200.

6. A. Walter Litz, *Introspective Voyager* (New York: Oxford University Press, 1972), p. 100.

7. Doggett, *Thought*, p. 129.

8. Emerson, "Nature," *Emerson's Complete Works* (Boston: Houghton Mifflin, 1929), I:7; hereafter Emerson will be cited by essay only.

9. Arthur Symons, *The Symbolist Movement in Literature* (1899; 1919 revision rpt. New York: E.P. Dutton, 1958), p. 72.

10. Bloom, *Stevens*, pp. 60–61.

11. Vendler, *Wings*, p. 285.

12. Bloom, *Stevens*, p. 63.

13. Louis Martz, *The Poem of the Mind* (Oxford: Oxford University Press, 1969), p. 202.

14. Bloom, *Stevens*, p. 63.

15. Walker, *Lyric*, p. 16.

16. The phrase occurs in "The Owl in the Sarcophagus" (*CP* 433), but the passage is by no means a gloss on the subject.

17. John Malcolm Brinnin as quoted in Vendler, *Wings*, p. 10.

18. William James, *The Varieties of Religious Experience* (1904; rpt. New York: Mentor, 1958).

19. See Margharita Laski, *Ecstasy* (Bloomington: Indiana University Press, 1962); Mircea Eliade, *Shamanism* (Princeton, N.J.: Princeton University Press, 1964); I. M. Lewis, *Ecstatic Religion* (Harmondsworth: Penguin Books, 1971); Richard Alpert, *Be Here Now* (Albuquerque: Lama Foundation, 1971); Charles T. Tart, ed., *Altered States of Consciousness* (New York: Doubleday, 1972); hereafter cited as Tart, *Altered States*.

20. For instance, see Thomas Weiskel, *The Romantic Sublime* (Balti-

more: Johns Hopkins University Press, 1976) and Stuart Ende, *Keats and the Sublime* (New Haven, Conn.: Yale University Press, 1976).

21. Vendler, *Wings*, p. 5.

Chapter 3.   *Four Types of Mysticism*

1. Charles T. Tart, "Preliminary Notes on the Nature of Psi Processes," in *The Nature of Human Consciousness*, Robert E. Ornstein, ed. (San Francisco: W.H. Freeman, 1968), p. 469. Tart pursued these views in *Transpersonal Psychologies* (New York: Harper and Row, 1975).

2. For an introduction to Buddhist magic, see Edward Conze, *Buddhism: Its Essence and Development* (1951; rpt. New York: Harper and Row, 1975), pp. 83–85; hereafter cited as Conze, *Buddhism*. See also discussions of Tantric Buddhism in Blofeld and Guenther.

3. Plato, *The Apology, Platonis Opera*, vol. I (Oxford: Clarendon, 1900), 22b.

4. William Blake, "A Vision of the Last Judgement," *Blake: Complete Writings* (London: Oxford University Press, 1966), p. 617.

5. Yung-chia (d. 713), trans. D. T. Suzuki, quoted in Frits Staal, *Exploring Mysticism* (Berkeley and Los Angeles: University of California Press, 1975), p. 159; hereafter cited as Staal, *Mysticism*.

6. Edmund Spenser, *Faerie Queene*, book I, canto IX, *The Poetical Works of Edmund Spenser* (Oxford: Oxford University Press, 1909), 2:111.

7. Quoted in Lucien Stryk, Takashi Ikemoto and Taigan Takayama, *Zen Poems of China and Japan: The Crane's Bill* (New York: Doubleday, 1973), p. xxix; hereafter cited as Stryk, Ikemoto and Takayama, *Zen Poems*.

8. Virginia Woolf, *Moments of Being* (New York: Harcourt, Brace, 1976). pp. 65, 67.

9. Yung-chia, quoted in Chung-Yuan, *Original Teachings*, p. 11.

Chapter 4.   *Meditative Perception: "The Course of a Particular"*

1. *OP* 96–97. Holly Stevens in *The Palm at the End of the Mind* corrected "air" to "ear" in the penultimate line, thereby restoring the original reading (*Hudson Review*, Spring 1961) and the more sensible one.

2. Chung-Yuan, *Teachings*, p. 59.

3. Kasamatsu and Hirai, "An Electroencephalographic Study on the Zen Meditation" (1966; rpt. in Tart, *Altered States*). Other useful studies of the physiology of meditation in Tart: Deikman, "Experimental Meditation," pp. 203–24; Anand et al., "Some Aspects of Electroencephalographic Studies in Yogis," pp. 515–19; Kamiya, "Operant Control of the EEG Alpha Rhythm" etc., pp. 519–29. See also Nowlis and Kamiya, "The Control of Electroencephalographic Alpha Rhythms" etc., in *Psychophysiology* 6, no. 4

(1970), and Wallace and Benson, "The Physiology of Meditation," *Scientific American,* February 1972. For a book-length study, see Tomio Hirai, M.D., *Zen and the Mind* (Tokyo: Japan Publications, 1978).

4. Quoted in Tart, *Altered States,* p. 507. (The quotation is correct; the writers are Japanese.)

5. Quoted in ibid., p. 511.

6. Quoted in ibid., p. 517.

7. Ibid., pp. 497–98.

8. Conze, *Buddhism,* p. 127.

9. Ibid., p. 134.

10. Ibid., p. 132.

11. Chung-Yuan, *Teachings,* p. 80.

12. Conze, *Buddhism,* p. 134.

13. Quoted in Chung-Yuan, *Teachings,* p. 202.

14. Quoted in ibid., p. 299.

15. Harold Henderson, *An Introduction to Haiku* (New York: Doubleday, 1958), p. 38. This is a widely respected set of translations, with helpful notes. Hereafter cited as Henderson, *Haiku.*

16. Chung-Yuan, *Teachings,* p. 93.

17. Lucien Stryk and Takashi Ikemoto, eds. and trans., *Zen: Poems, Prayers, Sermons, Anecdotes, Interviews* (New York: Doubleday, 1965), p. 12; hereafter cited as Stryk and Ikemoto, *Zen.* The Poem is a *waka* on "Void in Form" from "The Heart Sutra."

Chapter 5.   The Structure of Meditative Experience

1. "Subject B," quoted in Arthur J. Deikman, "Experimental Meditation," in Tart, *Altered States,* p. 208.

2. "Subject A," quoted in ibid., p. 208.

3. Daniel Goleman, *The Varieties of the Meditative Experience* (New York: E.P. Dutton, 1972), p. xx; hereafter cited as Goleman, *Meditative Experience.*

4. Quoted in ibid., p. xiv.

5. Especially Wallace and Benson, 1972. See ch. 4, n. 3, above.

6. Staal, *Mysticism,* p. 110.

7. Conze, *Meditation,* p. 113.

8. Goleman, *Meditative Experience,* p. 14.

9. Conze, *Buddhism,* pp. 100–01.

10. For a discussion of Theravadic views on "calmness," "right concentration" and the "ultimate goal" of nirvana, see Guenther, *Abhidharma,* p. 60.

11. Quoted in Tart, *Altered States,* p. 205.

12. Quoted in ibid., p. 206.

13. Quoted in ibid., pp. 208–09.

14. Quoted in ibid., pp. 211–12.
15. Quoted in ibid., p. 211.
16. Quoted in ibid., p. 220.
17. Quoted in ibid., p. 211.
18. Quoted in ibid., p. 215.
19. Quoted in ibid., p. 209.
20. Quoted in ibid., p. 211.
21. Quoted in ibid., pp. 215–16.
22. Quoted in ibid., p. 216.
23. Quoted in ibid., p. 216.
24. Quoted in ibid., p. 220.
25. Quoted in Peter Brazeau, *Parts of a World: Wallace Stevens Remembered* (New York: Random House, 1983), p. 239; hereafter cited as Brazeau, *Stevens Remembered.*

Chapter 6.   The Middle Way: "A Clear Day and No Memories"

1. Quoted in Conze, *Buddhism,* p. 43.
2. Ibid., p. 14.
3. Bhikshu Sangharakshita, *A Survey of Buddhism* (1957; rpt. Boulder, Colo.: Shambhala, 1980), p. 96. Sangharakshita's is a long, detailed introduction to Buddhism with a Mahayana bias; Conze's 1951 work is easier and shorter. Both books are weak on Tantric, Chinese and Japanese traditions, for which Blofeld, Guenther, Chung-Yuan, Suzuki and many other recent works might be consulted.
4. Guenther, *Abhidharma,* p. 9.
5. Ibid., p. 20.
6. Staal, *Mysticism,* p. 149.
7. Ibid., p. 13.
8. Conze, *Buddhism,* p. 13.
9. Ibid., p. 32. There is a new Nyingma Edition of the Tantra in English, Shambhala, 1983.
10. Staal, *Mysticism,* p. 99.
11. Chung-Yuan, *Teachings,* p. 7.
12. Staal, *Mysticism,* p. 158.
13. Conze, *Buddhism,* pp. 130–31.
14. Ibid., p. 132.
15. Staal, *Mysticism,* p. 36. See also Staal, p. 45; Chung Yuan, *Teachings,* pp. 10–11; and Sangharakshita, *A Survey of Buddhism,* pp. 301–14.
16. Conze, *Buddhism,* p. 20.
17. Guenther, *Abhidharma,* pp. 193–94.
18. Conze, *Buddhism,* p. 134.
19. Conze, *Buddhism,* p. 137.

20. Quoted in Paul Reps and Nyogen Senzaki, *Zen Flesh, Zen Bones* (Kakuan section originally published 1935; rpt. New York: Doubleday Anchor, n.d.), pp. 134–55.

21. Quoted in Conze, *Buddhism,* p. 130.

22. Wan-ja T'ung-Che, quoted in Chung-Yuan, *Teachings,* p. 53.

23. Ma-tsu (d. 788), quoted in Chung-Yuan, *Teachings,* p. 130.

24. Chung-Yuan, *Teachings,* p. 48.

25. Ibid., p. 140.

26. Tomio Hirai, *Zen and the Mind* (Tokyo: Japan Publications, 1978), p. 103; hereafter cited as Hirai, *Zen.*

27. Chung-Yuan, *Teachings,* p. 165.

28. Ibid., p. 143.

29. T.R.V. Murti, quoted in ibid., p. 4.

30. Chung-Yuan, *Teachings,* p. 34.

31. Guenther, *Abhidharma,* p. 71.

32. Ibid., p. 112.

33. Chung-Yuan, *Teachings,* p. 59.

34. Nan Chuan, quoted in Garma C. C. Chang, *The Practice of Zen* (1959; rpt. New York: Harper & Row, 1970), p. 18; hereafter cited as Chang, *Practice.*

35. Fa-yung, quoted in Chung-Yuan, *Teachings,* p. 21.

36. For instance, a Yoga text labels the lower levels of consciousness "the scattered (ksipta), the confused (mudha), the distracted (viksipta)" (Staal, *Mysticism,* p. 119).

Chapter 7.   The Meditative Stevens: "The Latest Freed Man"

1. Quoted in Brazeau, *Stevens Remembered,* p. 213.

2. Guenther, *Abhidharma,* p. 95.

3. See William Bevis, "The Arrangement of Harmonium," *English Literary History* 37, no. 3 (Sept. 1970), 456–73.

4. Chung-Yuan, *Teachings,* p. 141.

5. Muso (1275–1352), quoted in Stryk and Ikemoto, *Zen,* p. 4.

6. Brazeau, *Stevens Remembered,* p. 27n, 32.

7. Guenther, *Abhidharma,* p. 74.

Chapter 8. The Physiology of Meditation

1. Richard E. Byrd, *Alone* (London: Putnam, 1938), p. 121; hereafter cited as Byrd, *Alone.*

2. Quoted in Walter F. Prince, *Noted Witnesses for Psychic Occurrences* (Boston: Lippincott, 1928), p. 144.

3. Byrd, *Alone,* pp. 130–31.

4. R. K. Wallace and H. Benson, "The Physiology of Meditation," *Scientific American,* February 1972, p. 158.

5. Hirai, *Zen,* p. 108.

6. In the general neurophysiology of this chapter I have tried to be conservative, using the lowest common denominators between texts. Remarks not traced to specific sources are consonant with: Colin Blakemore, *Mechanics of the Mind* (Cambridge: Cambridge University Press, 1977); hereafter cited as Blakemore, *Mechanics of the Mind; The Brain, A Scientific American Book* (San Francisco: W.H. Freeman, 1979); Francis Leukel, *Introduction to Physiological Psychology,* 3d ed., (St.Louis: Mosby, 1976); Donald Stein and Jeffrey Rosen, *Basic Structure and Function in the Central Nervous System* (New York: Macmillan, 1974). The definitions of *self,* however, are my own.

7. Jose Delgado, *Physical Control of the Mind* (New York: Harper & Row, 1969), p. 50.

8. See Leo V. Dicara, "Learning in the Autonomic Nervous System," Ralph Ezios, "Implications of Physiological Feedback Training," and Nowlis and Kamiya, "The Control of Electroencephalographic Alpha Rhythms," all reprinted in *The Nature of Human Consciousness,* ed. Robert Ornstein (San Francisco: Freeman, 1973), pp. 335, 376, 387.

9. Arthur J. Deikman, "Implications of Experimentally Induced Contemplative Meditation" (1966), quoted in Staal, *Mysticism,* p. 118. See also Deikman, "Deautomatization and the Mystic Experience" (1966) in Tart, *Altered States,* pp. 25ff.

10. Byrd, *Alone,* p. 122.

11. Henderson, *Haiku,* pp. 19–20.

12. Hirai, *Zen,* p. 103.

13. Roland Fischer, "A Cartography of the Ecstatic and Meditative States," *Science* 174, no. 4012 (Nov. 1971), 897–903.

14. Ibid.

15. Goleman, *Meditative Experience,* p. 38.

16. Byrd, *Alone,* pp. 122–23.

Chapter 9. Self and Will

1. Wilder Penfield, *The Mystery of the Mind* (Princeton, N.J.: Princeton University Press, 1975), p. 19; hereafter cited as Penfield, *Mind.*

2. Ibid., p. 20.

3. Blakemore, *Mechanics of the Mind.*

4. Guenther, *Abhidharma,* p. 144.

5. Ibid., p. 47.

6. From the *Visuddhimagga,* quoted in Conze, *Meditation,* p. 152.

7. Penfield, *Mind,* pp. 52–53.

8. Ibid., p. 18.

9. Ibid., p. 77.
10. Guenther, *Abhidharma*, p. 83.

Chapter 10. Language, Mind, and No-Mind

1. Staal, *Mysticism*, p. 179.
2. Bhikshu Sangharakshita, *A Survey of Buddhism* (1957; rpt. Boulder, Colo.: Shambhala, 1980), p. 96.
3. Helen Vendler, *Part of Nature, Part of Us* (Cambridge, Mass: Harvard University Press, 1980), p. 11.
4. Tsung Kao, quoted in Chang, *Practice*, p. 89.
5. Guenther, *Abhidharma*, p. 6.
6. Chung-Yuan, *Teachings*, p. x.
7. Staal, *Mysticism*, p. 35.
8. Ibid., pp. 25ff.

Chapter 11. The Tragedy of Desire in "Esthétique du Mal"

1. The same equation of generation, time, and pain can be found in the opening of "Credences of Summer," written three years later (*CP* 372–78). The images of generation—mothers, fathers, lovers—represent the world of passing time, which is the enemy of a meditative ability to live in the present moment "beyond which there is nothing left of time." Furthermore, in "Credences" the images of generation are "false disasters," only imagined, suggesting that the historical world is *maya,* illusion, and only the moment "now" is real.

Chapter 12. Turn of the Century

1. André Breton, "Manifesto of Surrealism," in *Manifestoes of Surrealism,* trans. Seaver and Lane (Ann Arbor: U. of Michigan Press, 1969), p. 34; hereafter cited as Seaver and Lane, *Manifestoes.* Many thanks to Sara Miller and Peter Russell for observations on surrealists, dadaists, and Mallarmé.
2. Stephane Mallarmé, *Selected Prose Poems, Essays and Letters,* trans. Bradford Cook (Baltimore, Md.: Johns Hopkins Press, 1956), p. 93. For a typically difficult use of *le néant* in Mallarmé, see the poem "Ses Ondes pures."
3. Tristan Tzara, "Lecture on Dada" in *The Dada Painters and Poets,* ed. Robert Motherwell (New York: Wittenbaorn, Schultz, 1951), p. 247.
4. Tristan Tzara, in Seaver and Lane, *Manifestoes,* p. 251.
5. André Breton, *Le Surrealisme et la peinture* (Paris: Gallimard, 1965), p. 373.

6. Rick Fields, *How the Swans Came to the Lake* (Boulder, Colo.: Shambhala Press, 1981), p. 69. Hereafter cited as Fields, *Swans*.

7. Quoted in Welbon, *Nirvana*, p. 167.

8. Quoted in ibid., p. 165.

9. Fields, *Swans*, p. 42.

10. Ibid., p. 86. Fields tells in some detail the delightful story of Blavatsky and Olcott.

11. Ibid., p. 97.

12. Ibid., p. 103.

13. Quoted in ibid., p. 102.

14. Ibid., p. 135.

15. Walt Whitman, "The Errand-Bearers" in *The New York Times*, June 27, 1860, and later revised to this "Broadway Pageant" in *Leaves of Grass*. The seed grows past "bonze, brahmin, and llama" in the first version to return to "Asia, the all-mother" in the final text.

16. Fields, *Swans*, p. 124.

Chapter 13.   Yeats's Chatterji

1. William Butler Yeats, *The Trembling of the Veil* (1922), rpt. in *The Autobiography of William Butler Yeats* (New York: Macmillan, 1965), p. 117. Hereafter cited as Yeats, *Autobiography*.

2. Quoted in Frank Tuohy, *Yeats* (New York: Macmillan, 1976), p. 34. Hereafter cited as Tuohy, *Yeats*.

3. Yeats, *Autobiography*, p. 116.

4. Ibid.

5. Ibid., p. 117.

6. Ibid., p. 60.

7. Ibid., p. 61.

8. Quoted in Tuohy, *Yeats*, p. 35.

9. Ibid.

10. The first version of Yeats's poem is quoted in Richard Ellmann, *The Identity of Yeats* (Oxford: Oxford University Press, 1964), pp. 44–45. Hereafter cited as Ellmann, *Identity*.

11. Quoted in ibid., pp. 234–35.

12. Ibid., p. 46.

13. Tuohy, *Yeats*, p. 36.

14. Quoted in ibid., p. 201.

15. Ibid., p. 213.

16. Quoted in ibid., p. 208.

17. Shree Purohit Swami and W. B. Yeats, *The Ten Principal Upanishads* (London: Faber & Faber, 1937), p. 9.

18. Quoted in Tuohy, *Yeats*, p. 213.

Chapter 14.   Santayana's Angels

1. George Santayana, *Interpretations of Poetry and Religion* (New York: Harper and Brothers, 1957), pp. 13–15.
2. Ibid., p. 15.
3. Ibid., p. 18.
4. Ibid., p. 19.
5. Ibid., p. 20.

Chapter 15.   Pound's Cathay

1. Pound's letter and useful comments appear in William Pratt, *The Imagist Poem* (New York: Dutton, 1963), pp. 31–32.
2. Hugh Kenner, *The Pound Era* (Berkeley: University of California Press, 1971), p. 197. Hereafter cited as Kenner, *Pound*.
3. Fields, *Swans*, p. 161.
4. Quoted in ibid., p. 153.
5. Ibid., p. 158.
6. Fenellosa, quoted in ibid., p. 158.
7. Pound, quoted in ibid., p. 153.
8. Kenner, *Pound*, p. 225.
9. Fenellosa, quoted in ibid., p. 225.
10. Ibid., p. 210.
11. Pound, quoted in ibid., p. 174.
12. Quoted in Wai-lim Yip, *Ezra Pound's Cathay* (Princeton, N.J.: Princeton University Press, 1969), pp. 21–22.
13. Quoted in Sanford Schwartz, *The Matrix of Modernism* (Princeton, N.J.: Princeton University Press, 1985), p. 132; hereafter cited as Schwartz, *Matrix*.
14. Quoted in Timothy Materer, *Vortex* (Ithaca, N.Y.: Cornell University Press, 1979), p. 65; hereafter cied as Materer, *Vortex*.

Chapter 16.   Stevens' Readings

1. See for instance Wang Wei's "Retreat at Mount Chung-Nan" and Bynner's note in *The Jade Mountain* (New York: Knopf, 1929), pp. 195, 266.
2. Arthur Morrison, *Illustrated Catalogue for an Exhibition of Japanese Prints* (London, Fine Arts Society, 1909). There is a copy of this catalogue in the New York Public Library.
3. Arthur Morrison, *Guide to an Exhibition of Japanese and Chinese Paintings* (London's British Museum Trustees, 1914), p. 6.
4. Morrison, *Illustrated Catalogue*, p. 2.
5. Quoted in Brazeau, *Stevens Remembered*, p. 137.

Chapter 17. Stevens' Walks

1. See Brazeau, *Stevens Remembered*, pp. 207, 231, 239, 243.
2. Quoted in Stryk and Ikemoto, *Zen Poems*, p. 90.
3. Dogen (1200–1253), quoted in ibid., p. 81.
4. Brazeau, *Stevens Remembered*, p. 197.
5. Chung-Yuan, *Teachings*, pp. 47–9.
6. Guenther, *Abhidharma*, p. 86.
7. Ibid., p. 9.
8. Staal, *Mysticism*, p. 45.
9. Chung-Yuan, *Teachings*, p. 44.

Chapter 18. Overlooking Nothing: The Critics

1. J. Hillis Miller, "Wallace Stevens' Poetry of Being," in Pearce and Miller, *Act*, p. 157.
2. Louis Martz, *The Poem of the Mind* (Oxford: Oxford University Press, 1969), p. 202.
3. Richard A. Macksey, "The Climates of Wallace Stevens," in Pearce and Miller, *Act*, p. 217.
4. Richard A. Macksey in Pearce and Miller, *Act*, p. 200. Macksey's article explores Stevens' "nothing" in relation to a nonmeditative reading of Valery and Heidegger.
5. Ibid., p. 62.
6. Ibid., p. 1.
7. Ibid., p. 63.
8. Ibid., p. 63.
9. Bloom, *Stevens*, p. 240.
10. Vendler, *Wings*, p. 220.
11. Welbon, *Nirvana*, p. 27.
12. Vendler, *Wings*, pp. 285–86.
13. For instance, see Tart, *Altered States*, pp. 218 ff; Staal, *Mysticism*, pp. 105–07; Hirai, *Zen*, pp. 134–35; Stryk and Ikemoto, *Zen*, p. xxx.
14. Hsiang-yen (c. 900), quoted in Chung-Yuan, *Teachings*, p. 189.
15. Doggett, *Thought*, pp. 8–9.
16. Staal, *Mysticism*, p. 72.
17. Conze, *Buddhism*, p. 39.
18. For a critique of Zaehner, see Staal, *Mysticism*, pp. 67ff.
19. Ibid., p. 160.
20. Guenther, *Abhidharma*, p. 141.
21. Buson (1715–1783), quoted in Stryk, Ikemoto and Takayama, *Zen Poems*, p. xliii.

22. Henderson, *Haiku*, p. 93.
23. Quoted in Stryk, Ikemoto and Takayama, *Zen Poems*, p. 157.
24. Ibid., p. xxxviiiff.
25. Staal, *Mysticism*, p. 111.
26. Chang, *Practice*, p. 203.
27. Vendler, *Wings*, p. 13.

Chapter 19.   *Fragments and Change*

1. William H. Pritchard, *Lives of the Modern Poets* (New York: Oxford University Press, 1980), p. 190.
2. Bloom, *Stevens*, p. 168.
3. Chung-Yuan, *Teachings*, p. 197.
4. Quoted in Schwartz, *Matrix*, p. 123.
5. Perloff, *Poetics*, p. 156.
6. Staal, *Mysticism*, p. 129.
7. Han-shan, quoted in Chang, *Practice*, p. 114.
8. Quoted in Chang, *Practice*, pp. 113, 115.
9. Perloff, *Poetics*, pp. 61–62.

Chapter 20.   *Opus 130 and the Politics of Emotion*

1. Harold Truscott, *Beethoven's Late String Quartets* (London: Dobson, 1968), p. 16; hereafter cited as Truscott, *Beethoven's Late Quartets*.
2. Quoted in Perloff, *Dance*, p. 163.
3. "Der Schwer Gefasste Entschluss. Muss es sein? Es muss sein! Es muss sein!" For a discussion, see George Marek, *Beethoven* (New York: Crowell, 1969), p. 608.
4. Truscott, *Beethoven's Late Quartets*, p. 9.
5. Ibid., pp. 86–87.
6. Ibid., p. 87.
7. Ibid.
8. Philip Radcliffe, *Beethoven's String Quartets* (1965; rpt. Cambridge: Cambridge University Press, 1978), pp. 124–26.
9. Wayne Fields, "Beyond Definition: A Reading of *The Prairie*," in *James Fenimore Cooper*, ed. Fields (Englewood Cliffs, N.J.: Prentice-Hall, 1979), p. 109.
10. Quoted in Vendler, *Wings*, p. 306.
11. Jerry Waldo, *Ragtime* (New York: Hawthorne, 1976), pp. 4–6.
12. Ibid., p. 14.
13. Ibid., p. 15.
14. Ibid., p. 13.

15. William Wees, *Vorticism and the English Avant-garde* (Toronto: University of Toronto Press, 1972), p. 49.

16. Ibid., p. 51.

17. Ibid.

18. Dick Katz, quoted in *The Smithsonian Collection of Classic Jazz*, ed. Martin Williams (Washington, D.C.: The Smithsonian Institution, 1973), p. 26.

19. Quoted in ibid., p. 33.

20. Truscott, *Beethoven's Late Quartets*, p. 330.

21. Stryk and Ikemoto, *Zen*, p. 323.

Chapter 21.   *Four Types of Form*

1. Barbara Herrnstein Smith, *Poetic Closure* (Chicago: University of Chicago Press, 1968), p. 109; hereafter cited as Smith, *Closure*.

2. Kenneth Burke, *Counter-Statement* (New York: Harcourt, Brace, 1931), p. 157.

3. Ibid., pp. 158–59.

4. Burke, *Counter-Statement*, p. 158.

5. Ibid.

6. Smith, *Closure*, pp. 98–99.

7. Burke, *Counter-Statement*, p. 159.

8. William Faulkner, *The Sound and the Fury* (New York: Random House, 1929), p. 94.

9. See, for instance, Louis Simpson, *Three on the Tower* (New York: Morrow, 1975), pp. 146ff.

10. Chang, *Practice*, p. 203.

11. Shinzen Young, quoted in Robinson and Johnson, *The Buddhist Religion*, 3d ed. (Belmont, Calif.: Wadsworth, 1982), p. 231.

12. Quoted in Brazeau, *Stevens Remembered*, p. 175.

13. Quoted in Hughes, *The Shock of the New* (New York: Knopf, 1981), p. 174.

14. Chang, *Practice*, p. 43.

Chapter 22.   *The Comedy of Consciousness*

1. Quoted in Brazeau, *Stevens Remembered*, p. 211.

2. Sigmund Freud, quoted with interesting comments in Staal, *Mysticism*, pp. 132–33, emphasis added.

Postscript

1. Perloff, *Dance,* p. 14.
2. Perloff, *Poetics,* p. 23.
3. Ibid., p. 4.
4. Quoted in Materer, *Vortex,* p. 208.
5. Quoted in Wees, *Vorticism,* p. 13.
6. Ibid., chs. 1–2.
7. C. K. Stead, *Pound, Yeats, Eliot and the Modernist Movement* (New Brunswick, N.J.: Rutgers University Press, 1986), ch. 7.
8. Donald Davie, *Ezra Pound* (Chicago: University of Chicago Press, 1975), p. 40.
9. Quoted in Kenner, *Pound,* p. 157.
10. Quoted in ibid., p. 159.
11. Quoted in ibid., p. 157.
12. Ibid., p. 153.
13. Ibid., p. 150.
14. From Emerson's "Nature" (Boston: Houghton Mifflin, 1957), p. 41.
15. Quoted in Kenner, *Pound,* p. 160.
16. Ibid., p. 171.
17. Quoted in Schwartz, *Matrix,* p. 148.
18. Davie, *Pound,* pp. 73ff.
19. Quoted in Materer, *Vortex,* p. 152.
20. Quoted in Schwartz, *Matrix,* p. 56.
21. Quoted in ibid.
22. Wees, *Vorticism,* pp. 82–83.
23. Quoted in Materer, *Vortex,* p. 91.
24. Quoted in Schwartz, *Matrix,* p. 121.
25. Quoted in ibid.
26. Quoted in Materer, *Vortex,* p. 207.
27. Quoted in Schwartz, *Matrix,* p. 66.
28. Jack London, *The Sea-Wolf* (New York: Macmillan, 1904), p. 58.
29. *Charles Ives' Memoirs,* ed. John Kirkpatrick (New York: W.W. Norton, 1972), p. 83.
30. Quoted in Richard Ellmann, *Eminent Domain* (London: Oxford University Press, 1967), p. 62.
31. Quoted in Frank Kermode, "Poet and Dancer Before Diaghilev," in *What Is Dance,* ed. Copeland and Cohen (New York: Oxford University Press, 1983), p. 145ff.
32. Kenner, *Pound,* p. 136.

Bibliography

Altieri, Charles. *Act and Quality.* Amherst: University of Massachusetts Press, 1981.

Anand, B. K., et al. "Some Aspects of Electroencephalographic Studies in Yogis." In *Altered States,* ed. Tart.

Arnheim, Rudolf. *Art and Visual Perception.* Berkeley and Los Angeles: University of California Press, 1954.

Baird, James. *The Dome and the Rock: Structure in the Poetry of Wallace Stevens.* Baltimore: Johns Hopkins Press, 1968.

Bates, Milton. *Wallace Stevens: A Mythology of Self.* Berkeley and Los Angeles: University of California, Press, 1986.

Blakemore, Colin. *Mechanics of the Mind.* Cambridge: Cambridge University Press, 1977.

Blofeld, John. *The Tantric Mysticism of Tibet.* New York: E.P. Dutton, 1970.

Bloom, Harold. *Poetry and Repression.* New Haven, Conn.: Yale University Press, 1976.

Bloom, Harold. *Wallace Stevens: The Poems of Our Climate.* Ithaca, N.Y.: Cornell University Press, 1977.

Bloom, Harold, ed. *Romanticism and Consciousness.* New York: W.W. Norton, 1970.

Blyth, R. H. *Zen in English Literature and Oriental Classics.* 1942; rpt. New York: E.P. Dutton, 1960.

Borroff, Marie, ed. *Wallace Stevens: A Collection of Critial Essays.* Englewood Cliffs, N.J.: Prentice-Hall, 1963.

Brazeau, Peter. *Parts of a World: Wallace Stevens Remembered.* New York: Random House, 1983.

Breton, André. *Le Surrealisme et la peinture.* Paris: Gallimard, 1965.

Breton, André. "Manifesto of Surrealism." In *Manifestoes of Surrealism,* ed. and trans. Richard Seaver and Helen Lane. Ann Arbor: University of Michigan Press, 1969.

Brogan, Jacqueline Vaught. *Stevens and Simile: A Theory of Language.* Princeton, N.J.: Princeton University Press, 1986.

Burke, Kenneth. *Counter-Statement.* New York: Harcourt, Brace, 1931.

Burke, Kenneth. *Language as Symbolic Action.* Berkeley and Los Angeles: University of California Press, 1966.

Bynner, Witter. *The Jade Mountain.* New York: Knopf, 1929.

Byrd, Richard E. *Alone.* London: Putnam, 1938.

Chang, Garma C. C. *The Practice of Zen.* 1959; rpt. New York: Harper and Row, 1970.

Chung-Yuan, Chang. *Original Teachings of Ch'an Buddhism.* 1969; rpt. New York: Random House, 1971.

Cleary, Thomas, and J. C. Cleary. *The Blue Cliff Record.* 3 vols. Boulder, Colo., and London: Shambhala Press, 1977.

Conze, Edward. *Buddhism: Its Essence and Development.* 1951; rpt. New York: Harper and Row, 1975.

Conze, Edward. *Buddhist Meditation.* 1956; rpt. New York: Harper and Row, 1975.

Conze, Edward. *Selected Sayings from the Perfection of Wisdom.* 1955; rpt. Boulder, Colo.: Prajna Press, 1978.

Copeland, Roger, and Marshall Cohen, eds. *What Is Dance?* New York: Oxford University Press, 1983.

Davie, Donald. *Ezra Pound.* Chicago: University of Chicago Press, 1975.

DeBary, Theodore, ed. *The Buddhist Tradition.* New York; Random House, 1969.

Deikman, Arthur J. "Deautomatization and the Mystic Experience." In *Altered States,* ed. Tart.

Deikman, Arthur J. "Experimental Meditation." In *Altered States,* ed. Tart.

Delgado, Jose. *Physical Control of the Mind.* New York: Harper and Row, 1969.

Derrida, Jacques. *Of Grammatology.* Trans. G. C. Spivak. Baltimore, Md.: Johns Hopkins University Press, 1972.

Dicara, Leo V. "Learning in the Autonomic Nervous System." In *The Nature of Human Consciousness,* ed. Ornstein.

Dickson, G. Lowes. *Letters from John Chinaman.* London: R. Brimley Johnson, 1904.

Doggett, Frank. *Stevens' Poetry of Thought.* Baltimore, Md.: Johns Hopkins Press, 1966.

Doggett, Frank, and Robert Buttel, eds. *Wallace Stevens: A Celebration.* Princeton, N.J.: Princeton University Press, 1980.

Eagleton, Terry. *Literary Theory.* Minneapolis: University of Minnesota Press, 1983.

Eliade, Mircea. *The Sacred and the Profane.* Trans. Willard Trask. New York: Harcourt, Brace, 1959.

Eliade, Mircea. *Yoga: Immortality and Freedom.* Trans. Willard Trask. Princeton, N.J.: Princeton University Press, 1958.

Ellmann, Richard. *Eminent Domain.* London: Oxford University Press, 1967.

Ellmann, Richard. *The Identity of Yeats.* Oxford: Oxford University Press, 1964.

Ende, Stuart A. *Keats and the Sublime.* New Haven, Conn.: Yale University Press, 1976.

Ezios, Ralph. "Implications of Physiological Feedback Training." In *The Nature of Human Consciousness*, ed. Ornstein.

Fields, Rick. *How the Swans Came to the Lake: A Narrative History of Buddhism in America*. Boulder, Colo.: Shambala Press, 1981.

Fischer, Roland. "A Cartography of the Ecstatic and Meditative States," *Science* 174, no. 4012 (November 1971), 897–903.

Frye, Northrop. *Anatomy of Criticism: Four Essays*. Princeton, N.J.: Princeton University Press, 1957.

Frye, Northrop. *A Study of English Romanticism*. New York: Random House, 1968.

Goleman, Daniel. *The Varieties of the Meditative Experience*. New York: E.P. Dutton, 1972.

Guenther, Herbert V. *Philosophy and Psychology in the Abhidharma*. Berkeley, Calif., and London: Shambhala Press, 1976.

Hartmann, Ernest L. *The Functions of Sleep*. New Haven, Conn.: Yale University Press, 1973.

Henderson, Harold. *An Introduction to Haiku*. New York: Doubleday, 1958.

Herrigel, Eugen. *Zen in the Art of Archery*. New York: Pantheon, 1953.

Hines, Thomas J. *The Later Poetry of Wallace Stevens: Phenomenological Parallels with Husserl and Heidegger*. Lewisburg, Pa.: Bucknell University Press, 1976.

Hirai, Tomio. *Zen and the Mind*. Tokyo: Japan Publications, 1978.

Hughes, Robert. *The Shock of the New*. New York: Knopf, 1961.

Iser, Wolfgang. *The Implied Reader*. Baltimore, Md.: Johns Hopkins University Press, 1974.

James, William. *The Varieties of Religious Experience*. 1904; rpt. New York: Mentor, 1958.

Kamiya, Joe. "Operant Control of the EEG Alpha Rhythm." In *Altered States*, ed. Tart.

Kapleau, Philip. *The Three Pillars of Zen*. Boston: Beacon Press, 1967.

Kato, Bunno, et al., trans. *The Three Fold Lotus Sutra*. New York and Tokyo: Weatherhill/Kosei, 1975.

Kenner, Hugh. *The Pound Era*. Berkeley and Los Angeles: University of California Press, 1971.

Kermode, Frank. "Poet and Dancer Before Diaghilev." In *What Is Dance*, ed. Copeland and Cohen.

Kermode, Frank. *The Sense of an Ending: Studies in the Theory of Fiction*. New York: Oxford University Press, 1966.

Kirkpatrick, John, ed. *Charles Ives' Memoirs*. New York: Norton, 1972.

Kubose, Gyomay. *Zen Koans*. Chicago: Henry Regnery, 1975.

Laski, Margharita. *Ecstasy*. Bloomington: Indiana University Press, 1962.

Lentricchia, Frank. *After the New Criticism*. Chicago: University of Chicago Press, 1980.

Lentricchia, Frank. *The Gaiety of Language: An Essay on the Radical Poetics of W. B. Yeats and Wallace Stevens*. Berkeley and Los Angeles: University of California Press, 1968.

Leukel, Francis. *Introduction to Psychiological Psychology.* St. Louis: Mosby, 1976.

Lewis, I. M. *Ecstatic Religion.* Harmondsworth, Middlesex: Penguin Books, 1971.

Litz, A. Walter. *Introspective Voyager.* New York: Oxford University Press, 1972.

Macksey, Richard A. "The Climates of Wallace Stevens." In *The Act of the Mind,* ed. Pearce and Miller.

Magliola, Robert R. *Derrida on the Mend.* West Lafayette, Ind.: Purdue University Press, 1984.

Magliola, Robert R. *Phenomenology and Literature.* West Lafayette, Ind.: Purdue University Press, 1983.

Mallarmé, Stephane. *Selected Prose, Poems, Essays and Letters.* Ed. Bradford Cook. Baltimore, Md.: Johns Hopkins Press, 1956.

Marek, George. *Beethoven.* New York: Crowell, 1969.

Martz, Louis. *The Poem of the Mind.* Oxford: Oxford University Press, 1969.

Materer, Timothy. *Vortex.* Ithaca, N.Y.: Cornell University Press, 1979.

Merton, Thomas. *Mystics and Zen Masters.* New York: Dell, 1961.

Miller, J. Hillis. "Wallace Stevens' Poetry of Being." In *The Act of the Mind,* ed. Pearce and Miller.

More, Paul Elmer. *Shelburne Essays.* New York: Putnam's, 1909.

Morrison, Arthur. *Guide to an Exhibition of Japanese and Chinese Prints.* British Museum Trustees, 1914.

Morrison, Arthur. *Illustrated Catalogue for an Exhibition of Japanese Prints.* London: Fine Arts Society, 1909.

Naranjo, C., and R. Ornstein, eds. *On the Psychology of Meditation.* New York: Viking, 1971.

Okakura, Kakuzo. *The Ideals of the East.* 1903; rpt. London: J. Murray, 1920.

Ornstein, Robert E. *On the Experience of Time.* Harmondsworth, Middlesex: Penguin Books, 1969.

Ornstein, Robert E., ed. *The Nature of Human Consciousness.* San Francisco: W.H. Freeman, 1968.

Pearce, Roy Harvey. "Wallace Stevens: The Last Lesson of the Master." In *The Act of the Mind,* ed. Pearce and Miller.

Pearce, Roy Harvey, and J. Hillis Miller, eds. *The Act of the Mind,* Baltimore, Md.: Johns Hopkins Press, 1965.

Penfield, Wilder. *The Mystery of the Mind.* Princeton, N.J.: Princeton University Press, 1975.

Perloff, Marjorie. *The Dance of the Intellect.* Cambridge: Cambridge University Press, 1985.

Perloff, Marjorie. *The Poetics of Indeterminacy.* Princeton, N.J.: Princeton University Press, 1981.

Plato, *The Apology.* Vol. 1 of *Platonis Opera.* Oxford: Clarendon Press, 1900.

Poulet, Georges. *Studies in Human Time*. Trans. Elliott Coleman. Baltimore, Md.: Johns Hopkins Press, 1956.

Pratt, William. *The Imagist Poem*. New York: E.P. Dutton, 1963.

Prince, Walter F. *Noted Witnesses for Psychic Occurrences*. Boston: Lippincott, 1928.

Pritchard, William H. *Lives of the Modern Poets*. New York: Oxford University Press, 1980.

Radcliffe, Philip. *Beethoven's String Quartets*. 1965; rpt. Cambridge: Cambridge University Press, 1978.

Regeuiro, Helen. *The Limits of Imagination: Wordsworth, Yeats, Stevens*. Ithaca, N.Y.: Cornell University Press, 1976.

Reps, Paul, and Nyogen Senzaki. *Zen Flesh, Zen Bones*. 1935; rpt. New York: Doubleday Anchor, n.d.

Richardson, Joan. *Wallace Stevens*. New York: William Morrow, 1986.

Robinson, Richard, and W. Johnson. *The Buddhist Religion*. 3d ed. Belmont, Calif.: Wadsworth, 1982.

Rosen, Charles. *The Classical Style*. New York: Viking, 1971.

Sangharakshita, Bhikshu. *A Survey of Buddhism*. 1957; rpt. Boulder, Colo.: Shambhala Press, 1980.

Santayana, George. *Interpretations of Poetry and Religion*. New York: Harper and Brothers, 1957.

Sasaki, Ruth Fuller, trans. *The Record of Lin-chi*. Kyoto, Japan: Institute for Zen Studies, 1975.

Schwartz, Sanford. *The Matrix of Modernism*. Princeton, N.J.: Princeton University Press, 1985.

Shree Purohi Swami and W. B. Yeats. *The Ten Principal Upanishads*. London: Faber and Faber, 1937.

Simpson, Louis. *Three on the Tower*. New York: Morrow, 1975.

Smith, Barbara Herrnstein. *Poetic Closure*. Chicago: University of Chicago Press, 1968.

Spenser, Edmund. *The Faerie Queene*. Vol. 2 of *The Poetical Works of Edmund Spenser*. Oxford: Oxford University Press, 1909.

Staal, Frits. *Exploring Mysticism*. Berkeley and Los Angeles: University of California Press, 1975.

Stace, W. T. *Mysticism and Philosophy*. Philadelphia and New York: J.B. Lippincott, 1960.

Stead, C. K. *Pound, Yeats, Eliot, and the Modernist Movement*. New Brunswick, N.J.: Rutgers University Press, 1986.

Stein, Donald, and Jeffrey Rosen. *Basic Structure and Function in the Central Nervous System*. New York: Macmillan, 1974.

Stevens, Holly. *The Palm at the End of the Mind*. New York: Knopf, 1967.

Stevens, Holly, ed. *Souvenirs and Prophesies: The Young Wallace Stevens*. New York: Knopf, 1977.

Stryk, Lucien, and Takashi Ikemoto, eds. and trans. *Zen Poems: Prayers, Sermons, Anecdotes, Interviews*. New York: Doubleday, 1965.

Stryk, Lucien, Takashi Ikemoto, and Taigan Takayama. *The Crane's Bill: Zen Poems of China and Japan.* New York: Doubleday, 1973.

Symons, Arthur. *The Symbolist Movement in Literature,* rev. ed. 1919; rpt. New York: E.P. Dutton, 1958.

Tart, Charles T. *States of Consciousness.* New York: E.P. Dutton, 1975.

Tart, Charles T. *Transpersonal Psychologies.* New York: Harper and Row, 1975.

Tart, Charles T., ed. *Altered States of Consciousness.* New York: Doubleday, 1972.

Tibbetts, Paul, ed. *Perception: Selected Readings in Science and Phenomenology.* Chicago: Quadrangle, 1969.

Truscott, Harold. *Beethoven's Late String Quartets.* London: Dobson, 1968.

Tuohy, Frank. *Yeats.* New York: Macmillan, 1976.

Tzara, Tristan. "Lecture on Dada." In *The Dada Painters and Poets,* ed. Robert Motherwell. New York: Wittenbaorn, Schultz, 1951.

Underhill, Evelyn. *Mysticism.* 1911; rpt. New York: E.P. Dutton, 1961.

Vaihinger, Hans. *The Philosophy of As If.* Trans. C. K. Ogden. London: Routledge, 1924.

Vendler, Helen. *The Music of What Happens.* Cambridge, Mass.: Harvard University Press, 1988.

Vendler, Helen. *On Extended Wings: Wallace Stevens' Longer Poems.* Cambridge, Mass.: Harvard University Press, 1969.

Vendler, Helen. *Part of Nature, Part of Us: Modern American Poets.* Cambridge, Mass.: Harvard University Press, 1980.

Walker, David. *The Transparent Lyric.* Princeton, N.J.: Princeton University Press, 1984.

Wallace, R. K., and H. Benson. "The Physiology of Mediation." *Scientific American,* February 1972.

Watson, Burton, Trans. *Chuang Tzu: Basic Writings.* New York: Columbia University Press, 1964.

Wees, William. *Vorticism and the English Avant-garde.* Toronto: University of Toronto Press, 1972.

Weiskel, Thomas. *The Romantic Sublime.* Baltimore, Md.: Johns Hopkins University Press, 1976.

Welbon, Guy Richard. *The Buddhist Nivana and Its Western Interpreters.* Chicago: University of Chicago Press, 1968.

Welch, Holmes. *Taoism.* Boston: Beacon Press, 1957.

Woolf, Virginia. *Moments of Being.* New York: Harcourt, Brace, 1976.

Yeats, William Butler. *Autobiography.* New York: Macmillan, 1965.

Yip, Wai-Lim. *Ezra Pound's Cathay.* Princeton, N.J.: Princeton University Press, 1969.

Zaehner, R. C. *Zen, Drugs and Mysticism.* New York: Random House, 1972.

Index

Critical Essays in Modern Literature

The Fiction and Criticism of Katherine Anne Porter (revised)
Harry James Mooney, Jr.

The Fiction of J. D. Salinger (revised)
Frederick L. Gwynn and Joseph L. Blotner

Richard Wright: An Introduction to the Man and His Work
Russell Carl Brignano

The Hole in the Fabric: Science, Contemporary Literature, and Henry James
Strother B. Purdy

Reading the Thirties: Texts and Contexts
Bernand Bergonzi

The Romantic Genesis of the Modern Novel
Charles Schug

The Great Succession: Henry James and the Legacy of Hawthorne
Robert Emmet Long

The Plays and Novels of Peter Handke
June Schlueter

Yeats, Eliot, Pound and the Politics of Poetry: Richest to the Richest
Cairns Craig

After Innocence: Visions of the Fall in Modern Literature
Terry Otten

The Metafictional Muse: The Works of Robert Coover, Donald Barthelme, and William H. Gass
Larry McCaffery

The Grand Continuum: Reflections on Joyce and Metaphysics
David A. White

The Utopian Novel in America, 1886–1896: The Politics of Form
Jean Pfaelzer

Mind of Winter: Wallace Stevens, Meditation, and Literature
William W. Bevis